Penguin Education

Creativity
Edited by P. E. Vernon

Penguin Modern Psychology Readings

General Editor
B. M. Foss

Advisory Board

P. C. Dodwell
Marie Jahoda
S. G. M. Lee
W. M. O'Neil
R. L. Reid
Roger Russell
P. E. Vernon
George Westby

Creativity

Selected Readings

Edited by P. E. Vernon

Penguin Books

Penguin Books Ltd, Harmondsworth,
Middlesex, England
Penguin Books Inc., 7110 Ambassador Road,
Baltimore, Md 21207, U.S.A.
Penguin Books Australia Ltd, Ringwood,
Victoria, Australia

First published 1970
This selection copyright © P. E. Vernon, 1970
Introduction and notes copyright © P. E. Vernon, 1970

Made and printed in Great Britain by
Richard Clay (The Chaucer Press) Ltd,
Bungay, Suffolk
Set in Monotype Times New Roman

Contents

Part Six Stimulating Creativity 339

12 + 25.

Introduction

Several excellent symposia or collections of articles in the field of creativity have been published in the past ten years, notably by Anderson (1959), Gruber, Terrell and Wertheimer (1962), Mooney and Razik (1967), Stein and Heinze (1960), C. W. Taylor (1964a and b) and C. W. Taylor and Barron (1963). Useful general summaries are provided by Golann (1963), Barron (1965), Cropley (1967) and Tyson (1966). However these do not serve quite the same function as a book of Readings, which should sample major contributions of the past, as well as recent work. Naturally my choice in the present collection is arbitrary, but I believe fairly conventional rather than idiosyncratic. It is based on the following principles:

1. To show the range and variety of work in the area, both theoretical and applied, not glossing over the fact that much of it is controversial and indecisive.

2. To include many of the major names who are most often quoted, while at the same time trying to fill in the gaps between their articles or excerpts by less generally known contributions.

3. To give reasonable recognition to the work of British as well as American authors.

4. To avoid highly technical matter, which would presume considerable knowledge of, say, statistics.

This Introduction will attempt to indicate the main trends of psychological interest and importance,[1] and to provide a guide to suggested further reading. I say psychological, since I have excluded any discussion of what constitutes a great work of art or of scientific invention; these are matters of aesthetic criticism, or of theoretical or technological evaluation. Similarly art education or other forms of technical training are entirely omitted. The major, though by no means sole, emphasis is on differences between individuals in the abilities and personality characteristics

1. Considerable use has been made of my earlier articles (Vernon, 1964, 1967).

that underlie the production of artistic or scientific work which is generally recognized as creative and original. What various kinds of talents can be distinguished and, perhaps, measured? What are their origins? What promotes and what hinders their development?

It is just 100 years ago that Galton published his *Hereditary Genius* (1869), the first attempt at an empirical study of human abilities, which viewed men of genius, not as a kind of race apart, but as the extreme top end of a continuous distribution. However, the basic principles of measuring mental abilities were pioneered by Charles Spearman in London and Alfred Binet in Paris, in the first decade of the twentieth century. Though Galton himself thought of ability in terms of varied talents, combined with strong motivation, Spearman overemphasized the supreme importance of the general intelligence factor in all types of achievement; and both looked to heredity, rather than environment, as the source of greatness.

Now at the time when Galton was writing, society in general was little concerned about fostering or increasing its resources of men and women of outstanding ability. People were intrigued by the lives and tribulations of great artists, writers, scientists and leaders, but Thomas Gray was exceptional in his concern over 'mute inglorious Miltons' (1750). However, social reformers and politicians were beginning to realize that education was needed not merely for the aristocracy and the church but for the production of doctors, lawyers and the like, and even for the masses.

Since these first beginnings of the technological welfare society, European education has vastly extended its coverage and effectiveness. Particularly since the Second World War it has aimed to provide equality of opportunity, regardless of wealth or class. But it is still élitist in the sense that it differentiates according to the abilities and achievements that students actually manifest. We still assume, in other words, that genuine talent will make its way without requiring special encouragement, perhaps even that creative genius thrives on opposition and difficulties. Thus Europeans find some difficulty in understanding what all the fuss is about in America over creativity and 'the gifted child'. Nevertheless European educationists, like their American counterparts, are increasingly concerned as to whether current methods of teaching, testing and examining, at school and at university, may not unduly favour the conformist mentality and discourage spontaneous, independent thought among those children or students who might make future original contributions to the arts, sciences and technologies.

American education has always been more 'democratic', aiming to integrate diverse social groups and to reduce, rather than exacerbate, individual differences. Thus when L. M. Terman, profiting from Spearman's and Binet's contributions, embarked on his lifelong studies of intelligence, he deplored the lack of recognition and encouragement of brighter children in American schools. Both teachers and parents, it seemed, wanted to produce the conventional, socially well-adjusted child and viewed the unusually talented student with suspicion. Terman's work, together with Leta Hollingworth's (1926) studies of the difficulties of adjustment of very high-I.Q. children, made a considerable impact; and during the 1930s and 40s there was much experimentation with, and controversy over, schemes of 'acceleration', 'homogeneous grouping' or 'enrichment' of the curriculum. But it was the advent of Sputnik in 1957 that shocked America into asking whether its educational system was failing to produce sufficient original scientists to maintain its technological lead in the modern world.

Another turning point was J. P. Guilford's (1950) paper which pointed out that almost all the tests and achievement examinations used by American psychologists and educationists were 'convergent', that is, for each item there was one predetermined correct answer. Clearly these put the imaginative or independent thinker at a disadvantage. Creative thought is more likely to issue in a variety of new answers, in other words, to be divergent.

Many investigations of so-called creativity tests followed (see Part Four of this volume) together with a spate of publications on the need for early recognition of children with unusual ideas and talents, on tolerating and encouraging independent thinking and creative activities instead of repressing them because they upset the teacher's routine, on the possibilities of training students and industrial employees to develop their potential creative powers (see Part Six), and on the selection of research workers for creativity rather than for convergent types of achievement.

11

Whether this is a passing craze, or an educational revolution, time will show. As the Ammonses (1962) and others have pointed out, many of the prescriptions for encouraging creative development in children run directly counter to the manner in which creative geniuses in history were often reared.

Research has still not given a clear answer to such questions as whether creativity is an ability distinct from intelligence, or whether, as Thurstone (1952) and Guilford supposed, it involves a number of different primary mental abilities or factors. Nor do we know what kinds of tests, given in what manner, best predict future creative capacities of students and adult workers. A good deal of the confusion in this area arises from loose usage of terms like creative, original, imaginative, nonconformist, gifted, talented, genius, etc. Whereas some writers are talking about people like Mozart and da Vinci, or about highly productive and original artists or scientists of the present and future (say 1 in a 1000 of the population), others are referring to children or adults who score well on divergent thinking tests – a very different matter. Still others refer to the exceptionally able students from the top 1 or 2 per cent in I.Q. and achievement, or even to the top 20 per cent – the well-above average. Again there are many kinds, as well as degrees, of creativeness. Should we expect to be able to subsume a child's drawings or his father's gardening, under the same principles as Einstein's theory of relativity?

Let us go back to the beginning and look at a rather different aspect of the subject. To the layman, and indeed to the artist himself, the nature of the creative process is mysterious and unanalysable. It is difficult even to define creativity, though many have tried (cf. Ghiselin, 1952; I. A. Taylor, 1959), usually emphasizing novel combinations or unusual associations of ideas, and the point that such combinations must have social or theoretical value, or make an emotional impact on other people. To the psychologist, however, creative thinking is merely one of the many kinds of thinking which range from autistic fantasy and dreaming to logical reasoning. Indeed to some extent it seems to partake of both extremes (cf. McKellar, 1957; Vinacke, 1952). Many of the experiments that have been carried out on problem solving and blockages to novel solutions (e.g. Maier,

1930–31; Duncker, 1945; Wertheimer, 1959) are also relevant to creativity, and a few studies (e.g. Patrick, 1935, 1937) have attempted, not very successfully, to investigate creative production under laboratory conditions. Newell, Shaw and Simon (1962) have shown that most of the typical features of creative thinking, at least in mathematics and chess playing, are amenable to computer simulation. Further work along these lines and in information theory may well provide our best hope of progress in understanding the psychology of creative thought. Another possible mode of attack is through studies of the effects of hallucinogenic drugs (see Huxley, 1954). But though these release people from acquired inhibitions and conventional perceptual habits, there is little evidence, as yet, that they result in the production of worthwhile creative ideas.

So far we have considered creativity mainly as an ability and a form of cognitive activity. But throughout the history of its study a recurrent theme has been the underlying personality characteristics and emotional drives of the creative individual. ✓ According to John Dryden, 'Great wits are sure to madness near allied', and Lombroso (1891) considered genius as a manifestation of the diseased mind, accompanied by many signs of pathology. Kretschmer (1931) too spoke of a psychopathic element, combined with a high degree of talent, though he was more interested in the association of different types of genius with different physiques and temperaments. However, the first empirical investigation of the topic by Havelock Ellis (1904) showed very little psychosis among British men of genius, though minor nervous disorders and poor health in childhood were rather frequent. Cox's survey in the 1920s confirmed this (Cox, 1926), and emphasized the outstanding persistence and drive of great leaders, intellectuals and artists. Clearly generalizations are dangerous. Many men of genius in the past have shown psychotic or severe neurotic tendencies, and it is difficult to believe that they could have produced as they did had they been more normal. Many others have been eccentrics, rebels or emotionally unstable, while still others have lived full and very ordinary lives, though characterized by extreme devotion to their artistic or scientific work.

Our Readings include selections from Terman and Roe,

Freud and Rogers; while Part Five describes a number of investigations of living individuals, using tests and controlled interviews, which seem to yield a rather consistent picture of the personality and motivation of the creative scientist. Though too long to reproduce here, McClelland's (1962) synthesis of these findings with psychoanalytic theory is particularly worth reading. The creative artist is similar in some respects, but probably very different in others, and less progress has been made in studying him, presumably because he is less essential to technological survival. An unanswered question is why so few women have shown outstanding creativity in any field. Another fascinating problem is how the artist conveys in his pictures, writings or music his personal solutions to emotional conflicts, his insights into human nature, which give us aesthetic satisfaction through their effects on our own emotions. This adds a further complication, since it implies that creativity is always relative to a particular culture; it is not a product of the artist or scientist alone. There are very few who, like Shakespeare, appeal to something so universal in human nature as to retain their reputation over many generations and in diverse cultures. Even in the case of science and invention, where it is easier to judge that some insights are more seminal than others either for theoretical advance or for their practical utility, it is notorious that the value of original contributions is often not recognized at the time.

Some study has been given to cultural environments that favour or inhibit the production of sheer numbers of outstanding scientists or artists. J. M. Cattell (1906) initiated this approach by comparing the numbers of men of science born in different American states which varied in wealth, educational advance and social traditions. Others, such as Knapp (1963), have shown that certain universities or other institutions produce more creative research than others. While these differences are attributable largely to the quality of the students or staff they attract, we are beginning to get some understanding of the social and educational factors which go to make up the institutional 'climate'.

References

AMMONS, C. H., and AMMONS, R. B. (1962), 'How to prevent geniuses: McCurdy revisited', *Proc. Montana Acad. Sci.*, vol. 21, pp. 145–52.

ANDERSON, H. H. (ed.) (1959), *Creativity and its Cultivation*, Harper.

BARRON, F. (1965), 'The psychology of creativity', in T. M. Newcomb (ed.), *New Directions in Psychology*, vol. 2, Holt, Rinehart & Winston, pp. 1–134.

CATTELL, J. M. (1906), 'A statistical study of American men of science. III. The distribution of American men of science', *Science*, vol. 24, pp. 732–42.

COX, C. M. (1926), *Genetic Studies of Genius, Vol. II. The Early Mental Traits of Three Hundred Geniuses*, Stanford University Press.

CROPLEY, A. J. (1967), *Creativity*, Longmans, Green.

DUNCKER, K. (1945), 'On problem solving', *Psychol. Monogr.*, vol. 58, no. 270.

ELLIS, H. (1904), *A Study of British Genius*, Hurst & Blackett.

GALTON, F. (1869), *Hereditary Genius*, Macmillan, London, and Appleton.

GHISELIN, B. (1952), *The Creative Process: A Symposium*, University of California Press (Mentor Books edn, 1955).

GOLANN, S. E. (1963), 'Psychological study of creativity', *Psychol. Bull.*, vol. 60, pp. 548–65.

GRUBER, H. E., TERRELL, G., and WERTHEIMER, M. (eds.) (1962), *Contemporary Approaches to Creative Thinking*, Atherton Press.

GUILFORD, J. P. (1950), 'Creativity', *Amer. Psychol.*, vol. 5, pp. 444–54.

HOLLINGWORTH, L. (1926), *Gifted Children, Their Nature and Nuture*, Macmillan, New York.

HUXLEY, A. (1954), *The Doors of Perception*, Harper.

KNAPP, R. H. (1963), 'Demographic, cultural and personality attributes of scientists', in C. W. Taylor and F. Barron (eds.), *Scientific Creativity: its Recognition and Development*, Wiley, pp. 205–16.

KRETSCHMER, E. (1931), *The Psychology of Men of Genius*, Kegan Paul and Harcourt, Brace.

LOMBROSO, C. (1891), *The Man of Genius*, Walter Scott.

MAIER, N. R. F. (1930–31), 'Reasoning in humans', *J. comp. Psychol.*, vol. 10, pp. 115–43; vol. 12, pp. 181–94.

McCLELLAND, D. (1962), 'On the psychodynamics of creative physical scientists', in H. E. Gruber *et al.* (eds.), *Contemporary Approaches to Creative Thinking*, Atherton Press, pp. 141–74.

McKELLAR, P. (1957), *Imagination and Thinking*, Cohen & West.

MOONEY, R. L., and RAZIK, T. A. (eds.) (1967), *Explorations in Creativity*, Harper & Row.

NEWELL, A., SHAW, J. C., and SIMON, H. A. (1962), 'The process of creative thinking', in H. E. Gruber *et al.* (eds.), *Contemporary Approaches to Creative Thinking*, Atherton Press, pp. 63–119.

PATRICK, C. (1935), 'Creative thought in poets', *Arch. Psychol.*, vol. 26, pp. 1–74.

Introduction

PATRICK, C. (1937), 'Creative thought in artists', *J. Psychol.*, vol. 4, pp. 35–73.

STEIN, M. I., and HEINZE, S. J. (1960), *Creativity and the Individual*, Free Press.

TAYLOR, C. W. (ed.) (1964a), *Creativity: Progress and Potentiality*, McGraw-Hill.

TAYLOR, C. W. (ed.) (1964b), *Widening Horizons in Creativity*, Wiley.

TAYLOR, C. W., and BARRON, F. (eds.) (1963) *Scientific Creativity: its Recognition and Development*, Wiley.

TAYLOR, I. A. (1959), 'The nature of the creative process', in P. Smith (ed.), *Creativity: An Evaluation of the Creative Process*, Hastings House, New York, pp. 51–82.

THURSTONE, L. L. (1952), 'Creative talent', in L. L. Thurstone (ed.), *Applications of Psychology*, Harper, pp. 18–37.

TYSON, M. (1966), 'Creativity', in B. M. Foss (ed.), *New Horizons in Psychology*, Penguin Books, pp. 167–82.

VERNON, P. E. (1964), 'Creativity and intelligence', *Educ. Res.*, vol. 6, pp. 163–9.

VERNON, P. E. (1967), 'Psychological studies of creativity', *J. child Psychol. Psychiat.*, vol. 5, 153–64.

VINACKE, W. E. (1952), *The Psychology of Thinking*, Tavistock.

WERTHEIMER, M. (1959), *Productive Thinking*, Tavistock.

Part One Pioneer Empirical Studies

Francis Galton is recognized as the founder of psychological and mathematical studies of individual differences. Though we have space only for a summary of his best known work (Reading 1), this illustrates his approach to the scaling of human ability, and his emphasis on the genetic basis of talents, to the neglect of family upbringing and other influences. Terman and Cox showed the same bias in their title, *Genetic Studies of Genius*, but gave greater recognition to the role of personality factors, of favourable environment and conditions of schooling, in the fruition of talent. Their studies, both of eminent historical figures and of high-I.Q. children, demonstrated that outstanding ability is more often associated with superior personality characteristics than with emotional abnormality. We may criticize Terman for trusting too much to intelligence tests and teachers' ratings in selecting his children's sample, indeed even virtually identifying genius with high I.Q.; but he was responsible for the most extensive follow-up study in the history of psychology (see Reading 2).

Roe's investigations of living scientists (Reading 3) are less psychometric, more clinical, in their methodology. But her conclusions regarding their upbringing and personalities have been generally confirmed by later work.

1 M. I. Stein and S. J. Heinze

A Summary of Galton's *Hereditary Genius*

Excerpt from M. I. Stein and S. J. Heinze, *Creativity and the Individual*, Free Press, 1960, pp. 85–90.[1]

Galton maintains that mental capacities are hereditary, that they follow the laws of organic transmission and that these laws can be ascertained by careful observation. His book is devoted primarily to a demonstration of the hereditary linkages among persons of outstanding achievement in a variety of fields.

The book is divided into three major sections. In the first, the problems of classifying men according to their ability are discussed, and the approach employed in this work is described. In the second, the lineages of eminent personages are presented and tabulated. Men in nine fields of achievement are covered: judges, statesmen, commanders, literary men, men of science, poets, musicians, painters and divines. In the final section, Galton compares the results for the various fields and presents the conclusions that he feels they justify.

Natural ability is assumed to obey the 'law of deviation from an average', or in other words, to be normally distributed. Galton proposes fourteen classes of mental ability, 'each being separated from its neighbours by *equal grades*', covering the usual range of mental abilities above (classes A–G) and below (classes a–g) the average. A fifteenth and sixteenth class, labeled X and x represent the extremes of genius and idiocy. The natural ability referred to is not a simple intelligence factor, but is a composite of intelligence, motivation and power.

It is argued that eminence is an adequate index to natural ability since the truly able individual cannot be repressed by social obstacles. In addition, it is pointed out that English social life presents more restrictions than does American and yet

1. It may be noted that Stein and Heinze provide admirable abstracts of all the older literature on creativity [*Ed.*].

England has produced more truly eminent men. Finally, Galton notes that men who are aided by social advantages do not achieve eminence unless they are 'endowed with high natural gifts'. The relatives of Popes are especially cited as undistinguished, though given special advantages by the Pope. Galton concludes: 'I feel convinced that no man can achieve a very high reputation without being gifted with very high abilities; and I trust that reason has been given for the belief, that few who possess these very high abilities can fail in achieving eminence.'

The selection of subjects varied with the field under consideration. The English judges were selected from the *Lives of the Judges*, by Foss. Only those judges between 1660 and 1865 were considered. The statesmen were composed of the premiers beginning with the reign of George III and the men mentioned in Lord Brougham's *Statesmen of the Reign of George III*. No source for the list of commanders is given. However, Galton indicates that he has included only those commanders 'whose reputation has been tested by prolonged wars, or whose ascendency over others has been freely acknowledged'. The names of the literary men were taken from 'dictionaries'. Galton extracted those names which he found 'most prominent'. The scientists were also selected from biographical dictionaries, the men who had achieved 'enduring reputation' or who were 'otherwise well known' to the present generation being selected. No criterion of selection is given for the poets, musicians or artists. The divines included those covered in Middleton's *Biographia Evangelica*. Brief attention is also given to the ancestry of senior classics at Cambridge, outstanding oarsmen and wrestlers of the North Country.

Three grades of ability are dealt with: (a) illustrious men among whom 'many are as one in a million, and not a few as one of many millions. . . . They are men whom the whole intelligent part of the nation mourns when they die; who have, or deserve to have, a public funeral; and who rank in future ages as historical characters'; (b) eminent men – those who have 'achieved a position that is attained by only 250 persons in each million of men, or by one person in each 4000'; (c) the third and lower grade is that of English judges – their average ability 'cannot be rated as equal to that of the lower of the two grades' described above.

A total of 286 judges was studied. Thirty of these men were chancellor, and of the thirty, twenty-four had eminent relations. Of the remaining 256 judges, only ninety had eminent relations. Galton concludes: 'There is, therefore, abundant reason to conclude that the kinsmen of Lord Chancellors are far richer in natural gifts than those of other judges.'

The precise number of statesmen studied is not given. There were fifty-seven English statesmen and a 'small supplementary list, taken from various periods and other countries'. From this study, Galton concludes that the ablest statesmen had the largest number of able relatives; that the statesmen were more gifted than the judges, since they had more eminent relations than did the judges; and that the 'statesman's type of ability is largely transmitted or inherited' since many of the eminent relations were, themselves, statesmen.

In a separate chapter, Galton considers 'the causes of failure of issue of judges and statesmen'. He notes that many of the judges studied postponed marriage until they were elevated to the bench. Even so, the number of legitimate children of judges appears to be considerable. It was in the marriages of children and grandchildren that the cause for the extinction of the line was found. Galton points out that among English peers in general there is a preference for marrying heiresses, and these women have been 'peculiarly unprolific'. A comparison of the number of children from heiress and non-heiress marriages demonstrates this point.

In all, about fifty-nine commanders were studied. Of these, thirty-two had relationships of sufficient eminence to be tabulated. In this tabulation, Galton observes that the greater the eminence of the commander, the greater the number of eminent relations he had. The commanders are presumed to be a more able group than either the judges or statesmen, and it is observed that the commanders had a greater number of eminent relations than either of the other two groups. As in the case of statesmen, Galton concludes that the 'peculiar type of ability' required of a commander is inherited since several families of generals appear in his list.

The total number of literary people studied is not indicated. However, the relations of fifty-two are tabulated. Though Galton felt unqualified to decide who among the literary relatives of men of letters were themselves eminent, he does conclude that 'we may rest satisfied that an analysis of kinsfolk shows literary genius to be fully as hereditary as any other kind of ability we have hitherto discussed.'

The eminent relations of sixty-five scientific men are tabulated. Here Galton finds the group distinguished from those previously studied in three ways. Fewer of the fathers and grandfathers of the scientists were themselves eminent; the importance of the female line of inheritance was more marked; and a greater proportion of the sons of the most gifted became distinguished in their fathers' fields than was true among the judges, statesmen or literary men. Galton suggests that the mother is of particular importance in determining an eminent scientific career since it is she who teaches the son his basic attitude towards reality. She may either teach him an unquestioning acceptance of dogmatism or an attitude of inquiry and love of truth.

A total of fifty-six poets were studied, and of these at least 40 per cent were found to have eminently gifted relations. Particularly noteworthy, however, is the fact that eminent relations were largely confined to the poets' immediate families. Galton concludes, 'Poets are clearly not founders of families.' The rare combination of qualities required of the eminent poet is believed to be unstable in inheritance. Inheritance of the strong sensuous tastes of the poet without the controlling faculties may lead to complete failure.

Twenty-six of the 120 eminent musicians studied had illustrious relatives. As in the case of the poets, the eminent kin of the musicians were to be found primarily among the closest relatives. There was also a notable absence of eminent relations through the female line among the musicians.

The forty-two painters studied were all 'illustrious ancient' artists of the Italian, Spanish and Dutch schools. Eighteen of them had eminent relatives. Again, however, 'The rareness with which artistic eminence passes through more than two degrees of kinship, is almost as noticeable . . . as in the case of musicians and poets.'

In studying the lives of 196 divines, Galton concluded that 'they are not the founders of families who have exercised a notable influence on our history, whether that influence be derived from the abilities, wealth or social position of any of their members', that 'a pious disposition is decidedly hereditary', and that 'there are also frequent cases of sons of pious parents who turned out very badly'.

Comparing the results for the various groups studied, Galton summarizes:

The general uniformity in the distribution of ability among the kinsmen in the different groups, is strikingly manifest. The eminent sons are almost invariably more numerous than the eminent brothers, and these are a trifle more numerous than the eminent fathers. On proceeding further down the table, we come to a sudden dropping off of the numbers at the second grade of kinship, namely, at the grandfather, uncles, nephews and grandsons. . . . On reaching the third grade of kinship, another abrupt dropping off in numbers is again met with, but the first cousins are found to occupy a decidedly better position than other relations within the third grade.

Certain exceptions to the general results are noted. They include: (a) the small number of eminent sons of commanders; (b) the small number of eminent fathers of scientists – particularly as compared with the large number of eminent sons of the scientists; (c) the small number of eminent fathers of poets; and (d) the 'enormous' number of eminent sons of artists.

Having dealt with the exceptions, Galton concludes that:

If we say that to every ten illustrious men, *who have any eminent relation at all*, we find three or four eminent fathers, four or five eminent brothers, and five or six eminent sons, we shall be right in seventeen instances out of twenty-four; and in the seven cases where we are wrong, the error will consist of less than one unit in two cases (the fathers of commanders and men of literature), of one unit in four cases (the fathers of poets and the sons of judges, commanders and divines), and of more than one unit in the sole case of sons of artists.

From these results, Galton estimates the chances that a given relative of any of the *most* illustrious men will achieve eminence as follows: the chance of a father is 1 in 6; of a brother, 1 in 7; of each son, 1 in 4; of each grandfather, 1 in 25; of each uncle, 1 in 40; of each nephew, 1 in 40; and of each grandson, 1 in 29. For all more remote relatives, the chances are about 1 in 200, except for first cousins whose chances are about 1 in 100.

The relative capacities of male and female lines for transmitting ability are discussed in some detail. Galton concludes that eminent men are the offspring of good marriages and not just good paternal stock. However, the decidedly smaller number of transmissions along the female line suggests either an 'inherent incapacity in the female line for transmitting the peculiar forms of ability we are now discussing', or possibly 'the aunts, sisters, and daughters of eminent men do not marry, on the average, so frequently as other women'. He believes there is some evidence for this latter explanation.

As a matter of special interest, Galton investigated evidence concerning the constitutions of his eminent population. His observations led him to conclude that 'the gifted men consist of two categories – the very weak and the very strong'. The mortality curves were bi-modal, one group of men dying quite young and another at a much later age. The scientists lived longer than any other group and had decidedly fewer early deaths than the others.

Galton concludes his book with an attempt to apply the results of his study to a comparison of the abilities of different races and with a discussion of the development of types. He particularly stresses the need to build a race of greater average ability than that of the 'present time'. He is concerned that the demands of civilization upon the existing race are greater than its powers to perform. He concludes that:

The best form of civilization in respect to the improvement of the race, would be one in which society was not costly; where incomes were chiefly derived from professional sources, and not much through inheritance; where every lad had a chance of showing his abilities and, if highly gifted, was enabled to achieve a first-class education and entrance into professional life, by the liberal help of the exhibitions and scholarships which he had gained in his early youth; where marriage was held in as high honour as in ancient Jewish times; where the pride of race was encouraged (of course I do not refer to the nonsensical sentiment of the present day, that goes under that name); where the weak could find a welcome and a refuge in celibate monasteries or sisterhoods, and lastly, where the better sort of emigrants and refugees from other lands were invited and welcomed, and their descendants naturalized.

2 L. M. Terman

Psychological Approaches to the Biography of Genius

Excerpts from Part One of L. M. Terman, 'Psychological approaches to the study of genius', *Papers on Eugenics*, no. 4, 1947, pp. 3–20.[1]

Probably few words have acquired a greater variety of connotations than 'genius'. On this occasion I shall disregard the numerous meanings attached to the word in the first two thousand years of its history and call attention only to common usages in modern English.

In a popular sense genius is often used to designate some kind of mystical gift that cannot be explained by the ordinary laws of human nature. The scientist, of course, rejects this usage. Havelock Ellis and others have used the term as practically synonymous with eminence. Galton, while employing the criterion of eminence, follows Samuel Johnson in defining a genius as one who is endowed with superior intellectual ability. This definition is essentially identical with that given in Warren's *Dictionary of Psychological Terms*, 1934, and is the one I prefer.

The *sine qua non* of genius is the ability to acquire and to manipulate concepts, the shorthand symbols without which abstract thinking cannot proceed. However, there are many levels of aptitude for concept mastery and the question arises where genius may be said to begin. We have at one extreme Dr

1. This Reading may be regarded as a summary of L. Terman *et al.*, *Genetic Studies of Genius*, 5 vols., Stanford University Press.

Vol. I. *Mental and Physical Traits of a Thousand Gifted Children*, 1926.

Vol. II. *The Early Mental Traits of Three Hundred Geniuses*, 1926.

Vol. III. *The Promise Of Youth*, 1930.

Later two further volumes were published by L. Terman and M. H. Oden, which showed the continuing intellectual achievement and generally superior characteristics of the gifted group, although few, if any, could be regarded as geniuses.

Vol. IV. *The Gifted Child Grows Up*, 1947.

Vol. V. *The Gifted Group at Mid-Life*, 1959. [*Ed.*]

Field's laboratory rats which required thousands of trials and a good part of their lives to learn to respond to triangularity in visual stimuli; that is, to acquire one crude concept. At the other extreme are the Newtons and the Aristotles. The intermediate levels range upward through infra-human intelligence, average human intelligence and the superior grades that permit higher and higher levels of abstraction. Any line that may be drawn to demarcate genius is purely arbitrary. Whether one restricts the term to the ablest in many millions, in a few thousand or in a few hundred, does not matter provided the facts are stated.

Another problem is that of identifying the individuals who qualify at a particular level of genius chosen for investigation. I have referred to the criterion of eminence. Unfortunately, eminence as measured by popular acclaim or even by space in biographical dictionaries is influenced by other circumstances than intellectual achievement. The population it affords is the result of innumerable selective factors which vary from age to age and from culture to culture. The genius who survives as such has successfully run the gauntlet of premature death, the inanities of formal education, the social and ethical pressures of his immediate environment, and the more general cultural influences that have given direction and content to the civilization in which he was born. To study only the biographies of historic characters gives us a one-sided picture in that it tells us nothing about the potential geniuses who failed to achieve greatly. To complete the picture it is necessary not only to investigate the life histories of eminent persons but also to inaugurate researches that will proceed in the opposite direction. That is, we should identify early in life those individuals who are intellectually gifted, secure quantitative measures of their mental and physical traits, then follow their careers through life.

For twenty years parallel studies in these two directions have been in progress at Stanford University. On the one hand, the mental development of 300 eminent individuals has been traced backward to childhood; on the other hand, the development of more than 1300 intellectually superior subjects has been followed in the forward direction from childhood to early maturity. It is possible to give only a few highlights from these two lines of investigation.

I

I shall first review some of the more recent approaches to the biographical study of emiment persons. As you well know, the highly original publications of Francis Galton between 1869 (*Hereditary Genius*) and 1889 (*Natural Inheritance*) stimulated many interesting investigations on the origin and qualities of great men. Unfortunately, the methodology of these studies soon became stereotyped along statistical lines, with failure to take advantage of progress in individual psychology. It has long seemed to me that the writing of a biography is as much a psychological as an historical undertaking and that biographers fail as often from lack of psychological insight as from any other cause. Not infrequently an otherwise competent biographer over-looks crucial facts in his subject's mental life or else interprets them in ways that are psychologically unsound. It was a striking example of such erroneous interpretation that led me to apply to the Commonwealth Fund for a grant to finance a research on the early mental development of historical geniuses. At that time my study of California gifted children was under way and the possibility of cross-illumination from the two lines of approach seemed promising.

The erroneous interpretation referred to was found in Karl Pearson's *Life, Letters and Labours of Francis Galton* (Cambridge University Press, 1914–30). In a discussion of Galton's intellectual precocity Pearson had presented an extraordinary array of documentary evidence regarding his subject's early accomplishments. Francis learned to read at the age of two and a half years and wrote a letter before he was four that has been preserved. By the age of five he could read 'almost any English book' and some French, could cast up any sum in addition, had mastered all the multiplication table except the 9s and 11s, knew the table of English money and could tell time by the clock. Now it happens that all of these and several other dated performances of Galton have been standardized by psychologists on unselected children of different ages, and that the mental ages necessary for each performance is known. By the use of such norms it is possible in the case of Galton to estimate with considerable assurance the lowest I.Q. that would account for the facts. This was unquestionably in the neighbourhood of 200, a figure not equalled by more than one child in 50,000 of the generality. Yet Pearson was so unaware of the significance of the performances he had described as to assert: 'I do not think we can say more than that Francis Galton was a normal child with rather more than average ability.'

The research for which funds had been provided was carried out by Catharine Cox and two assistants. The first task was to select a group of eminent subjects in such a way as to avoid the bias that is sure to enter when selection is subjective and haphazard. Cox began with Cattell's list of the 1000 most eminent individuals of history as determined by the space devoted to them in biographical dictionaries. Taking the 500 most eminent of Cattell's list, she eliminated from this group those born before 1450, those who belonged to the hereditary aristocracy or nobility, and a few others, arbitrarily, whose eminence had little or no basis in intellectual achievement. This left her with 300 subjects.

Cox and her assistants combed the biographies of these subjects for data on early mental development as indicated by interests, education, school standing and school progress, friends and associates, reading, production and achievement. Special attention was given to evidence from documentary sources. The material thus assembled ran to 6000 typed pages. The evidence for each subject was then examined independently by three psychologists who were intimately acquainted with age norms of mental performance. Their task involved two things: (a) estimation of the minimum I.Q. that would account for a subject's childhood performances, and (b) a rating of the reliability of the evidence on which the I.Q. estimate was based. The averages of the three estimates for all individual subjects were the primary data for this part of the study.

It must be emphasized that the I.Q. as reckoned is an estimate of the lowest I.Q. that could reasonably account for the recorded facts; the actual childhood I.Q.s of historical geniuses are of course indeterminate.

For the entire group the estimated minimum I.Q.s ranged from 100 to 200, with an average of 155. The average is more than three standard deviations above the mean of the generality. Low estimates in the range of 100 to 120 I.Q. occurred only when there was little biographical information about the early years. The mean was highest for philosophers (170), and next highest for poets, novelists, dramatists and revolutionary statesmen (160). The lowest was for soldiers (125), the next lowest for artists (140) and musicians (145). The mean for scientists (155) was identical with the mean for the total group.

It will be understood, I trust, that I.Q. estimates of this kind are not to be taken too literally. For a majority of the subjects the information on which the estimates were based was far short of what could be desired. However, despite all inadequacies of the data I believe that the author's main conclusion is warranted: namely, that the genius who achieves highest eminence is one whom intelligence tests would have identified as gifted in childhood. The author warns us that the converse of this does not follow; we may not conclude that every child who tests high will become eminent. Her data suggest that those who do achieve greatly are characterized not only by superior intellectual ability but also 'by persistence of motive and effort, confidence in their abilities and great strength or force of character'.

That personality traits are influential in determining both the level and the direction of achievement cannot be doubted. We shall see later that this is certainly true of the gifted children I have studied. However, one must also take account of the part played by chance. For a given type of achievement to be possible one must be born not too far from a given time and place. It is an interesting game to try to imagine how differently any list of eminent persons might read if every one now in it had lived a generation or two earlier or later. The soldiers would nearly all bear strange names, perhaps a majority of the statesmen, especially revolutionary statesmen, and doubtless many of the writers and scientists.

Apart from time and place of birth, there are other chance factors in vast number that are capable of shaping the life of a gifted youth. Newton at fifteen had left school and was tending his mother's farm; but for the timely visit of an uncle who had attended Cambridge it is unlikely that he would ever have received the education that made possible his great discoveries. Victor Cousin was bred in the gutter and was illiterate at the age of ten when he happened to befriend a bully's victim in a street fight, with the result that the latter's mother sought him out and gave him an education. Faraday left school at thirteen, and at fourteen was apprenticed to a bookbinder. It was the reading of an article on electricity in an encyclopaedia given him to bind that first stimulated his interest in science. Even this would probably have got him nowhere had not Humphrey Davy been near to lend a helping hand.

In a study like that of Cox, special interest attached to certain eminent persons who have been cited as examples of childhood backwardness. In every one of these cases the facts clearly contradict the legend. Goldsmith was characterized by Samuel Johnson as 'a plant that flowered late', and a childhood teacher said of him in her old age, 'never was so dull a boy'. Actually Goldsmith was writing clever verse at the age of seven years and at eight was reading Ovid and Horace. His I.Q. was probably 140 or higher. Sir Walter Scott is said to have been a dunce when he attended the Musselburgh School. The facts are that he never attended this school, that when only seven years old he read widely in poetry and in his prose at this age used correctly such words as 'melancholy' and 'exotic', that by age ten he had collected a small library of ballads and that at thirteen he lay awake nights reading Shakespeare when he was supposed to be asleep. His I.Q. was at least 150.

Other alleged dullards represent a type often encountered in the old-fashioned Latin school, i.e. the youth who hated Latin and Greek but had a natural talent for science. Liebig, the founder of physiological chemistry, was the despair of his language teachers. At fifteen he left school and was apprenticed to an apothecary because he wanted to be a chemist. At seventeen he managed to enter a university and at twenty was awarded the Ph.D. degree. John Hunter, British surgeon and anatomist, left Latin school at thirteen and spent four apparently idle years roaming the woods and fields, 'watching the ants, the bees, the birds, the tadpoles and caddis-worms, pestering people with questions about which nobody knew or cared anything'. Alexander von Humboldt and his brother Wilhelm, two years older, were privately tutored along the usual classical lines. Wilhelm liked languages and was early recognized as gifted; Alexander, caring only for nature, was considered mentally slow. Both became eminent, but Alexander outstripped his brother.

In the cases just cited one notes a tendency for the direction of later achievement to be foreshadowed by the interests and preoccupations of childhood. I have tried to determine how frequently this was true of the 100 subjects in Cox's group whose childhood is best documented. Very marked foreshadowing was noted in the case of more than half of the group, none at all in less than a fourth. Macaulay, for example, began his career as historian at the age of six with what he called a 'Compendium of universal history', filling a quire of paper before he lost interest in the project. Goethe's literary juvenilia are perhaps the most remarkable that have ever been preserved. Ben Franklin before the age of seventeen had displayed nearly all the traits that characterized him in middle life; manual skill, scientific curiosity, religious heterodoxy, wit and buffoonery, political and business shrewdness and ability to write. At the age of seventy, when on a diplomatic mission in England, he dug up an article which he had written in his teens, published it practically without change, and created a political sensation. At eleven Pascal wrote a paper on sound and was so interested in mathematics that his father thought best to deprive him of books on this subject until he had first mastered Latin and Greek. Pascal secretly proceeded to construct a geometry of his own and covered the ground as far as the thirty-second proposition of Euclid. At fourteen Leibnitz was writing on logic and philosophy and composing what he called 'An alphabet of human thought'. He relates that at this age he took a walk one afternoon to consider whether he should hold the doctrine of substantial forms.

In working with data of this kind the investigator must of course be wary, for even under the pen of a conscientious biographer the childhood period is likely to be coloured by the halo of adult achievement. The evidence, however, is indisputable in the case of nearly all the musicians, and hardly less convincing in the case of mathematicians and artists. There are few great poets who did not show unusual poetic talent before the age of fifteen. [. . .]

The early interests and displays of special talent by Cox's subjects were often disregarded in the vocational guidance given them by parents and teachers. In no less than twenty of the 100 cases whose childhood is best known there was pressure to turn the subject into another field than that in which eminence was achieved. The destiny that half of these had to escape was the legal profession. Balzac's parents tried for five years to starve him into submission that they might make a lawyer of him. Dumas (père) was first destined for a military career, later for the priesthood and was finally apprenticed to a notary. When Victor Hugo was nineteen his father offered him an allowance if he would relinquish literature for a more substantial profession. Victor preferred to live in a garret and write. Coleridge's father wanted his son to be a parson, but fortunately the father died and the boy was reared by an uncle who recognized literary genius when he saw it.

The guidance of gifted children is made more difficult by their versatility. Intellect by its very nature is highly general, and it follows that to one who is intellectually superior many fields of achievement are possible if the requisite interests and drives are present. The versatility of a few geniuses has received considerable attention, but the less spectacular cases are overlooked. People like to believe that the genius as a rule is no better than the rest of us except in one particular. The facts are very different. Except in music and the arts, which draw heavily on specialized abilities, there are few persons who have achieved great eminence in one field without displaying more than average ability in one or more other fields.

Several years ago, one of my students, Ralph K. White, made a study of the versatility of Cox's 300 geniuses (see *J. soc. Psychol.*, 1931, pp. 460–89). Using the biographical information assembled by Cox, White and another psychologist rated each subject on the ability shown in twenty-three different fields. The results indicated that a majority of the subjects displayed more than ordinary ability in five to ten fields. The mean versatility index was highest for non-fictional writers, statesmen and philosophers (around 7·5); somewhat lower for scholars, religious leaders, scientists, poets, mathematicians, novelists and dramatists (around 6·7); much lower for soldiers and artists (4·3 and 4·0), and lowest of all for musicians (only 2·7).

White further analysed his ratings to see what abilities tended to appear together. It was found, for example, that science, mathematics, invention and handwork form a rather closely-knit group; poetry, novels and drama another. Philosophy, social theory, history and languages form a third but less compact structure. Religious leadership is allied with politics and administration, while musicians stand pretty much alone. One of the most interesting relationships is that between art and the science cluster. Leonardo da Vinci is here the supreme example.

Another approach to the biography of genius is by way of psychoanalysis, which investigates the motivational dynamics that shape the individual personality. The contributions from this direction now make up a vast literature difficult to appraise. To any but the most orthodox Freudian much of it will appear highly extravagant and far-fetched. Some of the contributions, however, appeal to the psychologist as in line with common observation. One does not have to accept the elaborate super-structure of symbolism erected by Freud to be convinced that psychoanalysis has profoundly influenced modern theories of personality. There are few psychologists who longer doubt that the crucial influences shaping the lives of some persons stem from their childhood experiences: for example, from parent–child conflicts or attachments, from sibling relationships, from the sense of not being wanted or from frustration in its myriad forms. It is impossible to understand the unsexed personality of John Ruskin without knowledge of his parental attachments, the rebellious spirit of Lord Byron without knowledge of his deformity and of his maternal conflicts, or the messiah complex of John Wesley without knowledge of the mother-inspired ideal to which he was moulded by family pressures. The phenomenon called Hitler surely is not to be explained in terms of extraordinary intellectual endowment, but rather in terms of personal frustrations, displaced hatreds and fanatical aggressions.

I believe there is factual basis for Lasswell's suggestion that the role of rebel or agitator is sometimes only a continuation of the child's fight against parental tyranny. Emma Goldman, with psychological insight unusual in autobiographies, calls attention to the possible relationship between her career as anarchist and the brutalities she suffered from her father in childhood; she did not think it accidental that one of her foremost associates among the anarchists had a similar background of domestic tyranny.

Lange-Eichbaum, a German psychiatrist, has emphasized the

importance of inner conflicts and tensions of whatever kind as stimulants to great achievement. He believes that without such irritants no one ever puts forth his maximum effort; that the personality happily adjusted to its environment and never stirred to action by opposition or frustration is foredoomed to obscurity. Examining from a psychiatric point of view the lives of a large group of historical geniuses this author concludes that the more eminent the subject the more marked the evidence of inner conflict bordering on the psychopathic. One would like to see this conclusion checked by a research commission composed of historians, psychiatrists and psychologists working with an objectively selected population.

In evaluation of these various approaches to the study of historical geniuses I wish to go on record as believing that all of them have merit enough to justify their further cultivation. At the same time, anyone who has attempted to draw conclusions from the fragmentary information that can be gleaned from biographical works is painfully aware of the limitations of his material. One's interpretations are at best only tentative and suggestive, lacking always the finality of positive proof. It is a relief, accordingly, to turn to the investigation of living subjects who may be studied first-hand at successive age levels with unlimited opportunity for correlating factual data in the individual's life history.

II

By the study and follow-up of intellectually superior children we can find out what such individuals are really like in early life and what kind of men and women they become. Data which I had been able to secure from tests and observations of about 100 gifted children between 1910 and 1920 suggested that many of the traditional beliefs on these points contained a preponderant element of superstition. It was obvious, however, that to secure anything like conclusive evidence would require an expensive study of a large and representative group of subjects.

By good fortune a grant was obtained from the Commonwealth Fund for an investigation of the desired scope. In 1922 a school population of more than a quarter of a million was sifted by methods which brought to light practically all the children capable of earning an I.Q. of 140 or higher, a score that is attained by only five or six children in 1000. More than 1050 subjects of this degree of intellectual superiority were located in the elementary grades and about 400 in high schools, a population large enough to yield reliable statistical constants and sufficiently free from sampling bias to provide a sound basis for generalization. What is true of this group should be true of any similarly selected group in any comparable culture.

Let it again be noted that the gifted child is here arbitrarily defined as one whose score in tested intelligence is equalled by about one child in 200 of the school population. Obviously the term 'genius' can be applied to subjects of this grade of mental superiority only in a very liberal sense. The population studied by Galton was twenty times as highly selected, since it included only the most eminent in 4000 of the generality. The American 'Who's Who' population is ten or twelve times as highly selected as my gifted group, and Cattell's galaxy of 1000 starred scientists is over a hundred times as aristocratic. It is necessary to hold these comparative figures in mind in order to appraise justly the life achievements of the subjects I have studied.

The data secured for this group in 1922 include for a majority of the subjects two intelligence scores; twelve scores from a four-hour test of school achievement; scores from three tests of character, personality and interests; thirty-four anthropometric measurements; the results of a one-hour medical examination; ratings by parents and teachers on twenty-five personality traits; and a large amount of case-history information supplied by parents, teachers and field assistants. What is the gifted child like when we find him?

The medical examination and anthropometric measurements showed the typical gifted child physically superior to the average. The tests of personality and character yielded scores far superior to those of average children of corresponding age. In school achievement the gifted subjects scored almost as high as in I.Q. A majority of them had in fact acquired a good mastery of the curriculum as far as two, three or even four school grades beyond that in which they were enrolled.

Marked unevenness in achievement was rare. Whereas the

mean I.Q. of the group was about 150, the mean achievement quotients in reading, arithmetic, language usage, spelling, science information, literary information, historical information and aesthetic information, were all in the narrow range between 137 and 152. The relative uniformity of these average scores establishes beyond question that a high degree of versatility is the rule in a group of this kind.

This is where our biographical study of gifted children began in 1922. It has now been under way long enough to give some indication of the probable life achievement of such a group. The thousand who were below high-school age in 1922 now range from twenty-two to thirty-two years, with a median of about twenty-seven. The 1922 high-school subjects range from twenty-nine to thirty-seven, with a median of thirty-three. I am still in contact with more than 95 per cent of the original group.

For several years after 1922 the subjects were followed by information blanks that were filled out and mailed to me annually by the parents and teachers. In 1928 a second grant from the Commonwealth Fund made it possible to have field assistants re-test most of the subjects and obtain a large amount of additional information through interviews with parents, teachers and the subjects themselves. The next follow-up was conducted chiefly by mail in 1936–7, but a liberal grant from the Carnegie Corporation a year ago has made it possible to keep three research associates in the field since last September testing and interviewing the subjects. As not all of the new data have yet been statisticized, most of the figures I shall report will be in round numbers subject to later corrections that will not materially affect the picture.

First a few vital statistics. The mortality rate of the group to date is below that of the generality of corresponding age. The same is true of the insanity rate. The incidence of suicide approaches more closely that of the generality.

At the present time nearly 71 per cent of the members of the group are or have been married, the proportion being about the same for men and women. The divorce rate is below that of the generality in California of corresponding age. Among those who have married, 43 per cent of the men and 55 per cent of the women married college graduates. The mean intelligence score of the subjects themselves is well above that of their spouses, but the latter also test high.

The group by 1940 had produced about 783 offspring. Tests given recently to 384 of these who are above the age of two years, have yielded a mean I.Q. of approximately 127, which represents about the expected regression towards the mean of the generality.

Has the intellectual superiority shown by this group in 1922 been maintained? In terms of intelligence test scores the answer is, on the whole, in the affirmative. The re-tests given during the past year showed a majority of the subjects close to the ninety-ninth percentile of the generality. This is true even of those whose careers have not been particularly successful. Although there are exceptions to the rule, the intellectually gifted individual can be identified almost as accurately in the third elementary grade as at age thirty.

With regard to educational achievement, the average member of the group enters high school at thirteen and college at seventeen. Nearly 90 per cent enter college and of those entering about 80 per cent graduate. Although averaging more than a year younger than their classmates, they engage more extensively in extra-curricular activities, receive more student-body honours and are several times as likely to graduate with distinction.

Approximately two-thirds of the men who graduate, and half of the women, go on for graduate work. Of some 300 men who have completed their graduate studies, about fifty have received a Ph.D. degree, about the same number a medical degree, about eighty-five a law degree, and about thirty-five a degree in engineering or architecture. Less than one-tenth as many women as men have obtained a graduate degree beyond the M.A. For the sexes combined the incidence of higher professional degrees is perhaps twenty or thirty times as great as for the general population.

In appraising the life achievements of these subjects it is necessary to take account of the severe economic depression that has spanned most or all of their adult years. This circumstance has made harder the way of many and has diverted some permanently from their educational goals.

The averaged earned income of the men at age thirty is around $3000 a year. About a dozen of the men are earning between $10,000 and $15,000 a year. In general, the women who are gainfully employed earn only about half as much as the men, and the maximum reached by women is only about one-fifth the maximum for men. Income, however, is a poor measurement of achievement, particularly in the case of young men just starting on their professional careers. Some of the most promising members of the group are at present (1940) earning less than $2500 a year.

Turning to other indications of achievement we find that about fifty of the men and a dozen of the women are teaching in colleges or universities. Seven of these are already executive heads of departments.

Publications by the total group number hundreds of articles in professional or technical journals, at least twenty books, and a vast number of short stories, popular articles and poems. The books include textbooks, scholarly treatises, a semi-popular book on invention, five volumes of fiction and two books of poems. Eighty or more patents have been issued to men of the group, none to any of the women.

We have seen in the case of historical geniuses that the direction of adult accomplishment is often foreshadowed during the early years. In order to find whether this is true of my gifted group the records of men in the various fields are being compared with respect to childhood hobbies, school marks, achievement test scores, amount and kinds of early reading, trait ratings by parents and teachers, early social adjustment and other variables. Although the analysis has not been completed, the data are showing more than chance agreement between some of these variables and the field of adult achievement. This is particularly true of those who have accomplished the most. Achievement in music, literature and art is almost always foreshadowed in some degree.

The range of success in my group is very wide for both sexes and at the present time extends downwards to occupations as humble as those of policeman, carpenter, gardener, gas station operator, department store floor-walker, store clerk, house-to-house canvasser, small rancher, seaman, telephone operator, typist and filing clerk. The question arises what factors other than intelligence are important determiners of achievement in such a group.

One, obviously, is sex. Although the women equal or excel the men in school achievement from the first grade through college, after school days are over the great majority cease to compete with men in the world's work. If they do not marry at once they accept whatever kind of respectable employment is at hand. After marriage they fall into the domestic role and only in exceptional cases seek other outlet for their talents. The woman who is a potential poet, novelist, lawyer, physician or scientist usually gives up any professional ambition she may have had and devotes herself to home, husband and children. The exclusive devotion of women to domestic pursuits robs the arts and sciences of a large fraction of the genius that might otherwise be dedicated to them. My data strongly suggest that this loss must be debited to motivational causes and to limitations of opportunity rather than to lack of ability.

Since the achievement of women is so largely determined by extraneous circumstances and is in any case so difficult to estimate, my investigation of the causes of success and failure has been confined to the male group. Three psychologists, working independently, examined the records of 600 men and rated each subject on life success. The criterion of 'success' was the extent to which a subject had made use of his superior intellectual ability. The judges were instructed to give very little weight to earned income.

On the basis of these ratings the men were tentatively classified into three groups, composing roughly the highest fourth, the middle 50 per cent and the lowest fourth. The highest and lowest fourths, or the A and C groups as we have called them, were then compared with respect to test scores of 1922 and 1928, family records, home environment, case histories, health data, trait ratings and many other items of information, in the hope that by reading the records backwards, so to speak, some light might be thrown on the factors that influence achievement.

The educational and occupational records of these two groups present a vivid contrast. Of the As, 98 per cent entered college and 90 per cent graduated; of the Cs, 70 per cent entered and only 50 per cent graduated. Three-fourths of the As but only a fifth of the Cs completed one or more years of graduate work. Among those graduating, nearly one-half the As but only 4 per cent of the

Cs were elected to Phi Beta Kappa or Sigma Xi. Half of the As but only 10 per cent of the Cs had received appointment to scholarships, fellowship or assistantships. In professional or semi-professional pursuits were 96 per cent of the As as compared with 28 per cent of the Cs. Although salary had been given little weight in the success ratings, the average earned income of the As was two and a third times that of the Cs.

Let us turn next to the childhood records and test scores of the two groups to see what facts or circumstances are associated with differences in life accomplishment. We note first that during the elementary school years the As and Cs were about equally successful. Their average grades were almost identical, and the average scores on a four-hour achievement test were only a trifle higher for the A group. In high school the groups began to draw apart as a result of lower grades in group C, but it was not until the college period that the slump of this group assumed alarming proportions. The slump cannot be blamed upon extra-curricular activities, for these were almost twice as common among the As as among the Cs. Nor can it be attributed to intellectual deterioration, for on every mental test, from 1922 to 1940, the average score of the Cs has been only a few points lower than that of the As. In a population so highly selected for intelligence that each person in it rates within the top one per cent of the generality, the differences in success must necessarily be due chiefly to non-intellectual factors.

For one thing, the family backgrounds of the two groups differed markedly. Nearly twice as many A parents as C parents had graduated from college, and a similar difference was found between the siblings of As and Cs. Fathers of the As were far more often in the professional classes. The important point here is that the educational tradition was stronger in families of the A group. In line with this is the fact that the Jewish element is three times as large among the As as among the Cs. The Jewish child is under heavy pressure to succeed, with the result that he accomplishes more per unit of intelligence than do children of any other racial stock.

Significant differences between the groups were found in the childhood data on emotional stability, social adjustments and various traits of personality. The case histories and trait ratings obtained from parents and teachers in 1922 reflect these differences clearly. All the 1922 trait ratings except those for health averaged lower for the C group. That is, fifteen or more years prior to the classification of these subjects on the basis of adult achievement, teachers and parents had been able to discern personality differences that would later characterize the two groups.

The A–C differences are further evidenced in the marital records. The incidence of marriage is higher in the A group and the age of marriage is lower. Moreover, the As marry better than the Cs; the A spouses score higher in intelligence tests and include nearly twice as large a proportion of college graduates. Especially significant is the contrast in marital adjustments, for the incidence of separation or divorce is only a third as high in the A group as in the C group. This difference extends even to the parents of the two groups, the incidence of separation or divorce being only half as great for A parents as for C parents.

The A–C differences in marital adjustments appear to be symptomatic of more basic differences in emotional stability and integration of personality. With the aid of funds from the National Research Council a special study is being made of marital adjustments in the entire gifted population. This has shown that the A group scores higher than the C group not only in present marital happiness, but also higher in a test designed to measure general happiness of temperament, or what might be called aptitude for happiness.

The facts just reported appear to be in direct opposition to the Lange-Eichbaum theory that great achievement is associated with emotional tensions which border on the abnormal. In my gifted group success is associated with emotional stability rather than instability, with absence rather than presence of disturbing conflicts, with happiness of temperament and with freedom from excessive frustration. This does not necessarily mean that the Lange-Eichbaum theory has been disproved. It is conceivable that the personality factors which make for ordinary achievement under ordinary conditions are different from those which make for eminence of a superlative order. The two approaches agree in the conclusion that beyond a certain high level of intellectual ability success is largely determined by non-intellectual factors and that the number of persons who are endowed with abilities equal to great achievement is immensely greater than the number who will attain eminence.

Looking forward to the future, I regard it as unlikely that more than three score of my 1450 subjects will attain to a national reputation or that more than a dozen or so will become really eminent. It would be surprising if even one of them a hundred years hence should be found among the thousand most eminent persons of history. In sheer intellectual ability, however, I am sure that my group overlaps Cattell's thousand most eminent persons of history. Although the group certainly contains no intellect at all comparable with that of a Newton or Shakespeare, I believe it contains many who are intellectual equals of Washington, the nineteenth most eminent in Cattell's list, and perhaps some who are not intellectually inferior to Napoleon, the most eminent man of all time.

These specific estimates are of course not amenable to objective proof. They are offered merely as illustrations of a larger truth that no one can doubt who has studied either a group of historical persons or a group of living gifted subjects: namely, that genius and eminence are far from perfectly correlated. Why they are so poorly correlated, what circumstances affect the fruition of human talent, are questions of such transcendent importance that they should be investigated by every method that promises the slightest reduction of our present ignorance. So little do we know about our available supply of potential genius; the environmental factors that favour or hinder its expression; the emotional compulsions that give it dynamic quality; or the personality distortions that make it dangerous! And viewing the present crisis in world affairs who can doubt that these things may decide the fate of a civilization?

3 Anne Roe

A Psychologist Examines Sixty-Four Eminent Scientists

Anne Roe, 'A psychologist examines sixty-four eminent scientists',
Scientific American, vol. 187, 1952, pp. 21–5. For a fuller description see
Anne Roe, *The Making of a Scientist*, Dodd Mead, 1952.

What elements enter into the making of a scientist? Are there
special qualities of personality, mind, intelligence, background or
upbringing that mark a person for this calling? Besides the natural
interest in these questions, they have a practical importance,
because the recruitment of qualified young people into science is
a growing problem in our society. Where and how shall we find
them?

During the past five years I have been making a study of the
attributes of a group of scientists and the reasons why they chose
this field of work. The most eminent scientists in the U.S. were
selected as subjects, since they are most likely to exemplify the
special qualities, if any, that are associated with success in research
science. They were selected by panels of experts in each field of
science. The study finally settled on a group of sixty-four eminent
men who agreed to participate – twenty biologists, twenty-two
physicists and twenty-two social scientists (psychologists and
anthropologists). A high percentage of them are members of the
National Academy of Sciences or the American Philosophical
Society or both, and among them they have received a staggering
number of honorary degrees, prizes and other awards.

Each of the sixty-four individuals was then examined exhaustive-
ly by long personal interviews and tests: his life history, family
background, professional and recreational interests, intelligence,
achievements, personality, ways of thinking – any information
that might have a bearing on the subject's choice of his vocation
and his success in it. Each was given an intelligence test and was
examined by two of the modern techniques for the study of personality: the Rorschach and the Thematic Apperception Test
(TAT). The Rorschach, popularly known as the inkblot test,

gives information about such things as the way the subject deals with problems, his manner of approach to them, the extent and efficiency of his use of rational controls, his inner preoccupations, his responsiveness to outside stimuli. The TAT gives information about attitudes toward family and society and self, about expectations and needs and desires, and something about the development of these.

My study was financed during the first four years by grants from the National Institute of Mental Health and is being continued this year under a Guggenheim Fellowship. It has developed a great deal of material, much of which has been published in technical detail in special journals. In this brief article it is possible only to recapitulate the high points.

There is no such thing, of course, as a 'typical' scientist. Eminent scientists differ greatly as individuals, and there are well-marked group differences between the biologists and the physicists, and between the natural scientists and the social scientists. Certain common patterns do appear, however, in the group as a whole, and the most convenient way to summarize these generalizations is to try to draw a picture of what might be called the 'average' eminent scientist.

He was the first-born child of a middle-class family, the son of a professional man. He is likely to have been a sickly child or to have lost a parent at an early age. He has a very high I.Q. and in boyhood began to do a great deal of reading. He tended to feel lonely and 'different' and to be shy and aloof from his classmates. He had only a moderate interest in girls and did not begin dating them until college. He married late (at twenty-seven), has two children and finds security in family life; his marriage is more stable than the average. Not until his junior or senior year in college did he decide on his vocation as a scientist. What decided him (almost invariably) was a college project in which he had occasion to do some independent research – to find out things for himself. Once he discovered the pleasures of this kind of work, he never turned back. He is completely satisfied with his chosen vocation. (Only one of the sixty-four eminent scientists – a Nobel prize winner – says he would have preferred to do something else: he wanted to be a farmer, but could not make a living at it.) He works hard and devotedly in his laboratory, often seven days a week. He says his work is his life, and he has few recreations, those being restricted to fishing, sailing, walking or some other individualistic activity. The movies bore him. He avoids social affairs and political activity, and religion plays no part in his life or thinking. Better than any other interest or activity, scientific research seems to meet the inner need of his nature.

Table 1

Field	Age at time of study		Average age at time of receiving college degrees	
	Average	Range	B.A.	Ph.D., Sc.D., M.D.
Biologists	51·2	38–58	21·8	26·0
Physical scientists	44·7	31–56	20·9	24·6
Social scientists	47·7	35–60	21·8	26·8

Average age of the subjects at the time of the study and at the time they received their degrees is given in this table. The upper age limit was set at sixty; the lower limit was determined by the eminence of the subjects.

This generalized picture represents only majority traits; there are, of course, many exceptions to it, not only in individual cases but by groups; the social scientists, for instance, tend to be by no means shy but highly gregarious and social. Let us now consider the differences between groups. I have separated the physicists into the theorists (twelve) and the experimentalists (ten), because these two groups differ sharply. The biologists (physiologists, botanists, geneticists, biochemists, and so on) are sufficiently alike to be grouped together, and so are the social scientists.

No standardized intelligence test was sufficiently difficult for these eminent scientists; hence a special test was constructed by the Educational Testing Service. To provide ratings on particular intellectual factors, the test was divided into three parts: verbal (seventy-nine items), spatial (twenty-four items) and mathematical (thirty-nine). (The mathematical test used was not difficult enough for the physicists, and several of them did not take it.)

While the group as a whole is characterized by very high average intelligence, as would be expected, the range is wide (see Table 5). Among the biologists, the geneticists and biochemists

45

do relatively better on the non-verbal test than on the verbal, and the other biologists tend to do relatively better on the verbal. Among the physicists there is some tendency for theorists to do relatively better on the verbal and for the experimentalists to do relatively better on the spatial test. Among the social scientists the

Table 2

Field	Visual	Verbal	Imageless	Totals
Biologists	10	4	3	17
Physicists	10	4	4	18
Psychologists and anthropologists	2	11	6	19
Totals	22	19	13	54

Imagery of the scientists was correlated with specialty. The natural scientists were strong in visual imagery; the social scientists, in verbal.

experimental psychologists do relatively better on the spatial or mathematical than on the verbal test, and the reverse is true of the other psychologists and the anthropologists.

On the TAT the social scientists tended to give much longer stories than the other groups did – verbal fluency is characteristic

Table 3

Profession of Father	Visual	Verbal	Imageless	Totals
Verbal	5	10	3	18
Non-verbal	8	2	2	12
Totals	13	12	5	30

Imagery of the father's profession was strongly influential. The numbers on the right side of this table refer to the imagery of the sons.

of them. The biologists were inclined to be much more factual, less interested in feelings and, in general, unwilling to commit themselves. This was true to a lesser extent of the physical scientists. The biologists and physical scientists manifested a quite remarkable independence of parental relations and were without guilt feelings about it, while the social scientists showed many dependent attitudes, much rebelliousness and considerable helplessness, along with intense concern over interpersonal relations generally. The biologists were the least aggressive (but rather stubborn) and the social scientists the most aggressive. The most striking thing about the TAT results for the total group, however, is the rarity of any indication of the drive for achievement that all of these subjects have actually shown in their lives.

Table 4

	Bio-logists	Experimental physicists	Theoretical physicists	Psycho-logists	Anthro-pologists	Totals
Professions	9	5	10	7	3	34
Research science	0	1	0	0	0	1
Physician	0	2	1	2	0	5
Lawyer	0	0	1	1	3	5
Engineer	0	0	3	2	0	5
Clergyman	2	0	1	0	0	3
Editor	2	0	0	0	0	2
College teacher	4	0	3	2	0	9
School teacher	0	2	0	0	0	2
School superintendent	1	0	0	0	0	1
Pharmacist	0	0	1	0	0	1
Business	8	1	2	4	5	20
Own business	4	0	2	2	4	12
Clerk, agent, salesman	4	1	0	2	1	8
Farmer	2	4	0	2	0	8
Skilled labor	1	0	0	1	0	2
Totals	20	10	12	14	8	64
Per cent professional	45	50	84	50	38	53

Occupations of the fathers of the sixty-four eminent scientists showed a strong bias in favor of the professions. This was especially true of the twelve theoretical physicists, ten of whose fathers had been professionals. The anthropologists were an exception: five out of eight came from business backgrounds. Four of the ten experimental physicists were the sons of farmers. None of the scientists were the sons of unskilled laborers.

On the Rorschach the social scientists show themselves to be enormously productive and intensely concerned with human beings; the biologists are deeply concerned with form, and rely strongly upon a non-emotional approach to problems; the physicists show a good deal of free anxiety and concern with space and inanimate motion. Again the social scientists, particularly the anthropologists, are the most freely aggressive.

Early in the course of the work it became apparent that there were some differences in habits of thinking, and a special inquiry was instituted along these lines. The data are unsatisfactory from many standpoints – there are no objective tests for such material, and I had to ask many leading questions in order to convey any idea of what I was after. Nevertheless rather definite and meaningful patterns did appear. The biologists and the experimental

Table 5

	No.	Verbal test		Spatial test		Mathematical test	
		Average	Range	Average	Range	Average	Range
Biologists	19	56·6	28–73	9·4	3–20	16·8	6–27
Experimental physicists	7	46·6	8–71	11·7	3–22		
Theoretical physicists	11	64·2	52–75	13·8	5–19		
Psychologists	14	57·7	23–73	11·3	5–19	15·6	8–27
Anthropologists	8	61·1	43–72	8·2	3–15	9·2	4–13
Total	59	57·7	8–75	10·9	3–22	15·9	4–27
Approximate I.Q. equivalents		163	121–77	140	123–64	160	128–94

Intelligence test results revealed minor variations among the specialties of the scientists. The theoretical physicists did best in the verbal test; the experimental physicists rated lowest. Both theoretical and experimental physicists did not take the mathematical test because it was not sufficiently difficult. Two anthropologists who took the verbal test did not take the other tests on the ground that they could not do them.

physicists tend strongly to dependence upon visual imagery in their thinking – images of concrete objects or elaborate diagrams or the like. The theoretical physicists and social scientists tend to verbalization in their thinking – a kind of talking to themselves. All groups report a considerable amount of imageless thinking, particularly at crucial points. Men whose fathers followed talkative occupations (law, ministry, teaching) are more likely to think in words.

The life histories of these sixty-four men show some general similarities, and there are patterns characterizing some of the subgroups. Geographical factors seem not to be particularly significant, except that only a few came from the South. The economic level was varied, ranging from very poor to well-to-do; among the anthropologists and the theoretical physicists a somewhat higher percentage came from well-to-do homes.

In several respects the scientists' backgrounds differ very much from the population at large. There are no Catholics among this group of eminent scientists; five come from Jewish homes and the rest had Protestant backgrounds. Only three of the sixty-four now have serious interest in any church; only a few even maintain church memberships.

Another striking fact is that 53 per cent of the scientists were the sons of professional men; not one was the son of an unskilled laborer and only two were sons of skilled workmen. Why do more than half of our leading scientists come from the families of professional men? It seems to me most probable, from more knowledge of the family situations of these men than I can summarize here, that the operative factor is the value placed by these families and their associates on learning – learning for its own sake. Most of the scientists developed intellectual interests at an early age.

Another remarkable finding is how many of them were their parents' first children. This proportion is higher than chance expectancy in all of the subgroups. Thirty-nine were first born; of the rest five were eldest sons and two who were second born were effectively the eldest because of the early death of the first child. For the most of the others there is a considerable difference in age between the subject and the next older brother (averaging five years). It seems probable that all this may point to the most important single factor in the making of a scientist – the need and ability to develop personal independence to a high degree. The independence factor is emphasized by many other findings: the subjects' preference for teachers who let them alone, their attitudes toward religion, their attitudes toward personal relations, their satisfaction in a career in which, for the most part, they follow their own interests without direction or interference. It is possible that oldest sons in our culture have a greater amount of independence or more indulgence in the pursuit of their own interests than other children have. On the other hand, there is some psychological evidence that first-born tend to be more dependent, on the average, than other children, and a good case could be made out for a hypothesis that reaction to this over-dependence produced the scientists' strong drive to independence.

The early extracurricular interests of these men were varied, but here, too, there are some general patterns. More of the physicists than of the other groups showed early interests directly related to their later occupations, but this seems quite clearly to be due to the common small-boy preoccupation in this country with physical gadgets – radio, Meccano sets and so on. The theoretical physicists were omnivorous readers, the experimentalists much less so. Among the social scientists many went through a stage of considering or even working toward a literary career. Half of the biologists showed some early interest in natural history, but for only five was it of an intense and serious sort, involving keeping field records of birds and flowers, and so on. Many of the biologists did not know during childhood of the possibility of a career in biology. This was even more true of the psychologists and anthropologists, since there are almost no boyhood activities related to professional social science.

It is of considerable interest that over half of these men did not decide upon their vocations until they were juniors or seniors in college. More important, perhaps, than when they decided, is why they decided. It certainly was not just a matter of always following an early bent. From fiddling with gadgets to becoming a physicist may be no great leap, but the attractions of theoretical physics are not so obvious or well known, nor are those of the social sciences or advanced biology. In the stories of the social scientists and of the biologists it becomes clear that the most important factor in the final decision to become a scientist is the discovery of the joys of research. In physics the discovery may come so gradually as not to be noticed as such, but in the other sciences it often came as a revelation of unique moment, and many of these men know just when and how they found it out. A couple of quotations will illustrate this:

I had no course in biology until my senior year in college. It was a small college and the teacher was about the first on the faculty with a Ph.D. It was about my first contact with the idea that not everything was known, my first contact with research. In that course I think my final decision was really taken. It was mainly that I wanted to do something in the way of research though I didn't know just what, but working out something new.

One of the professors took a group of us and thought if we wanted to learn about things, the way to do it was to do research. My senior year I carried through some research. That really sent me, that was the thing that trapped me. After that there was no getting out.

That research experience is so often decisive is a fact of very considerable importance for educational practice. The discovery of the possibility of finding things out for oneself usually came through experience in school with a teacher who put the students pretty much on their own.

There are other things in the general process of growing up that may have influenced the choice of career in subtle ways. One-fourth of the biologists lost a parent by death or divorce at an early age. This may have tended to shove them to greater independence. Among the theoretical physicists there was a high incidence of serious illness or physical handicaps during childhood, which certainly contributed to the feelings of isolation characteristic of them. Among the social scientists there is an unusually intense concern with personal relationships, which often goes back to family conflicts during childhood. A relatively large proportion of them seem to have come from homes in which the mother was dominant and the father inadequate in some way. The divorce rate among the social scientists in this study was remarkably high – 41 per cent.

Whereas the characteristic pattern among the biologists and physicists is that of the shy, lonely, over-intellectualized boy, among the social scientists the characteristic picture is very different. They got into social activity and intensive and extensive dating at an early age. They were often presidents of their classes, editors of yearbooks and literary magazines, frequently big shots in college. This contrast between the natural and social scientists was still evident after they grew up. It is true only in general, of course; even among the theoretical physicists there are some ardent party-goers.

The one thing that all of these sixty-four scientists have in common is their driving absorption in their work. They have worked long hours for many years, frequently with no vacations to speak of, because they would rather be doing their work than anything else.

Part Two Introspective Materials

Artists and scientists are seldom likely to be careful and reliable observers of their own mental processes and methods of work; and in music and painting it must be doubly difficult to describe the nature of inspiration verbally. Nevertheless a good deal of material is available to us from letters and biographies; and while this illustrates tremendous variations in the methods of different creative individuals, there also seems to be much in common, even between different types of artists or between artists and scientists, when allowance is made for the different media of expression. Note that all our authors refer to ideas coming to them from outside the realm of conscious thought, though all (except Mozart) also show that creation is not merely inexplicable, unconscious inspiration; that it involves lengthy elaboration and working out by a skilled craftsman.

Here we have two excerpts by composers, one by a writer and one by a mathematician. Ghiselin (1952) has provided a much more extensive collection and R. Harding (1940) a very comprehensive synthesis.

References
GHISELIN, B. (1952), *The Creative Process: A Symposium*, University of California Press.
HARDING, R. (1940), *An Anatomy of Inspiration*, Cass.

4 Wolfgang Amadeus Mozart

A Letter [1]

Excerpt from E. Holmes, *The Life of Mozart Including his Correspondence*, Chapman & Hall, 1878, pp. 211–13.

When I am, as it were, completely myself, entirely alone, and of good cheer – say, travelling in a carriage, or walking after a good meal, or during the night when I cannot sleep; it is on such occasions that my ideas flow best and most abundantly. *Whence* and *how* they come, I know not; nor can I force them. Those pleasures that please me I retain in memory, and am accustomed, as I have been told, to hum them to myself. If I continue in this way, it soon occurs to me how I may turn this or that morsel to account, so as to make a good dish of it, that is to say, agreeably to the rules of counterpoint, to the peculiarities of the various instruments, etc.

All this fires my soul, and, provided I am not disturbed, my subject enlarges itself, becomes methodized and defined, and the whole, though it be long, stands almost complete and finished in my mind, so that I can survey it, like a fine picture or a beautiful statue, at a glance. Nor do I hear in my imagination the parts *successively*, but I hear them, as it were, all at once (*gleich alles zusammen*). What a delight this is I cannot tell! All this inventing, this producing, takes place in a pleasing lively dream. Still the actual hearing of the *tout ensemble* is after all the best. What has been thus produced I do not easily forget, and this is perhaps the best gift I have my Divine Maker to thank for.

When I proceed to write down my ideas, I take out of the bag of my memory, if I may use that phrase, what has been previously collected into it in the way I have mentioned. For this reason the

---

1. The original translator, in 1825, supposed this letter to have been written in 1783, but this is obviously wrong as the quartets mentioned were composed later. Most authorities now believe the letter to have been written *c.* 1789.

committing to paper is done quickly enough, for everything is, as I have said before, already finished; and it rarely differs on paper from what it was in my imagination. At this occupation I can therefore suffer myself to be disturbed; for whatever may be going on around me, I write, and even talk, but only of fowls and geese, or of Gretel or Bärbel, or some such matters. But why my productions take from my hand that particular form and style that makes them *Mozartish*, and different from the works of other composers, is probably owing to the same cause which renders my nose so large or so aquiline, or, in short, makes it Mozart's, and different from those of other people. For I really do not study or aim at any originality.

5 Peter Ilich Tchaikovsky

Letters

Excerpts from R. Newmarch, *Life and Letters of Peter Ilich Tchaikovsky*, John Lane, 1906, pp. 274–5, 280–81, 311–12.

Florence, 17 February (1 March) 1878

You ask if in composing this symphony I had a special programme in view. To such questions regarding my symphonic works I generally answer: nothing of the kind. In reality it is very difficult to answer this question. How interpret those vague feelings which pass through one during the composition of an instrumental work, without reference to any definite subject? It is a purely lyrical process. A kind of musical shriving of the soul, in which there is an encrustation of material which flows forth again in notes, just as the lyrical poet pours himself out in verse. The difference consists in the fact that music possesses far richer means of expression, and is a more subtle medium in which to translate the thousand shifting moments in the mood of a soul. Generally speaking, the germ of a future composition comes suddenly and unexpectedly. If the soil is ready – that is to say, if the disposition for work is there – it takes root with extraordinary force and rapidity, shoots up through the earth, puts forth branches, leaves and, finally, blossoms. I cannot define the creative process in any other way than by this simile. The great difficulty is that the germ must appear at a favourable moment, the rest goes of itself. It would be vain to try to put into words that immeasurable sense of bliss which comes over me directly a new idea awakens in me and begins to assume a definite form. I forget everything and behave like a madman. Everything within me starts pulsing and quivering; hardly have I begun the sketch ere one thought follows another. In the midst of this magic process it frequently happens that some external interruption wakes me from my somnambulistic state: a ring at the bell, the entrance of my servant, the striking of the clock, reminding me that it is time to leave off.

Dreadful, indeed, are such interruptions. Sometimes they break the thread of inspiration for a considerable time, so that I have to seek it again – often in vain. In such cases cool headwork and technical knowledge have to come to my aid. Even in the works of the greatest master we find such moments, when the organic sequence fails and a skilful join has to be made, so that the parts appear as a completely welded whole. But it cannot be avoided. If that condition of mind and soul, which we call *inspiration*, lasted long without intermission, no artist could survive it. The strings would break and the instrument be shattered into fragments. It is already a great thing if the main ideas and general outline of a work come without any racking of brains, as the result of that supernatural and inexplicable force we call inspiration. [. . .]

Clarens, 5 (17) March 1878

It is delightful to talk to you about my own methods of composition. So far I have never had any opportunity of confiding to anyone these hidden utterances of my inner life; partly because very few would be interested, and partly because, of these few, scarcely one would know how to respond to me properly. To you, and you alone, I gladly describe all the details of the creative process, because in you I have found one who has a fine feeling and can understand my music.

Do not believe those who try to persuade you that composition is only a cold exercise of the intellect. The only music capable of moving and touching us is that which flows from the depths of a composer's soul when he is stirred by inspiration. There is no doubt that even the greatest musical geniuses have sometimes worked without inspiration. This guest does not always respond to the first invitation. We must *always* work, and a self-respecting artist must not fold his hands on the pretext that he is not in the mood. If we wait for the mood, without endeavouring to meet it half-way, we easily become indolent and apathetic. We must be patient, and believe that inspiration will come to those who can master their *disinclination*. A few days ago I told you I was working every day without any real inspiration. Had I given way to my disinclination, undoubtedly I should have drifted into a long period of idleness. But my patience and faith did not fail me, and to-day I felt that inexplicable glow of inspiration of which I told you; thanks to which I know beforehand that whatever I write to-day will have power to make an impression, and to touch the hearts of those who hear it. I hope you will not think I am indulging in self-laudation, if I tell you that I very seldom suffer from this disinclination to work. I believe the reason for this is that I am naturally patient. I have learnt to master myself, and I am glad I have not followed in the steps of some of my Russian colleagues, who have no self-confidence and are so impatient that at the least difficulty they are ready to throw up the sponge. This is why, in spite of great gifts, they accomplish so little, and that in an amateur way.

You ask me how I manage my instrumentation. I never compose in the *abstract*; that is to say, the musical thought never appears otherwise than in a suitable external form. In this way I invent the musical idea and the instrumentation simultaneously. Thus I thought out the scherzo of our symphony – at the moment of its composition – exactly as you heard it. It is inconceivable except as *pizzicato*. Were it played with the bow, it would lose all its charm and be a mere body without a soul. [. . .]

Kamenka, 25 June (7 July) 1878

Yesterday, when I wrote to you about my methods of composing, I did not sufficiently enter into that phase of work which relates to the working out of the sketch. This phase is of primary importance. What has been set down in a moment of ardour must now be critically examined, improved, extended, or condensed, as the form requires. Sometimes one must do oneself violence, must sternly and pitilessly take part against oneself, before one can mercilessly erase things thought out with love and enthusiasm. I cannot complain of poverty of imagination, or lack of inventive power; but, on the other hand, I have always suffered from my want of skill in the management of form. Only after strenuous labour have I at last succeeded in making the form of my compositions correspond, more or less, with their contents. Formerly I was careless and did not give sufficient attention to the critical overhauling of my sketches. Consequently my *seams* showed, and there was no organic union between my individual episodes. This was a very serious defect, and I only improved gradually as time went on; but the form of my works will never be *exemplary*, because, although I can modify, I cannot radically alter the essential qualities of my musical temperament. But I am far from believing that my gifts have yet reached their ultimate development. I can affirm with joy that I make continual progress on the way of self-development, and am passionately desirous of attaining the highest degree of perfection of which my talents are capable. Therefore I expressed myself badly when I told you yesterday that I transcribed my works direct from the first sketches. The process is something more than copying; it is actually a critical examination, leading to correction, occasional additions and frequent curtailments.

6 Stephen Spender

The Making of a Poem

Stephen Spender, 'The making of a poem', reprinted in B. Ghiselin
(ed.), *The Creative Process: A Symposium*, University of California
Press, 1952, pp. 112–25. First published 1946.

It would be inexcusable to discuss my own way of writing poetry
unless I were able to relate this to a wider view of the problems
which poets attempt to solve when they sit down at a desk or
table to write, or walk around composing their poems in their
heads. There is a danger of my appearing to put across my own
experiences as the general rule, when every poet's way of going
about his work and his experience of being a poet are different,
and when my own poetry may not be good enough to lend my
example any authority.

Yet the writing of poetry is an activity which makes certain
demands of attention on the poet and which requires that he
should have certain qualifications of ear, vision, imagination,
memory and so on. He should be able to think in images; he
should have as great a mastery of language as a painter has over
his palate, even if the range of his language be very limited. All
this means that, in ordinary society, a poet has to adapt himself,
more or less consciously, to the demands of his vocation, and
hence the peculiarities of poets and the condition of inspiration
which many people have said is near to madness. One poet's
example is only his adaptation of his personality to the demands of
poetry, but if it is clearly stated it may help us to understand other
poets, and even something of poetry.

Today we lack very much a whole view of poetry, and have
instead many one-sided views of certain aspects of poetry which
have been advertised as the only aims which poets should
attempt. Movements such as free verse, imagism, surrealism,
expressionism, personalism, and so on, tend to make people
think that poetry is simply a matter of not writing in metre or
rhyme, or of free association, or of thinking in images, or of a

kind of drawing room madness (surrealism) which corresponds to drawing room communism. Here is a string of ideas: Night, dark, stars, immensity, blue, voluptuous, clinging, columns, clouds, moon, sickle, harvest, vast camp fire, hell. Is this poetry? A lot of strings of words almost as simple as this are set down on the backs of envelopes and posted off to editors or to poets by the vast army of amateurs who think that to be illogical is to be poetic, with that fond question. Thus I hope that this discussion of how poets work will imply a wider and completer view of poets.

Concentration

The problem of creative writing is essentially one of concentration, and the supposed eccentricities of poets are usually due to mechanical habits or rituals developed in order to concentrate. Concentration, of course, for the purpose of writing poetry, is different from the kind of concentration required for working out a sum. It is a focusing of the attention in a special way, so that the poet is aware of all the implications and possible developments of his idea, just as one might say that a plant was not concentrating on developing mechanically in one direction, but in many directions, towards the warmth and light with its leaves, and towards the water with its roots, all at the same time.

Schiller liked to have a smell of rotten apples, concealed beneath the lid of his desk, under his nose when he was composing poetry. Walter de la Mare has told me that he must smoke when writing. Auden drinks endless cups of tea. Coffee is my own addiction, besides smoking a great deal, which I hardly ever do except when I am writing. I notice also that as I attain a greater concentration, this tends to make me forget the taste of the cigarette in my mouth, and then I have a desire to smoke two or even three cigarettes at a time, in order that the sensation from the outside may penetrate through the wall of concentration which I have built round myself.

For goodness sake, though, do not think that rotten apples or cigarettes or tea have anything to do with the quality of the work of a Schiller, a de la Mare or an Auden. They are a part of a concentration which has already been attained rather than the causes of concentration. De la Mare once said to me that he thought the desire to smoke when writing poetry arose from a need, not of a stimulus, but to canalize a distracting leak of his attention away from his writing towards the distraction which is always present in one's environment. Concentration may be disturbed by someone whistling in the street or the ticking of a clock. There is always a slight tendency of the body to sabotage the attention of the mind by providing some distraction. If this need for distraction can be directed into one channel – such as the odor of rotten apples or the taste of tobacco or tea – then other distractions outside oneself are put out of competition.

Another possible explanation is that the concentrated effort of writing poetry is a spiritual activity which makes one completely forget, for the time being, that one has a body. It is a disturbance of the balance of body and mind and for this reason one needs a kind of anchor of sensation with the physical world. Hence the craving for a scent or taste or even, sometimes, for sexual activity. Poets speak of the necessity of writing poetry rather than of a liking for doing it. It is spiritual compulsion, a straining of the mind to attain heights surrounded by abysses and it cannot be entirely happy, for in the most important sense, the only reward worth having is absolutely denied: for, however confident a poet may be, he is never quite sure that all his energy is not misdirected nor that what he is writing is great poetry. At the moment when art attains its highest attainment it reaches beyond its medium of words or paints or music, and the artist finds himself realizing that these instruments are inadequate to the spirit of what he is trying to say.

Different poets concentrate in different ways. In my own mind I make a sharp distinction between two types of concentration: one is immediate and complete, the other is plodding and only completed by stages. Some poets write immediately works which, when they are written, scarcely need revision. Others write their poems by stages, feeling their way from rough draft to rough draft, until finally, after many revisions, they have produced a result which may seem to have very little connexion with their early sketches.

These two opposite processes are vividly illustrated in two examples drawn from music: Mozart and Beethoven. Mozart thought out symphonies, quartets, even scenes from operas, entirely in his head – often on a journey or perhaps while dealing with pressing problems – and then he transcribed them, in their completeness, onto paper. Beethoven wrote fragments of themes in note books which he kept beside him, working on and developing them over years. Often his first ideas were of a clumsiness which makes scholars marvel how he could, at the end, have developed from them such miraculous results.

Thus genius works in different ways to achieve its ends. But although the Mozartian type of genius is the more brilliant and dazzling, genius, unlike virtuosity, is judged by greatness of results, not by brilliance of performance. The result must be the fullest development in a created esthetic form of an original moment of insight, and it does not matter whether genius devotes a lifetime to producing a small result if that result be immortal. The difference between two types of genius is that one type (the Mozartian) is able to plunge to the greatest depths of his own experience by the tremendous effort of a moment, the other (the Beethovenian) must dig deeper and deeper into his consciousness, layer by layer. What counts in either case is the vision which sees and pursues and attains the end; the logic of the artistic purpose.

A poet may be divinely gifted with a lucid and intense and purposive intellect; he may be clumsy and slow; that does not matter, what matters is integrity of purpose and the ability to maintain the purpose without losing oneself. Myself, I am scarcely capable of immediate concentration in poetry. My mind is not clear, my will is weak, I suffer from an excess of ideas and a weak sense of form. For every poem that I begin to write, I think of at least ten which I do not write down at all. For every poem which I do write down, there are seven or eight which I never complete.

The method which I adopt therefore is to write down as many ideas as possible, in however rough a form, in notebooks (I have at least twenty of these, on a shelf beside my desk, going back over fifteen years). I then make use of some of the sketches and discard others.

The best way of explaining how I develop the rough ideas which I use, is to take an example. Here is a notebook begun in

1944. About a hundred pages of it are covered with writing, and from this have emerged about six poems. Each idea, when it first occurs, is given a number. Sometimes the ideas do not get beyond one line. For example no. 3 (never developed) is the one line:

> A language of flesh and roses.

I shall return to this line in a few pages, when I speak of inspiration. For the moment, I turn to no. 13, because here is an idea which has been developed to its conclusion. The first sketch begins thus:

(a) There are some days when the sea lies like a harp
    Stretched flat beneath the cliffs. The waves
    Like wires burn with the sun's copper glow
        [all the murmuring blue
            every silent]
    Between whose spaces every image
    Of sky [field and] hedge and field and boat
    Dwells like the huge face of the afternoon.
    [Lies]
    When the heat grows tired, the afternoon
    Out of the land may breathe a sigh
    [Across these wires like a hand. They vibrate
    With]
    Which moves across those wires like a soft hand
    [Then the vibration]
    Between whose spaces the vibration holds
    Every bird-cry, dog's bark, man-shout
    And creak of rollock from the land and sky
    With all the music of the afternoon.

Obviously these lines are attempts to sketch out an idea which exists clearly enough on some level of the mind where it yet eludes the attempt to state it. At this stage, a poem is like a face which one seems to be able to visualize clearly in the eye of memory, but when one examines it mentally or tries to think it out, feature by feature, it seems to fade.

The idea of this poem is a vision of the sea. The faith of the poet is that if this vision is clearly stated it will be significant. The vision is of the sea stretched under a cliff. On top of the cliff there are fields, hedges, houses. Horses draw carts along lanes, dogs bark far inland, bells ring in the distance. The shore seems laden with hedges, roses, horses and men, all high above the sea, on a very fine summer day when the ocean seems to reflect and absorb the shore. Then the small strung-out glittering waves of the sea lying under the shore are like the strings of a harp which catch the sunlight. Between these strings lies the reflection of the shore. Butterflies are wafted out over the waves, which they mistake for the fields of the chalky landscape, searching them for flowers. On a day such as this, the land, reflected in the sea, appears to enter into the sea, as though it lies under it, like Atlantis. The wires of the harp are like a seen music fusing seascape and landscape.

Looking at this vision in another way, it obviously has symbolic value. The sea represents death and eternity, the land represents the brief life of the summer and of one human generation which passes into the sea of eternity. But let me here say at once that although the poet may be conscious of this aspect of his vision, it is exactly what he wants to avoid stating, or even being too concerned with. His job is to recreate his vision, and let it speak its moral for itself. The poet must distinguish clearly in his own mind between that which most definitely must be said and that which must not be said. The unsaid inner meaning is revealed in the music and the tonality of the poem, and the poet is conscious of it in his knowledge that a certain tone of voice, a certain rhythm, are necessary.

In the next twenty versions of the poem I felt my way towards the clarification of the seen picture, the music and the inner feeling. In the first version quoted above, there is the phrase in the second and third lines:

> The waves
> Like wires burn with the sun's copper glow.

This phrase fuses the image of the sea with the idea of music, and it is therefore a key phrase, because the theme of the poem is the fusion of the land with the sea. Here, then, are several versions of these one and a quarter lines, in the order in which they were written:

> (b)   The waves are wires
> Burning as with the secret song of fires.

> (c) The day burns in the trembling wires
> With a vast music golden in the eyes.

> (d) The day glows on its trembling wires
> Singing a golden music in the eyes.

> (e) The day glows on its burning wires
> Like waves of music golden to the eyes.

> (f) Afternoon burns upon its wires
> Lines of music dazzling the eyes.

> (g) Afternoon gilds its tingling wires
> To a visual silent music of the eyes.

In the final version, these two lines appear as in the following stanza:

> (h) There are some days the happy ocean lies
> Like an unfingered harp, below the land.

> Afternoon gilds all the silent wires
> Into a burning music of the eyes.

> On mirroring paths between those fine-strung fires
> The shore, laden with roses, horses, spires,
> Wanders in water, imaged above ribbed sand.

Inspiration

The hard work evinced in these examples, which are only a fraction of the work put into the whole poem, may cause the reader to wonder whether there is no such thing as inspiration, or whether it is merely Stephen Spender who is uninspired. The answer is that everything in poetry is work except inspiration, whether this work is achieved at one swift stroke, as Mozart wrote his music, or whether it is a slow process of evolution from stage to stage. Here again, I have to qualify the word 'work', as I qualified the word 'concentration': the work on a line of poetry may take the form of putting a version aside for a few days, weeks or years, and then taking it up again, when it may be found that the line has, in the interval of time, almost rewritten itself.

✓ Inspiration is the beginning of a poem and it is also its final goal. It is the first idea which drops into the poet's mind and it is the final idea which he at last achieves in words. In between this start and this winning post there is the hard race, the sweat and toil.

Paul Valéry speaks of the '*une ligne donnée*' of a poem. One line is given to the poet by God or by nature, the rest he has to discover for himself.

My own experience of inspiration is certainly that of a line or a phrase or a word or sometimes something still vague, a dim cloud of an idea which I feel must be condensed into a shower of words. The peculiarity of the key word or line is that it does not merely attract as, say, the word 'braggadocio' attracts. It occurs in what seems to be an active, male, germinal form as though it were the center of a statement requiring a beginning and an end, and as though it had an impulse in a certain direction. Here are examples:

A language of flesh and roses.

This phrase (not very satisfactory in itself) brings to my mind a whole series of experiences and the idea of a poem which I shall perhaps write some years hence. I was standing in the corridor of a train passing through the Black Country. I saw a landscape of pits and pitheads, artificial mountains, jagged yellow wounds in the earth, everything transformed as though by the toil of an enormous animal or giant tearing up the earth in search of prey or treasure. Oddly enough, a stranger next to me in the corridor echoed my inmost thought. He said: 'Everything there is man-made.' At this moment the line flashed into my head:

A language of flesh and roses.

The sequence of my thought was as follows: the industrial landscape which seems by now a routine and act of God which enslaves both employers and workers who serve and profit by it, is actually the expression of man's will. Men willed it to be so, and the pitheads, slag-heaps and the ghastly disregard of anything but the pursuit of wealth, are a symbol of modern man's mind. In other words, the world which we create – the world of slums and telegrams and newspapers – is a kind of language of our inner wishes and thoughts. Although this is so, it is obviously a language which has got outside our control. It is a confused language, an irresponsible, senile gibberish. This thought greatly distressed me, and I started thinking that if the phenomena created by humanity are really like words in a language, what kind of language do we really aspire to? All this sequence of thought flashed into my mind with the answer which came before the question: a language of flesh and roses.

I hope this example will give the reader some idea of what I mean by inspiration. Now the line, which I shall not repeat again, is a way of thinking imaginatively. If the line embodies some of the ideas which I have related above, these ideas must be further made clear in other lines. That is the terrifying challenge of poetry. Can I think out the logic of images? How easy it is to explain here the poem that I would have liked to write! How difficult it would be to write it. For writing it would imply living my way through the imaged experience of all these ideas, which here are mere abstractions, and such an effort of imaginative experience requires a lifetime of patience and watching.

Here is an example of a cloudy form of thought germinated by the word *cross*, which is the key word of the poem which exists formlessly in my mind. Recently my wife had a son. On the first day that I visited her after the boy's birth, I went by bus to the hospital. Passing through the streets on the top of the bus, they all seemed very clean, and the thought occurred to me that everything was prepared for our child. Past generations have toiled so that any child born today inherits, with his generation, cities, streets, organization, the most elaborate machinery for living. Everything has been provided for him by people dead long before he was born. Then, naturally enough, sadder thoughts colored this picture for me, and I reflected how he also inherited vast maladjustments, vast human wrongs. Then I thought of the child as like a pin-point of present existence, the moment incarnate, in whom the whole of the past and all possible futures *cross*. This word 'cross' somehow suggested the whole situation to me of a child born into the world and also of the form of a poem about his situation. When the word 'cross' appeared in the poem, the idea of the past should give place to the idea of the future and it should be apparent that the 'cross' in which present and future meet is the secret of an individual human existence. And here again, the unspoken secret which lies beyond the poem, the moral significance of other meanings of the word 'cross' begins to glow with its virtue that should never be said and yet should shine through every image in the poem.

This account of inspiration is probably weak beside the accounts that other poets might give. I am writing of my own experience, and my own inspiration seems to me like the faintest flash of insight into the nature of reality beside that of other poets whom I can think of. However, it is possible that I describe here a kind of experience which, however slight it may be, is far truer to the real poetic experience than Aldous Huxley's account of how a young poet writes poetry in his novel *Time Must Have a Stop*. It is hard to imagine anything more self-conscious and unpoetic than Mr Huxley's account.

Memory

If the art of concentrating in a particular way is the discipline necessary for poetry to reveal itself, memory exercised in a particular way is the natural gift of poetic genius. The poet, above all else, is a person who never forgets certain sense impressions which he has experienced and which he can re-live again and again as though with all their original freshness.

All poets have this highly developed sensitive apparatus of memory, and they are usually aware of experiences which happened to them at the earliest age and which retain their pristine significance throughout life. The meeting of Dante and Beatrice when the poet was only nine years of age is the experience which became a symbol in Dante's mind around which the *Divine Comedy* crystallized. The experience of nature which forms the subject of Wordsworth's poetry was an extension of a childhood vision of 'natural presences' which surrounded the boy Wordsworth. And his decision in later life to live in the Lake District was a decision to return to the scene of these childhood memories which were the most important experiences in his poetry. There is evidence for the importance of this kind of memory in all the creative arts, and the argument certainly applies to prose which is creative. Sir Osbert Sitwell has told me that his book *Before the Bombardment*, which contains an extremely civilized and satiric account of the social life of Scarborough before and during the last war, was based on his observations of life in that resort before he had reached the age of twelve.

It therefore is not surprising that although I have no memory for telephone numbers, addresses, faces and where I have put this morning's correspondence, I have a perfect memory for the sensation of certain experiences which are crystallized for me around certain associations. I could demonstrate this from my own life by the overwhelming nature of associations which, suddenly aroused, have carried me back so completely into the past, particularly into my childhood, that I have lost all sense of the present time and place. But the best proofs of this power of memory are found in the odd lines of poems written in note books fifteen years ago. A few fragments of unfinished poems enable me to enter immediately into the experiences from which they were derived, the circumstances in which they were written, and unwritten feelings in the poem that were projected but never put into words.

> ... Knowledge of a full sun
> That runs up his big sky, above
> The hill, then in those trees and throws
> His smiling on the turf.

That is an incomplete idea of fifteen years ago, and I remember exactly a balcony of a house facing a road and, on the other side of the road, pine trees, beyond which lay the sea. Every morning the sun sprang up, first of all above the horizon of the sea, then it climbed to the tops of the trees and shone on my window. And this memory connects with the sun that shines through my window in London now in spring and early summer. So that the memory is not exactly a memory. It is more like one prong upon which a whole calendar of similar experiences happening throughout years, collect. A memory once clearly

71

stated ceases to be a memory, it becomes perpetually present, because every time we experience something which recalls it, the clear and lucid original experience imposes its formal beauty on the new experiences. It is thus no longer a memory but an experience lived through again and again.

Turning over these old note books my eye catches some lines, in a projected long poem, which immediately re-shape themselves into the following short portrait of a woman's face:

> Her eyes are gleaming fish
> Caught in her nervous face, as if in a net.
> Her hair is wild and fair, haloing her cheeks
> Like a fantastic flare of Southern sun.
> There is madness in her cherishing her children.
> Sometimes, perhaps a single time in years,
> Her wandering fingers stoop to arrange some flowers –
> Then in her hands her whole life stops and weeps.

It is perhaps true to say that memory is the faculty of poetry, because the imagination itself is an exercise of memory. There is nothing we imagine which we do not already know. And our ability to imagine is our ability to remember what we have already once experienced and to apply it to some different situation. Thus the greatest poets are those with memories so great that they extend beyond their strongest experiences to their minutest observations of people and things far outside their own self-centredness (the weakness of memory is its self-centredness: hence the narcissistic nature of most poetry).

Here I can detect my own greatest weakness. My memory is defective and self-centred. I lack the confidence in using it to create situations outside myself, although I believe that, in theory, there are very few situations in life which a poet should not be able to imagine, because it is a fact that most poets have experienced almost every situation in life. I do not mean by this that a poet who writes about a Polar Expedition has actually been to the North Pole. I mean, though, that he has been cold, hungry, etc., so that it is possible for him by remembering imaginatively his own felt experiences to know what it is like to explore the North Pole. That is where I fail. I cannot write about going to the North Pole.

Faith

It is evident that a faith in their vocation, mystical in intensity, sustains poets. There are many illustrations from the lives of poets to show this, and Shakespeare's sonnets are full of expressions of his faith in the immortality of his lines.

From my experience I can clarify the nature of this faith. When I was nine we went to the Lake District, and there my parents read me some of the poems of Wordsworth. My sense of the sacredness of the task of poetry began then, and I have always felt that a poet's was a sacred vocation, like a saint's. Since I was nine I have wanted to be various things, for example, Prime Minister (when I was twelve). Like some other poets I am attracted by the life of power and the life of action, but I am still more repelled by them. Power involves forcing oneself upon the attention of historians by doing things and occupying offices which are, in themselves, important, so that what is truly powerful is not the soul of a so-called powerful and prominent man but the position which he fills and the things which he does. Similarly, the life of 'action' which seems so very positive is, in fact, a selective, even a negative kind of life. A man of action does one thing or several things because he does not do something else. Usually men who do very spectacular things fail completely to do the ordinary things which fill the lives of most normal people and which would be far more heroic and spectacular perhaps if they did not happen to be done by many people. Thus in practice the life of action has always seemed to me an act of cutting oneself off from life.

Although it is true that poets are vain and ambitious, their vanity and ambition is of the purest kind attainable in this world, for the saint renounces ambition. They are ambitious to be accepted for what they ultimately are as revealed by their inmost experiences, their finest perceptions, their deepest feelings, their uttermost sense of truth, in their poetry. They cannot cheat about these things, because the quality of their own being is revealed not in the noble sentiments which their poetry expresses, but in sensibility, control of language, rhythm and music, things which cannot be attained by a vote of confidence from an electorate, or by the office of Poet Laureate. Of course, work is tremendously important, but, in poetry, even the greatest labor can only serve to reveal the intrinsic qualities of soul of the poet as he really is.

Since there can be no cheating, the poet, like the saint, stands in all his works before the bar of a perpetual day of judgement. His vanity of course is pleased by success, though even success may contribute to his understanding that popularity does not confer on him the favorable judgement of all the ages which he seeks. For what does it mean to be praised by one's own age, which is soaked in crimes and stupidity, except perhaps that future ages, wise where we are foolish, will see him as a typical expression of this age's crimes and stupidity? Nor is lack of success a guarantee of great poetry, though there are some who pretend that it is. Nor can the critics, at any rate beyond a certain limited point of technical judgement, be trusted.

The poet's faith is therefore, firstly, a mystique of vocation, secondly, a faith in his own truth, combined with his own devotion to a task. There can really be no greater faith than the confidence that one is doing one's utmost to fulfil one's high vocation, and it is this that has inspired all the greatest poets. At the same time this faith is coupled with a deep humility because one knows that, ultimately, judgement does not rest with oneself. All one can do is to achieve nakedness, to be what one is with all one's faculties and perceptions, strengthened by all the skill which one can acquire, and then to stand before the judgement of time.

In my notebooks, I find the following prose poem, which expresses these thoughts:

Bring me peace bring me power bring me assurance. Let me reach the bright day, the high chair, the plain desk, where my hand at last controls the words, where anxiety no longer undermines me. If I don't reach these I'm thrown to the wolves, I'm a restless animal wandering from place to place, from experience to experience.

Give me the humility and the judgement to live alone with the deep and rich satisfaction of my own creating: not to be thrown into doubt by a word of spite or disapproval.

In the last analysis don't mind whether your work is good or bad so long as it has the completeness, the enormity of the whole world which you love.

Song

Inspiration and song are the irreducible final qualities of a poet which make his vocation different from all others. Inspiration is an experience in which a line or an idea is given to one, and perhaps also a state of mind in which one writes one's best poetry. Song is far more difficult to define. It is the music which a poem as yet unthought of will assume, the empty womb of poetry for ever in the poet's consciousness, waiting for the fertilizing seed.

Sometimes, when I lie in a state of half-waking half-sleeping, I am conscious of a stream of words which seem to pass through my mind, without their having a meaning, but they have a sound, a sound of passion, or a sound recalling poetry that I know. Again sometimes when I am writing, the music of the words I am trying to shape takes me far beyond the words, I am aware of a rhythm, a dance, a fury, which is as yet empty of words.

In these observations, I have said little about headaches, midnight oil, pints of beer or of claret, love affairs, and so on, which are supposed to be stations on the journeys of poets through life. There is no doubt that writing poetry, when a poem appears to succeed, results in an intense physical excitement, a sense of release and ecstasy. On the other hand, I dread writing poetry for, I suppose, the following reasons: a poem is a terrible journey, a painful effort of concentrating the imagination; words are an extremely difficult medium to use, and sometimes when one has spent days trying to say a thing clearly one finds that one has only said it dully; above all, the writing of a poem brings one face to face with one's own personality with all its familiar and clumsy limitations. In every other phase of existence, one can exercise the orthodoxy of a conventional routine: one can be polite to one's friends, one can get through the day at the office, one can pose, one can draw attention to one's position in society, one is – in a word – dealing with men. In poetry, one is wrestling with a god.

Usually, when I have completed a poem, I think 'this is my best poem', and I wish to publish it at once. This is partly because I only write when I have something new to say, which seems more worth while than what I have said before, partly because optimism about my present and future makes me despise my past. A few days after I have finished a poem, I relegate it to the past of all my other wasted efforts, all the books I do not wish to open.

Perhaps the greatest pleasure I have got from poems that I have written is when I have heard some lines quoted which I have not at once recognized. And I have thought 'how good and how interesting', before I have realized that they are my own.

In common with other creative writers I pretend that I am not, and I am, exceedingly affected by unsympathetic criticism, whilst praise usually makes me suspect that the reviewer does not know what he is talking about. Why are writers so sensitive to criticism? Partly, because it is their business to be sensitive, and they are sensitive about this as about other things. Partly, because every serious creative writer is really in his heart concerned with reputation and not with success (the most successful writer I have known, Sir Hugh Walpole, was far and away the most unhappy about his reputation, because the 'highbrows' did not like him). Again, I suspect that every writer is secretly writing for *someone*, probably for a parent or teacher who did not believe in him in childhood. The critic who refuses to 'understand' immediately becomes identified with this person, and the understanding of many admirers only adds to the writer's secret bitterness if this one refusal persists.

Gradually one realizes that there is always this someone who will not like one's work. Then, perhaps, literature becomes a humble exercise of faith in being all that one can be in one's art, of being more than oneself, expecting little, but with a faith in the mystery of poetry which gradually expands into a faith in the mysterious service of truth.

Yet what failures there are! And how much mud sticks to one; mud not thrown by other people but acquired in the course of earning one's living, answering or not answering the letters which one receives, supporting or not supporting public causes. All one can hope is that this mud is composed of little grains of sand which will produce pearls.

7 H. Poincaré

Mathematical Creation

Excerpt from H. Poincaré, *The Foundations of Science*
(trans. G. B. Halstead), Science Press, 1924, pp. 383–94. First
published in *Science et Méthode*, Flammarion, Paris, 1908.

The genesis of mathematical creation is a problem which should intensely interest the psychologist. It is the activity in which the human mind seems to take least from the outside world, in which it acts or seems to act only of itself and on itself, so that in studying the procedure of geometric thought we may hope to reach what is most essential in man's mind.

This has long been appreciated, and some time back the journal called *L'Enseignement Mathématique*, edited by Laisant and Fehr, began an investigation of the mental habits and methods of work of different mathematicians. I had finished the main outlines of this article when the results of that inquiry were published, so I have hardly been able to utilize them and shall confine myself to saying that the majority of witnesses confirm my conclusions; I do not say all, for when the appeal is to universal suffrage unanimity is not to be hoped.

A first fact should surprise us, or rather would surprise us if we were not so used to it. How does it happen there are people who do not understand mathematics? If mathematics invokes only the rules of logic, such as are accepted by all normal minds; if its evidence is based on principles common to all men, and that none could deny without being mad, how does it come about that so many persons are here refractory?

That not every one can invent is nowise mysterious. That not every one can retain a demonstration once learned may also pass. But that not every one can understand mathematical reasoning when explained appears very surprising when we think of it. And yet those who can follow this reasoning only with difficulty are in the majority: that is undeniable, and will surely not be gainsaid by the experience of secondary-school teachers.

And further: how is error possible in mathematics? A sane mind should not be guilty of a logical fallacy, and yet there are very fine minds who do not trip in brief reasoning such as occurs in the ordinary doings of life, and who are incapable of following or repeating without error the mathematical demonstrations which are longer, but which after all are only an accumulation of brief reasonings wholly analogous to those they make so easily. Need we add that mathematicians themselves are not infallible?

The answer seems to me evident. Imagine a long series of syllogisms, and that the conclusions of the first serve as premises of the following: we shall be able to catch each of these syllogisms, and it is not in passing from premises to conclusion that we are in danger of deceiving ourselves. But between the moment in which we first meet a proposition as conclusion of one syllogism, and that in which we reencounter it as premise of another syllogism occasionally some time will elapse, several links of the chain will have unrolled; so it may happen that we have forgotten it, or worse, that we have forgotten its meaning. So it may happen that we replace it by a slightly different proposition, or that, while retaining the same enunciation, we attribute to it a slightly different meaning, and thus it is that we are exposed to error.

Often the mathematician uses a rule. Naturally he begins by demonstrating this rule; and at the time when this proof is fresh in his memory he understands perfectly its meaning and its bearing, and he is in no danger of changing it. But subsequently he trusts his memory and afterward only applies it in a mechanical way; and then if his memory fails him, he may apply it all wrong. Thus it is, to take a simple example, that we sometimes make slips in calculation because we have forgotten our multiplication table.

According to this, the special aptitude for mathematics would be due only to a very sure memory or to a prodigious force of attention. It would be a power like that of the whist player who remembers the cards played; or, to go up a step, like that of the chess player who can visualize a great number of combinations and hold them in his memory. Every good mathematician ought to be a good chess player, and inversely; likewise he should be a good computer. Of course that sometimes happens; thus Gauss was at the same time a geometer of genius and a very precocious and accurate computer.

But there are exceptions; or rather I err; I can not call them exceptions without the exceptions being more than the rule. Gauss it is, on the contrary, who was an exception. As for myself, I must confess, I am absolutely incapable even of adding without mistakes. In the same way I should be but a poor chess player; I would perceive that by a certain play I should expose myself to certain danger; I would pass in review several other plays, rejecting them for other reasons, and then finally I should make the move first examined, having meantime forgotten the danger I had foreseen.

In a word, my memory is not bad, but it would be insufficient to make me a good chess player. Why then does it not fail me in a difficult piece of mathematical reasoning where most chess players would lose themselves? Evidently because it is guided by the general march of the reasoning. A mathematical demonstration is not a simple juxtaposition of syllogisms, it is syllogisms *placed in a certain order*, and the order in which these elements are placed is much more important than the elements themselves. If I have the feeling, the intuition, so to speak, of this order, so as to perceive at a glance the reasoning as a whole, I need no longer fear lest I forget one of the elements, for each of them will take its allotted place in the array, and that without any effort of memory on my part.

It seems to me then, in repeating a reasoning learned, that I could have invented it. This is often only an illusion; but even then, even if I am not so gifted as to create it by myself, I myself re-invent it in so far as I repeat it.

We know that this feeling, this intuition of mathematical order, that makes us divine hidden harmonies and relations, can not be possessed by every one. Some will not have either this delicate feeling so difficult to define, or a strength of memory and attention beyond the ordinary, and then they will be absolutely incapable of understanding higher mathematics. Such are the majority. Others will have this feeling only in a slight degree, but they will be gifted with an uncommon memory and a great power of attention. They will learn by heart the details one after another; they can understand mathematics and sometimes make applications, but they cannot create. Others, finally, will possess in a less or greater degree the special intuition referred to, and then not only can they understand mathematics even if their memory is nothing extraordinary, but they may become creators and try to invent with more or less success according as this intuition is more or less developed in them.

In fact, what is mathematical creation? It does not consist in making new combinations with mathematical entities already known. Any one could do that, but the combinations so made would be infinite in number and most of them absolutely without interest. To create consists precisely in not making useless combinations and in making those which are useful and which are only a small minority. Invention is discernment, choice.

How to make this choice I have before explained; the mathematical facts worthy of being studied are those which, by their analogy with other facts, are capable of leading us to the knowledge of a mathematical law just as experimental facts lead us to the knowledge of a physical law. They are those which reveal to us unsuspected kinship between other facts, long known, but wrongly believed to be strangers to one another.

Among chosen combinations the most fertile will often be those formed of elements drawn from domains which are far apart. Not that I mean as sufficing for invention the bringing together of objects as disparate as possible; most combinations so formed would be entirely sterile. But certain among them, very rare, are the most fruitful of all.

To invent, I have said, is to choose; but the word is perhaps not wholly exact. It makes one think of a purchaser before whom are displayed a large number of samples, and who examines them, one after the other, to make a choice. Here the samples would be so numerous that a whole lifetime would not suffice to examine them. This is not the actual state of things. The sterile combinations do not even present themselves to the mind of the inventor. Never in the field of his consciousness do combinations appear that are not really useful, except some that he rejects but which have to some extent the characteristics of useful combinations. All goes on as if the inventor were an examiner for the second degree who would only have to question the candidates who had passed a previous examination.

But what I have hitherto said is what may be observed or inferred in reading the writings of the geometers, reading reflectively.

It is time to penetrate deeper and to see what goes on in the very soul of the mathematician. For this, I believe, I can do best by recalling memories of my own. But I shall limit myself to telling how I wrote my first memoir on Fuchsian functions. I beg the reader's pardon; I am about to use some technical expressions, but they need not frighten him, for he is not obliged to understand them. I shall say, for example, that I have found the demonstration of such a theorem under such circumstances. This theorem will have a barbarous name, unfamiliar to many, but that is unimportant; what is of interest for the psychologist is not the theorem but the circumstances.

For fifteen days I strove to prove that there could not be any functions like those I have since called Fuchsian functions. I was then very ignorant; every day I seated myself at my work table, stayed an hour or two, tried a great number of combinations and reached no results. One evening, contrary to my custom, I drank black coffee and could not sleep. Ideas rose in crowds; I felt them collide until pairs interlocked, so to speak, making a stable combination. By the next morning I had established the existence of a class of Fuchsian functions, those which come from the hypergeometric series; I had only to write out the results, which took but a few hours.

Then I wanted to represent these functions by the quotient of two series; this idea was perfectly conscious and deliberate, the analogy with elliptic functions guided me. I asked myself what properties these series must have if they existed, and I succeeded without difficulty in forming the series I have called theta-Fuchsian.

Just at this time I left Caen, where I was then living, to go on a geologic excursion under the auspices of the school of mines. The changes of travel made me forget my mathematical work. Having reached Coutances, we entered an omnibus to go some place or other. At the moment when I put my foot on the step the idea came to me, without anything in my former thoughts seeming to have paved the way for it, that the transformations I had used to define the Fuchsian functions were identical with those of non-Euclidean geometry. I did not verify the idea; I should not have had time, as, upon taking my seat in the omnibus, I went on with a conversation already commenced, but I felt a perfect certainty. On my return to Caen, for conscience' sake I verified the result at my leisure.

Then I turned my attention to the study of some arithmetical questions apparently without much success and without a suspicion of any connection with my preceding researches. Disgusted with my failure, I went to spend a few days at the seaside, and thought of something else. One morning, walking on the bluff, the idea came to me, with just the same characteristics of brevity, suddenness and immediate certainty, that the arithmetic transformations of indeterminate ternary quadratic forms were identical with those of non-Euclidean geometry.

Returned to Caen, I meditated on this result and deduced the consequences. The example of quadratic forms showed me that they were Fuchsian groups other than those corresponding to the hypergeometric series; I saw that I could apply to them the theory of theta-Fuchsian series and that consequently there existed Fuchsian functions other than those from the hypergeometric series, the ones I then knew. Naturally I set myself to form all these functions. I made a systematic attack upon them and carried all the outworks, one after another. There was one however that still held out, whose fall would involve that of the whole place. But all my efforts only served at first the better to show me the difficulty, which indeed was something. All this work was perfectly conscious.

Thereupon I left for Mont-Valérien, where I was to go through my military service; so I was very differently occupied. One day, going along the street, the solution of the difficulty which had stopped me suddenly appeared to me. I did not try to go deep into it immediately, and only after my service did I again take up the question. I had all the elements and had only to arrange them and put them together. So I wrote out my final memoir at a single stroke and without difficulty.

I shall limit myself to this single example; it is useless to multiply them. In regard to my other researches I would have to say analogous things, and the observations of other mathematicians given in L'Enseignement Mathématique would only confirm them.

Most striking at first is this appearance of sudden illumination, a manifest sign of long, unconscious prior work. The role of this unconscious work in mathematical invention appears to me incontestable, and traces of it would be found in other cases where it is less evident. Often when one works at a hard question, nothing good is accomplished at the first attack. Then one takes a rest, longer or shorter, and sits down anew to the work. During the first half hour, as before, nothing is found, and then all of a sudden the decisive idea presents itself to the mind. It might be said that the conscious work has been more fruitful because it has been interrupted and the rest has given back to the mind its force and freshness. But it is more probable that this rest has been filled out with unconscious work and that the result of this work has afterward revealed itself to the geometer just as in the cases I have cited; only the revelation, instead of coming during a walk or a journey, has happened during a period of conscious work, but independently of this work which plays at most a role of excitant, as if it were the goad stimulating the results already reached during rest, but remaining unconscious, to assume the conscious form.

There is another remark to be made about the conditions of this unconscious work: it is possible, and of a certainty it is only fruitful, if it is on the one hand preceded and on the other hand followed by a period of conscious work. These sudden inspirations (and the examples already cited sufficiently prove this) never happen except after some days of voluntary effort which has appeared absolutely fruitless and whence nothing good seems to have come, where the way taken seems totally astray. These efforts then have not been as sterile as one thinks; they have set agoing the unconscious machine and without them it would not have moved and would have produced nothing.

The need for the second period of conscious work, after the inspiration, is still easier to understand. It is necessary to put in shape the results of this inspiration, to deduce from them the immediate consequences, to arrange them, to word the demonstrations, but above all is verification necessary. I have spoken of the feeling of absolute certitude accompanying the inspiration; in the cases cited this feeling was no deceiver, nor is it usually. But do not think this a rule without exception; often this feeling deceives us without being any the less vivid, and we only find it out when we seek to put on foot the demonstration. I have especially noticed this fact in regard to ideas coming to me in the morning or evening in bed while in a semi-hypnagogic state.

Such are the realities; now for the thoughts they force upon us. The unconscious, or, as we say, the subliminal self plays an important role in mathematical creation; this follows from what we have said. But usually the subliminal self is considered as purely automatic. Now we have seen that mathematical work is not simply mechanical, that it could not be done by a machine, however perfect. It is not merely a question of applying rules, of making the most combinations possible according to certain fixed laws. The combinations so obtained would be exceedingly numerous, useless and cumbersome. The true work of the inventor consists in choosing among these combinations so as to eliminate the useless ones or rather to avoid the trouble of making them, and the rules which must guide this choice are extremely fine and delicate. It is almost impossible to state them precisely; they are left rather than formulated. Under these conditions, how can one imagine a sieve capable of applying them mechanically?

A first hypothesis now presents itself: the subliminal self is in no way inferior to the conscious self; it is not purely automatic; it is capable of discernment; it has tact, delicacy; it knows how to choose, to divine. What do I say? It knows better how to divine than the conscious self, since it succeeds where that has failed. In a word, is not the subliminal self superior to the conscious self? You recognize the full importance of this question. Boutroux, in a lecture, has shown how it came up on a very different occasion, and what consequences would follow an affirmative answer.

Is this affirmative answer forced upon us by the facts I have just given? I confess that, for my part, I should hate to accept it. Re-examine the facts then and see if they are not compatible with another explanation.

It is certain that the combinations which present themselves to the mind in a sort of sudden illumination, after an unconscious working somewhat prolonged, are generally useful and fertile combinations, which seem the result of a first impression. Does it follow that the subliminal self, having divined by a delicate

H. Poincaré

intuition that these combinations would be useful, has formed only these, or has it rather formed many others which were lacking in interest and have remained unconscious?

In this second way of looking at it, all the combinations would be formed in consequence of the automatism of the subliminal self, but only the interesting ones would break into the domain of consciousness. And this is still very mysterious. What is the cause that, among the thousand products of our unconscious activity, some are called to pass the threshold, while others remain below? Is it a simple chance which confers this privilege? Evidently not; among all the stimuli of our senses, for example, only the most intense fix our attention, unless it has been drawn to them by other causes. More generally the privileged unconscious phenomena, those susceptible of becoming conscious, are those which, directly or indirectly, affect most profoundly our emotional sensibility.

It may be surprising to see emotional sensibility invoked *à propos* of mathematical demonstrations which, it would seem, can interest only the intellect. This would be to forget the feeling of mathematical beauty, of the harmony of numbers and forms, of geometric elegance. This is a true esthetic feeling that all real mathematicians know, and surely it belongs to emotional sensibility.

Now, what are the mathematic entities to which we attribute this character of beauty and elegance, and which are capable of developing in us a sort of esthetic emotion? They are those whose elements are harmoniously disposed so that the mind without effort can embrace their totality while realizing the details. This harmony is at once a satisfaction of our esthetic needs and an aid to the mind, sustaining and guiding. And at the same time, in putting under our eyes a well-ordered whole, it makes us foresee a mathematical law. Now, as we have said above, the only mathematical facts worthy of fixing our attention and capable of being useful are those which can teach us a mathematical law. So that we reach the following conclusion: the useful combinations are precisely the most beautiful, I mean those best able to charm this special sensibility that all mathematicians know, but of which the profane are so ignorant as often to be tempted to smile at it.

What happens then? Among the great numbers of combinations blindly formed by the subliminal self, almost all are without interest and without utility; but just for that reason they are also without effect upon the esthetic sensibility. Consciousness will never know them; only certain ones are harmonious, and, consequently, at once useful and beautiful. They will be capable of touching this special sensibility of the geometer of which I have just spoken and which, once aroused, will call our attention to them, and thus give them occasion to become conscious.

This is only a hypothesis, and yet here is an observation which may confirm it: when a sudden illumination seizes upon the mind of the mathematician, it usually happens that it does not deceive him, but it also sometimes happens, as I have said, that it does not stand the test of verification. Well, we almost always notice that this false idea, had it been true, would have gratified our natural feeling for mathematical elegance.

Thus it is this special esthetic sensibility which plays the role of the delicate sieve of which I spoke, and that sufficiently explains why the one lacking it will never be a real creator.

Yet all the difficulties have not disappeared. The conscious self is narrowly limited and as for the subliminal self we know not its limitations, and this is why we are not too reluctant in supposing that it has been able in a short time to make more different combinations than the whole life of a conscious being could encompass. Yet these limitations exist. Is it likely that it is able to form all the possible combinations, whose number would frighten the imagination? Nevertheless that would seem necessary, because if it produces only a small part of these combinations, and if it makes them at random, there would be small chance that the *good*, the one we should choose, would be found among them.

Perhaps we ought to seek the explanation in that preliminary period of conscious work which always precedes all fruitful unconscious labor. Permit me a rough comparison. Figure the future elements of our combinations as something like the hooked atoms of Epicurus. During the complete repose of the mind, these atoms are motionless, they are, so to speak, hooked to the wall; so this complete rest may be indefinitely prolonged without the atoms meeting, and consequently without any combination between them.

On the other hand, during a period of apparent rest and unconscious work, certain of them are detached from the wall and put in motion. They flash in every direction through the space (I was about to say the room) where they are enclosed, as would, for example, a swarm of gnats or, if you prefer a more learned comparison, like the molecules of gas in the kinematic theory of gases. Then their mutual impacts may produce new combinations.

What is the role of the preliminary conscious work? It is evidently to mobilize certain of these atoms, to unhook them from the wall and put them in swing. We think we have done no good, because we have moved these elements a thousand different ways in seeking to assemble them, and have found no satisfactory aggregate. But, after this shaking up imposed upon them by our will, these atoms do not return to their primitive rest. They freely continue their dance.

Now, our will did not choose them at random; it pursued a perfectly determined aim. The mobilized atoms are therefore not any atoms whatsoever; they are those from which we might reasonably expect the desired solution. Then the mobilized atoms undergo impacts which make them enter into combinations among themselves or with other atoms at rest which they struck against in their course. Again I beg pardon, my comparison is very rough, but I scarcely know how otherwise to make my thought understood.

However it may be, the only combinations that have a chance of forming are those where at least one of the elements is one of those atoms freely chosen by our will. Now, it is evidently among these that is found what I called the *good combination*. Perhaps this is a way of lessening the paradoxical in the original hypothesis.

Another observation. It never happens that the unconscious work gives us the result of a somewhat long calculation *all made*, where we have only to apply fixed rules. We might think the wholly automatic subliminal self particularly apt for this sort of work, which is in a way exclusively mechanical. It seems that thinking in the evening upon the factors of a multiplication we might hope to find the product ready made upon our awakening, or again that an algebraic calculation, for example a verification, would be made unconsciously – nothing of the sort, as observation proves. All one may hope from these inspirations, fruits of unconscious work, is a point of departure for such calculations. As for the calculations themselves, they must be made in the second period of conscious work, that which follows the inspiration, that in which one verifies the results of this inspiration and deduces their consequences. The rules of these calculations are strict and complicated. They require discipline, attention, will and, therefore, consciousness. In the subliminal self, on the contrary, reigns what I should call liberty, if we might give this name to the simple absence of discipline and to the disorder born of chance. Only, this disorder itself permits unexpected combinations.

I shall make a last remark: when above I made certain personal observations, I spoke of a night of excitement when I worked in spite of myself. Such cases are frequent, and it is not necessary that the abnormal cerebral activity be caused by a physical excitant as in that I mentioned. It seems, in such cases, that one is present at his own unconscious work, made partially perceptible to the over-excited consciousness, yet without having changed its nature. Then we vaguely comprehend what distinguishes the two mechanisms or, if you wish, the working methods of the two egos. And the psychologic observations I have been able thus to make seem to me to confirm in their general outlines the views I have given.

Surely they have need of it, for they are and remain in spite of all very hypothetical: the interest of the questions is so great that I do not repent of having submitted them to the reader.

Part Three **Theoretical Contributions**

It was largely on the basis of Poincaré's and other similar accounts that Graham Wallas (Reading 8) formulated his analysis of stages in creative thinking. This has been widely accepted, though also criticized as being over-rigid. By the 'art' of thought, Wallas means the development of greater skill and effectiveness through self-training of one's 'natural' thought process.

F. C. Bartlett (Reading 9) likewise regards thinking as consisting of high-level skills and shows that these are similar in many respects to complex psychomotor skills. Somewhat like Guilford (Reading 15) he distinguishes thinking in 'closed systems' from 'adventurous thinking'; and in Reading 9 he analyses the characteristics of adventurous thinking in experimental science, referring particularly to the development of research on infectious diseases and on reaction time.

To Sinnott (Reading 10), as a biologist, creativeness is a characteristic of all living matter; he traces its evolutionary development up to the human level. This most advanced stage is discussed in the excerpt. Cropley's book is a general survey of work on creativity, and in the chapter included here (Reading 11) he describes some of the cognitive characteristics of creative thinkers, showing the bearings of modern learning theory and of information theory.

The psychodynamic psychologist is, of course, particularly concerned with the role of unconscious impulses in creativity, and as early as 1908 Freud (see Reading 12) pointed out the relations between the work of the artist, ordinary day-dreaming and children's play. Later writers, however, have moved away from the notion, developed in Freud's

work on Leonardo da Vinci (1910), that creative work is a
kind of sublimation of repressed complexes. Thus Kubie (1958)
maintains that inspiration originates at the preconscious level,
and is more likely to be blocked by, than to derive from,
neurosis. While Carl Rogers, in Reading 13, sees creativity as a
process of self-realization of the unusually sensitive and
well-integrated personality.

References

FREUD, S. (1910), 'Leonardo da Vinci and a memory of his childhood',
    reprinted in J. Strachey (ed.), *The Standard Edition of the Complete
    Psychological Works of Sigmund Freud*, Hogarth Press, 1958,
    pp. 63–137.

KUBIE, L. S. (1958), *Neurotic Distortion of the Creative Process*,
    University of Kansas Press.

8 G. Wallas

The Art of Thought

Excerpts from G. Wallas, *The Art of Thought*, Jonathan Cape, 1926, pp. 79–96.

In this chapter, I shall ask at what stages in that thought process the thinker should bring the conscious and voluntary effort of his art to bear. Here we at once meet the difficulty that unless we can recognize a psychological event, and distinguish it from other events, we cannot bring conscious effort to bear directly upon it; and that our mental life is a stream of intermingled psychological events, all of which affect each other, any of which, at any given moment, may be beginning or continuing or ending, and which, therefore, are extremely hard to distinguish from each other.

We can, to some degree, avoid this difficulty if we take a single achievement of thought – the making of a new generalization or invention, or the poetical expression of a new idea – and ask how it was brought about. We can then roughly dissect out a continuous process, with a beginning and a middle and an end of its own. Helmholtz, for instance, the great German physicist, speaking in 1891 at a banquet on his seventieth birthday, described the way in which his most important new thoughts had come to him. He said that after previous investigation of the problem 'in all directions ... happy ideas come unexpectedly without effort, like an inspiration. So far as I am concerned, they have never come to me when my mind was fatigued, or when I was at my working table. ... They came particularly readily during the slow ascent of wooded hills on a sunny day.' Helmholtz here gives us three stages in the formation of a new thought. The first in time I shall call Preparation, the stage during which the problem was 'investigated ... in all directions'; the second is the stage during which he was not consciously thinking about the problem, which I shall call Incubation; the third, consisting of the appearance of the 'happy idea' together with the psychological events which immediately preceded and accompanied that appearance, I shall call Illumination.

And I shall add a fourth stage, of Verification, which Helmholtz does not here mention. [. . .] In the daily stream of thought these four different stages constantly overlap each other as we explore different problems. An economist reading a blue book, a physiologist watching an experiment, or a business man going through his morning's letters, may at the same time be 'incubating' on a problem which he proposed to himself a few days ago, be accumulating knowledge in 'preparation' for a second problem, and be 'verifying' his conclusion on a third problem. Even in exploring the same problem, the mind may be unconsciously incubating on one aspect of it, while it is consciously employed in preparing for or verifying another aspect. And it must always be remembered that much very important thinking, done for instance by a poet exploring his own memories, or by a man trying to see clearly his emotional relation to his country or his party, resembles musical composition in that the stages leading to success are not very easily fitted into a 'problem and solution' scheme. Yet, even when success in thought means the creation of something felt to be beautiful and true rather than the solution of a prescribed problem, the four stages of preparation, incubation, illumination and the verification of the final result can generally be distinguished from each other.

If we accept this analysis, we are in a position to ask to what degree, and by what means, we can bring conscious effort, and the habits which arise from conscious effort, to bear upon each of the four stages. I shall not, in this chapter, deal at any length with the stage of preparation. It includes the whole process of intellectual education. Men have known for thousands of years that conscious effort and its resulting habits can be used to improve the thought processes of young persons, and have formulated for that purpose an elaborate art of education. The 'educated' man can, in consequence, 'put his mind on' to a chosen subject, and 'turn his mind off' in a way which is impossible to an uneducated man. The educated man has also acquired, by the effort of observation and memorizing, a body of remembered facts and words which gives him a wider range in the final moment of association, as well as a number of those habitual tracks of association which constitute 'thought systems' like 'French policy', 'scholastic philosophy' or 'biological evolution', and which present themselves as units in the process of thought.

The educated man has, again, learned and can, in the preparation stage, voluntarily or habitually follow out rules as to the order in which he shall direct his attention to the successive elements in a problem. Hobbes referred to this fact when in the *Leviathan* he described 'regulated thought' and contrasted it with that 'wild ranging of the mind' which occurs when the thought process is undirected. Regulated thought is, he says, a 'seeking'. 'Sometimes', for instance, 'a man seeks what he has lost. . . . Sometimes a man knows a place determinate, within the compass whereof he is to seek; and then his thoughts run over all the parts thereof, in the same manner as one would sweep a room to find a jewel; or as a spaniel ranges the field, till he find a scent; or as a man should run over the alphabet, to start a rhyme.' A spaniel with the brain of an educated human being could not, by a direct effort of will, scent a partridge in a distant part of the field. But he could so 'quarter' the field by a preliminary voluntary arrangement that the less voluntary process of smelling would be given every chance of successfully taking place.

Included in these rules for the preliminary 'regulation' of our thought are the whole traditional art of logic, the mathematical forms which are the logic of the modern experimental sciences, and the methods of systematic and continuous examination of present or recorded phenomena which are the basis of astronomy, sociology and the other 'observational' sciences. Closely connected with this voluntary use of logical methods is the voluntary choice of a 'problem attitude' (*Aufgabe*). Our mind is not likely to give us a clear answer to any particular problem unless we set it a clear question, and we are more likely to notice the significance of any new piece of evidence, or new association of ideas, if we have formed a definite conception of a case to be proved or disproved. [. . .] And though I have assumed, for the sake of clearness, that the thinker is preparing himself for the solution of a single problem, he will often (particularly if he is working on the very complex material of the social sciences) have several kindred problems in his mind, on all of which the voluntary work of preparation has been, or is being done, and for any of which, at the illumination stage, a solution may present itself.

The fourth stage, of verification, closely resembles the first stage of preparation. It is normally, as Poincaré points out, fully conscious, and men have worked out much the same series of mathematical and logical rules for controlling verification by conscious effort as those which are used in the control of preparation.

There remain the second and third stages, incubation and illumination. The incubation stage covers two different things, of which the first is the negative fact that during incubation we do not voluntarily or consciously think on a particular problem, and the second is the positive fact that a series of unconscious and involuntary (or foreconscious and forevoluntary) mental events may take place during that period. It is the first fact about incubation which I shall now discuss, leaving the second fact – of subconscious thought during incubation, and the relation of such thought to illumination – to be more fully discussed in connexion with the illumination stage. Voluntary abstention from conscious thought on any particular problem may, itself, take two forms: the period of abstention may be spent either in conscious mental work on other problems, or in a relaxation from all conscious mental work. The first kind of incubation economizes time and is therefore often the better. We can often get more result in the same time by beginning several problems in succession and voluntarily leaving them unfinished while we turn to others, than by finishing our work on each problem at one sitting. A well-known academic psychologist, for instance, who was also a preacher, told me that he found by experience that his Sunday sermon was much better if he posed the problem on Monday, than if he did so later in the week, although he might give the same number of hours of conscious work to it in each case. It seems to be a tradition among practising barristers to put off any consideration of each brief to the latest possible moment before they have to deal with it, and to forget the whole matter as rapidly as possible after dealing with it. This fact may help to explain a certain want of depth which has often been noticed in the typical lawyer-statesman, and which may be due to his conscious thought not being sufficiently extended and enriched by subconscious thought.

But, in the case of the more difficult forms of creative thought, the making, for instance, of a scientific discovery, or the writing of a poem or play or the formulation of an important political decision, it is desirable not only that there should be an interval free from conscious thought on the particular problem concerned, but also that that interval should be so spent that nothing should interfere with the free working of the unconscious or partially conscious processes of the mind. In those cases, the stage of incubation should include a large amount of actual mental relaxation. It would, indeed, be interesting to examine, from that point of view, the biographies of a couple of hundred original thinkers and writers. A. R. Wallace, for instance, hit upon the theory of evolution by natural selection in his berth during an attack of malarial fever at sea; and Darwin was compelled by ill-health to spend the greater part of his waking hours in physical and mental relaxation. Sometimes a thinker has been able to get a sufficiency of relaxation owing to a disposition to idleness, against which he has vainly struggled. More often, perhaps, what he has thought to be idleness, is really that urgent craving for intense and uninterrupted day-dreaming which Anthony Trollope describes in his account of his boyhood.

One effect of such a comparative biographical study might be the formulation of a few rules as to the relation between original intellectual work and the virtue of industry. There are thousands of idle 'geniuses' who require to learn that, without a degree of industry in preparation and verification, of which many of them have no conception, no great intellectual work can be done, and that the habit of procrastination may be even more disastrous to a professional thinker than it is to a man of business. And yet a thinker of good health and naturally fertile mind may have to be told that mere industry is for him, as it was for Trollope in his later years, the worst temptation of the devil. Cardinal Manning was a man of furious industry, and the suspension of his industry as an Anglican archdeacon during his illness in 1847 was, for good or evil, an important event in the history of English religion. [. . .] [Wallas goes on to cite many other examples of the benefits of mental and physical relaxation, and the dangers of administrative duties and too much reading – Ed.]

So far in this chapter I have inquired how far we can voluntarily improve our methods of thought at those stages – preparation, incubation (in its negative sense of abstention from voluntary thought on a particular problem), and verification – over which our conscious will has comparatively full control. I shall now discuss the much more difficult question of the degree to which our will can influence the less controllable stage which I have called illumination. Helmholtz and Poincaré both speak of the appearance of a new idea as instantaneous and unexpected. If we so define the illumination stage as to restrict it to this instantaneous 'flash', it is obvious that we cannot influence it by a direct effort of will; because we can only bring our will to bear upon psychological events which last for an appreciable time. On the other hand, the final 'flash', or 'click', is the culmination of a successful train of association, which may have lasted for an appreciable time, and which has probably been preceded by a series of tentative and unsuccessful trains. The series of unsuccessful trains of association may last for periods varying from a few seconds to several hours. H. Poincaré, who describes the tentative and unsuccessful trains as being, in his case, almost entirely unconscious, believed that they occupied a considerable proportion of the whole incubation stage. [. . .]

But if our will is to control a psychological process, it is necessary that that process should not only last for an appreciable time, but should also be, during that time, sufficiently conscious for the thinker to be at least aware that something is happening to him. On this point, the evidence seems to show that both the unsuccessful trains of association, which might have led to the 'flash' of success, and the final and successful train are normally either unconscious, or take place (with 'risings' and 'fallings' of consciousness as success seems to approach or retire), in that periphery or 'fringe' of consciousness which surrounds our 'focal' consciousness as the sun's 'corona' surrounds the disk of full luminosity.[1] This 'fringe consciousness' may last up to the 'flash' instant, may accompany it and in some cases may continue beyond it. But, just as it is very difficult to

1. I take the word 'fringe' from William James, who says in *The Principles of Psychology*, vol. 1, p. 258 (Holt, 1890): 'Let us use the words *psychic overtone*, *suffusion* or *fringe*, to designate the influence of a faint brain-process upon our thought, as it makes it aware of relations and objects but dimly perceived.'

see the sun's corona unless the disk is hidden by a total eclipse, so it is very difficult to observe our 'fringe consciousness' at the instant of full illumination, or to remember the preceding 'fringe' after full illumination has taken place. As William James says: 'When the conclusion is there, we have always forgotten most of the steps preceding its attainment.' [. . .]

I find it convenient to use the term 'intimation' for that moment in the illumination stage when our fringe consciousness of an association train is in the state of rising consciousness which indicates that the fully conscious flash of success is coming. [. . .] If this feeling of intimation lasts for an appreciable time, and is either sufficiently conscious or can by an effort of attention be made sufficiently conscious, it is obvious that our will can be brought directly to bear on it. We can at least attempt to inhibit, or prolong or divert the brain activity which intimation shows to be going on. And, if intimation accompanies a rising train of association which the brain accepts, so to speak, as plausible, but would not without the effort of attention automatically push to the 'flash' of conscious success, we can attempt to hold on to such a train on the chance that it may succeed.

9 F. C. Bartlett

Adventurous Thinking

Excerpts from F. C. Bartlett, *Thinking: An Experimental and Social Study*, Allen & Unwin, 1958, pp. 131-7, 160-63.

The Characteristics of Experimental Thinking

Opportunism

Anybody who looks back over an experimental development which has continued for many years, can hardly fail to notice that it has pursued an exceedingly wobbly course. If the surveyor is himself an experimenter, he will know that the recorded wanderings are fewer and less extensive than those which actually occurred. Many a time it will seem strange that turning points of discovery were not reached much earlier. All of this remains odd, however, only to somebody who already has the more complete knowledge which the investigations themselves have gradually built up. [. . .]

The scientific experimenter is, in fact, by bent and practice, an opportunist. He has to build upon the facts – the 'sensible' facts as Harvey would say – which are available to him when he begins his work, and he must use them to discover other facts, advancing stage by stage towards that eventual understanding of causal relations which he seeks. To the onlooker who makes a study at an advanced stage of the work, the experimenter's thinking must often appear wasteful, directed so far as specific stages are concerned, but wandering in relation to final issues, remarkably uneconomical in the sense that what may take the experimenter years to establish may take the expositor only a few minutes to describe.

Method and instrument

Both of the instances that we have considered [see original text] have shown again and again that the experimenter cannot move beyond the point for which methods and instrumentation are available. He may sometimes invent them; more often he ádopts them from some source that may be well outside his own immediate interests.

The experimenter must be able to use specific methods rigorously, but he need not be in the least concerned with methodology as a body of general principles. Outstanding 'methodologists' have not themselves usually been successful experimenters.

Similarly, and for much the same reasons, the experimenter must, more and more as knowledge develops, be able to think with instruments. However 'pure' his aims may be he has to be able to practise a technique and to handle a technology. Far the most important aspect of the experimenter's need to master method and to handle apparatus is that in the majority of cases the method and the instrumentation are brought into his field of work from the outside. There is something about experimenting, sometimes even in its routine forms, which demands a variety of interests.

Siting problems

At all stages of experimental science one of the principal uses of apparatus has been to aid and improve observation. Also at all stages whenever any experiment is performed there is always a lot more to observe than it is worth while observing. Consequently one of the greatest requirements for successful experiments is to be able to 'pinpoint' problems. This is what optics and the use of special lenses and lens systems did for the very early bacteriologists, what developments of the microscope did for the later ones, and what genetics and radiation analysis are doing in the study of bacteriophage. It is what amplification of very small electrical discharges, and the development of electronic recording and computing instruments have done in the study of reaction-time phenomena. To know where to look, as much as how to look, is a necessary step in experiment. Very often, perhaps always, it is a step that becomes possible when methods, apparatus, hints, or established findings are taken over from some field different from that in which they are to be applied. The identification of problem sites of outstanding concentration and importance has over and over again played a very great part in directing experimental research.

Making openings

The experimenter used to be pictured as always on the look-out for a 'crucial experiment', and a crucial experiment was regarded as one which settled some question once and for all. It is perfectly true that, like all other thinkers, he is trying to reach conclusions, or terminal positions, which everybody else who has sufficient and sufficiently accurate information *must* accept. But this is neither all, nor is it the most important part of what he is trying to do, except in such cases, much more rare than is often supposed, in which, for the time being, his interests are narrowly practical ones. We saw how the prolonged course of experiments, in each of the cases we have studied, fell into phases, or stages, or periods. At intervals something happened which then set the main stream of research for a long time to come. There is no accident about this; it is the regular course for experimental thinking to take. Original experimental thinking fills up a gap in a manner that commands assent, but also opens up many other gaps either not suspected before or not before susceptible of exact filling which now the more routine experimental thinking can deal with.

One of the most important features of these turning points in experimental development is that they very often introduce methods and instrumentation new to the field of research involved, but already developed in some other region of investigation. But if the experimenter who does this has any original impact upon his science he always does more than this. He must adapt the new methods and instruments for use in his own field, and he must show that they can be used to reach a compelling answer to some current problems, and at the same time to lead on to a number of further problems. As we have seen from our two leading instances, and could readily confirm from many others, genuine advance usually means (a) the progressive pushing back of the boundaries of what are regarded as defined fields of investigation, (b) the establishment of smaller and smaller and also, as a rule, more and more units as centres of those causal relations and activities with which the particular scientific discipline concerned must deal, and (c) usually the identification of some of these units and groups of units as possessing differential functions that, in the next phase of development, are most likely to be worth investigation.

For example, Helmholtz brought into the study of nerve conduction the very method already established by the astronomers to measure the difference between one 'personal equation' and another. He adapted the method so that he could measure time differences of response within what could be called a single length of motor nerves, and he adapted the apparatus into his own form of myograph. He settled once and for all that discharge along motor nerve takes a measurable time. Implicit in his experiment were a very large number of new questions which sooner or later were now bound to be asked. Those concerning actual times taken by more complex mental processes could be tackled at once, and the 'mental chronometry' period which followed was a direct outcome of the astronomer's observations and Helmholtz's experiment. Obviously Helmholtz had left open very important questions of the nature of the nerve impulse and more accurate and analysed measures of its rate. These had to wait for a long time till suitable recording apparatus was available. Equally Helmholtz had left open the whole question of a succession of events within the total reaction time which might perhaps have important bearings upon complex behaviour. These also had to wait, partly because they were obscured by the theoretical wrappings that mental chronometry very soon provided for itself, and partly because, here, too, adequate recording instruments were lacking.

Original and routine thinking

The winding progress of any branch of experimental science is made up essentially of a relatively small number of original inquiries, which may be widely separated, followed, as a rule, by a very large number of routine inquiries. The most important feature of original experimental thinking is the discovery of overlap and agreement where formerly only isolation and difference were recognized. This usually means that when any experimental science is ripe for marked advance, a mass of routine thinking belonging to an immediately preceding phase has come near to wearing itself out by exploiting a limited range of technique to establish more and more minute and specialized detail. A stage has been reached in which finding out further details adds little or nothing to what is known already in the way of opening up unexplored relations. In fact the minute improvements in delicacy of measurement, and the like, with which the routine investigator must now be concerned are little, if anything, more than further descriptive items, and science cannot live on description alone.

However, at the same time, perhaps in some other branch of science, and perhaps in some hitherto disconnected part of what is treated as the same branch, there are other techniques generating their own problems, opening up their own gaps. An original mind, never wholly contained in any one conventionally enclosed field of interest, now seizes upon the possibility that there may be some unsuspected overlap, takes the risk whether there is or not, and gives the old subject matter a new look. Routine starts again.

If these general interpretations of the facts are accepted, I think three things follow.

There is no point in asking whether originality or routine plays the more important part in experimental science. Neither occurs without the other, or can so occur. All that we can say is that for every original mind a large number of routine minds must be set to work.

The conditions for original thinking are when two or more streams of research begin to offer evidence that they may converge and so in some manner be combined. It is the combination which can generate new directions of research, and through these it may be found that basic units and activities may have properties not before suspected which open up a lot of new questions for experimental study.

The thinker in the closed system is in the position of contemplating a finished structure. Very often this may be exceedingly complex and elaborate and the rules of its construction difficult to appreciate. The thinker is, however, in the position of a spectator searching for something which he must treat as being in some way 'there' all the time. His search is rational but it is often emotionally sustained, and if it is, the emotion is appropriate to that which is associated with the contemplation of form and beauty of form, and is aesthetic or akin to the aesthetic.

The experimental thinker is in the position of somebody who must use whatever tools may be available for adding to some structure that is not yet finished, and that he himself is certainly not going to complete. Because the materials that he must use have properties of their own, many of which he cannot know until he uses them, and some of which in all likelihood are actually generated in the course of their use, he is in the position of an explorer rather than that of a spectator. His thinking, too, is often emotionally sustained, and if it is, the emotion is one of those appropriate to the chase, to risk, to adventure and to sport.

These are some of the main features and conditions of the thinking of the experimental scientist in so far as they can be detected by a study of continued experiment, over fairly long periods, carried out by many research workers, on widely defined topics. [. . .]

The Principal Characteristics of Experimental Thinking

I can now attempt a summary statement of the main characters of experimental thinking as they have appeared in the last two chapters [not included here].

1. Experimental thinking comes as a relatively late development in the search for knowledge of the world, since it has to be based upon much prior accumulation, description and classification of observed facts, and upon the invention of special methods and usually special instruments for establishing controlled sequences among these facts.

2. The basic challenge to experiment comes when events and phenomena which have appeared to display differences to immediate observations are seen, or suspected, to possess overlap and agreements. Experiment sets out to account for the overlap, to determine its range, and to find where once again it breaks out into differences.

3. Experimental thinking from the beginning and all through submits to empirical control. It is therefore much more an

expression of specialized interests than is any other sort of thinking that we have considered so far.

4. Because of its empirical foundation and control, it is opportunist by nature. It must attempt to deal with highly complex situations and systems, the structural properties of which can be found out only as experiments proceed. In consequence both the individual experimenter, and the broad course of experimental progress itself, are apt to take a wandering course, and when temporary, or final, issues are reached the course taken generally looks to have been a very uneconomical one.

5. Much experimental thinking has to be in terms of methods and instruments, and this becomes more marked as, in any field of exploration, experiment itself develops. Over and over again the most outstanding scientific advances have been made when methods and instruments invented to deal with one set of problems have been taken over into areas with which they had little or nothing to do in their origin. This again means that successful experimental thinking almost always demands multiple interests, and it has much to do with the fact that experimental discoveries are often made long before they are actively developed.

6. Especially in early stages of specific experimental progress, some of the most important thinking of the experimental scientists concerns the pinpointing, or siting, of problems; this may do more than anything else to save the experimenter from losing himself in detail.

7. Like other forms of thinking, the experimental kind is set to reach issues in a step sequence which will compel assent from all normal people who are prepared to accept the experimental approach. But it is not satisfied with this; it must also achieve new openings.

8. The most important of all conditions of originality in experimental thinking is a capacity to detect overlap and agreement between groups of facts and fields of study which have not before been effectively combined, and to bring these groups into experimental contact. Any experimental science is likely to show successive prolonged phases of advance and consolidation as it progresses.

If we consider the case of the individual experimenter, the

following appear as important determining influences in his success:

(a) While the particular kind of subject matter which he takes up will depend mainly upon the direction of his interests and opportunities, he is unlikely to achieve very much unless his preparation takes him into potentially overlapping fields of scientific exploration.

(b) It is likely that the most critical early steps that he takes will be due to prompting coming from people, or from other sources, outside himself and his own planned beginnings of experiment.

(c) It is almost certain that as his work develops he will follow a great many more clues than he eventually uses. He must know when to stop trying a particular direction of experiment, and he must not be afraid to do this.

(d) Experimenting and interpreting the results of experiment are not normally processes laid out in a strict succession; they go on together. Usually, however, there are final steps specially directed to such interpretation and presentation of results as will display order and system in a mass of detail. It is not un-common for the individual experimenter to get very much held up at this stage and he may have to put his own results out of mind for a time. When this happens it may be because, once again, the most illuminating interpretations often come from outside the immediate experimental range.

(e) An experimenter must 'know' what dimensions of change it is likely to be most worth his while to select for experimental control. This seems to demand some 'superior sensitivity' to 'dead ends' – if the experiments get more or less near to them – and to the proximity of openings so many, so varied, and so general that if he proceeds he is likely to wander aimlessly.

(f) Prediction, as the experimenter uses it, can either take the form of pointing out the most likely lines for experimental development before they have been embarked upon, or of stating expected results from novel experiments on the assumption that certain general principles have been correctly formu-lated. The second form of prediction is always to some degree deductive and so it has some common characters with formal 'closed system' thinking. It may or may not involve probability calculations.

(g) Science in its advances moves towards measurement. The quantification possible in a great many instances, especially in biological fields, is statistical, and since at present in such cases the values assignable have to be determined by experiment, any experimenter working in these fields now needs enough statistical background to select and use appropriate methods, if he is to think effectively.

10 E. W. Sinnott

The Creativeness of Life

Excerpt from E. W. Sinnott, 'The creativeness of life', in H. H. Anderson (ed.), *Creativity and its Cultivation*, Harper, 1959, pp. 21–9.

The Higher Levels of Creativity in Man

Man has emerged into a much higher behavioral level than any other animal can reach. His memory is far more extensive. By this means and the invention of speech and written symbols he is able to use the accumulated experience of the past. Most of his goals are now fulfilled not by bodily actions but by mental ones. To gain knowledge is now one of his great ends. By seeking relationships between facts, he learns to recognize general uniformities and to relate particulars to them, thus acquiring ability to reason. He can prove that Socrates, being a man, must be mortal since all men are so. Thus he has come to deal in abstractions.

His inner environment is vastly richer than that of a beast and, as society develops, his outer environment becomes far more complex also. All these diversities, like the far simpler environmental changes at the embryological and instinctive levels, modify the goals that are set up within his living system. The interpretation of mental life, however rich and complex, as the seeking of a wide variety of changing goals in the organized pattern is therefore a defensible one. Consciousness, so often involved with the concept of mind, is a problem by itself which need not, I think, concern us here. Conscious purpose, desire, thought, is the *subjective experience* of behavioral goals set up in the living system to which our actions continually seek to conform.

Imagination

But there is one important element that must be added to this concept of the human mind, particularly as we consider its creativeness. The multiplication of man's behavioral goals and the increased complexity of his psychological patterns have enriched his mental life, but something else has been acquired during his upward progress. Gaining the power to accumulate experience and to reason was not enough to make him truly man. Another quality was necessary – the great gift of *imagination*. This is perhaps man's most distinctive trait, for it makes possible his creativeness. Here at last, we finally come more closely to grips with the theme of this study.

To achieve his goals, to satisfy the pattern of the desires that arise in him from the interaction between his wide genetic capacity and the increasing complications of his environment would not have been enough to account for the tremendous acceleration in man's progress since he became man. Frequently, human advancement has been stalled because something essential for its further development was missing. Sooner or later there was born in someone's mind a new idea which supplied the necessary element. Hence must have come the use of fire, communication by written symbols, the invention of the wheel and the bow, domestication of animals, and many more. These doubtless had no sudden origin but were the products of many minds; but they were all novelties that could not have appeared unless there had been someone who could *imagine* a situation never yet experienced, who could picture in his mind something he had not seen.

The Process of Creativity

The problem of creativeness comes down at last to that of how these new ideas have their origin. Much thought has been given to this matter by psychologists and other students of the creative process. Two major methods appear to be operative. One is primarily deductive – creativeness by direct frontal assault. It consists in marshaling the widest possible array of facts and ideas and then carefully searching for heretofore unrecognized relationships between them. This seems to be the method used by Edison, for example, in making his inventions, and by Einstein in the development of his theoretical ideas. But we can be sure that this is not the way in which at least the first steps in creativity, in either science or the arts, have generally been taken.

It is much more common for a new idea to arise almost spontaneously in the mind, often seemingly out of nothing and at a time when a person may be thinking of something quite different. A famous instance is the way in which one of Henri Poincaré's (1924) insights into mathematics came to him. He had been struggling for days with the problem of functions, to no conclusion. One night after drinking black coffee and being unable to sleep, ideas rose in his mind, he says, in crowds, colliding, sometimes interlocking, and finally making some stable combinations from which he discovered the existence of the Fuchsian functions. Shortly afterward, while on a geological excursion and with no thoughts of mathematics in his head, as he put his foot on the step of an omnibus the idea flashed into his mind that the transformations he had used were identical with those of non-Euclidean geometry, a profound insight.

Another notable example often cited of the solution of a scientific problem without conscious effort is Otto Loewi's proof of the chemical mediation of nerve impulses. This came to him vividly in a dream, but on awakening he could not remember the details of it! The next night, fortunately, the dream was repeated. This time, before going to sleep again he recorded it fully and in the laboratory the next day performed the critical experiment that proved the truth of the solution thus given him.

Lovers of A. E. Housman (1933) have read his essay on *The Name and Nature of Poetry* in which he describes how his verses often arose in his mind.

As I went along, thinking of nothing in particular, only looking at things around me and following the progress of the seasons, there would flow into my mind, with sudden and unaccountable emotion, sometimes a line or two of verse, sometimes a whole stanza at once, accompanied, not preceded, by a vague notion of the poem which they were destined to form part of. Then there would usually be a lull of an hour or so, then perhaps the spring would bubble up again.

Many poets have experiences such as these. Robert Frost told a friend of mine about one of his. One winter evening the poet had opened his front door and strode out into the snowy darkness for a breath of air when there came into his mind the whole of that lovely poem *Stopping by Woods on a Snowy Evening*. The strange pattern of rhymes continued in his mind through the verses as he wrote them down, and to bring the poem to a close he had to break the rhythm in the final quatrain.

Many other cases such as these are described in Ghiselin's (1952) book, *The Creative Process*, in Hutchinson's (1949) *How to Think Creatively*, and in other places. This sort of creativity is not common, but it is certainly far from rare. It has been found among all sorts of men and women who are faced with the need – sometimes the consuming, passionate desire – to gain a new insight into truth or beauty, to solve a problem in science, to bring to life a painting out of pigment, oil, and canvas, or to set a poem down in words.

Such inspirations, it is well recognized, rarely come unless an individual has immersed himself in a subject. He must have a rich background of knowledge and experience in it. In science, he must be laboring to find the answer to a problem or to bring a mass of apparently unrelated facts in his mind into a unity; in art, he must be dreaming and pondering about a painting or a piece of music which he feels is there but cannot quite be brought into existence; in poetry, he has an intense preoccupation with something beautiful but still vague which he is trying eagerly to express. He is wrestling to bring into actuality these cloudy, half-formed products of his imagination. Often along the way he will jot down notes or sketches or snatches of music or single lines of verse or a half-written story, steps toward the completion of his still inchoate theme. Then, in a time of relaxation or when something else is actively occupying his mind, the answer which he seeks, or at least the creative nub of it, will come sauntering into his mind as if spontaneously.

Sometimes, as we have seen, the whole answer to a scientific problem may thus appear, or the outline for an entire story, or a substantial bit of verse; but more commonly the initial inspiration is only the start and must be followed by long hours or days of labor in revising and reorganizing and completing the original flash of insight. Nevertheless, without this flash the creative process might never have been able to get started.

The Unconscious

What relation can there be, we now may ask, between the organizing, regulatory, goal-seeking processes in which we have sought the origin of mind and these creative activities which are man's particular glory? Evidently such creative imagination is especially active at the mind's unconscious level. Here mental work is being done. Here, quite without conscious participation, choices are being made and ideas fitted together into patterns.

Psychology has little to tell us yet of what is happening here. In dreams and half-dreaming states the mind is filled with a throng of images and fantasies. The whole unconscious presumably is occupied with such, their source lying in memory and the experiences of the past and perhaps also directly in the processes of life itself. Here, we should remember, is the place where matter, life, and mind are most inextricably mixed. Here the natural tendencies and predilections of living stuff come to expression. More than all, I think, here the organizing power of life fashions into orderly patterns the floating fantasies of the unconscious mind. Here, if anywhere, new patterns may be created.

All this sounds rather vague and mystical, and it does indeed touch on a frontier where almost nothing now is certainly known. It is not pure speculation, however. The creative processes that must be taking place in the unconscious may not be different from those in the conscious mind. A scientist, faced with a problem, marshals all the facts he can find that bear on it. Many relations among them seem meaningless, and such he rules out. Others have significance, and finally, by rearranging and organizing the facts, he is able to build a consistent pattern of ideas and to form a theory. Many psychologists believe that something not unlike this is taking place in the unconscious when an individual has been pondering a problem and seeking to solve it in his conscious mind. Among the throng of random images and ideas, the unconscious mind rejects certain combinations as unimportant or incompatible but sees the significance of others. By its means, order – intellectual, esthetic, perhaps spiritual order – is here distinguished from randomness. Thus the unconscious mind is able to solve problems and to lay at least the foundation for the construction of a poem or a work of art. These are new creations. They might have been produced by the conscious mind and often have been, through sheer force of mental labor; but the reason that such a frontal attack often fails seems to be that the free association, present in the unconscious, is blocked in various ways and the really creative new relationships therefore are not seen.

One must recognize the operation in the unconscious of such an organizing factor, for chance alone is not creative. Just as the organism pulls together random, formless stuff into the patterned system of structure and function in the body, so the unconscious mind seems to select and arrange and correlate these ideas and images into a pattern. The resemblance between the two processes is close. The concept is worth considering that the organizing power of life, manifest in mind as well as in body – for the two are hardly separable – is the truly creative element. Creativity thus becomes an attribute of *life*.

That mind actually does possess some such organizing power as this is suggested by the conclusions of Gestalt psychology. I am not competent to discuss these nor is this volume the place to do so, but it seems clear that mind, or whatever its physical correlate may be, when confronted with the throng of unassociated stimuli pouring into it from the organs of sense, is able to organize them, largely without conscious effort, into patterns or *Gestalten*. Mind has a truly morphogenetic quality about it. The patterns it makes are new things, not repetitions of something in the past. This specifically creative ability of mind should not be forgotten in any consideration of creativity in general.

For the unconscious thus to build something new requires an incentive, a goal to be achieved. In this strange creativeness we seem faced with a much less concrete sort of goal than the ones discussed earlier – a seeking not for food or for a mate or for preferment or to enjoy the pleasures of a game or the more refined ones of listening to a symphony, but for something still inchoate, unformed, which is seeking, so to speak, to reach expression. The invariable precursor of unconscious creativity is a strong conscious desire for something – the solution of a problem or the construction of a work of art when only hints or cloudy outlines are in the mind. This eager search is often accompanied by wrestlings of the spirit which leave the seeker exhausted and spent, but when he abandons it, the search is still pursued at the lower unconscious levels of his mind and there it often is successful. In such cases we seem to be witnessing not the operation of an *established* norm but its actual *creation*. The living system here is exercising its ability to integrate and organize a pattern out of formlessness, an achievement which rational thought, being somewhat removed from its primitive living source and bound with habit and convention, may be incapable of doing.

An act of unconscious creativeness is dramatic and conspicuous but relatively rare. It is difficult, however, to draw a line between such a process and others much more common, products of the conscious mind which we call acts of *creative imagination*. Here the unconscious may have a share, also, but the process is in consciousness. From this comes the creation of most works of art, at least in their final state, and the solution of most scientific problems. It is the mark of genius.

But how, in turn, can we distinguish between the constructive processes of the creative imagination and that image-forming which is such an important part of all mental life from childhood to old age? Imagination of this simple kind seems to be a characteristically human trait. Indeed, it is necessary if reason is to be fruitful, for most reasoning processes require assumptions, if nothing more, and these are constructive acts of the imagination.

The imaginative process doubtless did not come into being suddenly, but probably arose when man began to contemplate the possibility of achieving one goal rather than another. Perhaps when he first recognized the significance of the concept 'if', it was born. At any rate, its development seems to have gone hand in hand with that of rationality. These primitive forms of imagination, we can agree, are potentially creative though often not actually so. They have led, however, at the higher levels of man's mind, to what seems a truly creative process.

Conclusion

What, then, may we conclude as to the biological basis of creativity? Simply this, I think: that *life* itself is the creative

113

process by virtue of its organizing, pattern-forming, questing quality, its most distinctive character. In living things below man and in man's bodily structure, life is tied to a conservative and relatively rigid physical basis in the genetic constitution of the individual, necessary if the world of organisms is not to become mixed and chaotic. But when this same organizing quality is applied to behavior, its products are much more various; and when it operates in the unthinkable complexity of the human brain, with its billions of neurones and almost countless number of synapses, the possibilities of new mental patterns are almost infinite. Gerard (1946) has well described this situation in his essay, 'The biological basis of imagination'. Says he:

By such various mechanisms, then, great masses of nerve cells – the brain as a great unity – act together; and not merely do two or a billion units sum their separate contributions, but each is part of a dynamic fluctuating activity pattern of the whole. This is the orchestra which plays thoughts of truth and beauty, which creates imagination. . . . What a beautiful basis for making new gestalts or recombinations of sensory material!

Here is the field where the creative imagination operates, whether in the conscious or the unconscious mind. Imagination, we may say, is simply the basic formative quality of life, emerging at this highest level from its former dependence on a rigid material basis and free to express itself in high creativity. The material for these expressions, these new norms and patterns, may exist in many forms – in pigments on canvas, in musical notes, in words, or simply in ideas. However creativity may manifest itself in the affairs of men, it is in this inherent creativeness of life, I believe, that its ultimate source is to be found.

Such is my thesis. For some, the suggestions here presented will have little appeal. It is unorthodox biology that I have presented. Many biologists will look with disfavor on an extrapolation of the fact of organization, real though it is, into the realm of purpose and thus of mind, and they will be likely to regard as useless the attempt to see in it the germ of creativity. Psychologists, particularly of the tougher-minded sort, will criticize the argument as naïve and as offering to our understanding of creativeness little that is constructive. I cannot help feeling, however, that the roots of the various problems that have been discussed here will finally be found in an understanding of the nature of life. Biologists, like all good and conservative scientists, have hesitated to plunge into speculations which verge on the metaphysical, for both speculation and metaphysics are terms somewhat in disrepute in scientific circles today. But problems such as this one of creativeness are so involved with life that students of the science of life, whether they like it or not, are going to be impelled more and more to try to make some contribution toward their solution, if only to state the problems in more precise form. This chapter is a tentative step in that direction.

References
GERARD, R. W. (1946), 'The biological basis of imagination; with biographical sketch', *Scient. Month.*, vol. 62, pp. 477–99.
GHISELIN, B. (ed.) (1952), *The Creative Process: A Symposium*, University of California Press.
HOUSMAN, A. E. (1933), *The Name and Nature of Poetry*, Cambridge University Press.
HUTCHINSON, E. D. (1949), *How to Think Creatively*, Abingdon.
POINCARÉ, H. (1924), 'Mathematical creation', in *The Foundations of Science* (trans. G. B. Halstead), Science Press, pp. 383–94.

11 A. J. Cropley

S–R Psychology and Cognitive Psychology

Excerpt from A. J. Cropley, *Creativity*, Longmans, Green, 1967, pp. 34–43.

S–R Psychology and Cognitive Psychology

It is common, nowadays, to draw a contrast between those psychologists who see psychological processes as essentially involving the building up of associations between stimuli and responses (S–R theorists), and those who are chiefly concerned with the ways in which people take in, organize, store and eventually output information so that it can be readily retained and quickly retrieved (cognitive theorists). At the extreme the two kinds of psychology tend to concentrate on separate aspects of human functioning, the S–R theorists being concerned largely with learning in all its manifestations, cognitive theorists concentrating more on processes like thinking. However, the essential difference between the two points of view is not really one of different subject matter, but of differing approaches to the same phenomena. Thus, S–R psychologists are frequently also concerned with things like thinking, the nature of personality, the processes of forgetting, and so on, but they approach these topics in their own characteristic way. Similarly, cognitive psychologists may investigate learning phenomena. The difference between the two approaches to psychology lies, in fact, in the mechanisms they see as underlying psychological functioning, rather than in the subject areas they study.

Thus, S–R psychologists have attempted to account for the phenomena of creativity in their own way, which involves the notion that human behaviour is essentially a matter of building up links or bonds between stimuli and responses, although they are inclined to disagree among themselves concerning the mechanics of bond formation. In fact, within the general framework of the S–R approach, there are several theories of how creative thinking comes to occur: one or two of these will be outlined very briefly in the following paragraphs.

Some S–R Theories of Creativity

Mednick (1962) has advanced a theory of creativity which is of the associative sort. He defines creativity as involving the formation of associations between stimuli and responses which are characterized by the fact that the elements linked together are not normally associated. Thus, he suggests that divergent people tend to link stimuli with highly unlikely responses, whereas in most people any particular stimulus is usually linked with the response with which it has most frequently been paired in the past. In other words, highly divergent people are particularly skilful at linking together, in an effective way, aspects of their environment which, on the basis of experience, do not really belong together. In most people, such happy S–R linkages seldom occur, except perhaps by chance,[1] whereas they are more or less commonplace among highly creative individuals.

The Remote Associations Test

On the basis of this point of view, Mednick has designed a test of creativity. The Remote Associations Test (RAT), as he called it, assumes that highly creative individuals will make a greater number of associations to any stimulus word than will less creative people. In each item of Mednick's test, subjects are presented with three words which have some common association, and they are required to find a fourth word which has common associative links with all three stimulus words. The RAT has been roughly standardized by Mednick and was reported by him to correlate with faculty ratings of the creativity of students in an architectural design course, and with ratings of research creativity of post-graduate students in psychology. It was also shown that high RAT scorers tended to be more 'liberal' in their views than low scorers, and that they expressed

1. Hebb (1949, p. 219) has suggested that the term 'serendipity' is now well established as a label for fortuitous, happy combinations.

significantly more interest in creative occupations like journalism and art.

However, there is evidence, cited by the present author (Cropley, 1966), which suggests that the RAT is more related to conventional verbal skills than to divergent thinking, and that the associational theory of divergence is probably inadequate.

Instrumental Conditioning and Divergent Thinking

It is also possible to formulate an S–R theory of creativity in terms of instrumental conditioning. Basically, instrumental conditioning involves the building up of S–R bonds by rewarding responses which are desired and failing to reward, or even punishing, linkages which are not required. Many authors have emphasized the role of such differential reinforcement in the building up of patterns of behaviour in children, and emphasize that their behaviour is shaped by the particular patterns of re-inforcement received during the process of growing up. This point of view suggests that the extent to which a child is able to make creative responses will be heavily dependent on the extent to which he has been rewarded or punished for creative thinking during his past childhood, and implies that parents will have an important effect on the disposition towards creative thinking, as a result of their child-rearing practices. The possibility of such a relationship will be discussed in a later chapter.

Other S–R Approaches to Creativity

More recent S–R theories have placed great emphasis on the so-called 'mediating processes', and a number of complex formulations have been advanced which, while retaining their essentially S–R nature (by sticking to the idea that links between stimuli and responses are the basic units of human behaviour and even of higher-level intellectual processes), have proposed that there are various structures which intervene between the S-part and the R-part of the S–R bond. An example of one such formu-lation is that of Osgood (1953). However, all such attempts to account for the phenomena of creativity in terms of the S–R view ignore the individual himself as an important element in the connecting of environment and behaviour. The person becomes merely some kind of storage place which is at the mercy of the external world, and which is essentially passive. In fact, many psychologists reject such a view, and insist that the most interesting determinants of whether or not a person functions divergently or convergently lie, not in his conditioning history, but in his properties as a human being. Thus, in this conception, the individual is seen as actively engaged in the business of living, and creative thinking is linked to his personal properties, as well as to the power of his intellect.

The Cognitive Position

Hence, in contrast to S–R theories of creativity, cognitive theorists are chiefly concerned with the ways in which people organize information received from the world. The individual is regarded as actively at grips with his environment, not merely the passive recipient of whatever it chances to offer him. Different people possess differing ways of 'taking hold of' the external world; they receive information in characteristic ways, interpret it idiosyncratically, and store it in terms of all the information processed in the past. Intellectual functioning is thus seen as a highly unified process so that the attempt to break it down into discrete fragments in the S–R way is bound to be inadequate. Hence, in accounting for the appearance or absence of creative thinking, cognitive psychologists are concerned with differences between highly creative and highly convergent individuals in the characteristic ways in which they come to grips with their environment.

Consequently, as far as cognitive theorists are concerned, creativity represents not differing systems of associational bonds, but different ways of getting and handling information, and different ways of combining data in seeking effective solutions (different 'mind styles' if you like). Hence, the cognitive approach to creativity asks about the extent to which highly creative people are prepared to take risks in their thinking, about their willingness to take in large quantities of the information the environment has to offer (rather than to restrict themselves to a narrow, but safe, segment of it), about their capacity for quickly changing their point of view, and so on. The remainder of this section will be concerned with a discussion of the relationship between high levels of creative thinking and several such cognitive variables.

Creative Thinking and Data Coding

As Bruner (1957) has pointed out, any individual in contact with the external world is confronted with masses of data, too much, in fact, for him to handle. If he tries to take in everything, he suffers a good deal of 'cognitive strain' (Bruner and Olver, 1963, p. 134). What happens is that individual environmental events are tied in with previous events so that new data are seen, not as unique occurrences, but as part of a related sequence of events which the environment has been providing throughout life. Thus, a new datum is rendered 'meaningful' by being connected with past data which it resembles. This process of connexion is called 'coding', and a set of related data is called a 'category'. The point is that the external world is rendered meaningful by the linking of new events with past events which they resemble, and Bruner sees this as the chief kind of intellectual activity.

Now the contents of categories are built up through experience, so that, in members of the same culture, systems of categories tend to be highly similar. This in turn means that a given event will tend to be coded in a similar way by most members of a given culture – coding becomes highly stereotyped, in fact. Nonetheless, some people, despite their common cultural background, retain the capacity to make novel and unusual codings which manifest themselves as creative thinking.

Clearly, the more a person treats data which look to have nothing to do with each other as though they are related, the more likely he is to make data combinations which are unusual (i.e. to think creatively). The kind of person who codes in this broad way is referred to as a wide categorizer, while the opposite kind of person is called a narrow categorizer. People who make very fine discriminations between bits of input and who require high levels of similarity before they can see relationships (narrow categorizers), are inclined to store information as though it consisted of a large number of relatively unrelated, specific bits, and are thus unlikely to make the kind of cognitive leap involved in creative thinking. On the other hand, willingness to treat data whose connexion with each other is not immediately apparent as roughly equivalent would be particularly favourable to the appearance of creativity. Creative thinking thus looks to be related to width of categorizing.

In fact, this prediction of a relationship between width of coding and creativity, made on theoretical grounds, has been substantiated by empirical data. Wallach and Kogan (1965, p. 129) sorted out a sample of 151 fifth grade American children into high and low creativity groups and also into high and low I.Q. groups, then obtained scores from them on a number of cognitive variables, of which category width in the sense outlined on this page was one. Analysis of the scores of the seventy boys and the eighty-one girls separately indicated that, in both groups, there was a significant tendency for the more highly creative children to get higher scores on the category width test.

This finding was supported by an analysis of category width scores obtained in the present author's own study with Canadian children. The 320 children were subdivided, on the basis of their scores on the creativity measures, and two special subgroups selected. These consisted of the top 10 per cent of the total sample on creativity and the bottom 10 per cent on those measures. The highly creative 10 per cent of the children showed a marked tendency to get higher scores on category width than did the low creative 10 per cent. Thus, the empirical evidence supports the prediction made on theoretical grounds. Creative thinkers are, in fact, markedly broader in the width of their categories, so that they are able to see data equivalences which are not at all apparent to more convergent individuals.

Creativity and Cognitive Styles

In the previous section it was stressed that intellectual functioning may usefully be thought of as involving the build up of codes, in which information about the recurring regularities of the world is stored. In this conception, the emphasis is on individual differences in the way in which data is stored once it has got into an individual's data processing systems. However, it is apparent that the presence or absence of creative thinking might well be connected with differences in the way in which environmental information is taken in, in the first place. Different people go about the matter of getting data from their environment in differing ways, so that, for example, some people concentrate closely on a small portion of what is available for input while others attend, in a less punctilious way, to a wider sweep of information. Such differences in the ways in which different individuals go about taking in the world are, in fact, so pervasive and so well documented that a label for the phenomenon is in widespread use among psychologists. The characteristic way in which an individual goes about taking in information from the world is referred to as 'cognitive style'. The cognitive styles whose existence have been demonstrated include 'field dependence', 'scanning-focusing', 'levelling-sharpening', and a number of others.

Most cognitive styles, including the ones just mentioned, have in common the property that they involve a dichotomy between, on the one hand, taking the world in in large lumps and, on the other, selectively attending only to chosen portions of the environment. The dichotomy can be restated as being a matter of paying attention to as wide a range of environmental properties as possible, or selecting a few attributes of the environment and concentrating on processing them. The latter strategy has the advantage that one can select a few highly related and task-relevant pieces of information and focus attention on them. This makes for ease of coding and necessitates little accommodation (modifying of codes), but that state of affairs is achieved at the expense of losing the capacity to make rapid changes in one's cognitive structures. In other words, the highly selective kind of cognitive styles lead to stereotypy of intellectual functioning, but have an important advantage in that they make life much easier.

On the other hand, taking in as much information as possible involves the risk of cognitive strain, necessitates frequent modification of existing categories, and makes intellectual functioning a more arduous task. However, this state of affairs leads to good pay-offs in that it involves the advantages of being able to change one's existing mental structures very readily, of being able to relate widely different looking data and, in fact, of being in a state highly favourable to the appearance of creative thinking. Thus, those people whose cognitive style involves the least censoring of the information available in the external world are most likely to be creative thinkers.

Risk Taking

A cognitive variable which is closely related to category width, and also to cognitive styles involving readiness to accept the maximum amount of information from the external world, is that of risk taking. The convergent thinker has a pretty clear picture of just what goes with what. He knows what is logical, what not, and his world is a well organized and neat place in which he can expect to get along without too much strain. By contrast, the wide categorizer, who is prepared to attend to a broad variety of environmental information, must continually run the risk of making mistakes, or of looking foolish. He cannot rely on a set of well-worn, tried and trusted principles to carry him through, but must adjust himself continuously to all available data. In this process, he may often be wrong, or certainly out of step with most of his fellows, so that he must risk making errors and being censured. Some authors, like McClelland (1963, p. 184) and Roe (1963, p. 170) for example, regard such willingness to take risks as so important in creativity that they mention it as one of the critical attributes of the highly creative individual.

Very closely linked with the notion that the creative thinker is not afraid to take a risk with his ideas is a further related trait – creative people are willing to 'have a go', intellectually speaking. They will, for example, risk an intelligent guess in a problem situation, whereas convergent thinkers are much more inclined to report that the problem is simply insoluble when it becomes apparent that logic, rule, and principle will not provide a solution. The latter kind of thinkers may even refuse to go on, on the grounds that the situation is 'foolish'.

The possibility of a relationship between creativity and risk taking was tested by a further analysis of the Canadian junior high school data already referred to in chapter 2 [not included here] and in Anderson and Cropley (1966). The two subsamples consisting of the most creative 10 per cent and the least creative 10 per cent of the entire 320 students were compared on a risk taking test, and the results indicated that the highly creative thinkers were significantly more willing to take intellectual risks by, for example, having a guess in a problem situation and then backing their own guess in the absence of any better information, rather than playing it safe by making a neutral estimate and expressing no confidence whatsoever in it. These findings are important because they strongly suggest that there are cognitive differences between creative and convergent thinkers, and further suggest that these differences are connected with the fact that the highly creative thinker is, to put it plainly, prepared to think boldly.

Rigidity

Thinking of the creative individual as a wide categorizer who attends to a broad span of environmental events and is willing to take a chance on being wrong, of looking foolish, or of drastically having to revise his views, leads to a consideration of the role in creative thinking of rigidity and flexibility. The creative thinker is, above all, flexible and adaptable in his intellectual functioning. He is not committed to the preservation of an existing *status quo*, and is prepared to rearrange his thinking. On the other hand, the rigid individual is convinced of the logic and rightness of his existing view of the world. He is unwilling to make rapid or drastic changes in intellectual orientation, perhaps even incapable, and he clings firmly to what he 'knows' is right. In this latter kind of person, the intellectual flexibility which characterizes the creative individual is missing, and he functions in a highly convergent manner.

This section may thus be summarized by saying that highly creative individuals are characterized, in the cognitive domain, by:

1. Possession of wide categories.
2. Willingness to take risks.
3. Willingness to 'have a go'.
4. High levels of flexibility.

References

ANDERSON, C. C., and CROPLEY, A. J. (1966), 'Some correlates of originality', *Austr. J. Psychol.*, vol. 18, pp. 218–27.

BRUNER, J. S. (1957), 'On going beyond the information given', in *Contemporary Approaches to Cognition*, Harvard University Press.

BRUNER, J. S., and OLVER, R. R. (1963), 'The development of equivalence transformations in children', in J. C. Wright and J. Kagan (eds.), Basic cognitive processes in children, *Child Devel. Monogr.*, no. 86.

CROPLEY, A. J. (1966), 'Creativity and intelligence', *Brit. J. educ. Psychol.*, vol. 36, pp. 259–66.

HEBB, D. O. (1949), *The Organization of Behavior*, Wiley.

MCCLELLAND, D. C. (1963), 'The calculated risk: an aspect of scientific performance', in C. W. Taylor and F. Barron (eds.), *Scientific Creativity: Its Recognition and Development*, Wiley.

MEDNICK, S. A. (1962), 'The associative basis of creativity', *Psychol. Rev.*, vol. 69, pp. 220–32.

OSGOOD, C. E. (1953), *Method and Theory in Experimental Psychology*, Oxford University Press.

ROE, A. (1963), 'Psychological approaches to creativity in science', in M. A. Coler (ed.), *Essays on Creativity in the Sciences*, New York University Press.

WALLACH, M. A., and KOGAN, N. (1965), *Modes of Thinking in Young Children*, Holt, Rinehart & Winston.

12 S. Freud

Creative Writers and Day-Dreaming

S. Freud, 'Creative writers and day-dreaming', in J. Strachey (ed.),
Standard Edition of the Complete Psychological Works of Sigmund Freud,
vol. 9, Hogarth Press, 1959, pp. 143–53. First published 1908.

We laymen have always been intensely curious to know – like the
Cardinal who put a similar question to Ariosto – from what
sources that strange being, the creative writer, draws his material,
and how he manages to make such an impression on us with it
and to arouse in us emotions of which, perhaps, we had not even
thought ourselves capable. Our interest is only heightened the
more by the fact that, if we ask him, the writer himself gives us no
explanation, or none that is satisfactory; and it is not at all
weakened by our knowledge that not even the clearest insight into
the determinants of his choice of material and into the nature of
the art of creating imaginative form will ever help to make
creative writers of *us*.

If we could at least discover in ourselves or in people like ourselves an activity which was in some way akin to creative writing!
An examination of it would then give us a hope of obtaining the
beginnings of an explanation of the creative work of writers. And,
indeed, there is some prospect of this being possible. After all,
creative writers themselves like to lessen the distance between their
kind and the common run of humanity; they so often assure us
that every man is a poet at heart and that the last poet will not
perish till the last man does.

Should we not look for the first traces of imaginative activity
as early as in childhood? The child's best-loved and most intense
occupation is with his play or games. Might we not say that every
child at play behaves like a creative writer, in that he creates a
world of his own or, rather, rearranges the things of his world in a
new way which pleases him? It would be wrong to think he does
not take that world seriously; on the contrary, he takes his play
very seriously and he expands large amounts of emotion on it.

The opposite of play is not what is serious but what is real. In spite of all the emotion with which he cathects his world of play, the child distinguishes it quite well from reality; and he likes to link his imagined objects and situations to the tangible and visible things of the real world. This linking is all that differentiates the child's 'play' from 'phantasying'.

The creative writer does the same as the child at play. He creates a world of phantasy which he takes very seriously – that is, which he invests with large amounts of emotion – while separating it sharply from reality. Language has preserved this relationship between children's play and poetic creation. It gives (in German) the name of *Spiel* ('play') to those forms of imaginative writing which require to be linked to tangible objects and which are capable of representation. It speaks of a *Lustspiel* or *Trauerspiel* ('comedy' or 'tragedy': literally, 'pleasure play' or 'mourning play') and describes those who carry out the representation as *Schauspieler* ('players': literally 'show-players'). The unreality of the writer's imaginative world, however, has very important consequences for the technique of his art; for many things which, if they were real, could give no enjoyment, can do so in the play of phantasy, and many excitements which, in themselves, are actually distressing, can become a source of pleasure for the hearers and spectators at the performance of a writer's work.

There is another consideration for the sake of which we will dwell a moment longer on this contrast between reality and play. When the child has grown up and has ceased to play, and after he has been labouring for decades to envisage the realities of life with proper seriousness, he may one day find himself in a mental situation which once more undoes the contrast between play and reality. As an adult he can look back on the intense seriousness with which he once carried on his games in childhood; and, by equating his ostensibly serious occupations of today with his childhood games, he can throw off the too heavy burden imposed on him by life and win the high yield of pleasure afforded by *humour*.

As people grow up, then, they cease to play and they seem to give up the yield of pleasure which they gained from playing. But whoever understands the human mind knows that hardly anything is harder for a man than to give up a pleasure which he has once experienced. Actually, we can never give anything up; we only exchange one thing for another. What appears to be a renunciation is really the formation of a substitute or surrogate. In the same way, the growing child, when he stops playing, gives up nothing but the link with real objects; instead of *playing*, he now *phantasies*. He builds castles in the air and creates what are called *day-dreams*. I believe that most people construct phantasies at times in their lives. This is a fact which has long been overlooked and whose importance has therefore not been sufficiently appreciated.

People's phantasies are less easy to observe than the play of children. The child, it is true, plays by himself or forms a closed psychical system with other children for the purposes of a game; but even though he may not play his game in front of the grown-ups, he does not, on the other hand, conceal it from them. The adult, on the contrary, is ashamed of his phantasies and hides them from other people. He cherishes his phantasies as his most intimate possessions, and as a rule he would rather confess his misdeeds than tell anyone his phantasies. It may come about that for that reason he believes he is the only person who invents such phantasies and has no idea that creations of this kind are widespread among other people. This difference in the behaviour of a person who plays and a person who phantasies is accounted for by the motives of these two activities, which are nevertheless adjuncts to each other.

A child's play is determined by wishes: in point of fact by a single wish – one that helps in his upbringing – the wish to be big and grown up. He is always playing at being 'grown up', and in his games he imitates what he knows about the lives of his elders. He has no reason to conceal this wish. With the adult, the case is different. On the one hand, he knows that he is expected not to go on playing or phantasying any longer, but to act in the real world; on the other hand, some of the wishes which give rise to his phantasies are of a kind which it is essential to conceal. Thus he is ashamed of his phantasies as being childish and as being unpermissible.

But, you will ask, if people make such a mystery of their phantasying, how is it that we know such a lot about it? Well, there is a class of human beings upon whom, not a god, indeed, but a stern goddess – Necessity – has allotted the task of telling what they suffer and what things give them happiness. These are the victims of nervous illness, who are obliged to tell their phantasies, among other things, to the doctor by whom they expect to be cured by mental treatment. This is our best source of knowledge, and we have since found good reason to suppose that our patients tell us nothing that we might not also hear from healthy people.

Let us now make ourselves acquainted with a few of the characteristics of phantasying. We may lay it down that a happy person never phantasies, only an unsatisfied one. The motive forces of phantasies are unsatisfied wishes, and every single phantasy is the fulfilment of a wish, a correction of unsatisfying reality. These motivating wishes vary according to the sex, character and circumstances of the person who is having the phantasy; but they fall naturally into two main groups. They are either ambitious wishes, which serve to elevate the subject's personality; or they are erotic ones. In young women the erotic wishes predominate almost exclusively, for their ambition is as a rule absorbed by erotic trends. In young men egoistic and ambitious wishes come to the fore clearly enough alongside of erotic ones. But we will not lay stress on the opposition between the two trends; we would rather emphasize the fact that they are often united. Just as, in many altar-pieces, the portrait of the donor is to be seen in a corner of the picture, so, in the majority of ambitious phantasies, we can discover in some corner or other the lady for whom the creator of the phantasy performs all his heroic deeds and at whose feet all his triumphs are laid. Here, as you see, there are strong enough motives for concealment; the well-brought-up young woman is only allowed a minimum of erotic desire, and the young man has to learn to suppress the excess of self-regard which he brings with him from the spoilt days of his childhood, so that he may find his place in a society which is full of other individuals making equally strong demands.

We must not suppose that the products of this imaginative activity – the various phantasies, castles in the air and day-dreams – are stereotyped or unalterable. On the contrary, they fit themselves into the subject's shifting impressions of life, change with every change in his situation, and receive from every fresh active impression what might be called a 'date-mark'. The relation of a phantasy to time is in general very important. We may say that it hovers, as it were, between three times – the three moments of time which our ideation involves. Mental work is linked to some current impression, some provoking occasion in the present which has been able to arouse one of the subject's major wishes. From there it harks back to a memory of an earlier experience (usually an infantile one) in which this wish was fulfilled; and it now creates a situation relating to the future which represents a fulfilment of the wish. What it thus creates is a day-dream of phantasy, which carries about it traces of its origin from the occasion which provoked it and from the memory. Thus past, present and future are strung together, as it were, on the thread of the wish that runs through them.

A very ordinary example may serve to make what I have said clear. Let us take the case of a poor orphan boy to whom you have given the address of some employer where he may perhaps find a job. On his way there he may indulge in a day-dream appropriate to the situation from which it arises. The content of his phantasy will perhaps be something like this. He is given a job, finds favour with his new employer, makes himself indispensable in the business, is taken into his employer's family, marries the charming young daughter of the house, and then himself becomes a director of the business, first as his employer's partner and then as his successor. In this phantasy, the dreamer has regained what he possessed in his happy childhood – the protecting house, the loving parents and the first objects of his affectionate feelings. You will see from this example the way in which the wish makes use of an occasion in the present to construct, on the pattern of the past, a picture of the future.

There is a great deal more that could be said about phantasies; but I will only allude as briefly as possible to certain points. If phantasies become over-luxuriant and over-powerful, the conditions are laid for an onset of neurosis or psychosis. Phantasies, moreover, are the immediate mental precursors of the distressing symptoms complained of by our patients. Here a broad by-path branches off into pathology.

I cannot pass over the relation of phantasies to dreams. Our dreams at night are nothing else than phantasies like these, as we can demonstrate from the interpretation of dreams. Language, in its unrivalled wisdom, long ago decided the question of the essential nature of dreams by giving the name of 'day-dreams' to the airy creations of phantasy. If the meaning of our dreams usually remains obscure to us in spite of this pointer, it is because of the circumstance that at night there also arise in us wishes of which we are ashamed; these we must conceal from ourselves, and they have consequently been repressed, pushed into the unconscious. Repressed wishes of this sort and their derivatives are only allowed to come to expression in a very distorted form. When scientific work had succeeded in elucidating this factor of *dream-distortion*, it was no longer difficult to recognize that night-dreams are wish-fulfilments in just the same way as day-dreams – the phantasies which we all know so well.

So much for phantasies. And now for the creative writer. May we really attempt to compare the imaginative writer with the 'dreamer in broad daylight', and his creations with day-dreams? Here we must begin by making an initial distinction. We must separate writers who, like the ancient authors of epics and tragedies, take over their material ready-made, from writers who seem to originate their own material. We will keep to the latter kind, and, for the purposes of our comparison, we will choose not the writers most highly esteemed by the critics, but the less pretentious authors of novels, romances and short stories, who nevertheless have the widest and most eager circle of readers of both sexes. One feature above all cannot fail to strike us about the creations of these story-writers: each of them has a hero who is the centre of interest, for whom the writer tries to win our sympathy by every possible means and whom he seems to place under the protection of a special Providence. If, at the end of one chapter of my story, I leave the hero unconscious and bleeding from severe wounds, I am sure to find him at the beginning of the next being carefully nursed and on the way to recovery; and if the first volume closes with the ship he is in going down in a storm at sea, I am certain, at the opening of the second volume, to read of his miraculous rescue – a rescue without which the story could not proceed. The feeling of security with which I follow the hero through his perilous adventures is the same as the feeling with which a hero in real life throws himself into the water to save a drowning man or exposes himself to the enemy's fire in order to storm a battery. It is the true heroic feeling, which one of our best writers has expressed in an inimitable phrase: 'Nothing can happen to *me*!' It seems to me, however, that through this revealing characteristic of invulnerability we can immediately recognize His Majesty the Ego, the hero alike of every day-dream and of every story.

Other typical features of these egocentric stories point to the same kinship. The fact that all the women in the novel invariably fall in love with the hero can hardly be looked on as a portrayal of reality, but it is easily understood as a necessary constituent of a day-dream. The same is true of the fact that the other characters in the story are sharply divided into good and bad, in defiance of the variety of human characters that are to be observed in real life. The 'good' ones are the helpers, while the 'bad' ones are the enemies and rivals, of the ego which has become the hero of the story.

We are perfectly aware that very many imaginative writings are far removed from the model of the naïve day-dream; and yet I cannot suppress the suspicion that even the most extreme deviations from that model could be linked with it through an uninterrupted series of transitional cases. It has struck me that in many of what are known as 'psychological' novels only one person – once again the hero – is described from within. The author sits inside his mind, as it were, and looks at the other characters from outside. The psychological novel in general no doubt owes its special nature to the inclination of the modern writer to split up his ego, by self-observation, into many part-egos, and, in consequence, to personify the conflicting currents of his own mental life in several heroes. Certain novels, which might be described as 'eccentric', seem to stand in quite special contrast to the type of the day-dream. In these, the person who is introduced as the hero plays only a very small active part; he sees the actions and sufferings of other people pass before him like a spectator. Many of Zola's later works belong to this category. But I must point out that the psychological analysis of individuals who are not creative writers, and who diverge in some respects from the so-called norm, has shown us analogous variations of the day-dream, in which the ego contents itself with the role of spectator.

If our comparison of the imaginative writer with the day-dreamer, and of poetical creation with the day-dream, is to be of any value, it must, above all, show itself in some way or other fruitful. Let us, for instance, try to apply to these authors' works the thesis we laid down earlier concerning the relation between phantasy and the three periods of time and the wish which runs through them; and, with its help, let us try to study the connexions that exist between the life of the writer and his works. No one has known, as a rule, what exceptions to frame in approaching this problem; and often the connexion has been thought of in much too simple terms. In the light of the insight we have gained from phantasies, we ought to expect the following state of affairs. A strong experience in the present awakens in the creative writer a memory of an earlier experience (usually belonging to his childhood) from which there now proceeds a wish which finds its fulfilment in the creative work. The work itself exhibits elements of the recent provoking occasion as well as of the old memory.

Do not be alarmed at the complexity of this formula. I suspect that in fact it will prove to be too exiguous a pattern. Nevertheless, it may contain a first approach to the true state of affairs; and, from some experiments I have made, I am inclined to think that this way of looking at creative writings may turn out not unfruitful. You will not forget that the stress it lays on childhood memories in the writer's life – a stress which may perhaps seem puzzling – is ultimately derived from the assumption that a piece of creative writing, like a day-dream, is a continuation of, and a substitute for, what was once the play of childhood.

We must not neglect, however, to go back to the kind of imaginative works which we have to recognize, not as original creations, but as the refashioning of ready-made and familiar material (p. 131). Even here, the writer keeps a certain amount of independence, which can express itself in the choice of material and in changes in it which are often quite extensive. In so far as the material is already at hand, however, it is derived from the popular treasure-house of myths, legends and fairy tales. The study of constructions of folk-psychology such as these is far from being complete, but it is extremely probable that myths, for instance, are distorted vestiges of the wishful phantasies of whole nations, the *secular dreams* of youthful humanity.

You will say that, although I have put the creative writer first in the title of my paper, I have told you far less about him than about phantasies. I am aware of that, and I must try to excuse it by pointing to the present state of our knowledge. All I have been able to do is to throw out some encouragements and suggestions which, starting from the study of phantasies, lead on to the problem of the writer's choice of his literary material. As for the other problem – by what means the creative writer achieves the emotional effects in us that are aroused by his creations – we have as yet not touched on it at all. But I should like at least to point out to you the path that leads from our discussion of phantasies to the problems of poetical effects.

You will remember how I have said (pp. 128 ff.) that the day-dreamer carefully conceals his phantasies from other people because he feels he has reasons for being ashamed of them. I should now add that even if he were to communicate them to us he could give us no pleasure by his disclosures. Such phantasies, when we learn them, repel us or at least leave us cold. But when a creative writer presents his plays to us or tells us what we are inclined to take to be his personal day-dreams, we experience a great pleasure, and one which probably arises from the confluence of many sources. How the writer accomplishes this is his innermost secret; the essential *ars poetica* lies in the technique of overcoming the feeling of repulsion in us which is undoubtedly connected with the barriers that rise between each single ego and the others. We can guess two of the methods used by this technique. The writer softens the character of his egoistic day-dreams by altering and disguising it, and he bribes us by the purely formal, that is, aesthetic, yield of pleasure which he offers us in the presentation of his phantasies. We give the name of an *incentive bonus*, or a *fore-pleasure*, to a yield of pleasure such as this, which is offered to us so as to make possible the release of still greater pleasure arising from deeper psychical sources. In my opinion, all the aesthetic pleasure which a creative writer affords us has the character of a fore-pleasure of this kind, and our actual enjoyment of an imaginative work proceeds from a liberation of tensions in our minds. It may even be that not a little of this effect is due to the writer's enabling us thenceforward to enjoy our own day-dreams without self-reproach or shame. This brings us to the threshold of new, interesting and complicated enquiries; but also, at least for the moment, to the end of our discussion.

Excerpt from S. Freud, *A General Introduction to Psychoanalysis*, Boni & Liveright, 1920, pp. 326–7.

The artist is an incipient introvert who is not far from being a neurotic. He is impelled by too powerful instinctive needs. He wants to achieve honor, power, riches, fame and the love of women. But he lacks the means of achieving these satisfactions. So like any other unsatisfied person, he turns away from reality, and transfers all his interests, his libido, too, to the elaboration of his imaginary wishes, all of which might easily point the way to neurosis. A great many factors must combine to present this termination of his development; it is well known how often artists especially suffer from a partial inhibition of their capacities through neurosis. Apparently their constitutions are strongly endowed with an ability to sublimize and to shift the suppression determining their conflicts. The artist finds the way back to reality in this way. He is not the only one who has a life of imagination. The twilight-realm of phantasy is upheld by the sanction of humanity and every hungry soul looks here for help and sympathy. But for those who are not artists, the ability to obtain satisfaction from imaginative sources is very restricted. Their relentless suppressions force them to be satisfied with the sparse day dreams which may become conscious. If one is a real artist he has more at his disposal. In the first place, he understands how to elaborate his day dreams so that they lose their essentially personal element, which would repel strangers, and yield satisfaction to others as well. He also knows how to disguise them so that they do not easily disclose their origin in their despised sources. He further possesses the puzzling ability of molding a specific material into a faithful image of the creatures of his imagination, and then he is able to attach to this representation of his unconscious phantasies so much pleasurable gratification that, for a time at least, it is able to outweigh and release the suppressions. If he is able to accomplish all this, he makes it possible for others, in their return, to obtain solace and consolation from their own unconscious sources of gratification which had become inaccessible. He wins gratitude and admiration for himself and so, by means of his imagination, achieves the very things which had at first only an imaginary existence for him; honor, power and the love of women.

13 C. R. Rogers

Towards a Theory of Creativity

C. R. Rogers, 'Toward a theory of creativity', *ETC: A Review of General Semantics*, vol. 11, 1954, pp. 249–60. Reprinted in H. H. Anderson (ed.), *Creativity and its Cultivation*, Harper, 1959, pp. 69–82.

I maintain that there is a desperate social need for the creative behavior of creative individuals. It is this which justifies the setting forth of a tentative theory of creativity – the nature of the creative act, the conditions under which it occurs, and the manner in which it may constructively be fostered. Such a theory may serve as a stimulus and guide to research studies in this field.

The Social Need

Many of the serious criticisms of our culture and its trends may best be formulated in terms of a dearth of creativity. Let us state some of these very briefly:

1. In education we tend to turn out conformists, stereotypes, individuals whose education is 'completed', rather than freely creative and original thinkers.

2. In our leisure-time activities, passive entertainment and regimented group action are overwhelmingly predominant, whereas creative activities are much less in evidence.

3. In the sciences, there is an ample supply of technicians, but the number who can creatively formulate fruitful hypotheses and theories is small indeed.

4. In industry, creation is reserved for the few – the manager, the designer, the head of the research department – whereas for the many life is devoid of original or creative endeavor.

5. In individual and family life the same picture holds true. In the clothes we wear, the food we eat, the books we read, and the ideas we hold, there is a strong tendency toward conformity, toward stereotypy. To be original or different is felt to be 'dangerous'.

Why be concerned over this? If, as a people, we enjoy conformity rather than creativity, shall we not be permitted this choice? In my estimation such a choice would be entirely reasonable were it not for one great shadow which hangs over all of us. In a time when knowledge, constructive and destructive, is advancing by the most incredible leaps and bounds into a fantastic atomic age, genuinely creative adaptation seems to represent the only possibility that man can keep abreast of the kaleidoscopic change in his world. With scientific discovery and invention proceeding, we are told, at a geometric rate of progression, a generally passive and culture-bound people cannot cope with the multiplying issues and problems. Unless individuals, groups and nations can imagine, construct and creatively revise new ways of relating to these complex changes, the lights will go out. Unless man can make new and original adaptations to his environment as rapidly as his science can change the environment, our culture will perish. Not only individual maladjustment and group tensions but international annihilation will be the price we pay for a lack of creativity.

Consequently it would seem to me that investigations of the process of creativity, the conditions under which this process occurs, and the ways in which it may be facilitated, are of the utmost importance.

It is in the hope of suggesting a conceptual structure under which such investigations might go forward, that the following sections are offered.

The Creative Process

There are various ways of defining creativity. In order to make more clear the meaning of what is to follow, let me present the elements which, for me, are a part of the creative process, and then attempt a definition.

In the first place, for me as scientist, there must be something observable, some product of creation. Though my fantasies may be extremely novel, they cannot usefully be defined as creative. unless they eventuate in some observable product – unless they are symbolized in words, or written in a poem, or translated into a work of art or fashioned into an invention.

138

These products must be novel constructions. This novelty grows out of the unique qualities of the individual in his interaction with the materials of experience. Creativity always has the stamp of the individual upon its product, but the product is not the individual, nor his materials, but partakes of the relationship between the two.

Creativity is not, in my judgement, restricted to some particular content. I am assuming that there is no fundamental difference in the creative process as it is evidenced in painting a picture, composing a symphony, devising new instruments of killing, developing a scientific theory, discovering new procedures in human relationships or creating new formings of one's own personality as in psychotherapy. (Indeed it is my experience in this last field, rather than in one of the arts, that has given me special interest in creativity and its facilitation. Intimate knowledge of the way in which the individual remolds himself in the therapeutic relationship, with originality and effective skill, gives one confidence in the creative potential of all individuals.)

My definition, then, of the creative process is that it is the emergence in action of a novel relational product, growing out of the uniqueness of the individual on the one hand, and the materials, events, people, or circumstances of his life on the other.

Let me append some negative footnotes on this definition. It makes no distinction between 'good' and 'bad' creativity. One man may be discovering a way of relieving pain, whereas another is devising a new and more subtle form of torture for political prisoners. Both these actions seem to me creative, even though their social value is very different. Although I shall comment on these social valuations later, I have avoided putting them in my definition because they are so fluctuating. Galileo and Copernicus made creative discoveries which in their own day were evaluated as blasphemous and wicked, and in our day as basic and constructive. We do not want to cloud our definition with terms which rest in subjectivity.

Another way of looking at this same issue is to note that to be regarded historically as representing creativity, the product must be acceptable to some group at some point of time. This fact is not helpful to our definition, however, both because of the fluctuating valuations already mentioned and because many creative products have undoubtedly never been socially noticed, have disappeared without ever having been evaluated. So this concept of group acceptance is also omitted from our definition.

In addition, it should be pointed out that our definition makes no distinction regarding the degree of creativity, since this too is a value judgement extremely variable in nature. The action of the child inventing a new game with his playmates; Einstein formulating a theory of relativity; the housewife devising a new sauce for the meat; a young author writing his first novel – all of these are, in terms of our definition, creative, and there is no attempt to set them in some order of more or less creative.

The Motivation for Creativity

The mainspring of creativity appears to be the same tendency which we discover so deeply as the curative force in psycho-therapy – *man's tendency to actualize himself, to become his potentialities*. By this I mean the directional trend which is evident in all organic and human life – the urge to expand, extend, develop, mature, the tendency to express and activate all the capacities of the organism, to the extent that such activation enhances the organism or the self. This tendency may become deeply buried under layer after layer of encrusted psychological defenses; it may be hidden behind elaborate façades which deny its existence; it is my belief however, based on my experience, that it exists in every individual and awaits only the proper conditions to be released and expressed. It is this tendency which is the primary motivation for creativity as the organism forms new relationships to the environment in its endeavor most fully to be itself.

Let us now attempt to deal directly with this puzzling issue of the social value of a creative act. Presumably few of us are interested in facilitating creativity which is socially destructive. We do not wish, knowingly, to lend our efforts to developing individuals whose creative genius works itself out in new and better ways of robbing, exploiting, torturing, killing other individuals; or developing forms of political organization or art forms which lead humanity into paths of physical or psychological self-destruction. Yet how is it possible to make the necessary discrimination such that we may encourage a constructive creativity and not a destructive?

The distinction cannot be made by examining the product. The very essence of the creative is its novelty, and hence we have no standard by which to judge it. Indeed history points up the fact that the more original the product, and the more far-reaching its implications, the more likely it is to be judged by contemporaries as evil. The genuinely significant creation, whether an idea, or a work of art, or a scientific discovery, is most likely to be seen at first as erroneous, bad or foolish. Later it may be seen as obvious, something self-evident to all. Only still later does it receive its final evaluation as a creative contribution. It seems clear that no contemporary mortal can satisfactorily evaluate a creative product at the time that it is formed, and this statement is increasingly true the greater the novelty of the creation.

Nor is it of any help to examine the purposes of the individual participating in the creative process. Many, perhaps most, of the creations and discoveries which have proved to have great social value have been motivated by purposes having more to do with personal interests than with social value, while on the other hand history records a somewhat sorry outcome for many of those creations (various Utopias, Prohibition, etc.) which had as their avowed purpose the achievement of the social good. No, we must face the fact that the individual creates primarily because it is satisfying to him, because this behavior is felt to be self-actualizing, and we get nowhere by trying to differentiate 'good' and 'bad' purposes in the creative process.

Must we then give over any attempt to discriminate between creativity which is potentially constructive, and that which is potentially destructive? I do not believe this pessimistic conclusion is justified. It is here that recent clinical findings from the field of psychotherapy give us hope. It has been found that when the individual is 'open' to all of his experience (a phrase which will be defined more fully), then his behavior will be creative, and his creativity may be trusted to be essentially constructive.

The differentiation may be put very briefly as follows. To the extent that the individual is denying to awareness (or repressing, if you prefer that term) large areas of his experience, then his creative formings may be pathological or socially evil, or both.

To the degree that the individual is open to all aspects of his experience, and has available to his awareness all the varied sensings and perceivings which are going on within his organism, then the novel products of his interaction with his environment will tend to be constructive both for himself and others. To illustrate, an individual with paranoid tendencies may creatively develop a most novel theory of the relationship between himself and his environment, seeing evidence for his theory in all sorts of minute clues. His theory has little social value, perhaps because there is an enormous range of experience which this individual cannot permit in his awareness. Socrates, on the other hand, although also regarded as 'crazy' by his contemporaries, developed novel ideas which have proven to be socially constructive. Very possibly this was because he was notably non-defensive and open to his experience.

The reasoning behind this will perhaps become more clear in the remaining sections of this paper. Primarily however it is based upon the discovery in psychotherapy,

. . . that if we can add to the sensory and visceral experiencing which is characteristic of the whole animal kingdom the gift of a free and undistorted awareness of which only the human animal seems fully capable, we have an organism which is aware of the demands of the culture as it is of its own physiological demands for food or sex; which is just as aware of its desire for friendly relationships as it is of its desire to aggrandize itself; which is just as aware of its delicate and sensitive tenderness toward others as it is of its hostilities toward others. When man's unique capacity of awareness is thus functioning freely and fully, we find that we have, not an animal whom we must fear, not a beast who must be controlled, but an organism able to achieve, through the remarkable integrative capacity of its central nervous system, a balanced, realistic, self-enhancing, other-enhancing behavior as a resultant of all these elements of awareness. To put it another way, when man is less than fully man – when he denies to awareness various aspects of his experience – then indeed we have all too often reason to fear him and his behavior, as the present world situation testifies. But when he is most fully man, when he is his complete organism, when awareness of experience, that peculiarly human attribute, is most fully operating, then he is to be trusted, then his behavior is constructive. It is not always conventional. It will not always be conforming. It will be individualized. But it will also be socialized (Rogers, 1953).

The Inner Conditions of Constructive Creativity

What are the conditions within the individual which are most closely associated with a potentially constructive creative act? I see these as possibilities.

A. Openness to experience: extensionality

This is the opposite of psychological defensiveness, when to protect the organization of the self certain experiences are prevented from coming into awareness except in distorted fashion. In a person who is open to experience each stimulus is freely relayed through the nervous system, without being distorted by any process of defensiveness. Whether the stimulus originates in the environment, in the impact of form, color or sound on the sensory nerves, or whether it originates in the viscera, or as a memory trace in the central nervous system, it is available to awareness. This means that instead of perceiving in predetermined categories (trees are green; college education is good; modern art is silly) the individual is aware of this existential moment as *it* is, thus being alive to many experiences which fall outside the usual categories (*this* tree is lavender; *this* college education is damaging; *this* modern sculpture has a powerful effect on me).

This last suggests another way of describing openness to experience. It means lack of rigidity and permeability of boundaries in concepts, beliefs, perceptions, and hypotheses. It means a tolerance for ambiguity where ambiguity exists. It means the ability to receive much conflicting information without forcing closure upon the situation. It means what the general semanticist calls the 'extensional orientation'.

This complete openness of awareness to what exists at this moment is, I believe, an important condition of constructive creativity. In an equally intense but more narrowly limited fashion it is no doubt present in all creativity. The deeply maladjusted artist who cannot recognize or be aware of the sources of unhappiness in himself may nevertheless be sharply and sensitively aware of form and color in his experience. The tyrant (whether on a petty or grand scale) who cannot face the weaknesses in himself may nevertheless be completely alive to and aware of the chinks in the psychological armor of those with whom he deals. Because there is the openness to one phase of experience, creativity is possible; because the openness is *only* to one phase of experience, the product of this creativity may be potentially destructive of social values. The more the individual has available to himself a sensitive awareness of all phases of his experience, the more sure we can be that his creativity will be personally and socially constructive.

B. An internal locus of evaluation

Perhaps the most fundamental condition of creativity is that the source or locus of evaluative judgement is internal. The value of his product is, for the creative person, established not by the praise or criticism of others, but by himself. Have I created something satisfying to *me*? Does it express a part of me – my feeling or my thought, my pain or my ecstasy? These are the only questions which really matter to the creative person, or to any person when he is being creative.

This does not mean that he is oblivious to, or unwilling to be aware of, the judgement of others. It is simply that the basis of evaluation lies within himself, in his own organismic reaction to and appraisal of his product. If to the person it has the 'feel' of being 'me in action', of being an actualization of potentialities in himself which heretofore have not existed and are now emerging into existence, then it is satisfying and creative, and no outside evaluation can change that fundamental fact.

C. The ability to toy with elements and concepts

Though this is probably less important than A or B, it seems to be a condition of creativity. Associated with the openness and lack of rigidity described under A is the ability to play spontaneously with ideas, colors, shapes, relationships – to juggle elements into impossible juxtapositions, to shape wild hypotheses, to make the given problematic, to express the ridiculous, to translate from one form to another, to transform into improbable equivalents. It is from this spontaneous toying and exploration that there arises the hunch, the creative seeing of life in a new and significant way. It is as though out of the wasteful spawning of thousands of possibilities there emerges one or two evolutionary forms with the qualities which give them a more permanent value.

The Creative Act and its Concomitants

When these three conditions obtain, constructive creativity will occur. But we cannot expect an accurate description of the creative act, for by its very nature it is indescribable. This is the unknown which we must recognize as unknowable until it occurs. This is the improbable that becomes probable. Only in a very general way can we say that a creative act is the natural behavior of an organism which has a tendency to arise when that organism is open to all of its inner and outer experiencing, and when it is free to try out in flexible fashion all manner of relationships. Out of this multitude of half-formed possibilities the organism, like a great computing machine, selects this one which most effectively meets an inner need, or that one which forms a more effective relationship with the environment, or this other one which discovers a more simple and satisfying order in which life may be perceived.

There is one quality of the creative act which may, however, be described. In almost all the products of creation we note a selectivity, or emphasis, an evidence of discipline, an attempt to bring out the essence. The artist paints surfaces or textures in simplified form, ignoring the minute variations which exist in reality. The scientist formulates a basic law of relationships, brushing aside all the particular events or circumstances which might conceal its naked beauty. The writer selects those words and phrases which give unity to his expression. We may say that this is the influence of the specific person, of the 'I'. Reality exists in a multiplicity of confusing facts, but 'I' bring a structure to my relationship to reality; I have 'my' way of perceiving reality, and it is this (unconsciously?) disciplined personal selectivity or abstraction which gives to creative products their esthetic quality.

Although this is as far as we can go in describing any aspect of the creative act, there are certain of its concomitants in the individual which may be mentioned. The first is what we may call the Eureka feeling – 'This is *it*!' 'I have discovered!' 'This is what I wanted to express!'

Another concomitant is the anxiety of separateness.[1] I do not

1. For this and the idea in the following paragraph I am specifically indebted to my student and colleague, Mr Robert Lipgar.

believe that many significantly creative products are formed without the feeling, 'I am alone. No one has ever done just this before. I have ventured into territory where no one has been. Perhaps I am foolish, or wrong, or lost, or abnormal.'

Still another experience which usually accompanies creativity is the desire to communicate. It is doubtful whether a human being can create, without wishing to share his creation. It is the only way he can assuage the anxiety of separateness and assure himself that he belongs to the group. He may confide his theories only to his private diary. He may put his discoveries in some cryptic code. He may conceal his poems in a locked drawer. He may put away his paintings in a closet. Yet he desires to communicate with a group which will understand him, even if he must imagine such a group. He does not create in order to communicate, but once having created he desires to share this new aspect of himself-in-relation-to-his-environment with others.

Conditions Fostering Constructive Creativity

Thus far I have tried to describe the nature of creativity, to indicate that quality of individual experience which increases the likelihood that creativity will be constructive, to set forth the necessary conditions for the creative act and to state some of its concomitants. But if we are to make progress in meeting the social need which was presented initially, we must know whether constructive creativity can be fostered, and if so, how.

From the very nature of the inner conditions of creativity it is clear that they cannot be forced, but must be permitted to emerge. The farmer cannot make the germ develop and sprout from the seed; he can only supply the nurturing conditions which will permit the seed to develop its own potentialities. So it is with creativity. How can we establish the external conditions which will foster and nourish the internal conditions described above? My experience in psychotherapy leads me to believe that by setting up conditions of psychological safety and freedom, we maximize the likelihood of an emergence of constructive creativity. Let me spell out these conditions in some detail, labeling them as X and Y.

X. *Psychological safety*

This may be established by three associated processes.

Accepting the individual as of unconditional worth. Whenever a teacher, parent, therapist or other person with a facilitating function feels basically that this individual is of worth in his own right and in his own unfolding, no matter what his present condition or behavior, he is fostering creativity. This attitude can probably be genuine only when the teacher, parent, etc., senses the potentialities of the individual and thus is able to have an unconditional faith in him, no matter what his present state.

The effect on the individual as he apprehends this attitude is to sense a climate of safety. He gradually learns that he can be whatever he is, without sham or façade, since he seems to be regarded as of worth no matter what he does. Hence he has less need of rigidity, can discover what it means to be himself, can try to actualize himself in new and spontaneous ways. He is, in other words, moving toward creativity.

Providing a climate in which external evaluation is absent. When we cease to form judgements of the other individual from our own locus of evaluation, we are fostering creativity. For the individual to find himself in an atmosphere where he is not being evaluated, not being measured by some external standard, is enormously freeing. Evaluation is always a threat, always creates a need for defensiveness, always means that some portion of experience must be denied to awareness. If this product is evaluated as good by external standards, then I must not admit my own dislike of it. If what I am doing is bad by external standards, then I must not be aware of the fact that it seems to be me, to be part of myself. But if judgements based on external standards are not being made then I can be more open to my experience, can recognize my own likings and dislikings, the nature of the materials and of my reaction to them, more sharply and more sensitively. I can begin to recognize the locus of evaluation within myself. Hence I am moving toward creativity.

To allay some possible doubts and fears in the reader, it should be pointed out that to cease evaluating another is not to cease having reactions. It may, as a matter of fact, free one to react. 'I don't like your idea' (or painting, or invention, or writing) is not an evaluation, but a reaction. It is subtly but sharply different from a judgement which says: 'What you are doing is bad (or good), and this quality is assigned to you from some external source.' The first statement permits the individual to maintain his own locus of evaluation. It holds the possibility that I am unable to appreciate something which is actually very good. The second statement, whether it praises or condemns, tends to put the person at the mercy of outside forces. He is being told that he cannot simply ask himself whether this product is a valid expression of himself; he must be concerned with what others think. He is being led away from creativity.

Understanding empathically. It is this which provides the ultimate in psychological safety, when added to the other two. If I say that I 'accept' you, but know nothing of you, this is a shallow acceptance indeed, and you realize that it may change if I actually come to know you. But if I understand you, empathically, see you and what you are feeling and doing from your point of view, enter your private world and see it as it appears to you – and still accept you – then this is safety indeed. In this climate you can permit your real self to emerge, and to express itself in varied and novel formings as it relates itself to the world. This is a basic fostering of creativity.

Y. *Psychological freedom*

When a teacher, parent, therapist or other facilitating person permits the individual a complete freedom of symbolic expression, creativity is fostered. This permissiveness gives the individual complete freedom to think, to feel, to be, whatever is most inward within himself. It fosters the openness, and the playful and spontaneous juggling of percepts, concepts and meanings, which is a part of creativity.

Note that it is complete freedom of *symbolic* expression which is described. To express in behavior all feelings, impulses and formings may not in all instances be freeing. Behavior may in some instances be limited by society, and this is as it should be.

But symbolic expression need not be limited. Thus, to destroy a hated object (whether one's mother or a rococo building) by destroying a symbol of it, is freeing. To attack it in reality may create guilt and narrow the psychological freedom which is experienced. (I feel unsure of this paragraph, but it is the best formulation I can give at the moment which seems to square with my experience.)

The permissiveness which is being described is not softness or indulgence or encouragement. It is permission to be *free*, which also means that one is responsible. The individual is as free to be afraid of a new venture as to be eager for it; free to bear the consequences of his mistakes as well as of his achievements. It is this type of freedom responsibly to be oneself which fosters the development of a secure locus of evaluation within oneself, and hence tends to bring about the inner conditions of constructive creativity.

Putting the Theory to Work

There is but one excuse for attempting to discover conceptual order and stating it in a theory; that is to develop hypotheses from the theory which may be tested. By such testing profitable directions for action may be found, and the theory itself may be corrected, modified and extended. Thus if this theory which I have tentatively formulated is worthwhile, it should be possible to develop from it hypotheses which might be objectively tested in classes in the arts; in education outside the arts; in leadership training groups whether in industry or the military services; in problem-solving groups of any sort. Let me suggest a few of the general hypotheses which might be given more specific and operational form for any of the above groups. They would apply whether one was concerned with the development of creative artists or creative leaders; with originality of design or creative methods of problem solving.

Hypotheses regarding inner conditions

1. Individuals who exhibit a measurably greater degree of conditions A, B and C (openness, internal locus of evaluation, ability to toy with materials) will, over any given period of time

149

spontaneously form more products judged to be novel and creative, than a matched group who exhibit a lesser degree of A, B and C.

2. The products of the first group will not only be more numerous, but will be judged to be more significant in their novelty. (Such a hypothesis could be given operational definition in art classes, problem-solving groups, or leadership training groups, for example.)

3. Condition A (openness to experience) can be predicted from conditions B or C, which are more easily measurable. (It is not at all certain that this hypothesis would be upheld, but it would be worth careful investigation. If conditions A, B and C are highly intercorrelated, then they could jointly be predicted from the one which proved most easily measurable. Thus we might gain clues as to how we might less laboriously select graduate students, for example, with a high creative potential.)

Hypotheses regarding fostering constructive creativity

4. Given two matched groups, the one in which the leader establishes a measurably greater degree of conditions X1, X2, X3 and Y (psychological safety and freedom) will spontaneously form a greater number of creative products, and these products will be judged to be more significantly novel.

5. Conditions X1, X2, X3 and Y are not of equal importance in fostering creativity. By comparing different groups in which one or another of these conditions is emphasized or minimized it may be possible to determine which of these conditions is most effective in facilitating creativity.

6. A group in which conditions X1, X2, X3 and Y are established should, according to our theory, have more effective and harmonious interpersonal relationships than a matched group in which these conditions are present to a lesser degree. (The reasoning is that if creativity is all of a piece, then a group in which the fostering conditions are established should be more constructively creative in social relationships.)

7. The extent to which different groups in our culture provide the fostering conditions (X and Y) could be measured. In this way one could determine whether creativity is now being fostered to a greater degree by the family group, classes in schools and

colleges, bull sessions, social clubs and groups, interested groups, military groups, industrial groups. (One wonders how college classes would show up in such a comparison.)

Conclusion

I have endeavored to present an orderly way of thinking about the creative process, in order that some of these ideas might be put to a rigorous and objective test. My justification for formulating this theory and my reason for hoping that such research may be carried out is that the present development of the physical sciences is making an imperative demand upon us as individuals and as a culture for creative behavior in adapting ourselves to our new world if we are to survive.

Reference

ROGERS, C. R. (1953), 'Some directions and end points in therapy', in O. H. Mowrer (ed.), *Psychotherapy – Theory and Research*, Ronald Press, pp. 44–68.

Part Four Psychometric Approaches

Razik's article (Reading 14) both typifies American anxieties on the subject of creativity and gives a general outline of current work with tests. Actually a number of psychologists had experimented with tests of imagination and originality (e.g. Burt *et al.*, 1926; Hargreaves, 1927), and other talents in the 1920s and 30s. However Thurstone's multiple-factor theory and, still more, Guilford's complex 'model' of intellectual abilities, described in Reading 15, unleashed the flood of work on creativity tests in the 1950s and 60s.

An account of Getzels and Jackson's well-known study is included as Reading 16, together with a careful appraisal of its strengths and weaknesses by Burt (Reading 17). L. Hudson (Reading 18) delivers a slashing attack on the illogicalities of the creativity 'boom', having found in his own investigations a strong association between Guilford's convergent thinking and a student's commitment to a career in science, and between divergent thinking and preference for literary studies. However, better designed investigations than Getzels', such as Wallach and Kogan's (Reading 19), which paid greater attention to the conditions of administration and to the statistical consistency of the divergent thinking tests, continue to show that such tests are measuring something of psychological importance in children. And Shapiro, in South Africa, obtained very promising correlations between a well-constructed battery and the creativeness of a group of adult research scientists. In Reading 20 he discusses the extraordinarily difficult problem of setting up suitable criteria against which alleged tests of creativity can be validated.

References
BURT, C. L. *et al.* (1926), 'A study in vocational guidance', *Indust. Health Res. Board Rep.*, no. 33.
HARGREAVES, H. L. (1927), ' The " faculty " of imagination', *Brit. J. Psychol. Monogr. Suppl.*, no. 10.

14 T. A. Razik

Psychometric Measurement of Creativity

T. A. Razik, 'Psychometric measurement of creativity', in
R. L. Mooney and T. A. Razik (eds.), *Explorations in Creativity*,
Harper & Row, 1967, pp. 301–9.

When one considers the developments of recent years in the study
of creativity, one can see that grounds are gradually being laid
for progress in the development of educational programs for
creativity. Thus far, the major effort has had to go into recon-
ceiving the nature, nurture and measurement of creativity.
Major conceptual blocks have stood in the way.

One block has been the culturally inherited conception of
creativity as being that property of the genius which mysteriously
accounts for his uncommon ability and which, by definition, the
common man cannot understand or possess. Assumably, genius
is where one finds it; creativity is where one finds it, and little
can be done through education to affect it.

This conception was common in America, even through the
1930s when Progressive Education was a fairly widespread
movement and focused attention on creative qualities in children.
When teachers and parents observed that young children were
naturally curious, exploratory, experimental and capable of
fresh responses to their world, and the term 'creative' was often
used to summarize such observations, the connexion was not
made between such behavior in children and those of a similar
nature in adults of genius caliber. The child's world and the world
of the genius were taken as worlds apart.

Both were assumed to be something granted by nature, much
like the weather, and about which one could comment, but
actually do little. Against this prevailing view, the Progressive
Education Movement was discounted as romantic, sentimental
and soft. In the struggle of the Second World War, creativity
was forgotten.

In the post-war world, the subject came into prominence again, this time with a new orientation. The atomic bomb, closing the war, dramatized the power which science and technology had gained in setting new conditions for the further existence and development of men. Progress had gone so far in harnessing the powers of nature that man was clearly seen to be arranging for his own fate by the creative work of his own hands. Genius might account for the basic ideas on which new developments were possible, but thousands of men were involved in the further innovations necessary to deliver that power as it reached the people.

The atomic bomb had been created by a massive effort of many men, and the whole fabric of modern life was, in fact, being drastically altered by extensive efforts of organized institutions of government and industry. Sputnik catalysed the realization for Americans that further life and development would depend on having many creative men at work in a constant effort to transcend what had already been done with accomplishments still more novel and powerful. However creative our scientists and engineers had been previous to Sputnik, they would need to be more creative in the future; their numbers would have to be greatly increased. Ways would have to be found to identify such people, to support them, and to cultivate them. Young men showing the capability of being creative would need to be recruited.

In the presence of the Russian threat, 'creativity' could no longer be left to the chance occurrences of the genius; neither could it be left in the realm of the wholly mysterious and the untouchable. Men *had* to be able to do something about it; creativity *had* to be a property in many men; it *had* to be something identifiable; it *had* to be subject to the effects of efforts to gain more of it. Through necessity, the basic concept of creativity thus changed from something heretofore soft and sentimental to something hard and realistic, closely connected with hardware and survival, as are the machines of war and industrial production. Research on creativity became legitimized as a properly serious concern of the military, government and industry.

As work progressed in defining and identifying aspects of creative behavior in adults, the words and conceptions coming to be used could be recognized by educators as those commonly used to characterize the behavior of young children. The similarity was too obvious to be missed and, this time, there was need to see the connexion. If children came endowed with creative capacities, then the role of education, in serving the national need, would be to recognize these capacities and to develop them through the students' growing years into adulthood. In this way, cultivating creativity might be possible to provide for the vast numbers of people needed in the creative developments of the future. This could now be the vision of those educators who wanted to see education in this new role.

In a few years, the climate of public opinion thus changed with respect to creativity so that it could now be seen as a potential property of all men, potentially identifiable and subject to nurture through suitable education. Arriving here, however, there was another conceptual block standing in the way of educators who wanted to see education take on its new role as cultivator of creativity in the masses of students. This blockage centered, ultimately, in the measurements which educators used to guide their efforts.

What finally controls an institution are the values it holds for itself and the means which are used to determine whether or not the values are being attained through the efforts of the institution. This boils down, in the concrete world, to the specification of observables which denote the values desired and the degree of their achievement. This means, in baldest terms, the measurements which are used, for it is measurement which supplies the concrete specifications of the behaviors desired and also the means by which to judge their attainment. Schools are controlled, finally, by the measures they want to make, can make and do, in fact, make.

The basic measurements on which schools have come to depend are not measurements which include the new dimensions of creativity. These basic measures are those provided by the intelligence tests and the achievement tests, the former to judge the capacity of students for schoolwork and the latter to judge the progress students make on their way through the school program.

These tests have been developed in an era when the main focus of educators has been on the formation of the school as a social system. In the need to get our society organized into consistent institutional forms, the efforts of educators have been centered on organizing the school as a working, social assemblage. The development of the child has been less important than the development of a smoothly operating social mechanism. Narrow definitions of targets were helpful in such a situation. Intelligence came to be operationally defined as what the intelligence tests measure, these tests being largely validated on school success. Achievement tests came to be defined as what students could do on tasks set for them by the school system – tasks for which there were single, predetermined and 'right' answers.

Both intelligence and achievement tests have thus been tied to the narrow limits of those abilities which the school establishment values for its operation as a given social system. Divergent and creative responses and abilities not fitting to the school norm have not been measured, operationally valued nor rewarded in systematic ways. The development of the student as a growing creative creature has been neglected.

Educators who have wanted to promote education for creativity have, therefore, come face to face with a formidable problem. Traditional measurements are deeply rooted in school practice, as are the narrow concepts on which they are based. New measures and concepts, sufficiently strong to compete with the old, are required. Tests are needed which include the new dimensions and which are pragmatically useful to classroom teachers in spotting creative behaviors in students and in judging the progress of students (and hence the effectiveness of the teaching) in the development of creative abilities. Apart from the creation of such measures, it is highly improbable that any general progress can be made in reordering education so that it serves the needs of the nation in cultivating the creativity of its general population.

Understandably, progress at this basic level has been slow. Nevertheless, progress has been made in some of the most essential matters. The following serves to highlight some of the major accomplishments to date.

J. P. Guilford (1950), who opened the present era of research on creativity with his 1950 presidential address to the American Psychological Association, has effectively redefined intelligence so as to include creative behaviors. In seventeen years of consistent and cumulative effort since that date, he has evolved a battery of tests which operationally specify dimensions of intelligence that go far beyond what traditional tests of intelligence have included. Using factor analysis, he has isolated 120 separate, measurable abilities. Present intelligence tests measure six to eight of these abilities. By 1962 Guilford (see Taylor and Barron, 1963) was able to operationally specify sixty-one of the total 120.

Especially useful in clarifying creativity has been the distinction Guilford has made between abilities for divergent thinking and abilities for convergent thinking. Divergent thinking moves away, as it were, from responses already known and expected. Convergent thinking moves toward responses that fit to the known and the specified. The experimental tests used to measure creativity emphasize divergent thinking – originality, fluency of ideas, flexibility, sensitivity to defects and missing elements and the ability to elaborate and redefine. Traditional measures of intelligence emphasize convergent thinking – logical reasoning toward single, 'right' answers. Measures of creativity call for new ideas, an original or unconventional response, and breaking away from the beaten path.

Supported largely by Air Force grants and focusing on adults in military establishments, Guilford has demonstrated that concern for creativity in the national interest is a hard core concern that can be productively pursued. Having opened the field to the adult world, he has also opened the field to the world of children and youth, since his tests and his concepts are and have been directly usable by educators in devising further tests for use in school situations. His work has been the fountainhead for the work of many others, and his concepts, operationally displayed in the tests he provides, now make it quite impossible for educators or others to assume that they have measured intelligence when they have used traditional intelligence tests alone.

J. W. Getzels and P. W. Jackson, in their study of creative adolescents at the University of Chicago Laboratory School (1962), have directly assaulted the bastions of complacency in school practice by bringing into plain view the operational consequences of judging students on the basis of intelligence tests alone. Benefiting from Guilford's breakthrough and devising tests for creativity, they contrasted the abilities of students who scored high on I.Q. (but not on creativity) with students who scored high on creativity (but not on I.Q.). They were able to show that the cream of the student crop in creativity would have been missed if traditional measures of intelligence had alone been used to reveal the 'able students'. Creative students have something else and something more than the intelligence tests show. Sizable proportions of students have these abilities, but can go undetected, if reliance is placed on the traditional tests alone.

Getzels and Jackson (1962) also showed that it is not only the intelligence tests that are biased against the highly creative child, but also the teachers. When asked to rate students on the degree to which they would like to have them in class, teachers clearly preferred the high-I.Q. over the highly creative pupil, and this in spite of the fact that, in this particular study, the high-I.Q. students and the highly creative students were equally superior to other students in school achievement. The study also showed that the high-I.Q. child tends to hold a self-image consistent with what he feels the teacher would approve, seeking to conform to the projected values of the teacher; the creative pupil, on the other hand, tends to hold to a self-image consistent with his own projected values, often not conforming to the teacher's values. He considers high marks and goals that projectively lead to adult success in life less important than does a member of the high-I.Q. group. He has a much greater interest in unconventional careers than his less creative peers.

Much of what Getzels and Jackson discovered has been subsequently confirmed; some has been modified. Educational circles have finally realized that reliance cannot be placed on testing as usual and teaching as usual, if creativity is to be valued in education. What Guilford showed to be intellectually wrong in conceiving of intelligence in narrow terms, Getzels and Jackson showed to be also educationally wrong. The usual practices in school not only neglect creativity; they damage it.

Knowing the negative effects of the traditional with respect to creativity is not enough to produce the positive programs that are needed. Extensive pioneering work needs to be done to lay out the lines along which the new, and the more encompassing, can be built. Guilford, Getzels and Jackson had necessarily opened the positive to illuminate the negative, but it remained to E. Paul Torrance to carry the direct and visible attack significantly into the positive domain in educational practice.

Through extensive work done at the University of Minnesota, Torrance created measures and methods that are usable by teachers in classroom settings. His aim has been to serve the profession as widely as possible by giving to classroom teachers in the public schools the tools they need to be able to cultivate creativity in children through their daily teaching practices. Beginning his work with studies which confirmed and built from the contributions of Guilford, Getzels and Jackson, he constructed tests of creativity usable at several levels of education, but focused mainly on the elementary school. Involved in field contacts, workshops and training programs for teachers, he developed programs both for classroom teaching and for teacher training.

Whereas Getzels and Jackson had done their research on students in the upper range of the I.Q. scale and in a university laboratory school, Torrance worked with children of various levels of ability and in the public schools. Getzels and Jackson had demonstrated some correlation between I.Q. and creativity scores up to a certain level of I.Q., but had found no correlation beyond that point. Torrance, in comparable studies (1962), confirmed the finding and also discovered that above a 120 I.Q. there was no correlation between I.Q. and creativity. Torrance estimates that we miss about 70 per cent of our more creative youth when we depend solely on I.Q. tests to measure ability. Some type of creative talent may be found all along the 'normal' I.Q. range, even in children in the below-average group.

Confirming Getzels and Jackson on the attitudes of teachers toward the high-I.Q. student as compared to the high-creative, Torrance also found that teachers rate the high-I.Q. students as more desirable students, more ambitious and hardworking, less unruly and more friendly. A study, using sixty-two characteristics as measuring factors, was made by Torrance (1965) to obtain teachers' concepts of the ideal pupil. The study indicated that the teachers had a great deal of ambivalence toward the kind of pupil who could be described as highly creative. Among the

161

sixty-two characteristics, the teachers rated independence in thinking second, independence in judgement nineteenth and courage twenty-ninth. It was far more important to teachers that children be courteous than that they be courageous. It was also more important that children do their work on time, be industrious, be obedient, be popular among their peers, and have other traits of this kind than that they be courageous. Because of a limited concept of giftedness and an emphasis on academic prowess, it is quite natural that the child who answers questions correctly, produces what he is told and knows what the text-book says, is considered by teachers to be superior. The creative child often fails to fit this model.

Torrance's tests (1965) have no single, predetermined 'right' answers; several answers are possible and, usually, the more (and the more unique) the better. Complex tasks are called for: for example, the Product Improvement Test calls for novel ideas for improving objects such as children's toys. Generally, during the test the objects are available for the child's manipulation. The Ask-and-Guess Test calls for questions and hypotheses about causes and results related to a picture. The Just Suppose Test presents improbable situations accompanied by drawings and requires imaginative solutions. To get the most information from a minimum of testing time, the measures have been constructed to allow responses to be scored for more than one dimension of creativity.

Substantial as the beginnings have been, Torrance regards these tests as *only* a beginning. How many tasks, of what length, of what variety of stimuli, how modified for diverse ages and cultural backgrounds, how scored, etc. – these are continuing and pressing problems if educators, generally, are to have what they need for identifying and developing creative behaviors in their daily teaching. But, without question, educators can now concretely sense the positive meanings of creative measurements. Torrance has assembled and presented ample illustrations. Directions for progress are indicated. Teachers can take hold of the testing task at their levels of operation; the problem now focuses on helping teachers develop the conceptions and the skills which enable them to teach effectively for the kind of behaviors the tests test. Much help is needed if teachers throughout the country are to get what they need for effectively influencing masses of students.

The citadels for primary help in educating and reeducating teachers for creative education are the universities and the upper echelons of the teaching profession. Here, the requirements for granting help are that creativity be thoroughly understood and appreciated. The intellectuals want intellectual grounding for what they do. This calls for research in depth and an integral understanding of the phenomenon of the creative human being.

Donald W. MacKinnon and Frank Barron of the Institute for Personality Assessment, University of California at Berkeley, undertook extensive studies (see Brown, 1962) focused on the personality structure and experience pattern of highly creative adults who had become valuable creative producers for society. Outstanding creative architects, writers and scientists were given intensive testing. A wide variety of tests, test situations, depth interviews and observations were used. 'Intelligence', as measured by I.Q., and formal education were but a few of many considerations. The basic question studied was: 'What factors contribute to creativity?' Psychoanalytic, psychological and humanistic frames of reference were used in interpreting the data.

In accord with the findings of Getzels and Jackson, and Torrance, MacKinnon and Barron found no simple relation between I.Q. and creativity. (Most of their subjects were above the 'breaking point' of relationship, i.e. 120 I.Q.) On school grades, MacKinnon and Barron's data showed that the creative person rarely was a straight-A student; averages on grades ranged around B for the architects, and somewhere between C and B for research scientists. Many of the subjects had grades that would not admit them to graduate study today.

MacKinnon and Barron's subjects were men who had had their education in a period when admission requirements and grading standards were less stringent, and insistence on institutionalized education as a prerequisite to responsible positions was less emphasized than it is today. Complexity of knowledge and rapidity of change now require more years of preparation, and educational institutions now get a tighter and tighter hold on the channels of opportunity. The inference of MacKinnon and Barron's findings is inescapable – that our present identification methods may be keeping many of our potentially creative producers out of colleges and graduate schools and, among those admitted, grading practices may well be failing or discouraging many so that, though admitted, they do not graduate.

The measurements used in higher education to identify and evaluate students would appear to be as misleading and damaging to creative development as Getzels and Jackson, and Torrance, found them to be at elementary and secondary levels of education. The studies of MacKinnon and Barron make this clear for educators to see; reform is needed throughout the whole range of institutionalized education.

MacKinnon and Barron's studies also make clear the complexity of the task. The creative person is a many faceted creature who is difficult to serve through present systems. Such persons are original, independent, self-assertive, imaginative and sensitive. Their needs can be served only through practices that value, focus on and flexibly modify to honor their individual uniqueness. Professors who help them must be persons who can listen as well as talk, who enjoy being challenged as well as to challenge, who gain joy in life from the new structures of thought that form in their students' minds, as well as from new structures that form in their own minds.

Much opportunity needs be allowed for student expression. The curriculum can only be a tentative approximation for what, in fact, is required as students become engaged in it. The heart of the system can only be the active communication of creative minds that resonate to one another's needs and challenges. Creative learning requires creative teaching, and there is no substitute or short cut.

MacKinnon and Barron's studies do not amplify these points, but their findings make such points clear to those educators who are looking for the inferences. Creative practices are needed in all areas of university life. Certainly they are needed in those areas responsible for the education and reeducation of teachers in the public schools. Here, in the universities and the upper echelons of educational leadership, lies the staging area for any further significant advances in evolving the people needed for contemporary life.

Obviously, education in the universities, or elsewhere, is not going to develop in significant proportions apart from the inter-locked efforts of many men, supplying strength from many different directions. A vehicle is needed to invite cooperation, sharing of perspectives, research findings and resources.

One such vehicle of central importance has been the series of conferences organized by Calvin W. Taylor of the University of Utah. Five of these conferences (1955, 1957, 1959, 1961, 1962) were focused primarily on problems connected with identifying creative talent for the sciences and were supported by the National Science Foundation. The sixth (1964) was focused on the use of educational media as a means for creative education and was supported by the U.S. Office of Education. Seeking empirical and operational grounds on which to research creativity, these conferences (and publications from them) have established the researchability of the subject. They have effectively moved conceptions of creativity from vague abstractions to concrete referents which are visibly significant for guiding action in the selection and cultivation of creative personnel.

Oriented chiefly to needs for creative personnel at the upper echelons, i.e. in science, these concrete referents have, nevertheless, led naturally and easily to the connected concern for creativity in the education of youth. Designed primarily for research men, they serve the interests of university men who want an intellectual and research base for what they do. Educators at the university level who want to develop educational programs to cultivate creativity in their students may now do so, knowing that they have a substantial base from which to build.

Gradually, then, the groundwork is being laid for significant advances in the development of creative education. Unmentioned have been many notable conferences, agencies and programs, and many research contributions which should surely be included if we were attempting a broad survey. The purpose, however, has been to sketch a perspective of what has been accomplished to date by citing the most evident developments and the core of need which lies in the realm of measurements and methods by which educators can guide their daily activity.

Development at this level requires the active work of a community of research men; Taylor's conferences have helped to establish such a community. Movement in depth and breadth of understanding of creative persons is required; MacKinnon and Barron have opened up that domain. Instruments and correlative methods of teaching are required in forms usable and used by classroom teachers in the field; Torrance has met this need. Clear-cut recognition that traditional measurements and methods are not adequate is required; Getzels and Jackson have effectively dramatized this fact. Reconception of basic intelligence is required; Guilford has supplied this reconception.

These are substantial contributions. Because of them creative education has a source for its further development which is far ahead of the sources available to educators in any prior period of our history. These developments have charted out the field and secured the anchorages for the contributions of many others, present and future. American education is far from being effective in the development of creativity in the masses of students, but the solid beginnings are there.

References

BROWN, E. J. (1962), 'Highly intelligent but not necessarily highly creative', *School and Community*, vol. 49, p. 24.

GETZELS, J. W., and JACKSON, P. W. (1962), *Creativity and Intelligence: Explorations with Gifted Students*, Wiley.

GUILFORD, J. P. (1950), 'Creativity', *Amer. Psychol.*, vol. 5, pp. 444–54.

TAYLOR, C. W., and BARRON, F. (1963), *Scientific Creativity: Its Recognition and Development*, Wiley.

TORRANCE, E. P. (1962), *Guiding Creative Talent*, Prentice-Hall.

TORRANCE, E. P. (1965), *Rewarding Creative Behaviour*, Prentice-Hall.

15 J. P. Guilford

Traits of Creativity

J. P. Guilford, 'Traits of creativity', in H. H. Anderson (ed.), *Creativity and its Cultivation*, Harper, 1959, pp. 142–61.

When some time ago this author presented hypotheses concerning the component talents contributing to creativity (Guilford, 1950), he was subsequently amazed at the evidence of widespread interest in the subject. Incidentally, the interest seemed to be stronger from outside the field of psychology than from within its boundaries. There is undoubtedly in this country, and possibly also in others, an undercurrent of need felt for increased creative performance and a desire to know more about the nature of creativity itself. Boring (1950) has suggested that an unusually strong interest in the subject is an aspect of our *Zeitgeist*. The present symposium is one expression of it.

Reasons for the Interest in Creativity

If we ask ourselves the reasons for this element in our *Zeitgeist*, speculation leads to several suggestive conclusions. The most urgent reason is that we are in a mortal struggle for the survival of our way of life in the world. The military aspect of this struggle, with its race to develop new weapons and new strategies, has called for a stepped-up rate of invention. Having reached a state of stalemate with respect to military preparedness, we encounter challenges on all intellectual fronts, scientific and cultural as well as economic and political. Again and again, we have been shaken out of our lethargy and our complacency by new developments.

Other reasons probably arise from states of boredom. There is likely to be a period of relative boredom following a great war. Boredom has also been a creeping disease in modern industry, where men and women need to perform less and less like human beings. Their work no longer calls upon them, as formerly, for decisions and for constructive thinking. The advances in automation have not helped this situation. There is also boredom arising from increased leisure time. Fortunately, satiation with any condition usually leads to corrective measures. The best solution would seem to be to direct leisure-time activities into channels of creative effort, giving individuals a taste of the rewards that can come from such efforts.

The coming of the age of space is another force contributing to the upsurge in interest in creativity. It stirs the imagination and it calls for readjustments at an accelerated rate. Many of the adjustments that we are forced to make are to the accelerated technological advances, but many are also due to the social implications of those advances. In a world grown small so far as travel and communication are concerned and a world in which the exploding population competes ever more strongly for its resources, adjustments in the political and personal-relations areas call increasingly for imaginative solutions. From any aspect from which we may view the scene, the needs for creativity are enormous.

A Psychological Approach to Creativity

These needs have found psychology ill prepared. Some years ago, a professor of journalism came to the author asking what psychologists knew about creative thinking. He had a strong desire to develop talents for creative writing among his students. With considerable regret and chagrin, it was necessary to tell him that there was almost nothing that psychologists knew about the subject.

In large part this deficiency on the part of psychology may be attributed to the general adoption of its stimulus–response model. There is no questioning of the advances that psychology has made with this conceptual model. But when we come to the higher thought processes, particularly to problems of creative thinking, the limitations of the model become very apparent. In approaching these problems it becomes more important than elsewhere to develop concepts pertaining to what goes on within the organism. We are forced to draw inferences regarding these events from what we can observe in terms of stimuli and responses, but we can no longer describe those events adequately in terms of stimulus–response concepts, or even in terms of intervening-variable concepts of the Hullian types.

The prevailing, alternative approach is through an emphasis upon trait concepts. Traits are properties of individuals, and they are fruitfully investigated by an approach that emphasizes individual differences. A trait is any distinguishable, relatively enduring way in which one individual differs from another. The psychologist's interest, of course, is heavily weighted in the direction of behavior traits. Wherever we can point out a trait variable along which individuals differ systematically, it may be concluded that this variable pertains to some property that individuals possess in common but to different degrees. But the property may also apply to a way of functioning and hence it may provide a concept for describing the way in which the individual operates.

The most defensible way of discovering dependable trait concepts of this kind at present is that of factor analysis. Factor analysis starts with information regarding the concomitant variations of performances. To say that the interest is confined to performances would be incorrect, for the performances whose intercorrelations are investigated are obtained under experimental control of the situations that help to instigate them. By varying the kind of test both qualitatively and quantitatively we can arrive at more accurate interpretation of factors and delineation of their properties. Information regarding factors may often thus be used as information regarding basic psychological functions.

It is the purpose of this chapter, first, to give a very brief survey of the known primary traits that are believed to be related to creativity. Primary traits are found by factor analysis. The survey will include both aptitude and non-aptitude traits, among the latter being traits of temperament and of motivation. Second, the paper will point out what seems to be the place of the aptitudes for creativity within the general framework of intellect. In doing so, some predictions will be made concerning undiscovered aptitudes for creative thinking. Third, some relationships of the factors of creativity to evaluations of creative performance other

169

than those in the aptitude-test category will be mentioned, to indicate that the factors of creativity do have some support from other sources, including evaluations of everyday life performances.

Primary Traits Related to Creativity

The status of our information regarding the primary traits of creativity can perhaps be most meaningfully presented on the background of some hypotheses that were adopted for investigation in 1950.[1]

Aptitude for creative thinking

Guilford (1950) predicted that we should find a factor characterized as an ability to see problems; a generalized sensitivity to problems. Such a trait was found, and it is best indicated by tests asking examinees to state defects or deficiencies in common implements or in social institutions or to state problems created by common objects or actions. The factor has more recently been identified logically as belonging in the general category of evaluative abilities (Guilford, 1957a). The reason is that the act involved is essentially a judgement that things are not all right; that goals have not been reached; or that not everything to be desired has been achieved. Such a decision would play no constructive part in productive thinking, but without this step productive thinking would not get started.

It was hypothesized that fluency of thinking would be an important aspect of creativity. This is a quantitative aspect that has to do with fertility of ideas. Our results in the Aptitudes Project have verified and extended information concerning four fluency factors (Wilson *et al.*, 1954).

There is the factor of *word fluency*, first reported by Thurstone (1938). This is an ability to produce words each containing a specified letter or combination of letters. It is not easy to see where this ability would have much importance in creative work

1. Much of the information to be mentioned in succeeding pages comes from the project on Aptitudes of High-Level Personnel at the University of Southern California, under contract N6onr-23810 with the Office of Naval Research.

in everyday life, but Drevdahl (1956) *has* found it to be related in both science and arts students.

A factor of *associational fluency* is indicated best in a test that requires the examinee to produce as many synonyms as he can for a given word in limited time. In contrast to word fluency, where only letter requirements are to be observed, associational fluency involves a requirement of meaning for the words given. One would expect such an ability to be important to the average writer who wants to find a word to satisfy a particular meaning he has in mind and a quick running over of words in that area is an advantage. We are testing this hypothesis in a study of theme writing in freshman English.

A factor of *expressional fluency* is best measured by a test calling for the production of phrases or sentences. The need for rapid juxtaposition of words to meet the requirements of sentence structure seems to be the unique characteristic of tests of this ability. Whether the same ability pertains to oral speech we do not know, but there is some reasonable presumption of at least a moderate correlation between corresponding performances in writing and in oral speech. Although in writing one does not ordinarily work under pressure of time, the facility for framing sentences must be an important asset. In oral speech it should be of even greater importance, particularly for oratorical talents. It can be said that the possession of a high degree of expressional fluency, as measured by written tests, can apparently lead observers to the conclusion that the expressionally fluent person has a high degree of creativity. In one study, not yet published, ratings of men in several different traits of creativity tended to be correlated positively with scores for the factor of expressional fluency.

A trait of probably much wider usefulness is fluency in the production of ideas, or the factor of *ideational fluency*. This is the ability to produce ideas to fulfill certain requirements in limited time. A test of this factor may ask examinees to name objects that are hard, white and edible or to give various uses for a common brick, or to write appropriate titles for a given story plot. In scoring for this factor, sheer quantity is the important consideration; quality need not be considered so long as responses are appropriate.

There are certain stages in most problem solving where there must be a searching for answers. The problem as structured or defined provides the specifications for the solutions that are sought. Unless the specifications point to a unique solution, some searching and testing of alternative solutions is likely to occur. The scanning process is more likely to arrive at suitable solutions if it can elicit a greater number of possibilities. Thus ideational fluency probably plays an important role in problem solving, and many problems require novel solutions, which means creative thinking.

In 1950 it was hypothesized that creative thinkers are flexible thinkers. They readily desert old ways of thinking and strike out in new directions. A factor of flexibility of thinking was therefore predicted. We found two abilities, both of which seem to fit into this general category (Wilson *et al.*, 1954).

One of these factors has been called *spontaneous flexibility*. It is defined as the ability or disposition to produce a great variety of ideas, with freedom from inertia or from perseveration. In tests of this factor, the examinee shows his freedom to roam about in his thinking even when it is not necessary for him to do so. In naming uses of a common brick, he jumps readily from one category of response to another – the brick used as building material, as a weight, as a missile, or as a source of red powder, and so on. Rigid thinkers, on the other hand, tend to stay within one or two categories of response. Another example of spontaneously flexible thinkers in dealing with concrete material are those who see rapid fluctuations in ambiguous figures, such as the Necker outline cube or the staircase figure.

The other type of flexibility of thinking is called *adaptive flexibility* for the reason that it facilitates the solution of problems. This is shown best in a type of problem that requires a most unusual type of solution. The problem may appear to be soluble by means of more familiar or conventional methods, but these methods will not work. One task that calls for this kind of solution is based upon the familiar game involving matchsticks. The examinee is given a set of contiguous squares, each side formed by a match, and is told that he is to take away a certain number of matches, leaving a certain number of squares. He is not told that the squares must be all of the same size, but if he adopts this obvious assumption he cannot solve one or more problems, for the only satisfactory end result is a number of squares that differ in size. Persistence in wrong but inviting directions of thinking means low status on the factor of adaptive flexibility.

In the area of creativity one should certainly expect to find a trait of originality. It is indicated by the scores of some tests in which the keyed responses are weighted in proportion to their infrequency of occurrence in the population of examinees. Unusualness of responses, in a statistical sense, is one principle of measurement of *originality*.

The factor is also indicated by tests in which items call for remote associations or relationships; remote either in time or in a logical sense. If we ask examinees to list all the consequences they can think of in the event that a new discovery makes eating unnecessary, the number of remote consequences they give indicates originality, whereas the number of obvious consequences indicates ideational fluency. This means that it takes a quality criterion to indicate the extent of originality of which a person is characteristically capable.

A third way of indicating degree of originality in taking tests is the number of responses an examinee can give that are judged as being clever. The titles given for short-story plots, for example, can be rated as clever or not clever. The number of not-clever responses indicates ideational fluency whereas the number of clever responses indicates originality.

There is a growing suspicion that what we have called originality is actually a case of adaptive flexibility when dealing with verbally meaningful material, parallel to the factor of adaptive flexibility as now known, which pertains to tasks dealing with non-verbal material. In either case one must get away from the obvious, the ordinary or the conventional in order to make a good score.

In 1950 a factor of redefinition was hypothesized, which called for an ability to give up old interpretations of familiar objects in order to use them or their parts in some new ways. Factor analysis has well supported such a dimension of individual differences (Wilson *et al.*, 1954). Which of the following objects, or their parts, could best be adapted to making a needle: pencil, radish, shoe, fish, or carnation? The keyed (correct) response is 'fish', since a bone from a typical fish seems to be most readily adaptable for the purpose of making a needle. Improvising, in general, probably reflects the ability of *redefinition*. It has been suggested that a low status on this factor means the condition of 'functional fixity' or 'functional fixedness', which has been gaining in use to describe failure to solve problems in which improvising must occur, such as making a pendulum out of a string and pliers.

Another factor, which was predicted and found in a study of planning abilities (Berger, Guilford and Christensen, 1957) and which needs further verification and analysis, may be mentioned. This is a factor called *elaboration*. It was indicated by a test in which the examinee is given one or two simple lines and told to construct on this foundation a more complex object. The score is the amount of elaboration demonstrated. It is also indicated by a test in which the bare outline of a plan is given, the examinee to list all the minor steps needed to make the plan work. It is possible that two abilities are involved, one pertaining to elaboration of figural material and one pertaining to elaboration of meaningful material. If so, the two abilities are probably positively correlated.

Not all of our early expectations in the way of factors have been supported with results. We predicted a unitary ability to analyse and also a unitary ability to synthesize, in thinking. Both hypotheses were apparently given ample opportunity to be verified if they were true, but the results did not come out that way. This is one example showing that we do not always get out of a factor analysis what we put into it. The result will no doubt seem contrary to common sense, for in our thinking we do analyse and we do synthesize.

The result does not refute the existence of these two kinds of operations. What it does indicate is that individuals do not differ systematically from one another with respect to a general ability to analyse in connexion with many kinds of tasks nor do they differ systematically in a general ability to synthesize. In this sense, analysis and synthesis are like problem solving. Factor analysis has not detected a unitary ability to solve problems. A number of unitary abilities undoubtedly play roles in solving problems, but the combinations of them and their respective weights depend upon the kind of problem. A similar conclusion may be drawn with regard to analysing and synthesizing.

Non-aptitude traits related to creativity

There are many, no doubt, who would look for the chief secrets of creative performance outside the modality of aptitudes. There is no denying that traits of motivation and of temperament should be expected to have significant determining effects upon whether or not an individual exhibits creative performance. These modalities of personality are definitely to be investigated in this connexion. There has been little rigorously obtained information regarding the roles of such traits in creative performance, however. In her studies of leading artists and of leading scientists in several fields, Anne Roe found only one trait that stood out in common among individuals. This was a willingness to work hard and to work long hours (Roe, 1946, 1953). This is a trait that may contribute to achievement and eminence in any field, however. There is no indication that it has a unique relation to creativity. The trait also merely means a very high level of general motivation, of whose sources we are uncertain. We are thus left with the problem, and the need for more analytical studies is strongly indicated.

In the Aptitudes Project our attention has recently been given to questions of non-aptitude traits that might contribute to creative thinking. Already mentioned is the conclusion that spontaneous flexibility in thinking appears to be a freedom from perseveration, which is one form of rigidity, and that adaptive flexibility appears to be a freedom from persistence in using previously learned, futile methods of solution, another form of rigidity. This raises the question as to whether the flexibility–rigidity factors in thinking should be classified in the modality of aptitudes or in the modality of temperament traits or whether in these instances we have traits with both temperamental and aptitudinal aspects, depending upon how one looks at them.

We have speculated regarding whether originality is perhaps an attitude of unconventionality, which predisposes an individual not to perform in the usual or the popular manner, preferring idiosyncratic ways of behaving. Our research only touches upon this question. As for the fluency factors, there have been a number of hypotheses mentioned in the literature regarding possible relationships between fluency of thinking and certain traits of motivation and temperament (Guilford *et al.*, 1957).

Another reason for attention to these problems is the fact that factor analysis had previously indicated at least three primary traits of interest in different kinds of thinking, including interest in *reflective thinking*, *rigorous thinking* and *autistic thinking*. Would these interests be found related to thinking performances of various kinds? There had also been found a pair of primary interests in esthetic activities, one an interest called *esthetic appreciation* and the other *esthetic expression*. These interest variables might well be related to creative performance in the arts and possibly more generally in creative performance.

A recent factor-analytical investigation of thinking interests explored some hypotheses of still other possible variables (Guilford *et al.*, 1957). With the use of self-inventory scores, which has been the basis for the discovery of the interest variables just mentioned, we found indications of some of the expected variables. One factor could be identified as *tolerance of ambiguity*. This is a willingness to accept some uncertainty in conclusions and decisions and a tendency to avoid thinking in terms of rigid categories. Another factor was identified as an interest in or liking for *convergent thinking*. Convergent thinking, which will be more fully explained in the next section, involves thinking toward one right answer, or toward a relatively uniquely determined answer. A companion factor was defined as an interest in or liking for *divergent thinking*, a type of thinking in which considerable searching about is done and a number of answers will do. Still another factor was found but it could not be very definitely identified. It could be an interest in originality or in creativity in general, or it could possibly be identified with either esthetic expression or esthetic appreciation.

In order to examine the possibilities that any or all of these factors have any bearing upon creative output, we correlated scores for these variables with scores for performance on tests of fluency, flexibility and originality. It was possible, also, to correlate scores for a number of other inventory variables, involving other traits, with the same aptitude-test scores. Some of the more pertinent results will be very briefly mentioned. The conclusions are based upon statistically significant correlations, but the coefficients were all below 0·30.

From the results we may conclude that individuals who do well in tests of associational fluency tend to have a stronger need for adventure and they are more tolerant of ambiguity. This kind of result is interesting because to make a good score for associational fluency one must extend his list of synonyms to those that are only tenuously related to the given word. Individuals who are high on scores for ideational fluency are inclined to be more impulsive, more ascendant, and more confident and to have a stronger appreciation of creativity. Individuals who show more than ordinary signs of nervousness and depression are likely to be slightly lower on tasks requiring ideational fluency, but they show no handicaps on other types of fluency tests. The population in which the study was made probably included none who reached the pathological level in those temperamental traits. Those who score higher in tests of expressional fluency are inclined to be more impulsive, to appreciate esthetic expression and to like reflective thinking.

Measures of originality show relationships to a number of non-aptitude traits, but none very strong, so far as our results go. The original person tends to be more confident and tolerant of ambiguity and to like reflective and divergent thinking and esthetic expression. The unoriginal person is inclined to be more meticulous and to feel a need for discipline. There is no indication that the original person is necessarily less inclined toward cultural conformity, which includes moral aspects. The hypothesis that originality rests upon an attitude of unconventionality is not supported. These results do not mean that for particular individuals there may not be such an association, but they do mean that in a general population the association is no more common than the lack of association.

The relations of the two flexibility factors to traits of rigidity were mentioned above. There were no other relationships found for the flexibility factors except some indication that persons high on spontaneous flexibility are likely to have a strong need for variety. The flexible person of this type rather obviously shows variety of directions in his work on tests.

The fact that all of these relationships were studied in the context of psychological testing should be emphasized. With motivation generally at a high pitch in taking tests, examinees have less room for showing very strong relationships between performance on those tests and any of the non-aptitude traits. Performances in daily life might well be found more strongly related to many of these traits of motivation and temperament.

Creativity and the Structure of Intellect

There has always been considerable interest in the relation between creativity and intelligence, particularly the extent to which the latter can account for the former. Unfortunately, 'intelligence' has never been uniquely defined. Furthermore, accumulating evidence indicates that intelligence is a multi-dimensional affair, with many components having been discovered by factor analysis. Our next question is whether the abilities that seem to be components of creative talent can be regarded as components of intelligence. If so, have they any significant status among the intellectual abilities?

Principles of the structure of intellect

After considering all the known factors that could be regarded as belonging in the intellectual category, including the abilities of fluency, flexibility and originality as well as sensitivity to problems, the author proposed a system of those factors and called it a 'structure of intellect' (Guilford, 1956b, 1957a). The principles of that system will be very briefly reviewed here and some important, general revisions will be suggested toward a comprehensive theory of intellect. The creative-thinking abilities find logical places within the system.

There are some forty-seven known factors of intellect. An examination of their properties has suggested that they can be put into a three-way classification, demonstrating three principles by which they can be organized. First, the recognized dimensions of intellect can be grouped in three categories according to the kind of material or content of thought. One kind of material may be called *figural*, for it is in the form of perceived elements or objects with their various properties. Visual objects such as lines and forms have properties of shape, size, color, texture, gradations, and so on. Auditory elements are in the form of rhythms, melodies and speech sounds. There are also tactual and kinesthetic materials, but the factor-analytical exploration of tests involving such materials has been practically non-existent. We might say that the abilities pertaining to the use of figural material constitute a general category of *concrete intelligence*.

Second, we have material that can be called conceptual or *semantic*. It consists of meanings, in verbalized form. The best-recognized tests of intelligence have been composed of verbal material and word meanings have been somehow involved.

Third, our aptitudes research has forced us to recognize a class of abilities to deal with what we have called *symbolic* material. Examples of such materials are numbers, syllables, words (word structures, not meanings) and all kinds of code material. Such elements have no natural meanings. Convention attaches uses and meanings to them arbitrarily. The alphabet and the number system provide convenient properties that make possible their uses in a multitude of ways. Aptitudes for mathematics and for languages probably rest heavily upon the symbolic abilities. The abilities pertaining to either semantic or symbolic materials would qualify for the commonly recognized category of 'abstract intelligence', but since they form two distinct classes, it is best to speak of the categories of *semantic intelligence* and *symbolic intelligence*, respectively.

The second major principle of classification is according to the kind of operations that are performed upon the materials of thought. There are five recognized general kinds of operations, all five kinds apparently applying to each of the three kinds of materials. One class of abilities has to do with the achievement of cognitions of various kinds. These factors may be called discovery abilities, but they also pertain to rediscovering and recognition of elements and of things derived from them. We recognize figural objects, symbolic objects and meanings. The recognition of word meanings is the essence of the factor of *verbal comprehension*, the dominating component in all verbal-intelligence tests.

Another group of aptitude factors is made up of memory abilities. There seems to be a different memory ability parallel to each cognition ability, in so far as the memory abilities are known. Two other groups have to do with the production of other information from given information by means of thinking processes. One of these groups has been identified as *convergent thinking* and the other as *divergent thinking*. Convergent thinking proceeds toward a restricted answer or solution. If asked: 'What is the opposite of high?' you would probably respond with 'Low.' This is an example of convergent thinking. If asked: 'What is two times five plus four?' you would have no other alternative than to say 'Fourteen.' But if you were asked to give a number of words that mean about the same as 'low', you could produce several different responses, all satisfying the requirement, such as 'depressed', 'cheap', 'degraded', and the like, and you would be correct. In this example we have an instance of divergent thinking.

The fifth class of intellectual abilities pertains to making evaluations of information and of conclusions or other responses derived from given information. We may question our cognitions and things we recall as well as our solutions to problems and we arrive at decisions as to whether they are correct, suitable, or adequate, and so on. Such abilities come in the category of *evaluation*.

When we apply certain operations to certain kinds of materials, we come out with products of various kinds. The third major way of classifying intellectual abilities is according to the product involved. The product may be a unit of thought, such as a figure, a symbolic structure or a concept. The product may be a class of units or it may be a relation between units. It may be a pattern, a system or a Gestalt of some kind, composed of units. Or it may be an implication, as when we make a prediction from the information that is available. Each of these kinds of product – units, classes, relations, systems and implications – has its own primary abilities. Although it is not certain that all five classes of products apply to all kinds of material combined with all kinds of operations, there is enough similarity recognized at this stage to justify the prediction that when more is known we shall be able to apply the same product categories throughout. We may have to add a sixth category that has to do with changes or transformations, since such a product now applies in connexion with some kinds of operations. Thus it appears that each primary, intellectual ability represents a kind of crossroad or intersection of a certain kind of operation, applied to a certain kind of material, yielding a certain kind of product.

A Comprehensive Theory of Intellect

If we apply common categories of materials, operations and products throughout the range of intellectual abilities, we can represent the structure of intellect in the form of a three-dimensional diagram (see Figure 1). Figure 1 is a geometric model presented to represent a comprehensive theory of human intellect.

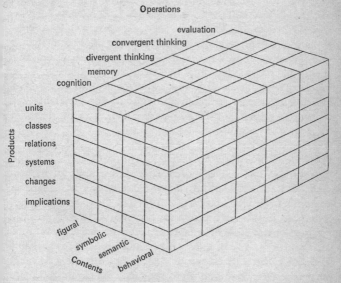

Figure 1 Theoretical model for the complete 'structure of intellect'

Shown in Figure 1 is provision for a fourth kind of material, namely, *behavioral*. There are no factor-analytical results that would justify such a category of intelligence, but there is enough information from other sources to justify the addition of such a class of factors in theory. Over thirty years ago, Thorndike proposed that there is a social intelligence distinct from abstract intelligence and from mechanical intelligence (Thorndike *et al.*, 1927). Today there is new interest in the explorations of 'empathy', which probably falls within the same category.

The implications of a behavioral category in the structure of intellect are very interesting. It was pointed out earlier that there is a concrete intelligence, a symbolic intelligence and a semantic intelligence, all of which are now supported by known factors. Since there are so many parallels among these three areas of intellect, it is reasonable to suggest that the same operations and products apply in the area of social intelligence or empathy. This would mean that we should look for abilities involving cognition of behavioral units, also of classes, relations, systems and implications. There would be parallel memory abilities where behavioral matters are concerned, also parallel abilities to think productively regarding behavioral matters, and abilities to evaluate the results of any of these operations. It would seem reasonable to hypothesize that all such kinds of operations and products apply in the area of social or behavioral events. As a possible variation, we should also consider the possibility that there are different abilities in connexion with one's own behavior and with the behavior of other persons.[2]

The place of aptitudes contributing to creative performances

To return to the abilities more clearly related to creativity, it is apparent that the traits of fluency, flexibility and originality come in the general category of divergent thinking. The factor known as sensitivity to problems, however, has been placed in the category of evaluation and the factor of redefinition in the category of convergent thinking, as stated earlier. It is probably true that other abilities outside the divergent-thinking category also make their contributions to productive thinking. We might arbitrarily define creative thinking as divergent thinking, but it would be incorrect to say that divergent thinking accounts for all the intellectual components of creative production.

There are a number of divergent-thinking abilities predicted by the system in the structure of intellect but not yet discovered, particularly in the figural and symbolic columns. Presumably these would have more to do with creative thinking in the arts (Guilford, 1957b) and in mathematics, whereas the known divergent-thinking abilities, being mostly in the verbal column, have more to do with creative thinking in the humanities, the

2. I am indebted to Philip R. Merrifield for this suggestion.

sciences, and in everyday affairs. Divergent-thinking abilities in the behavioral column should be useful in contributing to better human relations, whether between persons or on the political or industrial scenes or in international affairs.

Validity and Problems of Training

Some information on validity

Our work in the Aptitudes Project has been devoted almost entirely to basic research, with the belief that what we need most at this time is more intimate and thorough understanding of the nature of intellect and its components. We have not been without concern and interest with regard to the general applicability of our factorial concepts and we are frequently challenged in this regard. We, as well as others, have made a number of studies that bear on the question of the significance of the primary traits of creative aptitude from other than the factor-analytical point of view.

The information on validity is scattered and much of it was obtained incidental to studies with broader objectives. The construct validity of our tests of originality was well demonstrated by a study reported by Barron (1955). A hundred Air Force officers were assessed during a three-day period of observation and among other things were rated for degree of originality. A total score from tests of originality correlated 0·55 with the average ratings. Drevdahl (1956) found that a score for originality correlated 0·33 with instructor's ratings of originality of students in the arts and in the sciences.

One should not expect a great deal of predictive validity for test scores representing the factor of originality in connexion with course grades. Hills (1955) found an average correlation of −0·02 for an originality test in connexion with grades in several small classes in upper-division and graduate mathematics courses. Recently we have found an average correlation of 0·27 between a test of originality and average grades in science and mathematics for two groups of engineering students of about a hundred each.

There is little evidence, as yet, that the factors of verbal fluency have general predictability for academic or technical performances. A score for expressional fluency correlated 0·25 with grades in a course in astronomy, for some unknown reason (Guilford, 1956a). A score for ideational fluency correlated 0·37 with performance of aircraft engineers whose chief work was in designing aircraft parts and the criterion was rate of increase in pay over a limited period of time (Guilford, 1956a).

The factor of adaptive flexibility has consistently shown some small relationships to performance in mathematics and in one instance to achievement in physics (Guilford, 1956a). Hills (1955) found the average correlation with achievement in mathematics to be 0·33 and we have found the relation to grades in physics to be 0·23. Among aircraft engineers a score for adaptive flexibility correlated 0·31 with the criterion of rate increase in pay (Guilford, 1956a). Quantitative thinking that involves relatively novel problems seems generally to be related to adaptive flexibility.

A study of creativity of graduate engineers was made by Sprecher (1957). With criteria including ratings of inventiveness and also performance on original, technical problems, multiple correlations involving a few tests of the creativity factors were found in the range from 0·3 to 0·5.

Tests of creative factors did not predict which employees would contribute ideas in a suggestion box, but it was found that many other determiners were at work. For example, some creative individuals had incidental reasons for not offering contributions (Chorness and Nottelmann, 1957). The same tests were found to correlate significantly with some evaluations of the expressive aspects of teaching performance (Chorness and Nottelmann, 1956). Scores from the same tests were found to be related to incidence of certain kinds of creative hobbies as reported in biographical-information inventories (Gerry, DeVeau and Chorness, 1957).

Training for creativity

There has been considerable popular interest in training individuals for increased creativity. A large number of courses have been instituted in this country whose aim is to develop creativity of individuals, some of the courses being in universities, some in industry and some in governmental agencies. The methods of instruction have been somewhat varied, for no one knows at this stage what are the most effective ways of bringing about greater creative performance. The brainstorming method introduced by Osborn (1953) is one of the common devices. Although it is reported to bring about increased quantity of thinking production and to have some lasting, beneficial effects upon participants, there have been almost no reports of rigorous experiments designed specifically to test these impressions.

There are indications that some methods of training, at least, lead to increased originality of performance at the expense of fluency. Using a combination of training methods, including Osborn's brainstorming procedure and Arnold's (1954) 'out-of-this-world' exercise, Gerry, DeVeau and Chorness (1957) found that there were significant gains in scores for originality but probably some losses in scores for ideational fluency. In some unpublished data on ten-year-old children, it appears that a short course on creative writing was also followed by higher performance on tests of originality and lower on tests of ideational fluency, as compared with a matched, control group. A finding that bears indirectly upon the same problem is that when examinees are instructed to give clever titles to story plots in a test they tend to lose in total productivity but to gain in the number of clever responses as well as in the average level of rated cleverness as compared with examinees who have instructions that say nothing about cleverness (Christensen, Guilford and Wilson, 1957). The general implication from these few studies is that attention to creativity and efforts to increase it are likely to yield improvements in quality of responses at the expense of quantity. In everyday life, where there is much more time available than there is in tests of fluency, a slackened rate of flow of ideas should probably cause little concern.

Summary

This paper has attempted briefly, first, to point out some of the reasons for the spontaneous interests that have sprung up in recent years in connexion with the subject of creativity. It has suggested reasons for psychology's general postponement of serious investigations of the subject and has emphasized the importance of a trait approach to the subject in order to find the necessary working concepts.

There followed a brief review of aptitude traits that belong most clearly logically in the area of creativity and that have been discovered by factor analysis, many of them within the past ten years. These include factors of fluency of thinking and of flexibility of thinking, as well as originality, sensitivity to problems, redefinition and elaboration.

A number of relationships between certain non-aptitude traits and creative performance in tests have been indicated. The two forms of flexibility of thinking seem clearly to be opposites to two forms of rigidity in thinking. Redefinition seems logically opposite to the quality known as 'functional fixedness'. Other traits of temperament and of motivation seem to bear small relationships to performances in tests of fluency, flexibility and particularly tests of originality.

Most of the aptitude factors identifiable as belonging in the category of creativity are classifiable in a group of divergent thinking abilities. These abilities, by contrast to convergent thinking abilities, emphasize searching activities with freedom to go in different directions, if not a necessity to do so in order to achieve an excellent performance. Convergent-thinking activities proceed toward one right answer, or one that is more or less clearly demanded by the given information.

Other abilities contributing to creative performances find their places, also, in a three-dimensional, solid figure, in which the primary abilities are distinguished in terms of the kinds of material dealt with, the kinds of operations applied to the material, and the kinds of products resulting. It is theorized that a whole area of abilities, comprising what has sometimes been called 'social intelligence' and sometimes 'empathy', will be found parallel to other areas now distinguished along the lines of materials of thought – figural, symbolic and semantic.

A limited number of studies of validity tend to indicate that tests of some of the creative-thinking factors, such as adaptive flexibility and originality, have both construct validity and predictive validity.

Efforts made toward improving creativity through training have given informal indications of some measure of success. Experiments tend to indicate that training yields some improvement in performance on tests of originality but some possible loss on tests of ideational fluency. Awareness of the nature of the traits of creativity should provide a much better basis than formerly for systematic methods of education in this important area.

References

ARNOLD, J. E. (1954), *Creative Seminar Notes*, Creative Engineering Laboratory, M.I.T.

BARRON, F. (1955), 'The disposition toward originality', *J. abnorm. soc. Psychol.*, vol. 51, pp. 478–85.

BERGER, R. M., GUILFORD, J. P., and CHRISTENSEN, P. R. (1957), 'A factor-analytic study of planning abilities', *Psychol. Monogr.*, no. 435.

BORING, E. G. (1950), 'Great men and scientific progress', *Proc. Amer. Phil. Soc.*, vol. 94, pp. 339–51.

CHORNESS, M. H., and NOTTELMANN, D. A. (1956), The predictability of creative expression in teaching, *Air Force Personnel and Training Research Center, Lackland Air Force Base, Texas, Research Report*, no. AFPTRC-TN-56-130.

CHORNESS, M. H., and NOTTELMANN, D. A. (1957), The prediction of creativity among Air Force civilian employees, *Air Force Personnel and Training Research Center, Lackland Air Force Base, Texas, Research Report*, no. AFPTRC-TN-57-36.

CHRISTENSEN, P. R., GUILFORD, J. P., and WILSON, R. C. (1957), 'Relations of creative responses to working time and instructions', *J. exp. Psychol.*, vol. 53, pp. 82–8.

DREVDAHL, J. E. (1956), 'Factors of importance for creativity', *J. clin. Psychol.*, vol. 12, pp. 21–6.

GERRY, R., DEVEAU, L., and CHORNESS, M. (1957), A review of some recent research in the field of creativity and the examination of an experimental workshop, *Training Analysis and Development Division, Lackland Air Force Base, Texas, Project*, no. 56-24.

GUILFORD, J. P. (1950), 'Creativity', *Amer. Psychol.*, vol. 5, pp. 444–54.

GUILFORD, J. P. (1956a), 'The relation of intellectual factors to creative thinking in science', in C. W. Taylor (ed.), *The Identification of Creative Scientific Talent*, University of Utah, pp. 69–95.

GUILFORD, J. P. (1956b), 'The structure of intellect', *Psychol. Bull.*, vol. 53, pp. 267–93.

GUILFORD, J. P. (1957a), A revised structure of intellect, *Report of the Psychological Laboratory, University of Southern California*, no. 19.

GUILFORD, J. P. (1957b), 'Creative abilities in the arts', *Psychol. Rev.*, vol. 64, pp. 110–18.

GUILFORD, J. P., *et al.* (1957), The relations of creative thinking aptitudes to non-aptitude personality traits, *Report of the Psychological Laboratory, University of Southern California*, no. 20.

HILLS, J. R. (1955), The relations between certain factor-analyzed abilities and success in college mathematics, *Report of the Psychological Laboratory, University of Southern California*, no. 15.

OSBORN, A. F. (1953), *Applied Imagination: Principles and Procedures of Creative Thinking*, Scribner.

ROE, A. (1946), 'The personality of artists', *Educ. psychol. Measmt*, vol. 6, pp. 401–8.

ROE, A. (1953), 'A psychological study of eminent psychologists and anthropologists, and a comparison with biological and physical scientists', *Psychol. Monogr.*, no. 352.

SPRECHER, T. B. (1957), An investigation of criteria for creativity in engineers, *Doctoral Dissertation, University of Maryland*.

THORNDIKE, E. L., *et al.* (1927), *The Measurement of Intelligence*, Bureau of Publications, Teachers College, Columbia University.

THURSTONE, L. L. (1938), 'Primary mental abilities', *Psychometr. Monogr.*, no. 1.

WILSON, R. C., GUILFORD, J. P., CHRISTENSEN, P. R., and LEWIS, D. J. (1954), 'A factor-analytical study of creative thinking abilities', *Psychometrika*, vol. 19, pp. 297–311.

16 J. W. Getzels and P. W. Jackson

The Highly Intelligent and the Highly Creative
Adolescent [1]

J. W. Getzels and P. W. Jackson, 'The highly intelligent and the
highly creative adolescent: a summary of some research findings', in
C. W. Taylor and F. Barron (eds.), *Scientific Creativity: Its Recognition
and Development*, Wiley, 1963, pp. 161–72.

'Giftedness' in children has most often been defined as a score on
an intelligence test, and typically the study of the so-called gifted
child has actually been the study of children with high I.Q.s.
Implicit in this unidimensional definition of giftedness, it seems
to us, are several types of confusion, if not outright error.

First, there is the limitation of the I.Q. metric itself, which not
only restricts our perspective of the more general phenomenon
but places on the one concept a greater theoretical and predictive
burden than it was intended to carry. For all practical purposes,
the term 'gifted child' has become synonymous with the expression 'child with a high I.Q.', thus blinding us to other forms of
potential excellence.

Second, we have frequently behaved as if the intelligence test
alone represented an adequate sampling of *all* intellectual
functions. For example, despite the recent work on cognition
and creativity, the latter concept is still generally treated as if it
applied only to performance in one or more of the arts. In effect,
the term 'creative child' has become synonymous with the
expression, 'child with artistic talents', thus limiting our attempts
to identify and foster cognitive abilities related to creative
functioning in areas other than the arts.

And finally, third, there has been a failure to attend sufficiently
to the difference between the *definition* of giftedness as given by
the I.Q. and the variations in the *value* placed upon giftedness as
so defined. It is often taken for granted, for example, that the
gifted child is equally valued by teachers and by parents, in the
classroom and at home; that he is considered an equally good

1. A full report of the work is contained in Getzels and Jackson (1962).

prospect by teachers and by parents to succeed as an adult; and that children themselves *want* to be gifted. It is demonstrable that none of these assumptions can be held without question. Empirical data indicate that the gifted child is *not* equally valued by teachers and by parents, in the classroom and at home; he is *not* held to be an equally good prospect to succeed as an adult; and children themselves do *not* necessarily want to be gifted, at least not in the traditional sense of the term.

Despite its longevity, there is nothing inevitable about the use of the I.Q. in defining giftedness. Indeed, it may be argued that in many ways this definition is only an historical happenstance – a consequence of the fact that early inquiries in this field had the classroom as their context and academic achievement as their major concern. If we moved the focus of inquiry from the classroom setting, we might identify qualities defining giftedness for other situations just as the I.Q. did for the classroom. Indeed, even without shifting our focus of inquiry, if we only modified the conventional criteria of achievement, we might change the qualities defining giftedness even in the classroom. For example, if we recognized that learning involves the production of novelty as well as the memorization of course content, then measures of creativity as well as the I.Q. might become appropriate in defining characteristics of giftedness.

The series of studies, of which the one we shall describe below is a part, is based on the foregoing considerations. Broadly speaking, these studies attempt to deal not only with intelligence as the quality defining giftedness but also with such other qualities as creativity, psychological health and morality. Comparisons between groups of adolescents who are outstanding in these qualities serve as the basic analytic procedure of the research.

Problem

The central task we set ourselves in the specific part of the research we shall present here was to differentiate two groups of adolescents – one representing individuals very high in measures of intelligence but *not* as high in measures of creativity, the other representing individuals very high in measures of creativity but *not* as high in measures of intelligence – and to compare the two groups with respect to the following questions:

1. What is the relative achievement – achievement as defined by learning in school – of the two groups?

2. Are the two groups equally preferred by teachers?

3. What is the relative need for achievement – as measured by McClelland's Index of Need: Achievement on the Thematic Apperception Test – of the two groups?

4. What are the personal qualities the two groups prefer for themselves?

5. What is the relation between the personal qualities preferred by the two groups for themselves and the personal qualities they believe teachers would like to see in children?

6. What is the relation between the personal qualities preferred by the two groups for themselves and the personal qualities they believe lead to 'success' in adult life?

7. What is the nature of the fantasy productions of the two groups?

8. What are the career aspirations of the two groups?

Identifying the Experimental Groups: Subjects, Instruments, Procedures

The experimental groups were drawn from 449 adolescents of a Midwestern private secondary school on the basis of performance on the following instruments:

1. Standard I.Q. tests. Either a Binet, a Wechsler Intelligence Scale for Children, or a Henmon–Nelson score was available for each adolescent. The scores obtained from the WISC and the Henmon–Nelson were converted by regression equation to comparable Binet I.Q.s.

2. Five creativity measures. These were taken or adapted from either Guilford or Cattell, or constructed especially for the study, as follows:

(a) Word association. The subject was asked to give as many definitions as possible to fairly common stimulus words, such as 'bolt', 'bark', 'sack'. His score depended upon the absolute number of definitions and the number of different categories into which these definitions could be put.

(b) Uses for things. The subject was required to give as many uses as he could for objects that customarily have a stereotyped function attached to them, such as 'brick' or 'paper-clip'. His score depended upon both the number and the originality of the uses which he mentioned.

(c) Hidden shapes. The subject was required to find a given geometric form that was hidden in more complex geometric forms or patterns.

(d) Fables. The subject was presented with four fables in which the last lines were missing. He was required to compose three different endings for each fable: a 'moralistic', a 'humorous' and a 'sad' ending. His score depended upon the appropriateness and uniqueness of the endings.

(e) Make-up problems. The subject was presented with four complex paragraphs each of which contained a number of numerical statements, for example, 'the costs involved in building a house'. He was required to make up as many mathematical problems as he could that might be solved with the information given. His score depended upon the number, appropriateness, and complexity of the problems.

On the basis of the I.Q. measure and a summated score on the five creativity instruments, the two experimental groups were formed as follows:

1. The high-creativity group. These were subjects in the top 20 per cent on the creativity measures when compared with like-sexed age peers, but *below* the top 20 per cent in I.Q. ($N = 26$).

2. The high-intelligence group. These were subjects in the top 20 per cent in I.Q. when compared with like-sexed age peers, but *below* the top 20 per cent on the creativity measures ($N = 28$).

With the experimental groups thus defined it is possible to approach each of the research questions in turn.[2]

2. As might be expected, the creativity measures and I.Q. were not independent, the correlation between the two ranging from 0·12 to 0·39.

Question 1: What is the relative school achievement of the two groups?

As the data in Table 1 indicate, the results were clear cut and striking. Despite the similarity in I.Q. between the high creatives and the school population, and the twenty-three-point difference

Table 1

Means and Standard Deviations of Highly Creative and Highly Intelligent Groups on Experimental Variables

		Total population* ($N = 449$)	High I.Q. ($N = 28$)	High creative† ($N = 24$)
I.Q.	$\overline{X}$	132·00	150·00§	127·00
	s	15·07	6·64	10·58
School achievement	$\overline{X}$	49·91	55·00§	56·27§
	s	7·36	5·95	7·90
Teacher-preference	$\overline{X}$	10·23	11·20‡	10·54
ratings	s	3·64	1·56	1·95
Need for achievement	$\overline{X}$	49·81	49·00	50·04
(T = scores)	s	9·49	7·97	8·39

* For the purposes of comparison the scores of each experimental group were extracted from the total population before *t*-tests were computed.
† Two subjects omitted because of incomplete data.
‡ Significant at the 0·01 level.
§ Significant at the 0·001 level.

in mean I.Q. between the high creatives and the high I.Q.s, the achievement scores of the two experimental groups were *equally superior* to the achievement scores of the school population as a whole.

It was evident at this point that the cognitive functions assessed by our creativity battery accounted for a significant portion of the variance in school achievement. Moreover, since our creative students were not in the top of their class by I.Q. standards, their superiority in scholastic performance places them in the rather suspect category of so-called 'over-achievers'. This dubious classification often implies that the observed I.Q.-achievement discrepancy is a function of motivational (as opposed to cognitive) variables. It is assumed that the motivational elements pushing the student to outdo himself, as it were, are linked in varying degree to pathological conditions. We would raise the issue, at least for our present group, of whether it is motivational pathology or intellectual creativity that accounts for their superior scholastic achievement. Indeed, we wonder whether the current studies of cognitive functions other than those assessed by standard I.Q. tests do not underscore the need for re-examining the entire concept of 'over-achievement'.

Question 2: Which of the two groups was preferred by teachers?

To answer this question we asked the teachers to rate all students in the school on the degree to which they enjoy having them in class. The ratings of the two groups were then compared with those of the entire school population.

The results, which are shown in Table 1, were again quite clear cut. The high-I.Q. group stands out as being more desirable than the average student; the high-creative group does not. It is apparent that an adolescent's desirability as a student is not a simple function of his academic standing. Even though their academic performance, as measured by achievement tests, is equal, the high-I.Q. student is preferred over the average student, whereas the high-creative student is not.

This finding leads one to suspect either that there are important variables, in addition to the purely cognitive ones, that distinguish the experimental groups, or that the discriminating cognitive functions are themselves differently preferable in the classroom. Actually, these alternatives should not be posed as either–or, since, as we shall demonstrate, evidence can be adduced which tends to support both points of view.

Question 3: What is the relative need for achievement of the two groups?

In effect, we wanted to know here whether the superior school achievement of the high creatives – by I.Q. standards, their so-called 'overachievement' – could be accounted for by differences in motivation to achieve. To answer this question we administered six of the McClelland *n* achievement stimulus pictures. Each picture was shown on a screen for twenty seconds, and the subjects were given four minutes in which to write their responses. The results are presented in Table 1 and show no differences in need for achievement between the high creatives, the high I.Q.s and the total school population.

This failure to find differences does not, of course, mean that differences in motives do not exist. We could, and did, use other assessment procedures aimed at identifying motivational and attitudinal differences between the experimental groups. The next group of three questions deals with our efforts in this direction.

Question 4: What are the personal qualities that the two groups prefer for themselves?

Question 5: What is the relation between the personal qualities preferred by the two groups for themselves and the personal qualities they believe teachers prefer for them?

Question 6: What is the relation between the personal qualities preferred by the two groups for themselves and the personal qualities they believe lead to 'success' in adult life?

Answers to these questions were obtained from data provided by an instrument called the Outstanding Traits Test. This instrument contains descriptions of thirteen children, each exemplifying some desirable personal quality or trait. For example, one child is described as having the highest I.Q. in the entire school, another as being the best athlete, another as having the best sense of humor, another as being the best looking, and another as being the most creative person in the school.

Our subjects ranked these thirteen children in three ways: (a) on the degree to which they would like to be like them; (b) on the degree to which they believed teachers would like them; (c) on the degree to which they believed people with these various qualities would succeed in adult life.

The entire population of the school almost without exception ranked 'social skills' first as the quality in which they would like to be outstanding, and 'athletics', 'good looks', 'high energy level' and 'health' last. In view of this very high agreement, we reranked the responses, omitting the uniformly ranked qualities. The findings we are reporting here are on the reranked data.

The high I.Q.s ranked the qualities in which they would like to be outstanding in the following order: (1) character, (2) emotional stability, (3) goal directedness, (4) creativity, (5) wide range of interests, (6) high marks, (7) I.Q., (8) sense of humor. The high creatives ranked the qualities in the following order: (1) emotional stability, (2) sense of humor, (3) character, (4·5) wide range of interests, (4·5) goal directedness, (6) creativity, (7) high marks, (8) I.Q. Most noteworthy here is the extraordinarily high ranking given by the creative group to 'sense of humor', a ranking which not only distinguishes them from the high-I.Q. group (who ranked it last) but from all other groups we have studied.

Perhaps the most striking and suggestive of the differences between the two groups are observed in the relation of the qualities they want for themselves to the qualities they believe lead to adult success and the qualities they believe teachers favor.

For the high-I.Q. group, the rank-order correlation between the qualities they would like to have themselves and the qualities making for adult success was 0·81; for the high creativity group it was 0·10. For the high-I.Q. group, the correlation between the qualities they would like to have themselves and the qualities they believe teachers favor was 0·67; for the high-creativity group it was (minus) −0·25. The data are presented in Table 2.

In effect, where the high-I.Q. adolescent wants the qualities he believes make for adult success and the qualities that are similar to those he believes his teachers like, the high-creative adolescent favors personal qualities having no relationship to those he believes make for adult success and are in some ways the reverse of those he believes his teachers favor.

These findings reflect directly on the answers to two earlier questions – the one on teacher ratings and the one on the relationship between creativity and school achievement. If the desirability of students in the classroom is related to the congruence or discrepancy between their values and their teacher's values, then in the light of the above data it is hardly surprising that our high-I.Q. students are favored by teachers more than

Table 2

Rank-Order Correlations among Subsections of the Outstanding Traits Test

Components of correlations	Subjects	
	I.Q. (N = 28)	Creative (N = 26)
'Personal traits believed predictive of success' and 'personal traits believed favored by teachers'	0·62	0·59
'Personal traits preferred for oneself' and 'personal traits believed predictive of adult success'	0·81	0·10
'Personal traits preferred for oneself' and 'personal traits believed favored by teachers'	0·67	−0·25

are our creative students. Furthermore, if the motivational impetus represented by a concern with adult success and a desire to emulate the teacher is absent or weak among creative students, the observed relationship between creativity and school achievement becomes all the more significant.

Question 7: What is the nature of the fantasies of the two groups?

In addition to scoring the *n* achievement protocols conventionally for the single achievement theme, we analysed the *total content* of the stories. We first sorted 'blind' forty-seven protocols written by matched creative and non-creative subjects. This blind sorting resulted in only seven misplacements. Using the categories suggested by this sorting, we then systematically analysed the protocols of the two experimental groups. The analysis showed striking differences in the fantasy productions of the high I.Q.s and the high creatives. The creatives made significantly greater use of 'stimulus-free themes', 'unexpected endings', 'humor', 'incongruities' and 'playfulness'. The data are presented in Table 3.

Table 3

Categorization of Fantasy Productions of Highly Creative and Highly Intelligent Groups

Content-analysis categories	High I.Q.		High creativity		χ^2
	(N = 28)		(N = 24)		
	Frequency*	%	Frequency*	%	
Stimulus-free theme	11	39	18	75	5·31 † ‡
Unexpected ending	17	61	22	92	5·05 †
Presence of humor	7	25	17	71	9·16 §
Presence of incongruity	10	36	17	71	5·06 ‡
Presence of violence	13	46	18	75	3·27
Playful attitude toward theme	9	32	21	89	14·04 §

* Numbers in the frequency column represent the subjects whose fantasy productions fit the corresponding categories.

† Yates correction was applied in the computation of chi squares.

‡ Significant at the 0·05 level.

§ Significant at the 0·01 level.

Here, for example, in response to the stimulus picture perceived most often as a man sitting in an airplane reclining seat returning from a business trip or professional conference, are case-type stories given by a high-I.Q. subject and a high-creative subject.

The high-I.Q. subject: Mr Smith is on his way home from a successful business trip. He is very happy and he is thinking about his wonderful family and how glad he will be to see them again. He can picture it, about an hour from now, his plane landing at the airport and Mrs Smith and their three children all there welcoming him home again.

The high-creative subject: This man is flying back from Reno where he has just won a divorce from his wife. He couldn't stand to live with her anymore, he told the judge, because she wore so much cold cream on her face at night that her head would skid across the pillow and hit him in the head. He is now contemplating a new skid-proof face cream.

Or one more, this in response to the stimulus-picture most often perceived as a man working late (or very early) in an office:

The high-I.Q. subject: There's ambitious Bob, down at the office at 6.30 in the morning. Every morning it's the same. He's trying to show his boss how energetic he is. Now, thinks Bob, maybe the boss will give me a raise for all my extra work. The trouble is that Bob has been doing this for the last three years, and the boss still hasn't given him a raise. He'll come in at 9.00, not even noticing that Bob had been there so long, and poor Bob won't get his raise.

The high-creative subject: This man has just broken into this office of a new cereal company. He is a private-eye employed by a competitor firm to find out the formula that makes the cereal bend, sag and sway. After a thorough search of the office he comes upon what he thinks is the current formula. He is now copying it. It turns out that it is the wrong formula and the competitor's factory blows up. Poetic justice!

Recall that these stories were written in group sessions, often more than a hundred adolescents in the same room, with the maximum writing time four minutes per story. 'Skid-proof face cream!' 'Cereal that will bend, sag and sway!' It seems to us that it is this ability to restructure stereotyped objects with ease and rapidity – almost 'naturally' – that is the characteristic mark of our high-creative as against our high-I.Q. subjects.

One other characteristic is well illustrated by a number of the stories. This is a certain mocking attitude on the part of the creatives toward what they call the 'all-American boy' – a theme that is almost never mentioned by the high I.Q.s. Here, for example, are two responses to the stimulus picture most often perceived as a high school student doing his homework:

The high-I.Q. subject: John is a college student who posed for the picture while doing his homework. It is an average day with the usual amount of work to do. John took a short break from his studies to pose for the pictures, but he will get back to his work immediately after. He has been working for an hour already and he has an hour's more work to go. After he finishes he will read a book and then go to bed. This work which he is doing is not especially hard but it has to be done.

The high-creative subject: The boy's name is Jack Evans and he is a senior in school who gets Cs and Bs, hates soccer, does not revolt against convention and has a girl friend named Lois, who is a typical sorority fake. He is studying when someone entered the room whom he likes. He has a dull life in terms of anything that is not average. His parents are pleased because they have a red-blooded American boy. Actually, he is horribly average. He will go to college, take over his dad's business, marry a girl, and do absolutely nothing in the long run.

This 'anti-red-blooded boy' theme is also quite consistent with the creatives' rejection of 'success', which was mentioned earlier.

Question 8: What are the career aspirations of the two groups?

We have just begun the analysis of the data in this area. But this much is already clear – the two groups do indeed give different occupational choices and career aspirations. The data are presented in Table 4.

Table 4

Quantity and Quality of Occupations Mentioned by the Experimental Groups on Direct and Indirect Sentence Completion Tests*

Test	Group	Number of occupations mentioned			Unusual occupations	
		Total	$\overline{X}$	s	Number mentioned	Number of Ss mentioning
Direct	I.Q. (N = 28)	51	1·82†	1·09	6	5‡
	Creative (N = 26)	68	2·61†	1·41	24	16‡
Indirect	I.Q. (N = 28)	100	3·57‡	1·81	12	10†
	Creative (N = 26)	130	5·00‡	1·80	29	17†

* *t* was used to test differences between means in the fourth column; χ^2 was used to test differences between frequencies in the seventh column.

† Significant at 0·10 level.

‡ Significant at 0·01 level.

When the two groups were asked, on sentence-completion type questionnaires, to report the kinds of occupations they would like to have, the high creatives mentioned a significantly greater variety of occupations than did the high I.Q.s. When the types of occupations mentioned are divided into conventional and unconventional career categories – for example, doctor, engineer, businessman, were classified as conventional; inventor, artist, spaceman, disc jockey, as unconventional – 18 per cent of the high I.Q.s give unconventional career aspirations; 62 per cent of the high creatives give such aspirations.

Discussion

Several conceptual formulations may be adduced to account for the present data. In the context of this conference, however, we suggest that Guilford's factors of convergent and divergent thinking are highly relevant. Discussing the production of tests to assess these factors, Guilford (1957) states:

In tests of convergent thinking there is almost always one conclusion or answer that is regarded as unique, and thinking is to be channeled or controlled in the direction of that answer. . . . In divergent thinking, on the other hand, there is much searching about or going off in various directions. This is most easily seen when there is no unique conclusion. Divergent thinking . . . [is] characterized . . . as being less goal-bound. There is freedom to go off in different directions. . . . Rejecting the old solution and striking out in some new direction is necessary, and the resourceful organism will more probably succeed.

It seems to us that the essence of the performance of our creative adolescents lay in their ability to produce new forms, to risk conjoining elements that are customarily thought of as independent and dissimilar, to 'go off in new directions'. The creative adolescent seemed to possess the ability to free himself from the usual, to 'diverge' from the customary. He seemed to enjoy the risk and uncertainty of the unknown. In contrast, the high-I.Q. adolescent seemed to possess to a high degree the ability and the need to focus on the usual, to be 'channeled and controlled' in the direction of the right answer – the customary. He appeared to shy away from the risk and the uncertainty of the unknown and to seek out the safety and security of the known.

Furthermore, and most important, these differences do not seem to be restricted to the cognitive functioning of these two groups. The data with respect to both intellectually oriented and socially oriented behavior are of a piece, and the findings with regard to each of the eight questions can be put into the same conceptual formulation. The high I.Q.s tend to converge upon stereotyped meanings, to perceive personal success by conventional standards, to move toward the model provided by teachers, to seek out careers that conform to what is expected of them. The high creatives tend to diverge from stereotyped meanings, to produce original fantasies, to perceive personal success by unconventional standards, to seek out careers that do not conform to what is expected of them.

Turning to the social implications of this research and, indeed, of the great bulk of research dealing with creativity, there seems to be little doubt as to which of these two personal orientations receives the greater welcome in the majority of our social institutions. Guilford (1957), who quite clearly perceived this social bias, states:

[Education] has emphasized abilities in the areas of convergent thinking and evaluation, often at the expense of development in the area of divergent thinking. We have attempted to teach students how to arrive at 'correct' answers that our civilization has taught us are correct. This is convergent thinking. ... Outside the arts we have generally discouraged the development of divergent-thinking abilities, unintentionally but effectively.

It is, we believe, unfortunate that in American education at all levels we fail to distinguish between our convergent and divergent talents – or, even worse, that we try to convert our divergent students into convergent students. Divergent fantasy is often called 'rebellious' rather than 'germinal'; unconventional career choice is often labeled 'unrealistic' rather than 'courageous'. It is hoped that present work in cognition will help modify some of the stereotypic attitudes regarding children's thinking.

References
GETZELS, J. W., and JACKSON, P. W. (1962), *Creativity and Intelligence: Explorations with Gifted Students*, Wiley.
GUILFORD, J. P. (1957), A revised structure of intellect, *Report of the Psychological Laboratory, University of Southern California*, no. 19.

17 C. L. Burt

Critical Notice

C. L. Burt, 'Critical notice: the psychology of creative ability',
British Journal of Educational Psychology, vol. 32, 1962,
pp. 292–8. A review of J. W. Getzels and P. W. Jackson, *Creativity
and Intelligence: Explorations with Gifted Students*, Wiley, 1962.

The interest in what is now commonly termed 'creativity' goes
back to Galton's pioneer studies of the intellectual characteristics of men of genius. Nearly all the eminent men in his list –
the scientists, statesmen and military commanders, quite as
much as the poets, painters or writers of fiction – were distinguished by the originality of their ideas – the 'fluency and freedom of their associations'; and he was particularly anxious to
determine in what ways the free and fluent imaginations of the
genius differed from those of the insane, the delirious, the drug-
addict and the mere day-dreamer. The earliest attempts to provide an adequate theory of the subject came from the leading
critics of the current associationist doctrines, notably Ward and
Stout, and were based chiefly on the results of introspective
analysis. Stout, in his *Manual*, distinguished two main types of
'ideation' – 'serial' (or 'reintegrative') and 'divergent'; only
the former – the type of thinking in which the revived experience
is reinstated either completely or in part – could be explained by a
psychology based solely on the principle of 'association by
temporal contiguity'. A few contemporary associationists –
notably Bain – had sought to supplement the traditional theory
by recognizing a second principle, namely, 'association by
similarity'. But similarity is not a mode of association; it is a
relation. And Stout's own explanation was a development of
Thomas Brown's principle of 'relational suggestion', or (as
Spearman later termed it) 'the eduction of relations and correlates'. This he took to be the real key to the creative processes
of genius, and illustrated by apt examples from poets like Tennyson and Browning and scientists like Newton.

From an empirical standpoint, however, perhaps the important contribution of the British school was the attempt to attack the problem experimentally by the methods of factor analysis. Galton's original plan for systematic mental testing had included tests for what he called 'higher mental processes'; and several of his earlier disciples endeavoured to construct practicable tests of 'productive thinking' along lines suggested by these intro-spective studies. Moore and I, for example, ventured to introduce (among other methods) what we called the 'analogies test' (based on Stout's theory of relational suggestion), as well as Galton's Test of Free Association (to measure 'fluency') and Binet's Inkblot Test (to measure 'apperception'). Further tests were devised by Garnett, Webb and several of Spearman's research students. Hargreaves in a Monograph Supplement to the *British Journal of Psychology* (1927) published an elaborate re-search on 'The faculty of imagination'; and Spearman summed up his own views in a small volume on *The Creative Mind* (Apple-ton, 1930).

Most of the British work was carried out with children of school age. In America a number of workers tried somewhat similar procedures to assess creative ability both in younger children and in adults. The second edition of Whipple's *Manual of Mental and Physical Tests* (1915) describes the Analogies Test and a new test for Uncontrolled Association; and his chapter on 'Tests of imagination and invention' includes the Inkblot Test and a Test for Linguistic Invention. Chassell devised a number of suggestive 'Tests for originality' to be used with adults (*J. educ. Psychol.*, vol. 7, 1916, pp. 317 ff.); and Simpson in a paper on 'Creative imagination' (*Amer. J. Psychol.*, vol. 23, 1922, pp. 234 ff.) sought to demonstrate its relative independence of intelligence. However, the increasing domination of behaviour-istic theories diverted attention to those types of mental activity – or (as they preferred to say) of human behaviour – which could be interpreted in terms of the simple principles of mechanical association. Concepts like 'imagination' or 'productive think-ing' savoured too much of discredited introspectionist doctrines, and were deliberately excluded from behaviourist textbooks.

The revival of American interest in 'creativity' seems to have started with Professor Guilford's presidential address to the American Psychological Association, which dealt specifically with that subject ('Creativity', *Amer. Psychol.*, vol. 5, 1950, pp. 444 ff.); and most of the newer American work in that field has been inspired, directly or indirectly, by the researches of Guilford and his collaborators at the University of South California. Their work has been concerned almost entirely with adults, particularly with what they call 'high-level personnel'. The same holds true of the inquiries undertaken by Professor Calvin Taylor and his fellow workers at the University of Utah, although their researches have dealt chiefly with 'scientific creativity'. Of the various studies carried out on pupils of school age, the most influential have been those of J. W. Getzels, Professor of Educational Psychology in the University of Chicago. He and his associates have been interested more especially in the creative capacities exhibited by young adolescents. Much of their work has been repeated with younger children by Professor Torrance, Director of Educational Research at the University of Minnesota, who is himself one of the most active investigators in this field.

The volume now published by Professor Getzels and his colleague, Professor Jackson, describes in detail the most important of their various researches. In a prefatory note they relate how, in 1957, Professor Chase, Chairman of the Department of Education in their University, called a meeting of the faculty to discuss the need for research on giftedness. The outcome was the first of the studies reported in this book. It was the work of a co-operative team, financed in part by a grant from the United States Office of Education. The investigators began by asking what particular qualities are generally regarded as most characteristic of the gifted child, and most likely to be prognostic of adult success. As a result of questionnaires addressed to teachers and parents, they concluded that the most important qualities could be classified under four broad headings – intelligence, creativity, emotional adjustment and moral character. The first pair in their view designate contrasted types of 'cognitive excellence', and the second pair contrasted types of 'psychosocial excellence'. Accordingly they decided to select four groups of pupils – each pre-eminently distinguished by one or other of these four characteristics, and subject them to a systematic study.

The first and larger part of their volume is devoted to an

investigation of the two main types of cognitive activity as thus defined. The hypothesis which they set themselves to verify is that suggested in Guilford's address on 'Creativity': 'If the correlations between intelligence test scores and many types of creative processes are only moderate or low – and I predict they will be – it is because the primary abilities represented in the tests are not all-important for creative behaviour, and some of the primary abilities important for creative behaviour are not represented in the tests.' To assess intelligence they used the scores obtained with the Binet, WISC or Henmon–Nelson tests. To measure creativity five special tests were devised (based partly on the earlier work of Guilford) – 'completing fables', 'making up problems', 'hidden shapes', 'word association' and 'uses for things'.

The pupils chosen for intensive study were the boys and girls attending the senior classes of a private school in Chicago, ranging from the sixth grade up to the senior year of high school. Those selected comprised twenty-eight adolescents falling within the top 20 per cent in a test of intelligence (average I.Q. 150) but below the top 20 per cent in tests of creativity, and twenty-six falling within the top 20 per cent as judged by the tests of creativity but below the top 20 per cent in the test of intelligence (average I.Q. only 127). The greater part of their research consists in the attempts to determine 'what the pupils so selected are like as *students*, as *individuals* and as *members of their family*'; and a variety of supplementary tests and inquiries were carried out to discover in what ways, if any, the two contrasted groups differed when studied from each of these three aspects.

In tests of school attainments, the pupils in the 'creative' group, in spite of their relatively low intelligence, were, if anything, slightly superior to those in the 'intelligent' group. In tests of 'verbal' and 'non-verbal imaginative production' they revealed more humour, playfulness and wit, and a greater fondness for aggressive and violent situations: most of them were liable to 'break away from the stimulus', using it chiefly as a point of departure for free self-expression. In behaviour and in aspiration, e.g. in their choice of careers, they tended to diverge more widely both from the expectations of their teachers and from the patterns dictated by conventional standards. It is, therefore, scarcely surprising that, when the teachers were invited to rate the children for 'desirability', it was, on the whole, the pupils in the 'intelligent' group who were assessed as the most desirable members in a classroom. There were marked differences in the home backgrounds. Most of the fathers and more than half of the mothers of the 'intelligent' group had received a 'graduate training': in more than 60 per cent of the cases the fathers' occupational status is described as 'university teaching, research or editing'. Among the 'creative' group about 50 per cent of the fathers appear to have been engaged in 'business' – nearly three times as many as in the 'intelligent' group. The parents of the 'intelligent' group exercised greater 'critical vigilance' in regard to their children's day-to-day life and choice of friends, and were able to provide them with a more 'bookish' environment. The main conclusion seems to be that the attitudes both of teachers and of the more academic types of parent tend to favour the educable pupil rather than the creative pupil, and to repress instead of fostering any incipient inclination towards originality or enterprise.

Even so, what the authors consider to be the most puzzling phenomenon of all remains unexplained – the fact that the 'creative' group, despite their inferior home background, their inferior intelligence and their inferior behaviour in the classroom, actually score higher marks in the educational tests. This unexpected success, we are told, 'places them, as such phenomena are handled to-day, not in the category of "gifted children", but in the pejorative category of "overachievers"'. Accordingly, faced with this 'logical dilemma', the investigators are led 'to raise the specific issue whether it is an emotional or motivational *pathology*, or a *distinctive intellectual ability*, that accounts for the superior scholastic performance'. The first alternative – the appeal to 'psychopathology' – they very rightly reject: indeed, in this country few would take such an explanation seriously. The hypothesis which the investigators themselves prefer is that there are two distinct types of cognitive ability, which they call 'intelligence' and 'creativity' respectively. 'On the perennial question of whether the observed differences are the product of nature or nurture,' they say, they would 'agree with Guilford on adopting a position midway between the two extremes.' In this, once again, they are unquestionably correct. Education cannot create creativity, but it can do much to encourage and develop it.

However, what I want chiefly to question is the notion that there are two separate groups or types each characterized by a distinctive kind of intellectual ability. This method of interpreting the results seems a natural consequence of the factorial theory favoured by most American investigators – namely, that the mind on its intellectual side is composed of a number of 'primary abilities', and that the factors obtained from the kind of correlation matrix which at first sight suggests a 'general factor', ought always to be 'rotated' to secure a 'simple structure' of group factors only. Before we accept such a hypothesis we must scrutinize a little more closely the data and the arguments on which it rests. In selecting the so-called 'intelligent' group the investigators apparently relied on a single I.Q. procured from the records office of the school. Moreover, the test was applied, not at the time of inquiry, but when the pupils first entered the school, nor was it the same for every pupil. Hence, the assessments so obtained must have a rather low reliability. And in any case a test of the type employed, as the authors themselves observe in another part of their book, can 'rarely account for more than one-quarter of the variance in such crucial factors as school achievement and academic performance'. From this they infer that 'the common type of intelligence test' fails to 'sample all or at least a sufficiently broad range of known cognitive abilities'; it can only represent 'a rather narrow band of intellectual activities'; and, they add, 'it thus discourages observation of other types of cognitive functioning'.

Nevertheless, this of itself hardly suffices to prove that there is no such thing as a general factor underlying all known cognitive processes. It merely shows that the 'common type of intelligence test' provides a very inadequate measure of that factor. But this is a conclusion which has been stressed over and over again in the pages of this journal. Many of the constituent items that make up such tests depend largely on memory, particularly on verbal memory; they give an undue advantage to the well-taught child from the cultured home; and they 'tend to select children of an analytic or reproductive type rather than those of an intuitive or productive type'.

Unlike the intelligence tests, those used for testing 'creativity' were devised and applied specially in the course of the research; and, instead of just one test, five were used. The authors print a table of intercorrelations for boys and girls, based on 533 cases. Each of the tests of creativity correlates positively with the test of intelligence, two of them to the extent of 0·37 or 0·38. The authors themselves describe these figures as 'fairly low', and would evidently have us believe that their results fully confirm Guilford's prediction. But the correlations of the various tests of creativity among themselves are not much higher; moreover, as we have seen, the reliability of the intelligence test must have been rather low, and the children tested were themselves by no means a complete or random sample of the general population. In the table, taken as a whole, all the coefficients are positive; and, with one doubtful exception among the girls, each of the thirty figures is statistically significant. With both sexes a single general factor would fully account for the correlations observed; when the effects of the general factor have been eliminated, not one of the residual correlations is numerically larger than 0·10, and none is statistically significant. Indeed, the new tests for 'creativity' would form very satisfactory additions to any ordinary battery for testing the general factor of intelligence. In the earliest types of intelligence test the child had to invent his own reply; in most present-day tests alternative answers are suggested, and the child has merely to decide which is correct. This (as has often been pointed out) reduces spontaneity to a minimum; and an entirely different type of test-problem is needed to redress the balance.

However, when we examine the nature of the tests proposed by Professor Getzels and his colleagues for assessing creativity, and the way in which they are marked, it seems highly probable that they are biased in favour of those particular individuals whose special aptitudes are of a productive rather than a merely re-productive type. And in any case there can be no doubt whatever that these new tests have succeeded in eliciting supplementary activities that are rarely tapped by the usual brands of intelligence test. That this is so can readily be demonstrated by partialling out the influence of those particular processes measured by the 'intelligence' test: we then find that there still remains a set of positive partial correlations between the tests of creativity which are in nearly every case statistically significant.

But, no matter how reliable or how accurate our assessments of the general factor may be, we can certainly agree that this factor by itself could only account for part of 'the variance in such crucial performances as scholastic achievement'. Motivational factors must be almost equally important; and special abilities and special disabilities would have considerable weight. In this country, I take it, few educational psychologists would imagine that a single I.Q. based on a 'common type of intelligence test' would yield all the relevant information required: the real reason why such tests are nowadays so widely used is, not that they are thought to provide adequate or perfect assessments in themselves, but simply because they form the cheapest, most practicable and most easily standardized means of estimating a child's 'educable capacity'. If, however, as Professor Getzels and his colleagues have apparently found, 'talent-hunters' in America still trust too exclusively to a single type of test, then we may willingly agree that their criticisms are well founded.

This section of their book ends with a detailed discussion of the theoretical nature of creativity. They briefly review various speculative conceptions put forward by different schools of psychology – the associationist, the Gestalt, the psychoanalytic, etc.; but they entirely overlook the conclusions reached by previous experimentalists in this country. The main results have already been summarized in an earlier issue of this journal (*Brit. J. educ. Psychol.*, vol. 9, pp. 180ff. and refs.). Here, therefore, I need merely note the more important points in which the British studies seem to differ from the American.

To begin with, it has always been a standing principle with British psychologists to provide, whenever possible, some evidence for the reliability and the validity of the tests used. Parallel versions of each new test, for example, are applied to the same group; and, unless the correlation indicates a high degree of self-consistency, the test is usually rejected without further ado. If reliable, the test is then applied either to a group of individuals varying widely in the quality to be assessed and the test-results are correlated with the ratings of a trustworthy observer; or it may be applied to two contrasted groups, selected as possessing a high or a low degree of the quality in question; or, best of all perhaps, a predictive validation may be eventually obtained on the basis of the after-histories of the children tested. All this, of course, implies that we have already decided on a plausible criterion which will furnish a basis for the ratings, the selection or the later re-assessments – by no means an easy problem in the case of so vague a concept as 'creativity'. Most teachers, for example, tend to limit the term to pupils who show artistic talent or have a gift for imaginative writing: they forget that originality may be equally important in practical or scientific fields of work. Professor Getzels and Professor Jackson, however, apparently expect us to accept their tests as both reliable and valid without any direct or objective evidence.

Nevertheless, here is a collection of ingenious tests, carefully compiled, and the authors may reasonably retort that the critic is free to check the reliability and validity for himself. The British work, by comparison, is still at the preparatory stages. Much of it has been merely exploratory, based chiefly on factorial studies, which, it is assumed, should form the necessary preliminary to the construction of a reliable and valid battery of tests.

The chief conclusions are as follows. First, taking 'creativity' to mean *useful* creative activities, most British investigators seem agreed that in all of them general intelligence is an essential, and indeed the most important, constituent. Mere creativity without intelligence, as Galton long ago pointed out, would be all but worthless. Guilford, in a passage quoted by our authors, remarked, that most of the problems set in an intelligence test have 'a unique and an expected answer': 'Charles is taller than Henry. John is taller than Charles. Who is the shortest?' Here, he says, the examinee's thought-processes are intended to 'converge' on a solution which is already decided, and must be the same for all. A test of creativity, say Getzels and Jackson, requires the answers to 'diverge': it measures 'the ability to deal *inventively* with the verbal or numerical symbols or with object-space relations'. But is there any merit in *mere* invention – in suggesting that

211

Charles is the shortest, or that twice two are six just because the answers would be 'divergent'? What I have called 'useful creativity' must involve the ability to deal, not only inventively, but also rationally with the material supplied.

Spearman, indeed, went so far as to maintain that all 'creativeness or originality' depends solely on the 'eduction of correlates', and is, therefore, merely a manifestation of 'general intelligence': 'no special creative power exists' (*The Abilities of Man*, Macmillan, London, 1927, p. 187). However, nearly every other investigator in this country has found evidence for a distinct group factor – a factor for 'productive' as distinct from 'reproductive imagination'. To that extent the British investigators agree with the American. But they differ from the American in holding that this supplementary factor is not to be regarded as a simple faculty or 'primary ability': it is itself highly complex, and capable of further factorizations into a number of constituent subfactors.

1. The contributory factor most frequently reported is what Galton termed 'fluency', i.e. an unusual flow of associated ideas: the creative mind (if I may borrow a phrase from Binet) seems to be 'always pullulating with new notions'. Further, fluency itself has several different forms – verbal, visual, associative, ideational.

2. A second factor, all too frequently confused with the former, is a factor for 'divergent' association (in Stout's narrower sense rather than Guilford's). 'Fluency' might almost be defined in purely quantitative terms – by the number or speed with which ideas are suggested; 'divergence' depends on the qualitative nature of the ideas, and is measured by their variety. In 'serial' or 'redintegrative' association, the whole idea or situation which forms the stimulus tends to reproduce the whole idea or situation which was formerly associated with it; in 'divergent' association only a part of the initial stimulus is operative, and what is recalled may be merely a part of some other situation previously associated with it. Hobbes long ago provided the classical illustration: 'in a discourse of our present civil war what could seem more impertinent than to ask (as one did) what was the value of a Roman penny?' (*Leviathan*, I, iii). The operative element in the stimulus was the deliverance of one's master

to the enemy; the element recalled were the thirty denarii received by Judas as the reward for the most infamous of betrayals.

3. A third component, often overlooked, is a factor for what may be called 'receptivity'. It is this that largely distinguishes the inventiveness of the genius from the spurious originality of the crank, the eccentric and dreamer. The genius does not merely think of new solutions; he perceives new problems; he sees the familiar in a novel light: he does *not* treat the 'stimulus' solely as a 'point of departure'.

4. Finally, a factor noted by several investigators is one which they variously describe as 'insight', 'intuitive synthesis' or (in James's phrase) 'sagacity'. The true genius does not seize on just *any* distinctive part in the initial situation, nor does he reproduce just *any* distinctive element in the associated idea. He singles out what is most relevant or essential. What may be termed the 'analytic' type of mind – the type that is usually selected by the ordinary intelligence test – commonly reaches the right solution by patient analysis and step-by-step ratiocination; the 'synthetic' type jumps at it by a kind of impressionistic comprehension. Older British writers generally accounted for the process in terms of what Stout and others called 'apperception', and it was for this reason that 'apperception tests' were introduced into several of the earlier batteries. There is, however, yet a further complication. A number of investigators have reported that several of the factors, usually one or more of the first three, show an appreciable correlation with temperamental factors. The creative child, it is said, is active, alert and exploratory; and these, it is maintained, are characteristics of an extravertive disposition.

The relative independence of the subsidiary factors I have named seems demonstrated by the fact that they mature (and often decline) at different ages or stages in the development of the child. 'Fluency' appears earliest of all; during the primary school period it frequently diminishes and revives again in early adolescence. 'Receptivity' may also show itself at a fairly early age. The other two factors have been reported only in studies of older children. Moreover, different factors predominate in differing degrees in different individuals. The creativity of a scientific genius like Newton or Faraday differs widely from that of an artistic genius like Michaelangelo or Beethoven; the fertility of Dickens is different from that of Thackeray or George Eliot; the originality of Browning from that of Tennyson or Blake. For all these reasons, therefore, we must, I think, conclude that the weight of the evidence is strongly against the somewhat simplified interpretation proposed by Professor Getzels and Professor Jackson – namely, that there are just 'two basic cognitive or intellective modes', the 'creative' and the 'intelligent', and, similarly, two distinct types of 'gifted students'. Nevertheless, their survey of the subject and their own experimental studies remain full of interesting and suggestive points; and their tests, which are set out in full in an appendix, should be invaluable to future investigators.

The second part of their book describes a shorter study, dealing with what they term 'psychomotor excellence'. The need for some such inquiry, so they explain, was suggested by 'the shift in our social and educational goals from values emphasizing "character" to those emphasizing "adjustment"'. They contrast 'the relatively hedonistic present-time orientation of our culture' and 'the traditional work-success ethic' which dominated the 'moral climate' of American homes and American schools throughout the nineteenth century. They might perhaps have noted the still more striking contrast between 'present-time orientation' and the moral outlook of the early Pilgrim Fathers. To demonstrate that much of the change has taken place during our own life time they have selected two specimen periods – between the two wars, and since the last war, and compared the publications listed in the *Education Index*. During the first period they point out the number of references under the heading 'Adjustment' were only half as numerous as those under the heading 'Character' or 'Character training'; during the post-war period they were six times as numerous, and the references to character training dropped from 369 to only fifty-two.

In their own inquiry they have adopted much the same procedure as before. Two sets of tests were constructed and applied. These, it was hoped, would pick out first those pupils who were 'high in moral character but not in adjustment' and, secondly, those who were 'high in adjustment but not in character'. The two groups were then compared for intelligence, school attainments, teacher ratings, and home background. In tests of intelligence and of verbal and numerical attainments, the average scores of the 'moral' group were actually higher than those of the 'adjusted' group. However, in the intelligence test the difference was too small to be significant. Thus, although the average I.Q. for both groups was nearly the same, the 'moral' group had made much greater progress in their school work. But some of the children in the 'moral' group had started school earlier; and their mothers were sterner disciplinarians and more critical of their children's behaviour. In the occupations and the economic status of the parents there was little difference; the majority of those in the 'moral' group lived in apartments and had changed their residence rather frequently, whereas most of those in the 'adjusted' group lived in houses. There was, too, no discernible difference in the teachers' ratings for 'desirability'; but the number of pupils having 'qualities of leadership', is said to have been somewhat higher in the 'adjusted' group.

Once again, however, the groups compared were extremely small – only twenty-seven boys or girls in each, all from the same school. Considering that the interviews with each mother lasted two to three hours, the information obtained seems rather meagre. Instead of securing factual data relating to the education, occupation, socio-economic class, attendance at church or chapel, or the like, the investigators were primarily interested in what they call 'the mother's perceptions of her child'. By far the most illuminating portions of the inquiry are the case-studies and the verbatim answers, storyettes and essays collected from typical individuals in either group. It appears that 'adjusted' individuals tend, on the whole, to 'seek experiences that are immediately gratifying rather than eventually rewarding, to prefer social interaction to personal achievement, and, where there is a conflict of ideals, to sacrifice moral obligations to interpersonal harmony'; the individuals in the 'moral' group tend to reverse these trends, and to assert their own autonomy. In short, 'adjustment' is the 'analogue' in the sphere of 'psychosocial behaviour' corresponding to 'intelligence' in the sphere of 'cognitive behaviour'; both are essentially adaptive. Character, on the other hand, is the analogue of creativity; both are distinctive of an original and individualistic type of child.

In view of the limited range of the two sets of inquiries, they must be regarded (to use the author's own description) merely as 'exploratory studies'. Nevertheless, they throw into clear relief two important characteristics which present-day education tends to neglect. Let us, therefore, hope that, in the near future, their investigations will be enlarged and extended, and that similar researches will be planned and carried out by teachers and psychologists in this country.

18 L. Hudson

The Question of Creativity

Excerpt from L. Hudson, 'The question of creativity', in *Contrary Imaginations*, Methuen, 1966, pp. 100–115. (Penguin books edn, 1967)

I wish now to discuss a topic tangential to that of convergence and divergence: originality, or as psychologists have it, 'creativity'. Whatever the logical connexion between convergence or divergence and originality, psychologists are prone to view the topics as one and the same. Many psychologists, particularly American ones, see the diverger as potentially creative, and the converger as potentially uncreative. My own view, and my thesis in this chapter, is that the two topics must be carefully distinguished, otherwise we cannot begin to see how subtle the interconnexions really are. I shall offer a commentary on the recent American research on 'creativity' and, in doing so, try to distinguish between certain beliefs about creativeness and the evidence from which these are supposed to spring.

'Creative', it must first be established, is an adjective with widespread connotations:

'Tell me, how did you happen to get into inspirational writing?' He pondered for a moment before replying. 'Well, it was sort of a call,' he said reflectively. 'I had my own business up in Hollywood, a few doors from Grauman's Egyptian, on the Boulevard. We eternalized baby shoes – you know, dipped them in bronze for ashtrays and souvenirs. The work was creative, but somehow I felt I wasn't realizing my potentialities' (Perelman, 1959, p. 472).

In some circles 'creative' does duty as a word of general approbation – meaning, approximately, 'good'. It is rather the same with its derivative noun, 'creativity'. This odd word is now part of psychological jargon, and covers everything from the answers to a particular kind of psychological test, to forming a good relationship with one's wife. 'Creativity', in other words, applies to all those qualities of which psychologists approve. And like so many other virtues – justice, for example – it is as difficult to disapprove of as to say what it means.

As a topic for research, 'creativity' is a bandwagon; one which all of us sufficiently hale and healthy have leapt athletically aboard. It represents a boom in the American psychological industry only paralleled by that of programmed learning. Thus a topic, interesting in its own right, becomes fascinating, too, as an example of scientific fashion at work. One of the odd features of such vogues is that the ideas on which they are based are often old ones. That for programmed learning began some twenty-five years after Pressey invented the teaching machine; and the 'creativity' movement's heritage is longer still. Real creativity, excellence in the arts and sciences, has been a centre of psychologists' curiosity since their subject began. The present burgeoning is not a new phenomenon, but a return to a subject which has titillated the psychological fancy for a hundred years or more. Yet, apart from the vast increase in the scale of such research, and the generalization of 'creativity' to cover all aspects of human life, the work of the last fifteen years does also reveal a slight shift of focus: away from the romantic, humanistic figure of the artist-genius, towards the successful physical scientist. The causes of this shift are not fully understood. But two factors, at least, one can distinguish: a diffuse cultural ground-swell, elevating the scientist from the status of technician to that of culture hero; and a more specific concern on the part of the American nation with the state of their armaments industry. The first, though real enough, we can only guess about. The second factor can be traced to some extent to Sputnik.[1] This alerted American opinion, official and otherwise, to the emergence of Russia as a major technological force; and stimulated a search for more first-rate, home-grown physical scientists. The result has been the investment of previously unheard of sums of money in the quest for scientific talent.

Here, though, one meets an intriguing paradox. On the face of it, one would expect this preoccupation with physical science, and more specifically with scientific productivity, to tell against

1. Roe's work, however, and much of Guilford's, was published before Sputnik, not after.

the 'tender-minded' progressive traditions within psychology and to tell in favour of the 'tough-minded' scientific behaviourists and mental testers. In fact, though, the overriding character of the 'creativity' literature is one of enlightened, progressive humanism: we read not of ruthless conditioning for sophomores, but of sympathetically oriented teachers nurturing the creative impulse. This deserves a better explanation than I can offer. My guess would be that the post-Sputnik scare put the prevalent 'hard' scientific disciplines within psychology to a test which they failed. Mental testers were expected, and perhaps expected themselves, to apply scientific method to the problem of the original scientist and to produce a practical solution. (Psychologists understand their fellow men and scientific psychologists understand them scientifically.) But in this case the trick did not work. In terms of their test scores, good scientists turned out to be virtually indistinguishable from mediocre ones (see Harmon, 1958, 1959; Mackinnon, 1962a and b; Roe, 1953).

One wonders how the mental testers could have deceived themselves about the potentialities of their tests. Or were they so deceived? My belief is that during the 1930s and 1940s mental testers did in fact slip gradually away from the difficulties of prediction and explanation, into a state of false academic calm; and that this lapse was partially induced by the factor analytic theories which had been in vogue for the previous twenty years [see ch. 1, not included in this excerpt]. But, whatever the true account of all this, the 'creativity' movement has served in practice as a platform for the 'progressives'; and it represents the end of the isolation of the mental testing discipline from the rest of psychology. It has encouraged, too, a spirit of speculation, and of co-operation between one discipline and another. Mental testers and psychoanalysts publish cheek by jowl and so, too, do sociologists, anthropologists, demographers, administrators, teachers, historians of science, cyberneticists and many more besides. That a state of scholastic divorce from reality should be superseded by one of hectic freedom is surely to be applauded. At least the dangers of the situation are apparent. Under the old régime, critics could rarely master the necessary (or unnecessary) technical paraphernalia with which the concept of intelligence was surrounded; and, hence, tended to keep their doubts to themselves. Nowadays, it is clear to most, with or without technical knowledge, not only that the 'creativity' boom is, itself, a manifestation of fashion, but that the assertions of the psychologists concerned are frequently expressions of a particular psychological tradition rather than of dispassionate fact.[2]

Six Maxims

What is left after a fashion has swept through a particular area of psychology is usually a handful of important new facts, and what might be described as 'research maxims'. These are influential, imprecise and often misleading views about the general drift of events in a field of research. In the sphere of 'creativity', I detect six:

1. That the conventional intelligence test is outdated.

2. That in place of the conventional intelligence test, we now have tests of 'creativity'.

3. That despite the existence of 'creativity' tests, the factors which determine an individual's creativeness are personal not intellectual.

4. That originality in all spheres is associated with the same personal type – the diverger.

5. That convergence is a form of neurotic defence, while divergence is not. Divergence leads to all the good things in life, personal, as well as professional; convergence achieves the second at the expense of the first.

6. That conventional education is antipathetic to the diverger. Hence it jeopardizes the nation's supply of creative talent. Hence education should become more progressive.

2. An interesting discussion of the various psychological approaches to creativeness is given by Miller (1964). He distinguishes five: (a) the tradition, strong in mental testing ten years ago, that creative thinking is logical thinking; (b) associationism; (c) Gestalt psychology; (d) the psychodynamic approach, emphasizing the role of the unconscious; and (e) the cybernetic. It is the fourth of these, I suggest, which is the dominant one, and the one which gives the 'creativity' literature its progressive tone. A remarkable (if somewhat alarming) instance of the cybernetic approach is Simon's work (Newell, Shaw and Simon, 1962) on the use of computers to solve mathematical and scientific problems.

Few psychologists would stand by any one of these maxims without qualification. Nevertheless, they have currency in popular thinking on the subject, and in the minds of psychologists when they are off their guard.[3]

1. The downfall of the intelligence test

That the conventional intelligence test has failed to predict who will do outstanding work in science (or any other field) there is little question. MacKinnon's work is the most telling in this respect. He finds little or no connexion between adult I.Q. and adult achievement above a minimum level, which lies somewhere in the region of I.Q. 120. That is to say, nearly all of his eminent men and women produced scores above this level; but amongst them, the relation between I.Q. and originality was virtually nil. A mature scientist with an adult I.Q. of 130 is as likely to win a Nobel Prize as is one whose I.Q. is 180. MacKinnon comments (1962b, p. 488):

Over the whole range of intelligence and creativity there is, of course, a positive relationship between the two variables. No feeble-minded subjects have shown up in any of our creative groups. It is clear, however, that above a certain required minimum level of intelligence which varies from field to field and in some instances may be surprisingly low, being more intelligent does not guarantee a corresponding increase in creativeness. It just is not true that the more intelligent person is necessarily the more creative one.

A similar point is made ten years earlier by Roe (1953, p. 52):

Indeed there are a number of subjects for whom none of the test material would give the slightest clue that the subject was a scientist of renown.[4]

Admittedly, all such evidence about famous adults suffers a crucial weakness – the one already discussed in chapter 2 [not included here]. Such men may have abilities which they do not

3. Lest I be thought to attack straw men, the reader is recommended to read any handful of the dozens of books and hundreds of articles published during the last ten years with the word 'creativity' in their titles.
4. Roe here refers not just to intelligence tests but to a whole battery of testing techniques: the Rorschach and Thematic Apperception projective methods, Minnesota Multiphasic Personality Inventory, Strong Vocational Interests Blank, and so on.

choose to display. Or alternatively, they may only think efficiently when they care profoundly about what they are doing. Either way, it is quite likely that the greater a man's achievements, the less intellectually 'promiscuous' he will become. Evidence about adult abilities needs therefore to be viewed with circumspection. (If we ask a man to show us his braces, and he refuses, it does not follow that he supports his trousers with string.) On the other hand, we can by no means discount such evidence. And if anyone nurtured the belief that intellectual distinction was related closely to I.Q., MacKinnon's evidence must disabuse him.

However, the intelligence test cannot be discarded. Tests of this kind perform perfectly well the function for which they were originally conceived: the rapid and impersonal assessment of intellectual ability in the population as a whole. As Getzels and Jackson (1962, p. 3) remark, the I.Q. test is probably the best single measure we have. American Army psychologists showed that tests performed their task surprisingly well during the First World War; they have continued to do so ever since. British research on the 11-plus examination proves this. Over a wide spectrum of ability the intelligence test gives quite a good indication of a child's ability at school.[5] Difficulties arise only when the I.Q. is thought of as a precise measure of mental 'horsepower'. It is nothing of the sort; nor has factual evidence ever suggested otherwise. The chances of Smith (I.Q. 90) passing G.C.E. 'O' level are much lower than those of Jones (I.Q. 110). But it does not follow that all boys of I.Q. 110 will do better at 'O' level than all boys of I.Q. 90. Nor does it follow that because professional people score well on I.Q. tests that the more successful professional people have higher I.Q.s than the less.

The relation of I.Q. to intellectual distinction seems, in fact, highly complex. As far as one can tell, the relation at low levels of I.Q. holds quite well. Higher up, however, it dwindles; and

5. Just how valid the 11-plus is, it is not easy to tell. Vernon (1957) argues that the error involved is 5 per cent either way: or, to express the same statistic in different terms, that a quarter of the grammar school places each year are awarded in error. However, this estimate is certainly too favourable. It is based on correlations between the 11-plus and G.C.E. 'O' level results, themselves a poor index of true intellectual ability.

above a certain point, a high I.Q. is of little advantage. However, there are differences between one occupation and another, the relationship dwindling lower down the I.Q. scale in some subjects than in others. In the arts, for instance, it seems to peter out lower down than in science. For practical purposes, therefore, it might be fruitful to distinguish, for each occupation or subject, both the I.Q. levels above which a strength in I.Q. is not an advantage in real efficiency; and also lower limits, below which a weakness in I.Q. becomes incapacitating. Where one sets such limits depends, of course, on the criteria one has in mind. For argument's sake, we might define success academically: a good second class degree at Oxford or Cambridge; or, in more worldly terms, a successful novel or a good piece of scientific research. Granting these standards, I would guess that the lower limit in science lies in the region of I.Q. 115; and that a high I.Q. is of little advantage above I.Q. 125. The lower limit for the arts escapes me, because the 11-plus ensures that few boys with I.Q.s below 110 enter my sample in the first place. It probably lies somewhere in the area of I.Q. 95–100; and the upper point in the region of I.Q. 115.

Why should this relationship between I.Q. and real accomplishment peter out? Obviously, no one knows. But there are two simple explanations. First, (as the third research maxim asserts), that above a certain level of I.Q., motivation is of over-riding importance. Second, that the intellectual skills measured by I.Q. tests are too simple – and that if they were based on more complex skills, their predictive effectiveness would increase. As illustration of this second point, take the analogy of spelling. A man who cannot spell at all cannot write a novel. But once his ability to spell reaches a certain level, the restrictions which his inability imposes upon him largely disappear. Some of the most eloquent and literary of novelists, Scott Fitzgerald for example, spelt atrociously. In the same way, Einstein was comparatively only a mediocre mathematician, and Darwin was virtually innumerate. It may be that this argument applies to intelligence tests as well. However, this proposition, as I shall try to show later in this chapter, is not as simple as it seems.

Returning once more to the first research maxim, it seems that the downfall has affected not the I.Q. tests, but certain naïve and mystic notions about them: the belief that, armed with such tests, the psychologist could probe the innermost recesses of our minds, and predict our future accomplishments unerringly. In fact, they are a useful technique for measuring a particular kind of reasoning, and tell us, cheaply and quite accurately, which members of the normal population are, broadly speaking, clever, and which not. Responsible mental testers may protest that they, as responsible testers, have never suggested otherwise. But this would be disingenuous. Thousands of psychologists have been suggesting otherwise for several decades; and, moreover, have neglected to collect the evidence that would prove their suggestion (and the implicit power which it bestows on the tester) false. It has taken us fifty years to discover (or, at least, to publicize) what could have been ascertained overnight: that there are highly intelligent men and women who are not particularly good at intelligence tests; and men and women who are outstandingly good at intelligence tests who are not outstandingly good at anything else. We can scarcely now complain if our enemies take this failure as evidence of our lack, either of candour, or of native wit.

2. 'Creativity' tests

Open-ended tests are known throughout the United States as 'creativity' tests. Yet, as far as I can discover, there is scarcely a shred of factual support for this. The nearest we come to direct evidence is in the work of MacKinnon (1962a and b). He found that creative scientists, architects and novelists were prone to give unusual responses to a word association test; indeed, that unusualness of mental association was one of the best indices of an individual's originality in his professional work. However, the correlation is not high ($r = 0.50$ amongst architects), and applies particularly to associations which are unusual as opposed to rare. The highly creative members of MacKinnon's samples produced, it seems, not bizarre or remote associations, but relatively ordinary ones in large numbers.[6] He also found differences

6. MacKinnon (1962b), p. 490. MacKinnon defines an unusual association as one produced by less than 10 per cent and more than 1 per cent of the normal population: a rare association as one produced by 1 per cent or less.

between creative and non-creative on the Barron–Welsh Art test. On this, the creative were much more likely to prefer visual patterns which are complex and asymmetrical (see Barron, 1958; MacKinnon, 1962b, p. 488).

The issue of whether 'creativity' tests measure creativeness has been further confused by certain commentators. Getzels and Jackson have been taken to task for suggesting that the kind of ability measured by their open-ended tests is not closely linked with I.Q. In this they follow Guilford, the factor analyst, who claims to have isolated a very large number of intellectual factors, convergent and divergent reasoning being only two among them (Guilford, 1956). This assertion has caused a rapid closing of British ranks, and some American ones, too. Ostensibly, the point at issue is whether or not Getzels and Jackson's work refutes the general factor theory of intelligence. Burt (1962; see also Vernon, 1964), particularly, has argued that it does not. He is doubtless correct; but seems, in his eagerness to defend the general factor theory, to have missed a vital point. Whether or not they express it with sufficient clarity, the import of Getzels and Jackson's evidence is not that the general factor theory of intelligence is mistaken, but that for many practical purposes, it is irrelevant. The crucial fact, it emerges from Getzels and Jackson's work and my own, is that a knowledge of a boy's I.Q. is of little help *if you are faced with a formful of clever boys*. The boy with the lowest I.Q. in the form is almost as likely to get the top marks as the boy with the highest. It is this simple, but disruptive, implication that English critics of Getzels and Jackson have overlooked. They land, claws extended, on a technical red herring.[7]

7 Where this leaves us regarding factorial theories of mental ability, I am not sure. If one wishes to predict or explain the behaviour of any individual or group of individuals, what one needs are good primary data: pertinent tests, and detailed evidence about the choices the individuals actually face. If a boy wishes to study either mathematics or biology, one needs norms showing his chances of success in either field. Where the general (or any other) factor theory of intelligence comes in to such a process of detailed prediction I cannot quite see. Factorial theories of the intellect may be a useful stimulus to the construction of new tests, as they clearly have been in Guilford's case; but my impression is that for explanatory or predictive purposes they are unhelpful. In all probability, though, the minimum I.Q. score for comprehension of the general factor theory's significance is very high, and I do not meet it.

3. Personal factors not intellectual ones are crucial

This, of all six maxims, is the one with the best factual foundation. Long ago, in the context of Terman's *Genetic Studies of Genius*, Cox (1926, p. 187) remarked:

... high but not the highest intelligence, combined with the greatest degree of persistence, will achieve greater eminence than the highest degree of intelligence with somewhat less persistence.

Roe concurs; and so, too, does MacKinnon (1962b, p. 493):

Our data suggest, rather, that if a person has the minimum of intelligence required for mastery of a field of knowledge, whether he performs creatively or banally in that field will be crucially determined by non-intellective factors.

If they are right, the policy of devising new and better tests of high grade intelligence is a mistaken one. What we need, instead, are better tests of personality. Although this is a sensible deduction from the evidence, it is not logically binding. It does not follow, because we have not found a test of reasoning which predicts research ability, that such a test could not be devised. There may still be a case for better tests of reasoning: as they now stand mental tests are, after all, primitive affairs, and the skills they test are exceedingly simple. When we ask a scientist to complete a verbal analogy for us, or a numerical series, we are asking him to perform a skill insultingly trivial compared with those he uses in his research: when he grasps a theory; reviews the facts for which it is supposed to account; decides whether or not it does so; derives predictions from it; devises experiments to test those predictions; and speculates about alternative theories of his own and other people's. In all these manoeuvres he exercises skills of a complexity greater than we can readily comprehend.

And these intellectual operations are beyond us not simply because they are too complex. They depend, firstly, on huge accumulations of experience; and, secondly, upon the fact that the individual concerned cares intensely about what he is doing. Without training and experience, these complex skills do not exist. As I have remarked in chapter 2 [not included here] mature reasoning does not occur in a vacuum, but at the end of a lengthy and subtle development. Before he enters his training, the scientist (or, of course, any other brainworker) has potentialities rather than accomplishments. What matter, at this stage, are the factors which predispose him to pursue a given line of work, and enable him to benefit from it. Once he has become a mature scientist our ability to measure his intellectual skills with tests (rather than by reading his published works) becomes academic. The whole point of testing, in other words, lies in measuring those qualities which predispose a man to follow a particular bent. Some of these may be a matter of intellectual ability; but, in all probability, the majority do lie – as Cox, Roe and MacKinnon suggest – within the sphere of personality.

4. Divergers are potentially creative, convergers are not

Much writing on creativity rests on the assumptions that creative people are open, flexible and unconventional, and that the un-creative are inflexible and authoritarian. On this argument, it is the divergers (and perhaps all-rounders) who break new ground, while the convergers plod along cautiously in the rear. My own evidence suggests that this assumption is mistaken. Moreover, the two outstanding studies of originality amongst adults, those of Roe and MacKinnon, indicate that the relation between divergence and creativeness is bound to be complex (see MacKinnon, 1962a and b; Roe, 1951a, b and c, 1953). Both studies were based on famous people who subjected themselves voluntarily to psychological examination. This encompassed details of personality, attitude and biography, as well as intellectual ability. Roe restricted her sample to scientists (physical, biological and social); MacKinnon included architects and writers as well. Both command attention as studies of individuals who are distinguished beyond any reasonable doubt. 'Creative', in the context of these studies, for once carries its true connotation, their subjects being amongst the most able and intellectually productive in the world. I shall discuss their findings more fully in chapters 7 and 8 [not included here]. For the time being, it is enough to note that the findings of these two remarkable pieces of research conflict, and the conflict is one which must be resolved. Roe reports that eminent research workers in physical science strongly resemble the converger; MacKinnon that creative men and women in all fields are more divergent than their non-creative colleagues. These two conclusions can only be reconciled by assuming that the openness and uninhibitedness to which MacKinnon refers exist within a relatively narrow range. On this argument, all scientists are inhibited, the creative ones less so, the non-creative more. One can only make sense of this evidence, in other words, by assuming an intellectual spectrum in which each occupation (littérateur, historian, psychologist, biologist, physicist, and so on) attracts individuals of a particular personal type. The convergers are naturally attracted towards one end of the spectrum and the divergers to the other. Each field has its own waveband of emotional openness; only within the range of openness which each waveband affords are certain degrees of openness or restriction more conducive to good work than others.

The platitudes which ache to be released from this complex literature are the ones about the original scientist being the scientist who possesses some of the divergent qualities of the artist; and the successful artist being the one who enjoys some of the rigour and dedicated single-mindedness of the scientist. This notion accords neatly with Kuhn's analysis of scientific invention – that it depends upon a tension between the forces of tradition and revolution (see Kuhn, 1962, 1963). His analysis is one which, I am convinced, is applicable to most of the arts as well. It is compatible with both MacKinnon's findings and Roe's; and also with the evidence set out in chapters 2, 3 and 4 of the present text [not included here].

5. Convergers are neurotic, divergers not

Psychoanalysts frequently assume that we are psychologically healthy in so far as we have access to our own unconscious impulses. And the psychologists interested in 'creativity' also assume that because the diverger appears more emotionally open than the converger, he is automatically the healthier of the two. I have argued in chapter 5 [not included here] that the diverger's openness may be deceptive: that, in many cases, he merely defends himself against his feelings by a different (and perhaps less effective) means. There is no doubt, though, whatever the merits or demerits of the diverger's internal policies, that he does entertain emotions, whereas the converger frequently turns his back on them. This denial of the personal aspects of life seems – to many, at least – self-evidently neurotic. I am not at all sure that this is so. The conventional view has been expressed pithily by Freud. Asked what was the proper end of man, he is said to have replied: '*Lieben und arbeiten*' – to love and to work.[8] This is a noble ideal, and one which expresses every psychoanalyst's ambition, both for his clients and for himself. On the other hand it is a goal which not many achieve. Freud's own life illustrates the difficulty well. It is widely acknowledged that Freud advanced our theoretical knowledge of sex to a greater extent than anyone else, before or since. He was also a devoted husband and parent. Yet, according to his biographer, he enjoyed only somewhat cursory sexual relations with his wife, and experienced no sexual interest in any other woman (see Jones, 1961, p. 359). His life, in other words, is a refutation of his own ideals. One might argue that his choice of subject-matter and his zeal in pursuing it were both a product of his personal deficiency. Or, conversely, that his personal deficiency was the price that he paid for his intellectual trepidation. Either way, though, the paradox exists: and such things, as Freud himself would have remarked, are not accidents.[9]

It is arguable that physical scientists do evade personal issues; and possibly, too, that the novelist's urge to write stems from a failure to accept everyday reality for what it is. Both could be seen as 'immature'. But the standards against which such comparisons are made are exceedingly exalted – and the

8. Quoted by Erikson (1963), p. 264. Erikson emphasizes that Freud here refers specifically to genital sexuality, not merely to a more diffuse uxoriousness.

9. To reject the *lieben und arbeiten* view as impracticable is not to embrace its opposite, the view that productive thought is necessarily a product of neurosis: 'Great wits are sure to madness near alli'd. And thin partitions do their bonds divide' (John Dryden). This popular belief has been blamed on Seneca: 'Nullum magnum ingenium sine mixtura dementiae fuit.' In fact, though, he seems to have referred to the Platonic notion of divine inspiration, not insanity; and has ever since been misinterpreted. The belief that 'everything great in the world comes from neurotics' has been described by Lionel Trilling as one of the characteristic notions of our culture; but such evidence as we possess suggests that it is untrue.

psychologist's position in such bandying of value judgements is itself exposed. Of the physical scientist, the very worst that one can say is that he is a robot: he turns his back on a wide range of human experience more or less completely. Of the novelist, that he is an emotional prostitute, a man retailing the events of his own private life to please his public, or for money. The psychologist, on the other hand, does something considerably more odd: he tries to make sense of human behaviour by reifying it. People are described as though they were mechanisms; their experiences are reduced to numbers. He may even make a virtue of discussing human beings as though they were rats. The physical scientist denies his emotions; the novelist exploits them; the psychologist dismantles them. Whatever the moral, it is not that some occupational groups are more neurotic than others. Although convergers and divergers use different tactics in dealing with the pressures of work and emotional experience, one tactic is not necessarily better or worse than the other. Each has its characteristic strengths and weaknesses; and the neurotic is not the man who adopts a particular intellectual and personal style, but the one who, having adopted a style, suffers its weaknesses without enjoying its strengths.

Indeed, the present maxim may be an instance of psychological doctrine accumulating by a process of projection. As Roe (1953 p. 50) points out:

It is likely that the kind of person who has gone into social science may have had a biasing effect on the theories produced by social scientists, particularly with regard to the desirable or the mature personality. Practically all current psychological theory of development stresses strongly the central importance in any life of the richness of personal relations as a basis for 'adjustment'. But the data of this study demonstrate, and it seems to me quite conclusively, that a more than adequate personal and social adjustment in the larger sense of an adjustment which permits a socially extremely useful life and one which is personally deeply satisfying, is not only possible, but probably quite common, with little of the sort of personal relations which psychologists consider essential. Many of the biological and physical scientists are very little concerned with personal relations, and this is not only entirely satisfactory to them, but it cannot be shown always to be a compensatory mechanism (nor are compensatory mechanisms necessarily undesirable).

It can also apparently be satisfactory to others who are closely associated with them. That divorces are so much commoner among the social scientists is of interest in this connexion.

I shall suggest in the next chapter [not included here] that the crux of a psychologist's life lies in a conflict of a particular kind between the intellectual aspects of life and the emotional. If this is so, what more natural than that he should see the struggle to reconcile these elements as a proper activity, and project its successful solution as the goal for Everyman?

6. Conventional education is hostile to creativity. Progressive education is not

It is arguable that current educational practice in England and America stunts children's creative impulses. This conclusion is backed, or seems to be backed, by a number of important facts. MacKinnon (1962b) finds that his creative individuals were often undistinguished academically. This is supported by my own evidence about the degree classes gained at Oxford and Cambridge by groups of distinguished Englishmen: Fellows of the Royal Society, Doctors of Science at Oxford and Cambridge, High Court Judges, Cabinet Ministers. In each of these groups, poor degree classes were quite frequent. At Cambridge, for example, there was no relation between a research student's degree class and his chances, later on, of becoming an F.R.S. or a D.Sc. Fully a third of the future F.R.S.s at Cambridge had gained a second or worse at some time during their university careers; and the proportion amongst future D.Sc.s was over a half. In their final degrees at Oxford or Cambridge, some 54 per cent of future High Court Judges gained seconds, thirds or fourths; and the equivalent figure for future Cabinet Ministers was 66 per cent.[10] MacKinnon also reports that the creative members of his sample were frequently disliked by their teachers; and that they were frequently unhappy. Getzels and Jackson (1962) report similar reactions of teachers to their 'high creatives'. Teachers dislike 'high creatives', even when they are academically successful, and prefer teaching the more docile 'high I.Q.s'.

10. For a more detailed account, see Hudson (1958, 1960, 1961).

That conventional education is uncongenial to independent spirits seems to me incontestable; also, that much of what passes for education in this country and the United States is a waste of everyone's time, pupils and teachers alike. On the other hand, such conclusions are not entailed by the evidence that we now possess. The harsh fact remains that MacKinnon's eminent men are eminent; that men like Darwin and Einstein, who were unhappy or undistinguished at school, nevertheless produced the theories of evolution and relativity, respectively. This datum is open to at least three interpretations. The one drawn by some is that Einstein and Darwin survived through luck (or genius), but that thousands of others (of equal or nearly equal potentialities) are yearly oppressed and extinguished. MacKinnon's eminent are the lucky ones that got away. The second interpretation is that the unhappiness of these great men was a causal factor in making them great. Had they not suffered at school, they would have lead comfortable, mediocre lives like the rest of us. The third interpretation is that their unhappiness was concomitant but not causal: they were unhappy because they were remarkable, but their unhappiness did not affect their creative potentialities one way or the other.

What one makes of these alternatives is largely a matter of taste. My own suspicion is that progressive schools do make most children happier than authoritarian ones; but that they withdraw from children the cutting edge that insecurity, competition and resentment supply. Here the progressive dream comes home to roost. If we adjust children to themselves and each other, we may remove from them the springs of their intellectual and artistic productivity. Happy children simply may not be prepared to make the effort which excellence demands. Whether or not my suspicions about progressive education are justified, it is clear that we cannot use the 'creativity' literature as a stick with which to beat academic education of a more leisurely kind, whether on the lines of certain English public schools or those of the American high school. These may be inept, without 'driving out creativity'. Indeed, they may provide precisely the background of mild conformity and incompetence which reinforces the potentially original child's conviction of his own worth. They provide the ideal background against which to rebel. The conscious nurture of children's creative potentialities may still be a worthwhile operation, but not because it produces more and better brainworkers. It may be worthwhile because, quite simply it makes school a more enjoyable place to be. And this, in its turn, may lead children a little nearer the 'rich emotional life' which is every progressive psychologist's wistful dream.

References

BARRON, F. (1958), 'The psychology of imagination', *Scient. Amer.*, vol. 199, pp. 150–63.

BURT, C. (1962), 'Critical notice: the psychology of creative ability', *Brit. J. educ. Psychol.*, vol. 32, pp. 292–8.

COX, C. M. (1926), *Genetic Studies of Genius, Vol. II. The Early Mental Traits of Three Hundred Geniuses*, Stanford University Press.

ERIKSON, E. H. (1963), *Childhood and Society*, 2nd edn, Norton.

GETZELS, J. W., and JACKSON, P. W. (1962), *Creativity and Intelligence: Explorations with Gifted Students*, Wiley.

GUILFORD, J. P. (1956), 'The structure of intellect', *Psychol. Bull.*, vol. 53, pp. 267–93.

HARMON, L. R. (1958), A follow-up study of A.E.C. fellowship candidates, *National Research Council, Technical Report*, no. 13.

HARMON, L. R. (1959), Validation of fellowship selection instruments against a provisional criterion of scientific accomplishment, *National Research Council, Technical Report*, no. 15.

HUDSON, L. (1958), 'Undergraduate academic record of Fellows of the Royal Society', *Nature*, vol. 182, p. 1326.

HUDSON, L. (1960), 'Degree class and attainment in scientific research', *Brit. J. Psychol.*, vol. 51, pp. 67–73.

HUDSON, L. (1961), Arts/science specialization, unpublished Ph.D. Dissertation, Cambridge University.

JONES, E. (1961), *The Life and Work of Sigmund Freud*, Hogarth Press. (Penguin Books edn, 1964.)

KUHN, T. S. (1962), *The Structure of Scientific Revolutions*, Chicago University Press.

KUHN, T. S. (1963), 'The essential tension: tradition and innovation in scientific research', in C. W. Taylor and F. Barron (eds.), *Scientific Creativity: Its Recognition and Development*, Wiley, pp. 341–54.

MACKINNON, D. W. (1962a), 'The personality correlates of creativity: A study of American architects', *Proceedings of the Fourteenth International Congress on Applied Psychology*, Munksgaard.

MACKINNON, D. W. (1962b), 'The nature and nurture of creative talent', *Amer. Psychol.*, vol. 17, pp. 484–95.

MILLER, G. A. (1964), 'Review of *The Act of Creation* by A. Koestler', *Scient. Amer.*, vol. 211, p. 145.

NEWELL, A., SHAW, J. C., and SIMON, H. A. (1962), 'The process of creative thinking', in H. E. Gruber *et al.* (eds.), *Contemporary Approaches to Creative Thinking*, Atherton Press, pp. 63–119.

PERELMAN, S. J. (1959), *The Most of S. J. Perelman*, Heinemann.

ROE, A. (1951a), 'A psychological study of physical scientists', *Genet. Psychol. Monogr.*, vol. 43, pp. 121–239.

ROE, A. (1951b), A psychological study of eminent biologists, *Psychol. Monogr.*, vol. 64, no. 331.

ROE, A. (1951c), 'A study of imagery in research scientists', *J. Person.*, vol. 19, pp. 459–70.

ROE, A. (1953), 'A psychological study of eminent psychologists and anthropologists and a comparison with biologists and physical scientists', *Psychol. Monogr.*, vol. 67, no. 352.

VERNON, P. E. (1957), *Secondary School Selection*, Methuen.

VERNON, P. E. (1964), 'Creativity and intelligence', *Educ. Res.*, vol. 6, pp. 163–9.

19 M. A. Wallach and N. Kogan

A New Look at the Creativity–Intelligence Distinction

M. A. Wallach and N. Kogan, 'A new look at the creativity–
intelligence distinction', *Journal of Personality*, vol. 33, 1965, pp. 348–69.
Adapted from M. A. Wallach and N. Kogan, *Modes of Thinking in
Young Children: A Study of the Creativity–Intelligence Distinction*,
Holt, Rinehart & Winston, 1965, pp. 409–18.

For several years we have been concerned with two modes of
thinking in young children, which, it turns out, bear directly
upon what has assumed the proportions of a controversy in
recent psychological history. The nature of the controversy
might be put somewhat as follows: is there an aspect of cognitive
functioning which can be appropriately labeled 'creativity' that
stands apart from the traditional concept of general intelligence?
A close appraisal of the quantitative findings available on this
subject led us to a pessimistic answer. We shall pass some of
these findings quickly in review. Our examination of this literature opened up to us, however, the possibility of a valid distinction between creativity and intelligence that had not, in our view,
been sufficiently pursued and developed. The next step, therefore,
was empirical research in terms of this distinction. Finally, if
creativity and intelligence could be validly distinguished, we were
interested in studying the possible psychological correlates that
might distinguish individual differences on these two dimensions
considered jointly. Specifically, we were concerned with correlates in such areas as the child's observed behavior in school and
play settings, his esthetic sensitivities, his categorizing and conceptualizing activities, his test anxiety and defensiveness levels.
We can, of course, give but an overview of this work. For a complete presentation, see Wallach and Kogan (1965).

We began with a simple question: does the relevant psychological literature support the assumption of a unified dimension of
individual differences describing more and less creative cognitive
behavior? To put this question another way, can one demonstrate
the existence of greater and lesser degrees of a cognitive capability that is like intelligence in regard to being a pervasive, broad

dimension, but yet is independent of intelligence, and which can appropriately be labeled 'creativity'? It is clear that to talk of 'creativity' is to imply a referent different from that of the general intelligence concept. If that is not intended, then the creativity label becomes quite superfluous. The typical evidence that we found on this issue led, however, to an opposite conclusion. Let us consider an example.

The volume by Getzels and Jackson (1962), *Creativity and Intelligence*, is perhaps the best known of recent efforts in the field. Five alleged tests of creativity were administered to large samples of students ranging in class from sixth grade through the end of high school. Four of the five creativity tests correlated significantly with I.Q. for the girls, and all five of these tests correlated significantly with I.Q. for the boys. Consider next the relationships among the instruments in the creative battery – that is, the question of whether they define a unitary dimension of individual differences. The Getzels–Jackson results showed that the five creativity tasks are virtually no more strongly correlated among themselves than they are correlated with intelligence. To give some averages, for boys the mean correlation is 0·26 between the creativity battery and I.Q., and is 0·28 among the tasks in the creativity battery; in the case of the girls, the corresponding mean correlations are 0·27 and 0·32. In sum, the creativity measures correlated with intelligence on the order of 0·3, and also correlated with each other on the order of 0·3. There is no evidence, in short, for arguing that the creativity instruments are any more strongly related to one another than they are related to general intelligence. The inevitable conclusion is that little warrant exists here for talking about creativity *and* intelligence as if these terms refer to concepts at the same level of abstraction. The creativity indicators measure nothing in common that is distinct from general intelligence. Inspection of the creativity battery reveals a quite varied range of materials, including measures of the ability to devise mathematical problems, to compose endings for fables, to detect embedded geometric figures, to think up word definitions and to imagine uses for an object.

Comparable examination of other research reports in the literature forced us to the same kind of conclusion. Our survey included the study of findings reported by Barron (1963), Cline, Richards and Abe (1962), Cline, Richards and Needham (1963), Flescher (1963), Guilford and his collaborators (Guilford and Christensen, 1956; Wilson *et al.*, 1954) and Torrance and his co-workers (Torrance, 1960, 1962; Torrance and Gowan, 1963). To give but one more example of the kind of outcome obtained, consider a recent study by Cline, Richards and Needham (1963). With high school students as Ss and seven creativity measures, the average correlation for boys between the creativity indexes and an I.Q. measure is 0·35, while it is 0·21 among the various creativity tests. For girls, the average correlation between the creativity tests and I.Q. is 0·33, while it is 0·24 among the seven creativity measures. Again and again in reviewing the research in this area, the evidence led to the conclusion that the various creativity measures utilized are almost as strongly, equally strongly, or even more strongly related to general intelligence than they are related to each other. The evidence in hand thus seemed not to permit the very type of conceptualization that Getzels and Jackson (1962) and other researchers were proposing: namely, that there exists a pervasive dimension of individual differences, appropriately labeled 'creativity', that is quite distinct from general intelligence. We should note that this same critical point has been made by Thorndike (1963) in a recent article.

Appropriate wielding of Occam's razor at this juncture thus dictated the tough-minded conclusion that little of any generality was being measured here beyond differences in the traditional notion of intelligence. Let us pose two issues, however, that made it seem premature to let the matter go at that. First, a potpourri of abilities was being assessed in the good name of 'creativity'; second, all of the work that we had seen failed to consider the implications of the social psychology of the assessment situation within which measurement of 'creativity' was attempted. Consider each of these points in turn.

If we return to the introspections of highly creative artists and scientists, one major focus emerges. The majority of the available introspective accounts have in common a concern with associative freedom and uniqueness. These accounts consistently stress the ability to give birth to associative content that is abundant and original, yet relevant to the task at hand rather than bizarre. The writer's classical fear of 'drying up' and never being able to produce another word, the composer's worry over not having another piece of music within him, the scientist's concern that he won't be able to think of another experiment to perform – these are but indications of how preoccupied creative individuals can become with the question of associative flow. Introspections about times of creative insight also seem to reflect a kind of task-centered, permissive or playful set on the part of the person doing the associating. Einstein refers to 'associative play' or 'combinatory play'. The person stands aside a bit as associative material is given freedom to reach the surface.

We would propose that the essentials of the creative process may be contained in the two elements just considered: first, the production of associative content that is abundant and that is unique; second, the presence in the associator of a playful, permissive task attitude. Given a task clear enough that bizarre associative products do not readily occur, and given a permissive context within which the person works, two variables should permit us to index individual differences in creativity: the number of associations that the person can generate in response to given tasks and the relative uniqueness of the associations that he produces.

One implication of this view is that productivity and uniqueness of associates should be related variables. Defining uniqueness as a relative infrequency of a given associative response to the task at hand for a sample of Ss, we would then expect stereotyped associates to come earlier and unique associates to come later in a sequence of responses. Such an expectation would also be consistent with recent work by Mednick (e.g. 1962). If unique associates tend to come later in time, then it becomes clear also that an appropriate assessment context will require freedom from the pressure of short time limits, and perhaps freedom from any temporal pressure at all. The postulated need for a permissive, playful attitude also implies the desirability of freedom from time pressure. Such temporal freedom is one aspect of what a permissive situation would involve. Permissiveness further connotes a relative lessening of valuational pressures – that is, a focus upon the task rather than upon the self, a relaxed entertaining of the possible rather than tense insistence upon an answer that must be correct if one is not to lose face. The Taoists, as discussed by Rugg (1963), have called such a relaxed attitude a state of 'letting things happen'. Clearly, we are describing a type of situation in which the individual does not feel that he is being tested, and hence does not feel that what he does will have a bearing upon his self-worth in the eyes of others.

The foregoing analysis of creativity hence suggests a concentration of assessment attempts in the area of associational processes, in contrast to the quite heterogeneous types of tasks that have received the 'creativity' label in studies of the kind touched upon earlier. This theoretical analysis also suggests that the assessment context must be quite different from the kind utilized in the studies that we have reviewed; there should be freedom from time pressure and there should be a playful, game-like context rather than one implying that the person is under test. Interestingly enough, the kind of context present in the case of *all* of the studies on creativity that we reviewed earlier has borne strong connotations that a test or examination is at issue; the creativity procedures invariably have been referred to as 'tests', they have been administered to large groups of students in a classroom, and temporal constraint has been present – either explicitly, through the use of relatively brief time limits, or implicitly, through the use of group administration procedures. In all of this work, there has been the evident assumption that a testing context, with its implication that the respondent is being evaluated in terms of some success–failure criterion, is quite appropriate for studying creativity. The associative approach to creativity that we have taken, however, with its emphasis upon an attitude of playful entertaining of possibilities in a task-centered rather than ego-centered environment, suggests otherwise.

At this point we were ready to begin some experimentation of our own. Following the prescriptions just stated, could one empirically define a dimension of individual differences that concerned the ability to produce many cognitive associates, and many that are unique? Would this dimension possess a substantial degree of generality across differences in types of tasks – for example, verbal *v.* visual kinds of procedural formats? Such a contrast was of special interest since the general intelligence concept is defined with respect to a kind of ability that manifests itself in visual (performance) as well as verbal types of tasks, and we were presuming to assess a characteristic possessing approximately the same level of generality as conventional intelligence. Finally, and most important, would the foregoing dimension of associational ability be independent of individual differences in the traditional area of general intelligence? If research findings could provide affirmative answers to these questions, then, and only then, would one be in a position to talk about a kind of thinking ability appropriately labeled *creativity*, with the evident implication of a characteristic different from general intelligence, but yet a characteristic which also possesses a substantial degree of generality across task variations.

Our work, conducted with 151 children comprising the entire fifth-grade population of a suburban public school system in a middle class region, took great pains to establish a game-like non-evaluational context for the administration of procedures. The *E*s, two young women, were introduced as visitors interested in children's games, and spent two initial weeks with each class gaining rapport with the children. This initial period of familiarization also provided the basis for observations leading to ratings of the children's behavior on various dimensions, to be discussed later. Great effort was expended in communicating to the children that the presence of the *E*s did not concern examinations or tests. The teachers and principals, furthermore, did their utmost to dissociate the *E*s from any concern with intellectual evaluation. Finally, it was our view that the establishment of a game-like context required the *E*s to work individually with each of the 151 children. We sedulously avoided group administration with its academic testing implications.

Five procedures formed the basis for our exploration of creativity in these children. They concerned the generation of five kinds of associates. Two variables were measured in the case of each: uniqueness of associates, and total number of associates. Some of the procedures were verbal, others were visual in nature. One verbal procedure, for example, requested the child to generate possible instances of a verbally specified class concept, such as 'round things', or 'things that move on wheels'. Here and for every other creativity procedure, the child is given as much time on each item as he desires. Number of unique responses to an item is defined as the number of responses given by only one child in the sample of 151 to the item in question. Total number of responses offered to an item is, of course, self-defining. For 'round things', for example, 'life savers' is a unique response, while 'buttons' is not. Another verbal procedure requests the child to think of possible uses for various objects presented orally, such as 'shoe' or 'cork'. 'To trap a mouse in', is a unique use suggested for 'shoe', while 'to throw at a noisy cat' is not. A third verbal procedure asks the child to propose possible similarities between two objects specified in verbal terms. For instance, one pair is 'train and tractor', another is 'milk and meat'. A unique response to 'milk and meat' was 'they are government-inspected', while 'they come from animals' was not unique. The visual procedures, in turn, requested the child to think of possible interpretations or meanings for each of various abstract visual patterns and line forms.

These procedures obviously owe a debt to the Guilford group. They are administered, however, in a carefully constructed game-like context, with each child taken individually and encouraged to spend as much time as he wishes, in a relaxed atmosphere, on every item. These administration arrangements were very different from those employed by the Guilford group. It should be emphasized, furthermore, that the use of a game-like context did not lead to a violation of the task constraints present in the various items of the procedure. Bizarre or inappropriate responses were exceedingly rare.

To assess the traditionally demarcated area of general intelligence, ten indicators were utilized. These included verbal and performance subtests from the Wechsler Intelligence Scale for Children (Wechsler, 1949); the School and College Ability Tests, which provide measures of verbal and quantitative aptitude (Cooperative Test Division, 1957a and b); and the Sequential Tests of Educational Progress, which provide yardsticks of achievement in various academic content areas (Cooperative Test Division, 1957c and d, 1959).

The ten creativity indicators – a uniqueness and a productivity measure for each of five procedures – proved to be highly reliable, in terms of both split-half and item-sum correlations. The reliabilities of the ten intelligence instruments, in turn, are known to be quite high. We now were in a position, therefore, to study the dimensionality of the creativity and intelligence indexes. The findings were as follows. Whether examining results for the sample as a whole, or separately for the seventy boys and the eighty-one girls, the ten creativity measures proved to be highly intercorrelated, the ten intelligence measures proved to be highly intercorrelated, and the correlation *between* the creativity and the intelligence measures proved to be extremely low. To provide an idea of the correlational magnitudes involved, the average correlation among the ten creativity measures is on the order of 0·4; the average correlation among the ten intelligence indicators is on the order of 0·5; and the average correlation between these two sets of measures is about 0·1.

We may conclude, therefore, that a dimension of individual differences has been defined here which, on the one hand, possesses generality and pervasiveness, but which, on the other hand, nevertheless is quite independent of the traditional notion of general intelligence. This new dimension concerns a child's ability to generate unique and plentiful associates, in a generally task-appropriate manner, and in a relatively playful context. It is a considerable surprise that such a dimension should prove to be quite independent of general intelligence, and it seems indeed appropriate to label this dimension 'creativity'. The independence of this dimension from general intelligence seems all the more intriguing for two reasons: first, the creativity procedures almost inevitably call upon verbal facility in some degree, and verbal facility is a very basic element of the general intelligence concept; second, the independence in question is found for elementary school children, and one would expect young children to show less differentiation in modes of cognitive functioning than adults.

In a sense, all that has been described thus far constitutes a prelude. Having isolated a mode of thinking in children that is pervasive, independent of intelligence, and appropriately described as a dimension of individual differences in 'creativity', we now wish to understand its psychological significance. The appropriate research strategy at this point seemed to require consideration of individual differences on the creativity and the intelligence dimensions taken *jointly*. That is, a child's location had to be defined with respect both to general intelligence and to creativity as we have conceived of it. It was necessary, in other words, to compose four groups of children within each sex: those high in both creativity and intelligence, those high in one and low in the other, and those low in both. In order to define these groups, a single creativity index score and a single intelligence index score were obtained for each child. These index scores were the summed standard scores of the ten measures in each respective domain. The distributions of creativity index scores and of intelligence index scores then were dichotomized at their respective medians, within sex, to yield the groups that exemplified the four possible combinations of creativity and intelligence levels. The two sexes, incidentally, were quite similar with regard to the distributions of these index scores. Since all cases were retained, rather than just the extremes, it is evident that the procedure used for composing creativity and intelligence combinations was a conservative one.

Consider now some of the psychological differences that we found to distinguish children who are both creative and intelligent, creative but not intelligent, intelligent but not creative, and neither creative nor intelligent.

To begin with, we turn to the behavior of these several groups of children in the school environment. The two Es made independent ratings of the children along specifically defined behavioral dimensions during an initial two weeks of observation in each class. This work was carried out prior to any further contact with the children, so that the ratings could not be influenced by the performances of the children on the various experimental procedures used in our research. Furthermore, no other possible sources of information about the children were made available to the raters during the observation period. In short, every effort was made to insure that the ratings would be unbiased.

It should also be mentioned that these rating dimensions possess high inter-rater reliability, a very important point that the use of two independent observers permitted us to establish. Without this kind of reliability, investigation of individual differences on these behavioral dimensions would have been fruitless.

The judges rated each child's status on a given dimension in terms of a nine-point scale. For example, one characteristic was defined in terms of the following question: 'To what degree does this child seek attention in unsocialized ways, as evidenced by such behavior as speaking out of turn, continually raising his hand, or making unnecessary noises?' The first, third, fifth, seventh and ninth points on the rating scale for this question were given the verbal labels 'never', 'seldom', 'sometimes', 'usually' and 'always', respectively. Other questions rated in the same manner included: 'To what degree does this child hesitate to express opinions, as evidenced by extreme caution, failure to contribute, or a subdued manner in a speaking situation?' 'To what degree does this child show confidence and assurance in his actions toward his teachers and classmates, as indicated by such behavior as not being upset by criticism, or not being disturbed by rebuffs from classmates?' 'To what degree is this child's companionship sought by his peers?' 'To what degree does this child seek the companionship of his peers?'

The preceding questions were focused upon issues of social behavior. Several questions of an achievement-centered nature also were included. These inquired about such matters as the following: 'How would you rate this child's attention span and degree of concentration for academic school work?' 'How would you rate this child's interest in academic school work, as indicated by such behavior as looking forward to new kinds of academic work, or trying to delve more deeply into such work?' For these questions, the first, third, fifth, seventh and ninth points of the rating scales were labeled 'poor', 'below average', 'average', 'good' and 'superior', respectively.

Let us look in some detail at the results for the girls. Those high in both creativity and intelligence show the least doubt and hesitation of all the groups, show the highest level of self-confidence, and display the least tendency toward depreciation of oneself and one's work. Concerning companionship, these girls are sought out by their peers more eagerly than is any other group, and this high intelligence, high creativity group also seeks the companionship of others more actively than does any other group. There is reciprocity in social relationships for the members of this group. With regard to achievement, this group shows the highest levels of attention span, concentration, and interest in academic work. In all of these respects, the high–high group obviously is reflecting highly desirable modes of conduct in both the social and the achievement spheres. Interestingly enough, however, this group also is high in regard to disruptive, attention-seeking behavior. The high–high children may well be brimming over with eagerness to propose novel, divergent possibilities in the classroom, in the face of boredom with the customary classroom routines. Against the context of classroom programs that emphasize equal participation by class members and academic values that are likely to center around the traditional intelligence dimension, the cognitive behavior reflected in high creativity levels in the case of these girls may well possess a nuisance value and exert a rather disruptive effect in the classroom situation.

Consider next the group high in creativity but low in intelligence. In many respects it turns out that this group is at the greatest disadvantage of all in the classroom – and, indeed, under more of a disadvantage than the group which is low in both creativity and intelligence. Those of high creativity but low intelligence are the most cautious and hesitant of all the groups, the least confident and least self-assured, the least sought after by their peers as companions, and in addition are quite avoidant themselves of the companionship of others. There is a mutuality of social avoidance in the case of these girls. In the academic sphere, they are the most deprecatory of their own work and the least able to concentrate and maintain attention. In terms of the ratings for disruptive attention-seeking, however, these girls are high, and in this one respect similar to the high creativity, high intelligence group. Most likely, however, the attention-seeking of these two groups is quite different in quality, given the highly different contexts of other behaviors in the two cases. While the disruptive behaviors of the high–high group suggest enthusiasm and overeagerness, those of the high creative, low intelligence group suggest an incoherent protest against their plight.

It affords an interesting comparison to turn next to the group low in both intelligence and creativity. These girls actually seem to be better off than their high creativity, low intelligence peers. The low–low group possesses greater confidence and assurance, is less hesitant and subdued, and is considerably more outgoing toward peers in social relationships than is the high creative, low intelligence group. The low–low group members appear to compensate for their poor academic performances by activity in the social sphere, while the high creative, low intelligence individuals, possessing seemingly more delicate sensitivities, are more likely to cope with academic failure by social withdrawal and a retreat within themselves.

Finally, we turn to the group high in intelligence but low in creativity. As in the case of the high–high group, these girls show confidence and assurance. In terms of companionship patterns, however, an intriguing difference emerges. While sought quite strongly as a companion by others, the girl in this group tends not to seek companionship herself. She also is least likely to seek attention in disruptive ways and is reasonably hesitant about expressing opinions. Attention span and concentration for academic matters, in turn, are quite high. The impression that emerges, then, is of a girl who is strongly oriented toward academic achievement, is somewhat cool and aloof in her social behavior but liked by others anyway, and is unwilling to take the chance of overextending or overcommitting herself; there is a holding back, a basic reserve.

These results make it clear that one needs to know whether creativity in a child is present in the context of high or low intelligence, and one needs to know whether intelligence in a child is present in conjunction with high or low creativity. It is necessary to consider a child's joint standing on both dimensions. One must seriously question, therefore, the Getzels and Jackson (1962) procedure of defining a 'high creative' group as children who are high in creativity *but* low in intelligence, and defining a 'high intelligent' group as children who are high in intelligence *but* low in creativity. If one wishes to establish generalizations about the nature of creativity and of intelligence as distinct characteristics, one cannot afford to ignore those children who are high in both and who are low in both.

Let us consider now some evidence in a different area – that of conceptualizing activities. This evidence will cast light on differences among the groups of boys. In one of our procedures, the child was asked to group pictures of everyday physical objects, and was requested to give the reason for his grouping in each case. Among the fifty objects pictured were, for example, a rake, a screwdriver, a telephone, a lamp-post, a candle. The groupings were to be carried out in terms of putting together things that seem to belong together. When this phase was completed, reasons for grouping were obtained. These reasons later were content-analysed – blindly, of course, with respect to the identities of the children – and the reliability of the content analysis system was evaluated by having all materials scored by two independent judges. Reliability was found to be quite high. Consider briefly now one of the content-analysis distinctions employed.

We were interested in contrasting relational or thematic reasons for grouping with reasons based upon abstracted similarities among the objects. In the latter type of reason, every object in the group is an independent instance of the label applied, whether the labels refer to shared physical properties or to shared conceptual properties. An example of the physical-descriptive type of category would be the label, 'hard objects', for a group consisting of a lamppost, a door and a hammer. An example of the conceptual-inferential type of category would be the label, 'for eating', in the case of a group containing a fork, a spoon, a cup and a glass. By a relational or thematic type of reason, on the other hand, we refer to a label deriving from the relationship among the objects in the group; no single object is an independent instance of the concept, but rather all of the objects in the grouping are required in order to define it. An example of a thematic category is the label, 'getting ready to go out', for a group consisting of a comb, a lipstick, a watch, a pocketbook and a door.

The distinctions just made derive from work carried out by Kagan, Moss and Sigel (1960, 1963), with certain modifications necessitated by the nature of the stimuli. It has typically been assumed by these investigators as well as by others that responding on a relational or thematic basis represents an intellectually inferior manifestation. This may well be true when the stimuli to be grouped are few in number and their thematic characteristics highly salient, as has been the case in the studies just cited. Thematizing under such circumstances may represent a passive global approach to the materials provided. In the procedure that we employed, however, a large number of stimuli – fifty in all – were present, and their nature as well as the instructional context were such as to reduce markedly the *Eindringlichkeit* or prominence of thematic relationships. The child was encouraged to group in terms of abstractions, since the instructions implied to him that similarity be used as the basis for sorting. In addition, the objects were commonplace physical things and there were many of them. Under these circumstances, it might well be the case that relational or thematic grouping would constitute a free-wheeling, unconventional type of response to the given task, in contrast to the more customary practice of sorting the objects in terms of common elements, whether such elements be physical or conceptual. Constraints arising from the nature of the stimuli would be considerably stronger in the case of groupings based upon shared physical or conceptual properties. Groupings based on relationships or themas, on the other hand, would permit greater free play for the evolving of unique combinations of stimuli. With these considerations in mind, let us turn to some results.

The findings for males point to a particularly clear phenomenon. The group of high intelligence but low creativity stands out as avoiding the use of thematic or relational bases for grouping. Rather, they concentrate on conceptual common elements. For whatever reasons – and the reasons may differ in the case of different groups – the other three groups are more willing to indulge in thematic forms of conceptualizing. It is the high intelligence, low creativity group that shows a disproportionate avoidance of thematizing. Such a finding reinforces the hypothesis that thematic responding may, under the conditions of the present procedure, represent a more playful, imaginative approach to the grouping task than does strict common-element sorting.

To suggest that the low incidence of thematizing by the high intelligence, low creativity group is evidence for an avoidance reaction, however, is to imply a further distinction. In principle, a low incidence could reflect either an inability to thematize or an avoidance of it. In another experimental procedure, however, we assessed the ability of the children to integrate a set of words into a unified theme in story telling: that is, in this new task, thematizing was required of the child. Under such conditions, the high intelligence, low creativity group thematizes as well as the group high in both creativity and intelligence. It is when the option not to thematize is available that thematizing drops out of the behavior of the high intelligent, low creative group. Such evidence, then, suggests that we are dealing with a disinclination to thematize on the part of this group, not an inability to thematize.

It has typically been proposed in work on cognitive development (e.g. Bruner and Olver, 1963) that the most mature cognitive functioning involves inferential abstraction – the kind of organizing that would be reflected in terms of sorting objects on the basis of shared conceptual properties. Thematizing has been considered a developmentally primitive response. Our findings suggest, however, that a more critical consideration may be the relative balance between conceptual-inferential and thematizing tendencies. Consider the results for the various groups of boys on the sorting task in somewhat more detail. For both of the high creativity groups, the relative incidence of thematizing *and* inferential-conceptual grouping is fairly high. For the high intelligence, low creativity group, the relative incidence of thematizing is quite low, while the relative incidence of inferential-conceptual sorting is quite high. Finally, for the low intelligence, low creativity group, the relationship is reversed; the incidence of thematizing is high, while the incidence of inferential-conceptual sorting is relatively low.

In sum, the creative boys seem able to switch rather flexibly between thematizing and inferential-conceptual bases for grouping; the high intelligence, low creativity boys seem rather inflexibly locked in inferential-conceptual categorizing and strongly avoidant of thematic-relational categorizing; finally, the low intelligence, low creativity boys tend to be locked within thematic modes of responding and relatively incapable of inferential-conceptual behavior. Parenthetically, it might be well to offer the reminder that the incidences of thematic and inferential-conceptual groupings both can be high since there also exists the third scoring category of grouping in terms of common physical elements.

When we consider some of our data concerning sensitivity to

the expressive potential of visual materials, a result similar to the thematizing findings is obtained for the high intelligence, low creativity group of girls. With line drawings of stick figures in various postures as stimuli, various emotional states were proposed to the child as possibilities for one or another figure, and the child indicated a willingness or disinclination to entertain each possibility. Let us focus our attention upon two kinds of affective labels for each stick figure: a label constituting a highly likely, conventional suggestion and a label representing a quite unlikely, unconventional possibility. Unconventional and likely emotional attributions for the various stick figures were defined with reference to the consensus of adult judges. Each of some twenty-four stick figures was offered to the child with one affective label upon each presentation. A different type of label would be proposed each time a given figure was presented, and a given figure was repeated only after all the others had been shown. More inappropriate and more appropriate kinds of labels for the various figures would be offered on a random schedule. Note that a choice is never forced between these two classes of emotional attributions. Each presentation involves one stick figure and one label, with the child requested to accept or reject the label as a descriptive possibility. The child thus is free to accept appropriate and unconventional emotional attributions, to reject both kinds, or to accept one kind and reject the other.

The main results with this procedure for the girls were as follows. Although the four groups did not differ in regard to their acceptance of appropriate or likely affective attributions for the stick figures, they differed in a particular way regarding acceptance of the unconventional attributions – the group high in intelligence but low in creativity exhibited a conspicuously low level of such acceptance. Although the rate of acceptance of such attributions by the other three groups was generally quite low (about 5 per cent), the high intelligence, low creativity group accepted virtually none at all. The comparability among the groups regarding acceptance of appropriate attributions acts as a control, indicating that the differential acceptance behavior just described relates to the entertainment of unconventional attributions in particular, rather than simply to the acceptance of any kind of affective labels. Furthermore, there is no relationship between degree of acceptance of unconventional and of appropriate attributions. It is safe to conclude, therefore, that an acquiescence or 'yea-saying' response set cannot account for the differential acceptance of unconventional attributions.

The implications of the present findings appear to be quite similar to the thematizing results considered before in the case of the boys. In both cases, the high intelligence, low creativity group is intolerant of unlikely, unconventional types of hypothesizing about the world. This particular group appears conspicuously loath to 'stick its neck out', as it were, and try something that is far out, unconventional, and hence possibly 'wrong'. It is of particular interest that the high intelligence, low creativity group of girls avoids entertaining the possibility of unconventional emotional attributions under the present experiment's conditions. Recall that the entertainment of such possibilities has no effect upon the availability for acceptance of the likely and highly appropriate possibilities; it is not an 'either–or' situation. The high intelligence, low creativity girls seem to be so attuned to error that even where appropriate responses are not sacrificed, they refuse to deviate from a critical standard of 'correctness'.

Consider next some of the other findings in the domain of expressive sensitivity. Included in this domain were tasks requiring free descriptions of stimuli with implicit emotive significance. We content-analysed these free descriptions in order to determine the extent to which a child would confine his descriptions to comments upon the physical and geometric characteristics of the various stimuli, as contrasted with the extent to which he would 'go beyond' such physical categories and discuss the affective or expressive connotations of such materials. In the case of both sexes, the ability to range beyond the physical and into the realm of affective content tended to be maximal in the group high in both creativity and intelligence. That creativity and intelligence both could contribute to such physiognomic sensitivity – responsiveness to 'inner' feeling states on the basis of perceivable externals – suggested that two processes could be jointly involved in the display of this sensitivity. On the one hand, the capacity to make inferential translations from one mode of experience to another seems to be reflective of the general intelligence concept; on the other hand, the associational freedom implied by the creativity concept evidently enhances the range of experience available for making inferential linkages.

Let us turn now to some evidence on how the children describe themselves with respect to general anxiety symptoms and to those symptoms experienced under the stress of tests or examinations. Consider the findings for the boys. Standard materials for assessing manifest anxiety and test anxiety were employed, deriving from the work of Sarason *et al.* (1960). The results are suggestive of a Yerkes–Dodson function. They are of the same nature for both general manifest anxiety and test anxiety. The level of anxiety is lowest for the group that is high in intelligence but low in creativity. Anxiety level is middling for the two groups that are high in creativity, regardless of intelligence level. Finally, anxiety level is highest for the group that is low in intelligence and low in creativity. The allusion to the Yerkes–Dodson law is made since creativity is found to be maximal in the presence of an intermediate level of anxiety. If anxiety is either too low or too high, then creativity is reduced. Just as interesting, however, are the particular conditions under which anxiety level is lowest. It is the group high in intelligence but low in creativity who, by self-report, are least anxious. At the other end of the dimension, with the highest anxiety scores, stands the group low in both intelligence and creativity.

What are the implications of these findings? First of all, they force us to question whether creativity should be conceptually associated with a state of maximal freedom from anxiety symptoms. It is not those children who are lowest in anxiety level, but those who report a moderate degree of anxiety, whom we find to be most creative in their thinking processes. Traditional conceptions of mental health place considerable emphasis upon anxiety as a debilitator of cognitive performance and as a signal of inappropriate or ineffective adjustment. This no doubt is true when anxiety reaches quite high levels. We need only remember that the strongest degree of anxiety is found in the most cognitively deprived group of children – those who are low both in general intelligence and creativity. However, it may also be the case that a modicum of anxiety is reflecting more the presence of sensitivity to internal states than the presence of disturbance. This should not be construed, of course, as acceptance of the old saw that neuroticism breeds creativity. However, the data in hand do suggest that it is equally unrealistic to assume that the most creative children are the happiest children. There may well be elements of obsessiveness present in the kind of associative freedom that leads to high creativity status. A playful contemplation of the possible, but also an obsessive, task-centered reluctance to put a problem aside may be involved in the production of many associates and of a large number of unique associates. Creativity need not be all sweetness and light, therefore, but may well involve a tolerance for and understanding of sadness and pain. To think otherwise is to fall prey to the rather widespread American stereotype that suffering is always a bad thing and is to be avoided at all costs.

One possible cost of the avoidance of suffering is evident in the group whose levels of general anxiety and of test anxiety are lowest – the group high in intelligence but low in creativity. This result may well stem from the fact that the group in question is the most closely attuned to the demands of the classroom environment. In that environment, traditionally defined intelligence and its manifestations in the form of high academic achievement most likely are heavily rewarded, while creativity may well be viewed as more of a disruption than a boon. The mode of operation of the high intelligence, low creativity child, therefore, may be such as to minimize the sources of possible conflict between himself and the school environment and to maximize the sources of reward from that environment. It is not surprising that such a close fit between individual and social context would be reflected in a minimal level of anxiety.

From the kinds of results that have been passed in review, pictures begin to emerge concerning the psychological nature of the children in the four cognitive groupings: high creativity, high intelligence; high creativity, low intelligence; low creativity, high intelligence; and low creativity, low intelligence. In addition to our quantitative studies, clinical accounts describing various children in the sample also have been prepared, and these clinical materials have tended to reinforce the conclusions derived from the experimental work. The case studies can be summarized in terms of the generalizations presented below. These will also serve to underline the major points of congruence between the clinical and the experimental sources of information concerning the four creativity and intelligence groupings.

High creativity, high intelligence: These children can exercise within themselves both control and freedom, both adult-like and child-like kinds of behavior.

High creativity, low intelligence: These children are in angry conflict with themselves and with their school environment, and are beset by feelings of unworthiness and inadequacy. In a stress-free context, however, they can blossom forth cognitively.

Low creativity, high intelligence: These children can be described as 'addicted' to school achievement. Academic failure would be perceived by them as catastrophic, so that they must continually strive for academic excellence in order to avoid the possibility of pain.

Low creativity, low intelligence: Basically bewildered, these children engage in various defensive maneuvers ranging from useful adaptations such as intensive social activity to regression such as passivity or psychosomatic symptoms.

In conclusion, this presentation has traced in outline form the history of our research on two modes of thinking in young children; modes which constitute quite different, but yet quite pervasive, dimensions of individual differences. Our work progressed from the definition and operationalization of the cognitive types in question to an investigation of their correlates in such areas as observable social and achievement-relevant behaviors, ways of forming concepts, physiognomic sensitivities, and self-described levels of general anxiety and test anxiety. From the findings obtained, it seems fair to conclude that the present definition of creativity denotes a mode of cognitive functioning that matters a great deal in the life of the child. Most critical of all for advancing our understanding is a consideration of the child's *joint* status with regard to the conventional concept of general intelligence and creativity as here defined.

References

BARRON, F. (1963), *Creativity and Psychological Health*, Van Nostrand.

BRUNER, J. S., and OLVER, R. R. (1963), 'Development of equivalence transformations in children', in J. C. Wright and J. Kagan (eds.), Basic cognitive processes in children, *Monogr. Soc. Res. Child Devel.*, vol. 28, no. 2 (serial no. 86), pp. 125–41.

CLINE, V. B., RICHARDS, J. M., JR, and ABE, C. (1962), 'The validity of a battery of creativity tests in a high school sample', *Educ. psychol. Measmt*, vol. 22, pp. 781–4.

CLINE, V. B., RICHARDS, J. M., JR, and NEEDHAM, W. E. (1963), 'Creativity test and achievement in high school science', *J. appl. Psychol.*, vol. 47, pp. 184–9.

COOPERATIVE TEST DIVISION (1957a), *Cooperative School and College Ability Tests: Technical Report*, Educational Testing Service.

COOPERATIVE TEST DIVISION (1957b), *SCAT: Directions for Administering and Scoring*, Educational Testing Service.

COOPERATIVE TEST DIVISION (1957c), *Cooperative Sequential Tests of Educational Progress: Technical Report*, Educational Testing Service.

COOPERATIVE TEST DIVISION (1957d), *STEP: Directions for Administering and Scoring*, Educational Testing Service.

COOPERATIVE TEST DIVISION (1959), *Cooperative Sequential Tests of Educational Progress: Teacher's Guide*, Educational Testing Service.

FLESCHER, I. (1963), 'Anxiety and achievement of intellectually gifted and creatively gifted children', *J. Psychol.*, vol. 56, pp. 251–68.

GETZELS, J. W., and JACKSON, P. W. (1962), *Creativity and Intelligence*, Wiley.

GUILFORD, J. P., and CHRISTENSEN, P. R. (1956), A factor-analytic study of verbal fluency, *Report of the Psychological Laboratory, University of Southern California*, no. 17.

KAGAN, J., MOSS, H. A., and SIGEL, I. E. (1960), 'Conceptual style and the use of affect labels', *Merrill–Palmer Quart.*, vol. 6, pp. 261–78.

KAGAN, J., MOSS, H. A., and SIGEL, I. E. (1963), 'Psychological significance of styles of conceptualization', in J. C. Wright and J. Kagan (eds.), Basic cognitive processes in children, *Monogr. Soc. Res. Child Devel.*, vol. 28, no. 2 (serial no. 86), pp. 73–112.

MEDNICK, S. A. (1962), 'The associative basis of the creative process', *Psychol. Rev.*, vol. 69, pp. 220–32.

RUGG, H. (1963), *Imagination*, Harper & Row.

SARASON, S. B., DAVIDSON, K. S., LIGHTHALL, F. F., WAITE, R. R. and RUEBUSH, B. K. (1960), *Anxiety in Elementary School Children*, Wiley.

THORNDIKE, R. L. (1963), 'Some methodological issues in the study of creativity', in *Proceedings of the 1962 Invitational Conference on Testing Problems*, Educational Testing Service, pp. 40–54.

Psychometric Approaches

TORRANCE, E. P. (1960), *Educational Achievement of the Highly Intelligent and the Highly Creative: Eight Partial Republications of the Getzels-Jackson Study*, Bureau of Educational Research, University of Minnesota.

TORRANCE, E. P. (1962), *Guiding Creative Talent*, Prentice-Hall.

TORRANCE, E. P., and GOWAN, J. C. (1963), *The Reliability of the Minnesota Tests of Creative Thinking*, Bureau of Educational Research, University of Minnesota.

WALLACH, M. A., and KOGAN, N. (1965), *Modes of Thinking in Young Children: a Study of the Creativity–Intelligence Distinction*, Holt, Rinehart & Winston.

WECHSLER, D. (1949), *Intelligence Scale for Children: Manual*, Psychological Corporation.

WILSON, R. C., GUILFORD, J. P., CHRISTENSEN, P. R., and LEWIS, D. J. (1954), 'A factor-analytic study of creative-thinking abilities', *Psychometrika*, vol. 19, pp. 297–311.

20 R. J. Shapiro

The Criterion Problem

Excerpt from R. J. Shapiro, 'Creative research scientists', *Psychologia Africana, Monograph Supplement*, no. 4, 1968, pp. 37–45.

The problem of the criterion, in essence, is simply the problem of how to identify the creative person or how to identify the creative worth of the products of an individual. This represents the most challenging aspect of all research into creativity. Without establishing objective criteria, all endeavours at devising predictors, investigating personality and cognitive characteristics, and venturing hypotheses about the creative process, are of questionable value.

It is no exaggeration to say, in the words of Taylor and Holland (1964, p. 31), that 'there is no more crucial problem in creativity than the criterion problem'.

One of the disheartening conclusions emerging from approximately fifteen years of intensive research is that little progress has been made on achieving acceptable criteria of creativity. As Taylor (1964, p. 9) puts it:

And yet the problem of the criteria of creativity – perhaps the most crucial problem in this field – has been studied less than any other aspect of our total problem. The criterion problem concerns the evaluation of the degree of creativeness of a product or a performance; it is quite separate from the prediction problem, in which the creative potential of people is estimated – for example, by means of test scores – and in which predictions about future creative performances are made, based upon the 'creative potential' estimate for each person. . . . The authors of this book agree that the criterion problem demands the highest priority and that the most serious consideration for research support should be given to any proposals for worthwhile work on criteria.

Although few workers have included objective external criteria in their research, most creativity studies are based on an assumption of some degree of validity. Some investigators, for example, assume that their subjects are creative purely on the strength of reputation. Thus, Lehman (1958) analysed the age level at which creative chemists contributed their greatest work. For measures of creativeness he used a criterion based on the number of different histories of chemistry which cited each chemist's work. Another procedure has been to accept the judgements of professionally qualified experts as a criterion of creative ability. Anne Roe (1951) has utilized this method in selecting eminent scientists as subjects for investigations into the relationship between life history, intellectual functions, personality characteristics, and the pursuit of a particular science as a profession. Finally, a general consensus of opinion sometimes serves as a criterion of eminence. Freud's publications on Leonardo da Vinci (1910) and Dostoevsky (1928) are studies of two individuals universally acclaimed as creative geniuses.

Most research, particularly that of recent years, has not concerned itself with famous or eminent persons, first, because of their comparative rarity and secondly, because of the current emphasis on developing predictive tests on large samples. Consequently, different techniques have had to be evolved for identifying subjects as creative or otherwise.

Ultimate and Concurrent Criteria

The main validation problem, facing the researcher, is related to the distinction between ultimate and concurrent criteria. An ultimate criterion of creative performance must obviously base itself on the total output of a scientist, but an individual's total productivity can only be evaluated retrospectively, either from the time of his death, or at least from the time when he has completed his life work.

A feasible means of establishing ultimate criteria is to test large samples containing subjects of apparent creative ability, and then to pursue long-term, follow-up studies (longitudinal validity) in the manner of Terman's work. A longitudinal validation study would obviously prove extremely valuable in providing definite and accurate assessments of predictive techniques, as well as furnishing conclusive evidence for many factors hypothesized to relate to creativity.

Unfortunately an ultimate criterion is an ideal, rather than a practical goal. The tremendous time lag and great expense necessary renders it impractical. This explains why all validation attempts have thus far been confined to the use of intermediate criteria.

Harmon (1963, p. 44) talks of working 'backwards from an "ultimate criterion" of an individual's total life production of scientific creations to earlier substitute criteria which might come soon enough in the person's life to serve as a practical means for validation of predictors'. He quite correctly cautions though, that as we regress from the ultimate criterion to earlier correlates, we move over gradually from criterion-type measures to predictor-type measures. Such measures, he concludes, cannot strictly be regarded as either criterion or predictors, but only as guiding landmarks.

Bearing these reservations in mind, we must look to measures of concurrent validity for assessing the accuracy of predictors of scientific creativity.

Concurrent validation methods fall into one of three classes:

1. The first type, represented by the work of Guilford, can be thought of as a type of content validity. Guilford has assumed that the factorial study of his tests is in itself a kind of validation (construct validity), and he has not yet attempted a correlation of the factor measures with practical outside criteria.

2. A second form of concurrent validity is to be found in those studies in which aptitude tests (such as those of Guilford) are used to dichotomize a sample into 'high' and 'low' creative sub-groups, for the purpose of comparing these extremes on other variables such as personality characteristics, etc. If significant differences are found, then the aptitude tests are assumed to have a degree of validity. The great majority of studies fall into this category.

In the author's opinion, both of these assumptions are somewhat shaky. As reported earlier, a number of investigators have demonstrated the failure of most available predictors (including Guilford's tests) when validated against external criteria.

The practice of assuming validity on the evidence of significant differences between subjects distinguished on the basis of test scores, leaves two questions unanswered. In the first place, the predictive instruments may, in fact, yield measures on variables not directly related, or perhaps supplementary, to creativity. Consequently the subjects might still be distinguished on several measures, but for the wrong reason. Secondly, and more likely, the tests may, in fact, measure creativity factors, but without establishing correlations with on-the-job criteria, one cannot say to what extent such creativity factors play a role in actual performance.

3. The third, and most satisfactory, method for establishing concurrent validity is to apply a battery of predictors and to correlate the resulting scores with external criteria of creativity.

Criterion Measurement

Basically, only two variables can be measured for criterion purposes: products and persons.

Products

The analysis of a scientist's creative products, in terms of quantity and quality, would seem to offer the best means of validating predictors. As noted earlier, such a method is best suited to the employment of ultimate criteria, but product evaluations are also utilized in intermediate criteria of performance.

Even as a basis for an ultimate criterion, the quantification of a scientist's products presents some difficulties. First, one must face the fact that a variety of products are possible, and it is no easy matter to determine their relative importance. Examples of scientific products include: patents, patent disclosures, journal publications, technical books, unpublished research reports, unprinted oral presentations, ideas, suggestions, technical inventions and new methods.

The most straightforward procedure is simply to add up the number of products for any scientist, and to use this summation as a criterion score. McPherson (1963) warns of the flaws in such a method. As an illustrative example, consider the problems pertaining to the use of number of patents as a criterion of research performance: some products have creative worth, but are not patentable; quality differs from patent to patent; it is easier to obtain patents in a new field, but difficult in a well-worked field; a scientist may not bother to patent his products.

Ideally, a qualitative evaluation of every product in a scientist's total output would yield the most accurate ultimate criterion. Again there are obstacles, the most obvious being that such an evaluation is a matter of human judgement and therefore liable to subjective bias. Despite this limitation, however, a careful assessment of the creative quality of products would probably produce the best possible ultimate criterion. McPherson (1963) recommends an analytical scheme for guiding judges in assessing products. He has adopted it from an existing patent law, designed to determine the 'inventivlevel' of patent applications.

The term 'inventivlevel' refers to a norm of creative quality used in deciding whether to accept or reject a patent application. Certain characteristics are considered in determining inventivlevel and these, McPherson believes, could be profitably used in assessing the creativeness of products for criteria purposes. The relevant characteristics are:

1. The realization of the product demanded intellectual activity which can best be defined as 'creative strength'.

2. Usefulness is the second essential characteristic of inventivlevel. A new product must be useful – it must represent a beneficial technological advance.

3. The invention must be new, in terms of overcoming special difficulties. The human response to an invention, so characterized, is typically one of surprise.

This characteristic of McPherson reminds the author of Bruner's definition of creativity (Bruner, 1962, p. 3): 'An act that produces effective surprise – this I shall take as the hallmark of a creative enterprise.' The effective surprise is not produced because a product is rare or bizarre, but because it has a quality of obviousness which results in a shock of recognition.

4. It is considered relevant that the inventor did an appreciable amount of experimenting before achieving his novel invention.

5. Inventivlevel is deemed to be present where a product is successfully achieved in a field characterized by a history of failure.

6. Credit is given if evidence indicates that other individuals in the same branch of activity were previously sceptical of the likelihood of success for a new development such as that particular invention.

7. There should have been a previously unfulfilled desire, now fulfilled by virtue of the birth of the new product.

Brogden and Sprecher (1964) propose several important steps that should be taken in research concerning scientific products:

1. The relation between amount of creative productivity and level of creativity should be investigated.

2. The relation between the diversity of an individual's products and the level of his creativity, should be investigated.

3. Scales for evaluating the level of creativity of products should be developed. One could base such a scale on a definition like Ghiselin's (1963, p. 42): 'Creative action ... alters the universe of meaning itself, by introducing into it some new element of meaning or some new order of significance, or more commonly both.'

4. As a by-product of step 3, abbreviated procedures for evaluating products should be worked out.

5. The scales developed should be validated against ratings of individuals who vary in their judged creativeness.

6. Official records, normally used for product evaluation, should be investigated to determine their adequacy, and when, where, and why they are in error.

Brogden and Sprecher (1964) also believe it important to distinguish between direct products and supplementary products. The former refers to products created as an end result of a definite research programme centred on a specific operational problem. Supplementary products are incidental discoveries, made by chance when one is not looking for them. They are supplementary in that they do not relate to the immediate problem, but may have use at a later date or in some other branch of research. The authors conclude that for criterion purposes, supplementary products having no relation to the immediate research goal, should 'be judged to be of very little value' (p. 164).

The present writer does not agree with this last view. Many of the greatest discoveries have come from scientists who, while working on a specific project, observed apparently unrelated phenomena and deviated to follow these to fruitful conclusions. Should such 'accidental' discoveries be regarded as relatively unimportant? Paradoxically, it may well be that only the exceptionally creative scientist would perceive implications in what others reject as inconsequential phenomena.

Persons

In view of the difficulties in assessing products, many criteria relate to persons instead. One approach, discussed earlier, is to assume creativity for subjects acknowledged as eminent producers.

Commonly, person evaluations are gained from supervisors, peers or from self reports, and the judgement usually refers to such variables as personality traits, on-the-job performance, work habits, etc.

At the outset there are two problems to consider which affect ratings by others. First, there is the obvious risk of personal bias distorting the ratings. Bloom (1963) suggests that descriptive rating questionnaires, based on findings from previous studies, should be used in order to minimize bias on the part of the raters. A second problem was suggested to the author by an investigation by Taylor, Smith and Ghiselin (1963), who found that scores obtained from different sources (immediate supervisors, laboratory chiefs, peer ratings, subjective scoring, official records) bore little relationship to each other. This means that some external criteria may be more accurate than others, or that different areas of information are contributed by different sources. Whatever the reason, it follows that criterion information should be obtained from more than one contribution, and that one should exercise caution in combining diverse criteria.

In a number of cases, ratings by others have proved valid as criteria. Buel's (1960) work is a good example. Laboratory supervisors were asked to anonymously describe their most and least creative research subordinates. No definitions of creativity were introduced, so that the descriptions were spontaneous and fully reflected the views of the supervisors. One hundred and forty-three statements (derived from the descriptions) served as microdefinitions of creativity, and were used as descriptive check-list items for rating personnel in a wide variety of research activities. The ratings were found to correlate positively with a number of other commonly used criteria.

Taylor and Holland (1964) mention two studies in which supervisory ratings correlated significantly with scores on various predictive measures, and one study in which peer nominations and rankings proved valid as criteria.

Donald Taylor (1963) made use of the Thurstone procedure of constructing attitude scales for devising supervisory check-list rating scales. A brief description of his method is worth reporting, since it influenced some of the criterion methods employed in the present investigation.

Taylor collected 206 statements relating to creativity and originality from a variety of authoritative sources. Forty-four judges independently sorted the statements into seven groups, according to a seven-point scale of creativity (from very low to very high). Frequency distributions were calculated for each statement, representing the piles into which it was sorted by the judges. The median of each distribution was taken as the scale value for each statement. Seventy-nine statements showing the least dispersion (least disagreement between judges) were finally selected, and from these, two sets of twenty-four statements were chosen in such a way as to cover the seven-point scale in as nearly equal steps as possible. These two sets provided equivalent forms of a check-list scale for rating creativity.

Supervisors rated a number of research scientists by simply checking every statement on the check-list that applied to or described each scientist. Significant correlations were obtained between these ratings and a number of tests of creative thinking.

One weakness in the study, which Taylor admits, is that he used college undergraduates as the judges who initially sorted the statements. It is likely that senior scientists would have been more accurate in assessing the creativity level of each statement.

The critical-incident technique, originated by Flanagan (1949), offers promise for constructing effective rating procedures.

'The critical-incident technique consists essentially in the collection of reports of behaviors which were critical in the sense that they made the difference between success and failure in the observed work situations. These critical incidents must represent actual observations of on-the-job behavior' (Flanagan, 1952, p. 378).

The first application of these methods was in an investigation of research personnel (Flanagan, 1949). Approximately 500 scientists were interviewed and provided a total of 3300 critical behaviours, i.e. actions, observed in others, which led to the solution of a particular research problem and, conversely, actions which hindered progress on that problem. The critical incidents (good and bad) are tabulated under a set of descriptive categories for future rating purposes.

The critical-incident method is comprehensive and thorough, and it might prove extremely sound as a technique for establishing objective creativity criteria. The main drawback is a practical one. A great deal of time must be expended by senior research personnel in constantly observing and reporting the activities of other personnel, so that accurate checks can be made on the numerous critical incidents as they occur from day to day.

Flanagan (1949) and Stoltz (1957) have indicated the importance of work habits in creative productivity, and Sprecher (1959, 1963, 1964) formulated a criterion based largely on work habits. In the first study (1959), Sprecher asked engineers to explain why men they had ranked highest in creativity differed from those ranked lowest. A content analysis confirmed the frequent finding that novelty of ideas is important, but it also revealed that work-habit characteristics are regarded as important factors of creativity. In his second study (1963) Sprecher proposed the actual rating form and scoring procedure which resulted from his investigations.

Jones (1964) asked managers to rate eighty-eight industrial scientists and technologists on each of twelve descriptors (e.g. analytical mindedness, communicativeness, idea mindedness, level of energy, liking for problems). The procedure used in rating and weighting these descriptors was taken from Sprecher, and Jones achieved significant positive correlations between this criterion and several predictors.

The author is impressed by Sprecher's emphasis on work habits and his suggestions for weighting them to provide criterion ratings. In the present study use is made of a work-habit inventory, the construction of which was influenced by Sprecher's work.

There is a good deal of evidence to suggest that creative individuals differ significantly from non-creative individuals on certain personality traits. It therefore appears somewhat surprising that, as Taylor and Holland (1964) point out, personality inventories have not proved successful as predictive instruments.

Van Zelst and Kerr (1954) remark on the fact that for many years there has been a preoccupation with external assessments of personality, but that these rarely predict criteria such as job success. They therefore advocate the use of self ratings rather than external assessments, basing their view on the assumption that the individual himself is best informed about his own personality. As an experiment they asked 514 scientists to rate themselves on a number of personality traits thought to relate to creativity. These ratings were correlated with a criterion of research productivity (number of publications and inventions), and it was found that 68 per cent of the validity coefficients were significant beyond the 1 per cent level.

The influence of this study can be seen in the present investigation, where personality inventories are employed for criterion rather than predictive purposes. Furthermore, it was decided to use self ratings, as well as supervisory ratings of personality.

General Methodological Considerations

Seldom do experimenters pay heed to the possibilities of bias effects in their criteria. Brogden and Taylor (1950) have classified the types of bias often unwittingly introduced into criterion construction. These are: criterion deficiency (omitting important elements); criterion contamination (introducing extraneous elements); criterion scale unit bias (inequality of scale units in the criteria); criterion distortion (improper weighting in combining criterion elements).

They warn researchers that such imperfections can considerably influence validity coefficients with the predictive battery, as well as possibly distorting estimates of criterion reliability. The present investigator paid particular attention to these sources of bias when devising his criteria measures.

Finally, it remains to note that recent research has demonstrated the complexity of the criterion problem. Taylor, Smith and Ghiselin (1963) used eight different sources to obtain data about the contribution of 166 scientists. These sources were: immediate supervisors, laboratory chiefs, peers, senior scientists, publications and research reports, official organizational records, the project researcher and the scientist himself.

The data were organized and processed to yield fifty-two scores on the contributions of the scientists. Thereafter, the fifty-two contribution scores were classified, by means of factor analysis, into fifteen relatively independent categories. The large number of different categories, fifteen, required for adequately classifying all the contribution scores, led the authors to the conclusion that the criterion problem is extremely complex. Of particular significance was the finding that some of the criterion variables incorporated areas of information normally disregarded in validity studies. It therefore follows that no single measure of creative performance will suffice on its own as an adequate criterion.

The complexity of creativity as a whole is borne out in further studies conducted by Taylor and Ellison (1964). They conclusively demonstrated that a complex battery of predictors, as well as multidimensional criteria, are necessary for tapping most of the diversity of factors operative in creative performance.

Brogden and Sprecher (1964) have been prompted by a consideration of the complexity of the problem to outline all the important variables that are involved in setting up criteria of creativity. Their scheme is valuable for any experimenter attempting to validate his methods, and it was instrumental in guiding the author in the present study.

References

BLOOM, B. S. (1963), 'Report on creativity research by the examiner's office of the University of Chicago', in C. W. Taylor and F. Barron (eds.), *Scientific Creativity: Its Recognition and Development*, Wiley, pp. 251–64.

BROGDEN, H. E., and SPRECHER, T. B. (1964), 'Criteria of creativity', in C. W. Taylor (ed.), *Creativity: Progress and Potential*, McGraw-Hill, pp. 155–76.

BROGDEN, H. E., and TAYLOR, E. K. (1950), 'The theory and classification of criterion bias', *Educ. psychol. Measmt*, vol. 10, pp. 159–86.

BRUNER, J. S. (1962), 'The conditions of creativity', in H. Gruber *et al.* (eds.), *Contemporary Approaches to Creative Thinking*, Atherton, pp. 1–30.

BUEL, W. D. (1960), 'The validity of behavioral rating scale items for the assessment of individual creativity', *J. appl. Psychol.*, vol. 44, pp. 407–12.

FLANAGAN, J. C. (1949), *Critical Requirements for Research Personnel: a Study of Observed Behaviors of Personnel in Research Laboratories*, American Institute for Research.

FLANAGAN, J. C. (1952), 'Principles and procedures in evaluating performance', *Personnel*, vol. 28, pp. 373–86.

FREUD, S. (1910), 'Leonardo da Vinci and a memory of his childhood', in J. Strachey (ed.), *The Standard Edition of the Complete Psychological Works of Sigmund Freud*, vol. 2, Hogarth, pp. 63–137.

FREUD, S. (1928), 'Dostoievski and parricide', in J. Strachey (ed.), *The Standard Edition of the Complete Psychological Works of Sigmund Freud*, vol. 21, Hogarth, pp. 177–94.

GHISELIN, B. (1963), 'Ultimate criteria for two levels of creativity', in C. W. Taylor and F. Barron (eds.), *Scientific Creativity: Its Recognition and Development*, Wiley, pp. 30–43.

HARMON, L. R. (1963), 'The development of a criterion of scientific competence', in C. W. Taylor and F. Barron (eds.), *Scientific Creativity: Its Recognition and Development*, Wiley, pp. 44–52.

JONES, F. E. (1964), 'Predictor variables for creativity in industrial science', *J. appl. Psychol.*, vol. 48, pp. 134–6.

LEHMAN, H. C. (1958), 'The chemist's most creative years', *Science*, vol. 127, pp. 1213–22.

MCPHERSON, J. H. (1963), 'A proposal for establishing ultimate criteria for measuring creative output', in C. W. Taylor and F. Barron (eds.), *Scientific Creativity: Its Recognition and Development*, Wiley, pp. 24–9.

ROE, A. (1951), 'A psychological study of physical scientists', *Genet. Psychol. Monogr.*, vol. 43, pp. 121–239.

SPRECHER, T. B. (1959), 'A study of engineers' criteria for creativity', *J. appl. Psychol.*, vol. 43, pp. 141–8.

SPRECHER, T. B. (1963), 'A proposal for identifying the meaning of creativity', in C. W. Taylor and F. Barron (eds.), *Scientific Creativity: Its Recognition and Development*, Wiley, pp. 77–88.

SPRECHER, T. B. (1964), 'Creativity and individual differences in criteria', in C. W. Taylor (ed.), *Widening Horizons in Creativity*, Wiley, pp. 336–50.

STOLTZ, R. E. (1957), 'Criterion dimensions in research productivity', *Amer. Psychol.*, vol. 12, p. 443.

TAYLOR, C. W. (1964), *Creativity: Progress and Potential*, McGraw-Hill.

TAYLOR, C. W., and ELLISON, R. L. (1964), 'Predicting creative performance from multiple measures', in C. W. Taylor (ed.), *Widening Horizons in Creativity*, Wiley, pp. 227–60.

TAYLOR, C. W., and HOLLAND, J. (1964), 'Predictors of creative performance', in C. W. Taylor (ed.), *Creativity: Progress and Potential*, McGraw-Hill, pp. 15–48.

TAYLOR, C. W., SMITH, W. R., and GHISELIN, B. (1963), 'The creative and other contributions of one sample of research scientists', in C. W. Taylor and F. Barron (eds.), *Scientific Creativity: Its Recognition and Development*, Wiley, pp. 53–76.

TAYLOR, D. W. (1963), 'Variables related to creativity and productivity among men in two research laboratories', in C. W. Taylor and F. Barron (eds.), *Scientific Creativity: Its Recognition and Development*, Wiley, pp. 228–50.

VAN ZELST, R. H., and KERR, W. A. (1954), 'Personality self-assessment of scientific and technical personnel', *J. appl. Psychol.*, vol. 38, pp. 145–7.

Part Five **Personality Studies**

Barron's article (Reading 21) provides further evidence that Guilford-type tests of creativity can be of value in some groups, though it is included mainly to illustrate the approach to creativity through personality characteristics. MacKinnon and his colleagues, at the Institute for Personality Assessment and Research at the University of California, have carried out a series of studies of groups of scientists, writers, inventors, etc., who had been picked out either as outstandingly creative, or as more routine workers. They applied a considerable variety of tests, interviews and other techniques. The results, as shown in the reading on architects (Reading 22), converge to a rather convincing picture, which is consistent with that described earlier by Roe, and with the independent investigations of R. B. Cattell (Reading 23).

C. W. Taylor, the energetic organizer of many conferences and projects and editor of several books in the field of creativity, has developed Biographical Inventory Tests which cover a wide range of interests, attitudes, personality characteristics, work methods, etc. (see Reading 24). Provided that the items have been validated repeatedly among highly creative and less creative research workers, this approach seems to offer greater promise for the selection of creative students, scientists and artists than does the aptitude test.

21 F. Barron

The Disposition towards Originality

F. Barron, 'The disposition toward originality', *Journal of Abnormal and Social Psychology*, vol. 51, 1955, pp. 478–85.

There has been a marked tendency in psychological research on originality to focus attention upon the single original act in itself, rather than upon the total personality of the originator. This is understandable, for the birth and development of the original idea are usually more immediately interesting and dramatically vivid than the birth and history of the man who had the idea. Newton's apple and Archimedes' tub and the well of Eratosthenes are thus naturally the circumstances with which we associate the remarkable insights of these original geniuses; we do not often ask ourselves whether these men were for the most part disposed to express or to suppress erotic impulses, or whether their emotions were fluent or turgid, or how subject to intense anxiety they were, or how much given to violent action. We tend to disembody the creative act and the creative process by limiting our inquiry to the creator's mental content at the moment of insight, forgetting that a highly organized system of responding lies behind the particular original response which, because of its validity, becomes an historical event.

There is good reason for believing, however, that originality is almost habitual with persons who produce a really singular insight. The biography of the inventive genius commonly records a lifetime of original thinking, though only a few ideas survive and are remembered to fame. Voluminous productivity is the rule and not the exception among individuals who have made some noteworthy contribution. Original responses, it would seem, recur regularly in some persons, while there are other individuals who do not ever depart from the stereotyped and the conventional in their thinking.

If, then, some persons are regularly original, whereas others are regularly unoriginal, it must be the case that certain patterns of relatively enduring traits either facilitate or impede the production of original acts. Rather than focusing on the immediate conditions which have triggered the original response, the present study was concerned with the underlying disposition toward originality which it may be presumed exists in those persons who are regularly original. The research was directed first of all toward identifying individuals who performed consistently in a relatively more or relatively less original way; when this had been done, the more original were compared with the less original in terms of personality organization. Independent evidence concerning the personalities of the Ss was obtained both through the use of standardized paper-and-pencil tests and through employment of the living-in assessment method, with its emphasis upon observation of the Ss through several days of informal social interaction, situational tests, group discussions, psychodrama, and the like. The observers were of course kept in ignorance of the scores earned by the Ss on tests of originality.

The Relativity of Originality

It is a basic assumption of this study that acts are original only in relation to some specified commonality. The original must be defined relative to the usual, and the degree of originality must be specified statistically in terms of incidence of occurrence. Thus the first criterion of an original response is that it should have a certain stated uncommonness in the particular group being studied. A familiar example of this in psychological practice is the definition of an original response to the Rorschach inkblots, the requirement there being that the response should, in the examiner's experience, occur no more often than once in 100 examinations.

In the present study, we propose to deal with a relatively low order of originality, its limits being set by the nature of the sampling of Ss. The Ss are 100 captains in the United States Air Force, and originality as discerned here is originality in relation to the usual responses of only 100 persons. Furthermore, these 100 persons are not themselves especially selected for originality in relation to the population in general. Nevertheless, as we shall show later, some of the 100 captains are regularly original in comparison with the remainder, whereas others are regularly unoriginal in relation to the entire group. Apart from their military status, the sample may be described as a group of normal, healthy young men, of average intelligence, socio-economically of the lower middle class in their pre-army background, and similar to young men in general in terms of the usualness and the unusualness of their responses to the tests of originality employed in this experiment.

A second criterion that must be met if a response is to be called original is that it be to some extent adaptive to reality. The intent of this requirement is to exclude uncommon responses which are merely random, or which proceed from ignorance or delusion. An example of the application of this second criterion may be taken from the scoring of one of the measures of originality used in this experiment: the measure is a count of the number of uncommon *and correct* anagram solutions to the test word 'generation'. Many *S*s did not hesitate to offer solutions that were incorrect, and that were usually unique. In such instances, the application of the second criterion of originality was straightforward and decisive. Not all the tests called for such purely cognitive responses with unambiguous denotative meaning, however: in the case of inkblot tests, for example, we come closer to the problems involved in evaluating fantasy or works of art, and verification cannot be had by recourse to a dictionary. Instead, when the examiner himself cannot 'see' the form pointed to by *S*s, he must have recourse to other psychologists who have given many Rorschachs and who can be considered fairly open to suggestions as to what the blots might reasonably look like. Consensual verification is thus sought for such imaginings. Poor forms, or uncommon responses which did not sufficiently respect the inkblot reality, were not credited as original in this study.

The Measurement of Originality

Eight test measures were accepted here as indicative of originality. They are described below. The first three of these measures are taken from the creativity battery developed by Guilford and his

275

associates in the Project on Aptitudes of High-Level Personnel at the University of Southern California. These three tests had significant loadings on the originality factor in the Guilford researches. Of the remaining five measures, two are derived from commonly used projective techniques, the Rorschach Psychodiagnostic and the Thematic Apperception Test; another is a commonly used anagram test; and the remaining two tests were devised by the writer.

1. Unusual uses. This test calls upon the subject to list six uses to which each of several common objects can be put. It is scored for infrequency, in the sample under study, of the uses proposed. Odd–even reliability in this sample is 0·77.

2. Consequences B. In this test, S is asked to write down what would happen if certain changes were suddenly to take place. The task for him is to list as many consequences or results of these changes as he can. The responses are scored according to how obvious the imagined consequences are, the less obvious responses receiving the higher scores. Interrater agreement is 0·71.

3. Plot titles B. Two story plots are presented, and S is asked to write as many titles as he can think of for each plot. The titles are rated on a scale of cleverness from 0 to 5. The number of titles rated 2, 3, 4 or 5 constitutes the cleverness score. Interrater agreement in this study is 0·43.

4. Rorschach O+. This is a count of the number of original responses given by S to the ten Rorschach blots and adjudged by two scorers, working separately, to be good rather than poor forms. Standard Rorschach administrative procedure is followed. Interrater agreement is 0·72, and only those responses scored by both scorers as O+ were credited.

5. Thematic Apperception Test: originality rating. Two raters, working independently of one another, rate the TAT protocols of the 100 S's on a nine-point scale, using approximate normal curve frequencies for each point along the scale. Interrater agreement is 0·70. The *S*'s score is the average of the two ratings.

6. Anagrams. The test word 'generation' is used, and the anagram solutions are scored for infrequency of occurrence in the sample under study. If *S* offers a solution that is correct and that is offered by no more than two other *S*s, he receives one point for originality. Total score is therefore the number of such uncommon but correct solutions.

7. Word Rearrangement Test: originality rating. In this test, *S* is given fifty words which were selected at random from a list of common nouns, adjectives, and adverbs. He is told to make up a story which will enable him to use as many as possible of the listed words. His composition is rated for originality on a nine-point scale, just as the TAT was. Interrater agreement in this instance is 0·67.

8. Achromatic inkblots. This is a set of ten achromatic inkblots constructed locally. The *S* is asked to give only one response to each blot. Responses are weighted according to their infrequency of occurrence in the sample under study, the more infrequent responses receiving the higher weights. Score is the sum of the weights assigned to *S*'s responses on all ten blots. Odd–even reliability is 0·43.

It is worth noting that all eight of these tests are free-response tests; the respondent is not presented with alternatives devised by the test maker, but must instead summon from within himself his own way of solving problems, seeing the blots, interpreting the pictures, putting together the words or letters, and so on. There is considerable latitude allowed for self-expression and for idiosyncratic interpretation.

Futhermore, diverse media are presented for the respondent to express himself through. The two inkblot tests allow for original visualization, or original perceptual organization of visual forms. The TAT and the Word Rearrangement Test permit originality of verbal composition to show itself. Consequences and Unusual Uses call for bright ideas in more or less discrete form. Plot

Titles evokes epigrammatic or sloganistic originality, while Anagrams requires a combination of word fluency and ease of perceptual reorganization.

If originality is indeed a dimension, and if some persons are regularly original whereas others are regularly unoriginal, we should expect the intercorrelations of these measures to be positive and to be statistically significant; we should not, however, expect the coefficients to be very high, for it is reasonable that the dimension of originality would have its variance apportioned to several media of expression. Even regularly original persons can be expected to be outstandingly original in only one or two ways. The extent to which these expectations are confirmed in the present study may be seen from Table 1, in which the Pearsonian correlation coefficients of all eight test measures with one another are given. (With an N of 100, a Pearsonian r is significant at the 0·05 level if it is 0·20 or greater; an r of 0·26 is significant at the 0·01 level.)

Table 1

Interrelations of Eight Originality Measures

Test measures	1	2	3	4	5	6	7	8
1. Unusual uses	—	0·42	0·37	0·08	0·17	0·29	0·06	0·17
2. Consequences B	0·42	—	0·46	−0·02	0·21	0·21	0·16	0·09
3. Plot titles B	0·37	0·46	—	0·17	0·26	0·17	0·16	0·07
4. Rorschach O+	0·08	−0·02	0·17	—	0·21	0·03	−0·05	0·17
5. TAT originality	0·17	0·21	0·26	0·21	—	0·36	0·41	0·02
6. Anagrams	0·29	0·21	0·17	0·03	0·36	—	0·33	0·38
7. Word rearrangement orig.	0·06	0·16	0·16	−0·05	0·41	0·33	—	0·09
8. Inkblot originality	0·17	0·09	0·07	0·17	0·02	0·38	0·09	—

As Table 1 shows, the correlations of the eight measures with one another tend to be positive and to be significantly different from zero. The inkblot tests alone appear to bear little relationship to the other measures; indeed, they do not even correlate significantly with one another. If the two inkblot tests are excluded, however, two-thirds of the intercorrelations of the remaining six measures are significant at the 0·05 level, and all are positive. Table 1 thus provides satisfactory evidence of the

expected coherence or regularity of the manifestations of
originality, with considerable reservations, however, concerning
the relevance of inkblot originality to the dimension here being
measured.

Since it is quite possible that originality is simply a multi-
factorial dimension in which certain factors bear little relationship to other factors but yet are positively related to the underlying dimension as a whole, it would probably be premature to
exclude the inkblot measures from this battery of tests of originality. Considerable doubt must be entertained concerning their
validity, however, and there is another piece of evidence which
reinforces the doubt. The staff psychologists who conducted the
three-day, living-in assessments were particularly interested in
two theoretically central variables which they sought to rate on
the basis of their observations: one of these variables was
originality (the other was personal stability). The correlations
between this final over-all rating on originality and the eight test
measures of originality are shown in Table 2. Also given in

Table 2

Relationship of Eight Test Measures to Rated
Originality and to Composite Test Originality

Test measures	9	10
1. Unusual uses	0·30	0·60
2. Consequences B	0·36	0·59
3. Plot titles B	0·32	0·62
4. Rorschach O+	0·18	0·38
5. TAT originality	0·45	0·59
6. Anagrams	0·22	0·62
7. Word rearrangement originality	0·45	0·51
8. Inkblot originality	0·07	0·46
9. Staff rating on originality	—	0·55
10. Composite test originality	0·55	—

Table 2 are the correlations of the eight measures individually
with a variable which is the sum of the standard scores earned by
each S on each of the eight tests; in other words, each test
measure is correlated with a composite of which it is itself a part.

The correlations thus show the relative contributions of each test to the total score on the battery of tests.

Table 2 provides evidence that the test battery is in substantial agreement with the staff psychologists who gave ratings on originality without knowledge of the test scores. The correlation of 0·55 between the test composite and the observers' ratings is encouraging evidence that inexpensive, objective, and efficient measurement of originality is possible.

Again, however, the inkblot measures have relatively little relationship to these composite variables. The staff rating of originality correlates significantly with six of the eight measures (well beyond the 0·01 level of significance with five of them); but neither the Rorschach originality nor the Inkblot originality is significantly related to the staff rating. As would be expected, these measures also have the least contribution to make to the test composite.

In spite of this situation, both inkblot measures were retained in the battery for purposes of identifying regularly original and regularly unoriginal Ss. The reasoning was as follows. On the face of it, uncommon responses to inkblots are original acts within the definition of originality being employed here. Tendencies toward uncommon visual perceptions are of course not readily recognized in ordinary social situations, since they have to be verbalized to be socially visible. Hence the failure of inkblot tests to correlate with the staff rating of originality, based on observations of social behavior alone, should be discounted. The lack of a verbal component in perceptual originality, and its conspicuous presence in the other originality tests, may also account for the relative independence of the inkblot tests in the test composite. Finally, if the inkblot measures contribute only error variance to the composite, their retention will result in failure of some true relationships to appear, but this will be an error on the conservative side; and if they do in fact contribute true variance not contributed by any other test, they may add appreciable validity to the picture of the personality correlates of originality. They were therefore retained for the purpose of identifying regularly original and regularly unoriginal subjects.

A dual criterion was now established for calling a given subject regularly original: he had to be at least one standard deviation above the mean on the test composite; and he had to be at least two standard deviations above the mean on at least one of the eight measures. Fifteen regularly original Ss were thus identified; more than half of them were at least two standard deviations above the mean on two or more of the eight tests.

For comparison purposes, the fifteen lowest scorers on the final distribution of summed standard scores were selected; all of these Ss also met the criterion of being at least two standard deviations below the mean on at least one of the eight measures. They will be referred to as the regularly unoriginal subjects.

Some Hypotheses Suggested by Previous Work

The existence of a very general attitude toward experience, of a sort which disposes toward complexity of outlook, independence of judgement and originality, has been suggested by the results of studies reported earlier by the present writer. It was found, for example, that individuals who refused to yield to strong pressure from their peers to concur in a false group opinion described themselves, on an adjective check list, as 'original' and 'artistic' much more frequently than did subjects who yielded to such group pressure. In addition, the independent (non-yielding) Ss showed a marked preference for complex and asymmetrical line drawings, as opposed to simple and symmetrical drawings. This preference for the complex and asymmetrical had been shown previously to be highly correlated both with the choice of art as a vocation and with rated artistic ability among art students. Furthermore, in a sample of Ph.D. candidates in the sciences, preference for the complex and asymmetrical figures proved to be significantly related to rated originality in graduate work. This same relationship was found among graduating medical school seniors who were rated for originality by their faculty. Other evidence indicated that the opposed preferences, for complexity or for simplicity, were related to a generalized experiential disposition: the preference for complexity is associated with a perceptual attitude which seeks to allow into the perceptual system the greatest possible richness of experience, even though discord and disorder result, while the preference for simplicity is associated with a perceptual attitude which allows into the system only as much as can be integrated without great discomfort and disorder, even though this means excluding some aspects of reality.

From all these considerations, certain hypotheses as to the characteristics of original persons were derived and put to the test in the present study. The hypotheses, and the ways in which they were tested, or partially tested, are described below.

Hypothesis 1

That original persons prefer complexity and some degree of apparent imbalance in phenomena.

Test 1a. The Barron–Welsh Art Scale of the Figure Preference Test. Preference for complex-asymmetrical figures earns the subject a high score.

Hypothesis 2

That original persons are more complex psychodynamically and have greater personal scope.

Test 2a. Psychiatric interviewer rating on 'complexity and scope as a person'. The Ss receiving high ratings are those who were diagnosed by a psychiatric interviewer, on the basis of a two-hour interview, as having a 'more complex personality structure and greater potential for complex ego-synthesis'. Ratings were on a nine-point scale with approximate normal curve frequencies being assigned to each point along the scale.

Hypothesis 3

That original persons are more independent in their judgements.

Test 3a. The Independence of Judgement Scale. On this inventory scale, which was developed against the criterion of actual behaviour in the Asch group pressure experiment in previous studies, high scores indicate similarity to persons who manifest independence.

Test 3b. A modification of the Asch group pressure experiment. This is a situational test in which Ss are put under pressure from their peers to agree to certain apparent group judgements. High scores indicate yielding to such pressures; regularly original persons should therefore have lower scores.

Hypothesis 4

That original persons are more self-assertive and dominant.

Test 4a. Dominance–submission ratings in a psychodramatic situation especially designed to elicit such tendencies in the subjects. Ratings were on a nine-point scale.

Test 4b. The Social Dominance Scale of the California Psychological Inventory. This is a thoroughly studied and validated scale for the measurement of dominance in real-life social situations.

Test 4c. Staff rating on dominance, based on three days of observation of social behaviour. Dominance was defined for the raters as follows: 'self-assurance, ascendance and self-confidence in dealing with others; forceful, authoritative, resolute, not easily intimidated'. A five-point rating scale was used.

Test 4d. The Self-Assertiveness Scale of the California Psychological Inventory.

Test 4e. The Phallicism Scale of the Personal Preference Scale. This scale is intended as a measure of the derivatives and residuals in the adult personality of propensities which were highly cathected in the phallic stage of psychosexual development. High scores indicate an emphasis on personal power and desire for recognition.

Hypothesis 5

That original persons reject suppression as a mechanism for the control of impulse. This would imply that they forbid themselves fewer thoughts, that they dislike to police themselves or others, that they are disposed to entertain impulses and ideas that are commonly taboo, and in general that they express in their persons the sort of indiscipline which psychoanalytic theory would ascribe to a libidinal organization in which derivatives of the early anal rather than of the late anal stage in psychosexual development predominate.

Test 5a. An index of suppression–expression on the Minnesota Multiphasic Personality Inventory is obtained by adding the T-scores on the Lie, Hysteria and K-scales and subtracting from that sum the sum of T-scores on Psychopathic Deviation and Hypomania. On this index, regularly original Ss should obtain lower scores.

Test 5b. The Policeman Interest Scale of the Strong Vocational Interest Blank. Although this is bound to be a somewhat derivative measure of the personality tendency toward suppression of outlawed impulse, it does at least reflect the similarity of the subject's interests to those of persons who are regularly employed at maintaining law, order and civil discipline – who, in short, seem vocationally suited to policing. Regularly original Ss should earn low scores.

Test 5c. The Early Anal and the Late Anal scales of the Personal Preference Scale (Grygier revision). If the scales are valid and the hypothesis is correct, regularly original Ss should score higher on Early Anal and lower on Late Anal than do regularly unoriginal Ss.

Test 5d. The Impulsivity Scale of the California Psychological Inventory. Since high scorers are those who express impulse readily, the regularly original Ss should earn higher scores than the regularly unoriginal Ss.

Test 5e. Staff rating: impulsivity. Again, regularly original Ss should receive higher ratings.

The group comparisons specified in these predictions are presented in detail in Table 3. As that table shows, twelve of the fifteen predictions proved correct. A fairly conservative criterion of confirmation was adopted: significance at the 0·05 level when

F. Barron

the two-tailed test was applied. The theoretical formulation suggested by the previous work on complexity–simplicity and on independence of judgement is substantially confirmed by these results.

Table 3

Tests of Hypotheses

Hypotheses	Originals (N = 15)		Unoriginals (N = 15)		t	P
	M	SD	M	SD		
1. Preference for complexity						
Test 1a. Barron–Welsh Art Scale	19·40	12·28	12·67	10·69	2·16	0·02
2. Complexity as a person						
Test 2a. Psychiatric rating: 'complexity as a person'	6·40	1·82	4·00	1·67	3·58	0·001
3. Independence of judgement						
Test 3a. Independence of Judgement Scale	9·60	1·67	8·00	2·94	1·74	0·05
Test 3b. Group pressure situation	5·00	1·87	8·60	1·80	3·93	0·001
4. Self-assertion and dominance						
Test 4a. Psychodrama: dominance rating	41·13	11·70	38·40	7·78	0·72	0·23
Test 4b. CPI: Social Dominance Scale	36·60	3·74	28·87	4·75	4·74	0·001
Test 4c. Staff rating: dominance	34·40	7·10	25·40	4·06	4·05	0·001
Test 4d. CPI: Self-Assertiveness Scale	15·73	1·44	15·07	2·74	0·78	0·22
Test 4e. PPS: Phallicism Scale (VIK)	13·20	2·37	9·13	4·27	3·08	0·01
5. Rejection of suppression; tendency toward expression of impulse						
Test 5a. MMPI: (L + Hy + K) − (PD + Ma)	43·47	26·24	58·87	12·30	1·78	0·045
Test 5b. SVIB: Policeman Interest Scale	44·67	9·87	55·00	10·81	−2·61	0·01
Test 5c. PPS: Early Anal Scale (IVB)	20·33	4·57	17·87	2·90	1·66	0·06
Late Anal Scale (VB)	23·53	4·59	26·80	4·85	−1·81	0·05
Test 5d. CPI: Impulsivity Scale	23·13	7·86	16·60	6·08	1·98	0·03
Test 5e. Staff rating: impulsivity	32·27	6·41	27·80	5·42	4·74	0·001

Discussion

The five major hypotheses in this study have been stated in terms derived directly from previous observations. There is another way of looking at them, however, which permits the results to be considered in somewhat other terms, and in a broader context. Since the hypotheses have already been stated and to some extent justified, it may be appropriate in discussing these results to venture somewhat beyond the literal meaning of the findings to date.

We have spoken here of the disposition toward originality, with originality being so measured as to be equivalent to the capacity for producing adaptive responses which are unusual. But unusualness of response may be considered a function as well of the objective freedom of an organism, where this is defined as the range of possible adaptive responses available in all situations. As the response repertoire of any given organism increases, the number of statistically infrequent responses, considered relative to the population of like organisms, will also increase. Thus the ability to respond in an unusual or original manner will be greatest when freedom is greatest.

Now freedom is related in a very special manner to degree and kind of organization. In general, organization, in company with complexity, generates freedom; the more complex the level of integration, the greater is the repertoire of adaptive responses. The tendency toward organization may, however, operate in such a fashion as to maintain a maladaptive simplicity. We are familiar in the political sphere with totalitarian states which depend upon suppression to achieve unity; such states are psychodynamically similar to the neurotic individual who suppresses his own impulses and emotions in order to maintain a semblance of stability. There are at hand enough case histories of both such organizations, political and private, to make it clear that the sort of unity and balance that depends upon total suppression of the claims of minority affects and opinions is maladaptive in the long run.

Suppression is a common way of achieving unity, however, because in the short run it often seems to work. Increasing complexity puts a strain upon an organism's ability to integrate phenomena; one solution of the difficulty is to inhibit the development of the greater level of complexity, and thus to avoid the temporary disintegration that would otherwise have resulted.

Originality, then, flourishes where suppression is at a minimum and where some measure of disintegration is tolerable in the interests of a final higher level of integration.

If we consider the case of a human being who develops strongly the disposition toward originality, we must posit certain personal characteristics and personal history which facilitated the development of such a disposition. In our hypotheses, the term 'dominance' was used to describe one trait of the regularly original individual. This may be translated as a strong need for personal mastery, not merely over other persons, but over all experience. It initially involves self-centeredness, which in its socialized form may come to be known as self-realization. One aspect of it is the insistence on self-regulation, and a rejection of regulation by others.

For such a person, the most crucial developmental crisis in relation to control of impulse comes at the anal stage of socialization. What our hypotheses have suggested is that there is a positive rebellion against the prohibition of unregulated anal production, and a carrying of the derivatives of anal indiscipline into adult life. The original person, in adulthood, thus often like things messy, at least at first; the tendency is toward a final order, but the necessary preliminary is as big a mess as possible. Viewed developmentally, the rejection of externally imposed control at the anal stage is later generalized to all external control of impulse, with the tendency toward socially unlicensed phallic activity, or phallic exhibitionism in its more derivative forms, being simply another expression of the general rejection of regulation of impulse by others, in favor of regulation of impulse by oneself.

The disposition toward originality may thus be seen as a highly organized mode of responding to experience, including other persons, society, and oneself. The socially disrated traits which may go along with it include rebelliousness, disorderliness, and exhibitionism, while the socially valued traits which accompany it include independence of judgement, freedom of expression, and novelty of construction and insight.

In this view, then the pervasive and unstereotyped unconventionality of thought which one finds consistently in creative individuals is related generically to a tendency to resist acculturation, where acculturation is seen as demanding surrender of one's personal unique, fundamental nature. This may, although it does not always, result in a rejection of conventional morality. From our study of these military officers as well as from extensive studies of individuals whose chosen goal in life is scientific and artistic creation, we conclude that there is by no means an abatement of the moral attitude in creative persons. On the contrary, they are characteristically aroused to wrath at the shoddy, the meretricious, and the unjust, and their feeling about creative power in themselves and others is in some sense religious. Very often their work, seen in the perspective of a lifetime of endeavor, is itself the creation of a cosmos of their own, as though each mind is progressively unfolding itself as life itself has.

The psychological conditions which make a society or an epoch creative and consistently original have been little studied, but it seems likely that social conditions analogous to those seen in individual creativity are important. Freedom of expression and movement, lack of fear of dissent and contradiction, a willingness to break with custom, a spirit of play as well as of dedication to work, purpose on a grand scale; these are some of the attributes which a creative social entity, whether vast or tiny, can be expected to have.

22 D. W. MacKinnon

The Personality Correlates of Creativity: A Study of
American Architects

Excerpts from D. W. MacKinnon, 'The personality correlates of
creativity: a study of American architects', in *Proceedings of the
Fourteenth Congress on Applied Psychology*, vol. 2, Munksgaard,
1962, pp. 11–39.

The Architect as Artist and Scientist

The decision to include architects among the professions to be
studied was based upon the assumption that they might as a
group reveal that which is most generally characteristic of
creativity and the creative person. Grossly oversimplifying the
profoundly complex one might, as has often been done, entertain
the notion that there are at least two kinds of creativity – artistic
and scientific – and that those who practice and excel in one of
these are, at least in some respects, different from those who labor
in the other. Yet it is clear that there are certain domains of
creative endeavor which require that the successful practitioner
be both artist and scientist. Surely architecture is such a field,
with its requirements that its designs meet the demands, as
described by Ruskin, of firmness, delight and commodity, or in
more modern language, the demands of technology, visual form
and planning. Yet surely the requirements of effective architecture are not limited to these three. One who studies a successfully
practicing architect will soon be impressed by his juggler-like
ability to combine, reconcile and exercise the diverse skills of
businessman, lawyer, artist, engineer and advertising man, to say
nothing of author-journalist, psychiatrist, educator and psychologist. In what other profession could one better observe the
multifarious expressions of creativity?

Identifying Creative Architects

We began our enterprise by asking a panel of experts, five
university professors of architecture each working independently,

to nominate the forty most creative architects in the United States. In addition to making nominations, panel members rated the creativity of each nominated architect on a five-point scale and wrote a summary evaluation of his work, indicating why he was nominated.

Had there been perfect agreement among the nominators, each would have mentioned the same forty. Actually they gave us eighty-six names. Thirteen of the architects were nominated by all five members, nine were nominated by four, eleven were nominated by three, thirteen by two, while forty were individual nominations by single panel members. Subsequently each panel member rated the creativity of those not nominated by him originally, provided he knew them well enough to do so.

On the basis of the average or mean rating of their creativity and the summary evaluations of their work, the nominated architects (known to us at this stage only by a disguising code number) were listed in the order in which we would invite them to participate in the study. Our hope was to win the cooperation of the first forty whom we invited, but to get forty acceptances sixty-four invitations had to be sent out.

The forty who accepted came to Berkeley in groups of ten, where they were subjects of a weekend-long intensive assessment. But what of the twenty-four who declined our invitation to be studied? Are they more or less creative than the forty who were willing to be assessed, or in no way different? When the nominating panel's ratings of creativity for the two groups were converted to standard scores and compared, the means were found to be identical: 50·0, standard deviation 9·9 for the twenty-four not assessed, as against 50·1, standard deviation 9·5 for the forty assessed architects.

To check further on this point we asked fourteen editors of the major American architectural journals, *Architectural Forum*, *Architectural Record*, *Journal of the American Institute of Architects* and *Progressive Architecture* to rank the sixty-four invited architects from most to least creative, and eleven did so. When mean rankings for the twenty-four versus the forty were converted to standard scores, the non-assessed group had a slightly higher mean score (51·9, SD 8·0) than the assessed sample (48·7, SD 6·1), but the difference is not statistically significant.

If we did not assess the forty most creative architects in the country, we at least can be assured of having studied a highly creative group of architects indistinguishable in their creativity from the group of twenty-four who declined to be studied. [. . .]

Sampling Widely the Profession of Architecture

But to have limited our study to the assessment of forty architects, each of whom was recognized as highly creative, would not have permitted us to say anything with confidence about the personality correlates of creativity. For the distinguishing characteristics of this sample – and there were many that we found – might well have nothing to do with their creativity. Obviously the design of our study required that the profession of architecture be widely sampled beyond the assessed forty in order to discover whether and to what extent the traits of creative architects are characteristic of architects in general or peculiar to those who are highly creative.

To this end the *Directory of Architects* published in 1955 was searched in order to select two additional samples of architects both of which would match the assessed sample of forty, which I shall now call architects I, with respect to age and geographic location of practice. The first of the supplementary samples, which I shall designate architects II, is composed of forty-three architects each of whom met the additional requirement that he had had at least two years of work experience and association with one of the originally nominated creative architects. The other additional sample, which I shall label architects III, is composed of forty-one architects none of whom has ever worked with any of the nominated creative architects.

By selecting three samples in this manner we hoped to tap a range of talent sufficiently wide to be fairly representative of the profession as a whole. In a first attempt to determine whether we had achieved this goal it seemed reasonable to assume that an approximate measure of an architect's creativeness might be the amount of space devoted to his work in the architectural literature. Accordingly two indices of publicity or prominence, and by inference also indices of creativity, were computed: (a) a weighted index of the number of articles by or about each architect and his work referenced in the *Architectural Index* for the years 1950–58, and (b) a weighted index of the number of pages devoted to each architect and his work for the same period.

Table 1 shows the mean scores for both of these indices for each of the three samples.

Table 1

Indices of Publicity or Prominence

| | Group | | |
	I	II	III
Articles by or about each architect, 1950–58	131	20	3
Pages	97	13	2

On both indices architects I are clearly superior to the other two samples. Architects II on both measures are between architects I and III, but much closer to the latter than to the former. [. . .]

In search of a better criterion, six groups of architects and experts on architecture were asked finally to rate on a nine-point scale the creativity of each of the 124 architects comprising the total sample of architects I, II and III whom they knew well enough to judge. Ratings of creativity were made for varying numbers of architects by five members of the original nominating panel (all professors of architecture in the University of California), by six editors of the major architectural journals, by nineteen professors of architecture distributed nation-wide, by thirty-two architects I, thirty-six architects II and twenty-eight architects III.

Table 2 shows the mean rating of creativity for each of the three groups of architects: architects I, 5·46; architects II, 4·25; and architects III, 3·54; the mean differences in rated creativity between groups I and II and groups II and III being significant beyond the 0·001 level, and also of course between I and III.

Having demonstrated that the three groups do indeed represent significantly different levels of creativity, we can examine data obtained from them to discover the personality correlates of creativity and more specifically the distinguishing characteristics of creative architects.

Unfortunately our data are not so extensive for architects II and III as for architects I. Where the latter group experienced a three-day-long assessment, the former groups, working independently and at home, spent some six or seven hours completing a selection of tests, questionnaires and inventories from our total assessment battery. Under these conditions, there were some tests, notably tests of intelligence and timed tests, which could not be administered.

Table 2

Mean Ratings of Creativity on Nine-Point Scale of 124 Architects Separated into Three Groups

Groups rated	Mean rating	SD	T-ratio	P Value
Architects I	5·46	0·43	10·795	≤0·001
Architects II	4·25	0·56	4·908	≤0·001
Architects III	3·54	0·74		

The Impression Made by Creative Architects

How are creative architects seen by psychological assessors? Following each three-day assessment, staff members checked on the Gough Adjective Check List (1960) those adjectives which in their opinion were especially descriptive of each architect. Adjectives which were checked by three or more of the ten staff members for 80 per cent or more of the architects most saliently describe our image of the creative architect. They are: alert, artistic, intelligent, responsible (checked for 100 per cent of the group); ambitious, capable (98 per cent); cooperative (95 per cent); civilized, dependable, friendly, pleasant, resourceful (92 per cent); active, confident, industrious, reliable (90 per cent); conscientious, imaginative, reasonable (88 per cent); enterprising, independent, interests wide (85 per cent); adaptable, assertive, determined, energetic, persevering, sincere (82 per cent); and

293

individualistic, serious (80 per cent). The impression which they make is obviously a highly favorable one.

Another method whereby we recorded our impressions was the 100-item Q-sort developed by Block (1961), consisting of psychodynamic descriptions of personal functioning which were sorted for each architect into nine piles ranging from those most descriptive to those least descriptive of him. Compositing the sortings made by each staff member yields the staff's composite image of the personality structure of the creative architect. Listed in Table 3 in rank order are the fifteen statements (out of 100) which we consider most descriptive of the creative architects – architects I.

Table 3

Rank	Item
1.	Enjoys esthetic impressions; is esthetically reactive.
2.	Has high aspiration level for self.
3.	Values own independence and autonomy.
4.	Is productive; gets things done.
5.	Appears to have a high degree of intellectual capacity.
6.	Genuinely values intellectual and cognitive matters.
7.	Concerned with own adequacy as a person, either at conscious or unconscious levels.
8.	Is a genuinely dependable and responsible person.
9.	Has a wide range of interests.
10.	Behaves in an ethically consistent manner; is consistent with own personal standards.
12.	Has social poise and presence; appears socially at ease.
12.	Enjoys sensuous experiences (including touch, taste, smell, physical contact).
12.	Is critical, skeptical, not easily impressed.
14.	Appears straightforward, forthright, candid in dealings with others.
15.	Is a talkative individual.

With the possible exception of the item in seventh rank, the image of the creative architect we have formed is a highly favorable one. There are, however, many facets of personality not revealed in any mere listing of adjectives and phrases; and so I turn now to a discussion of traits and dispositions revealed by creative architects in their performance on various assessment procedures.

Artistic Production and Creativity

A task set all subjects in our studies is the making of a mosaic (Hall, 1958). Supplied with a large selection of one-inch squares cut from twenty-two different colors of poster-board, the subject is asked to use these in any fashion he chooses to construct within a thirty-minute period a pleasing, completely filled-in 8 × 10 inch mosaic.

The mosaics made by all our creative subjects – architects, engineers, research scientists, mathematicians, novelists, essayists and poets – have been rated by a panel of experts on several dimensions: over-all artistic merit, good use of color, good use of form, originality, warmth and pleasingness. The raters were four members of the University of California faculty: two in the Department of Art and two in the Department of Decorative Art. Their ratings were averaged to provide a single rating for each mosaic on each of the six rated dimensions.

Since we checked 'artistic' for 100 per cent of the sample and sorted in first place the item 'enjoys esthetic impressions; is esthetically reactive', it will come as no surprise that the creative architects' mosaics received relatively high ratings, but there was considerable variation among them, and as one might also expect, there was a significant even though low positive correlation between the over-all artistic merit ratings of the mosaics made by the architects and their creativity as architects as judged by the editors, the correlation between the two being $+0.35$.

The creative architect 'appears to have a high degree of intellectual capacity'. That is the statement which held fifth rank in our Q-sorting for the group. Where creative architects stand among other groups with respect to intelligence is shown in Table 4, which presents the average scores earned by several groups on the Concept Mastery Test (Terman, 1956), a difficult, high level test of verbal intelligence. The creative architects earn a mean score of 113, scoring as a group five points below research scientists and twelve points above undergraduate students. But their individual scores range widely from thirty-nine to 179 (these are not I.Q. scores), and within the group the correlation of intelligence as measured by the Concept Mastery Test and creativity in architecture as rated by the experts is −0·08, not significantly different from zero.

Table 4

Mean Score and Standard Deviations for Various Groups on the Concept Mastery Test, Form T

Group	N	Mean	SD
Creative writers	20	156·4	21·9
Subjects of Stanford Gifted Study	1004	136·7	28·5
Women mathematicians	41	131·7	33·8
Graduate students	125	119·2	33·0
Research scientists	45	118·2	29·4
Creative architects (I)	40	113·2	37·7
Undergraduate students	201	101·7	33·0
Spouses of gifted subjects	690	95·3	42·7
Electronics engineers and scientists	95	94·5	37·0
Engineering college seniors	40	80·4	27·9
Military officers	344	60·3	31·6
Independent inventors	14	50·8	34·7

Certainly this does not mean that over the whole range of creative endeavor there is no correlation between intelligence and creativity. We have found no feeble-minded architects. Rather, it suggests that a certain amount of intelligence is required for creativity, but beyond that point being more intelligent or less intelligent is not crucially determinative of the level of an architect's creativeness. And, certainly, for an individual architect to be recognized for his creativity does not require that he be outstanding in verbal intelligence.

It may well be that spatial and other types of intelligence are far more important for the creativity of an architect than his verbal intelligence. On the Crutchfield (1958) version of the Gottschaldt Figures Test, which requires that one isolate and identify simple geometric figures that are imbedded or hidden in larger more complex figures, creative architects score higher than any other group we have studied. The Gottschaldt Figures

Test measures the ability to analyse and reorganize spatial patterns as well as a general flexibility and insightfulness in dealing with cognitive materials. In addition a stringent time limit of two minutes makes performance on the test a function of

Table 5

Mean Scores and Standard Deviations for Various Groups on the Gottschaldt Figures Test

Sample	N	Mean	SD
Creative architects (I)	40	15·7	4·4
Research scientists	45	15·5	3·7
Women mathematicians	41	13·7	4·4
Student writers	10	10·5	5·9
Military officers	100	9·7	4·9
Creative writers	20	7·4	4·4

one's ability to work quickly and effectively under stress and pressure. Table 5 shows the superior performance on this test of creative architects as compared with research scientists, mathematicians, military officers and professional writers.

Table 6

Mean Scores and Standard Deviations for Various Groups on the General Information Survey

Sample	N	Mean	SD
Research scientists	45	46·1	8·6
Medical school seniors	39	43·7	7·8
Creative architects (I)	40	42·2	6·6
Medical school applicants	70	40·7	7·6
Male university students	221	37·5	7·3
Military officers	311	36·5	8·8

One should not conclude, however, that the intelligence of creative architects is expressed only in narrow and rather specific skills and abilities. On the General Information Survey (Gough, 1954), as Table 6 shows, creative architects are among the highest scorers. This test consists of far-ranging factual questions about sports, music, literature, history, geography, drinks, restaurants, and the like, and is designed to assess an individual's general knowledge of the world and the culture in which he lives.

In brief, creative architects reveal themselves as broadly informed (remember, we checked 'interests wide' for them), who, if not outstanding in their performance on tests of verbal intelligence are, nevertheless, intellectually very competent. A distinction must be made between I.Q. intelligence and effective intelligence; and it is on the latter that creative architects excel. Yet, if verbal intelligence tests are not the special metier of creative architects, they are nonetheless highly verbal characters. The item which fell in fifteenth place (out of 100) in our Q-sort description of them was 'Is a talkative person'.

Values and Creativity

On the Allport–Vernon–Lindzey Study of Values (1951) designed to test in the individual the relative strength of the six values of men as described by Eduard Spranger, namely, theoretical, economic, esthetic, social, political and religious, architects I, as may be seen in Figure 1, score highest on esthetic and theoretical, and despite the success with which, as entrepreneurs, they carry out their architectural practice, their least valued value is the economic.

The esthetic and theoretical values are also the two highest values for architects II and III, but these values are less pronounced for them. Furthermore, the economic value, the lowest of all values for highly creative architects, is held significantly higher (at the 0·01 level) by architects III, and also by architects II. Indeed in the total sample of 124, the theoretical value correlates with the rated creativity of the architects +0·18, and esthetic value +0·35, and the economic value −0·48.

Jungian Typological Functions and Creativity

On the Myers–Briggs Type Indicator (1958), a test designed to place individuals in the scheme of personality types developed by Carl G. Jung, interesting similarities and differences among the three samples are revealed.

Within the framework of this test, it may be said that, whenever a person uses his mind for any purpose, he performs either an act of perception (he becomes aware of something) or an act of judgement (he comes to a conclusion about something). And most people are inclined to show a rather consistent preference for and greater pleasure in one or the other of these, preferring either to judge or to perceive.

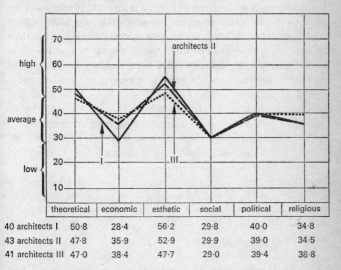

	theoretical	economic	esthetic	social	political	religious
40 architects I	50·8	28·4	56·2	29·8	40·0	34·8
43 architects II	47·8	35·9	52·9	29·9	39·0	34·5
41 architects III	47·0	38·4	47·7	29·0	39·4	38·8

Figure 1 Profiles of values for architects on the Allport–Vernon–Lindzey Study of Values

An habitual preference for the judging attitude may lead to some prejudging, and in any case to the living of a life that is controlled, carefully planned and orderly. A preference for the perceptive attitude results in a life that is more open to experience both from within and from without, and characterized by flexibility and spontaneity. A judging type will place more emphasis upon the control and regulation of experience, while a perceptive type is inclined to be more open and more receptive to all experience, seeking to know as much about life as possible. [. . .]

The outstanding creative architects (architects I) tend to be perceptive types, 58 per cent of them preferring perception to judgement. Among architects II and III, perceptive types are in the minority, there being 44 per cent in architects II and only seventeen per cent among architects III.

It is the other way around with judging. 81 per cent of architects III and 53 per cent of architects II are judging types, while only 40 per cent of architects I show a preference for judging.

Means for the three groups show the same progressions: in the case of perception 16·3 to 11·7 to 9·2 as one moves from the more to the less creative architects, and in the case of judgement means go from 18·1 to 15·3 to 12·4 as one moves from the less creative to the more creative groups.

The second preference in this scheme is for one of two types of perception: sense perception or sensation, which is a direct becoming aware of things by way of the senses v. intuitive perception or intuition, which is an indirect perception of the deeper meanings and possibilities inherent in things and situations.

Preliminary norms for this test suggest that in the United States three out of four persons will be classified as sense perceptives. They concentrate on things as they are experienced through their five senses, and they center their attention on existing facts. The one out of every four who perceives intuitively looks expectantly for a link or bridge between that which is given and present and that which is not yet thought of, focusing habitually upon possibilities.

Now there is no doubt that we would expect creative persons not to be stimulus- and object-bound but ever alert to the as-yet-not-realized. The fact that 100 per cent of the creative architects (architects I) are intuitive, when only an estimated 25 per cent of the American population are intuitive, is a striking finding. In view of this it is especially interesting to note that in the comparison samples intuition is less often the preferred mode of perception: 84 per cent of architects II and 59 per cent of architects III

Conversely, the percentage of sensation types progresses' from 0 per cent of architects I to 14 per cent of architects II to 39 per cent of architects III.

There is a corresponding progression of mean scores for the three samples on intuition (from 21·0 to 17·1 to 14·4) and on sensation (from 3·4 to 6·6 to 10·5), the differences being in each case at or beyond the 0·05 level of significance.

If we use sense perception to tell us what is and intuition to tell us what may be, we use thinking and feeling in judging and evaluating our experience. Thinking judgement or thinking is a logical process, aimed at an impersonal fact-weighing analysis. Feeling judgement or feeling is a process of appreciation and evaluation of things which gives them a personal and subjective value.

In general, artists show a preference for feeling, engineers a preference for thinking. Since architects have to be both artists and engineers and some are more of one and others more of the other, it is intriguing to discover that in both architects I and architects III the preference is about evenly divided between thinking and feeling.

The final preference in Jungian typology is the well-known one between introversion and extraversion. It is clear that architects as measured by this test favor introversion: 65 per cent of the creative architects (architects I), 67 per cent of architects II, and 63 per cent of architects III are introverts.

Just as there is no significant difference in the frequency of introverts from sample to sample, so also there is no significant difference in the mean scores on introversion and extraversion among the three groups.

Interpersonal Relations and Creativity

The finding that the majority of architects are introverts jibes with other test results and with our observations of the creative architects in the assessment setting. Though the professional duties of an architect require a great deal of interaction with others, this is not especially to the liking of the creative architect, who tends to be an introvert desiring aloneness and time for contemplative thought and creative activity. On one of our tests of interpersonal behavior, FIRO-B (Schutz, 1958), the creative architects revealed less desire to be included in group activities than any other group we have studied. Yet it is clear that when they have to interact with others they tend to do so in a dominant manner, with marked social presence, and often with consummate skill. Despite their wish to be left alone, paradoxically, or perhaps most understandably, on a measure of the desire to exert

301

and exercise control over others, creative architects score higher than any other professional group we have tested.

In the total sample of 124, the number of organizations to which architects belonged correlated −0·22 with their judged creativity. Correlations of certain scores on FIRO-B with the architects' rated creativity may also be noted. Scores on E^I (the expressed desire to include others in one's activities) correlate −0·44 with creativity, while scores on W^I (the expressed desire to be included in other's activities) correlate with creativity −0·26. W^c (the wish to be controlled by others) correlates −0·24 with creativity, while E^c (the desire to control others) correlates with creativity +0·34.

Preferences for Complexity and Creativity

The perceptiveness of the creative architect and his openness to richness and complexity of experience are revealed in several of his test performances.

The Barron–Welsh Art Scale of the Welsh Figure Preference Test (Barron and Welsh, 1952) presents to the subjects a set of sixty-two abstract line drawings which range from the simple and symmetrical to the complex and asymmetrical. In the original study which standardized this test some eighty painters from New York, San Francisco, New Orleans, Chicago and Minneapolis showed a marked preference for the complex, asymmetrical, vital and dynamic figures. A contrasting sample of non-artists revealed a marked preference for the simple and symmetrical drawings.

Table 7 shows how our three samples of architects performed on this test relative to the performance of each other and of other groups. Architects I, the forty nominated creative architects, earn a mean score of 37·1, testing very close to the artists, who scored 39·1. Then in descending order of preference for the complex and asymmetrical come writers (31·5), architects II (29·5), women mathematicians (27·0), architects III (26·1), research scientists (24·0), student engineers (21·5) and non-artists (13·9).

There is a pronounced difference in mean score between creative architects (architects I) and the comparison samples of architects unselected with respect to creativity (architects II and III) in their liking of the rich, complex and asymmetrical. Similarly, in the total sample of architects, scores on an Institute scale which measures the preference for perceptual complexity correlate $+0.48$ with rated creativity. If one considers the meaning

Table 7
Mean Scores and Standard Deviations for Various Groups
Barron–Welsh Art Scale

Group	N	Mean	SD
Artists	30	39·1	13·8
Architects I	40	37·1	9·8
Writers	20	31·5	12·5
Architects II	43	29·5	10·1
Women mathematicians	41	27·0	14·7
Architects III	41	26·1	12·1
Research scientists	45	24·0	12·3
Student engineers	40	21·5	11·8
Non-artists	300	13·9	7·6

of these preferences it is clear that creative architects are especially disposed to admit complexity and disorder into their perceptions without being made anxious by the chaos. They appear to have both a strong need and a superior capacity to achieve the most difficult and far-reaching ordering of the richness they are willing to experience.

These same traits are revealed by the architects in their making of mosaics. With twenty-two different colors available, some select the fewest possible (one used only one color, all white), while others seek to make order out of the largest number possible. And there is a significant though low positive correlation of $+0.38$ between the number of colors which an architect chooses in making a mosaic and his architectural creativity as rated by the experts.

Life History Correlates of Creativity

Turning now to the life histories of our subjects, we may ask what kinds of experiences nurtured their creativity.

It is clear from their reports that certainly not all of them had the kind of happy homes and favorable life circumstances so generally thought to be conducive to sound psychological development. Some underwent brutal treatment at the hands of sadistic fathers. These, to be sure, constitute the minority, but they appear today no less creative than those whose fathers offered them quite satisfactory male figures with whom easy identification could be made, though there is some evidence that they are not as effective or as successful in the financial and business aspects of their profession as the others.

Settling upon their life careers came early for some, one of whom already at four had decided he wanted to be an architect. Others were slow in coming to a professional identity, not deciding until several years past college that architecture was what they wanted to practice. In the case of several of these, the choice of a life profession was made the more difficult by virtue of the fact that they possessed so many skills and interests, providing them with the possibility of many quite different careers. Several were painters and sculptors before they became architects and some of them continue today these other artistic pursuits in a professional and not merely a vocational fashion along with their architectural practice.

Almost without exception one or both of the parents were of artistic temperament and considerable skill. Often it was the mother who in the architect's early years fostered his artistic potentialities by her own example as well as her tuition. And also, almost without exception the creative architects manifested considerable interest and skill in drawing and painting.

Independence and Creativity

In school and college the creative architects were tolerably good students, but in general not outstanding if one may judge from their academic grades. In college they averaged about a B. But what most clearly appears to have characterized their college careers was the independence with which they worked.

In work and courses which caught their interest they could turn in an A performance, but in courses that failed to strike their imagination, they were quite willing to do no work at all. In general, their attitude in college appears to have been one of profound skepticism. They were unwilling to accept anything on the mere say-so of their instructors. Nothing was to be accepted on faith or because it had behind it the voice of authority. Such matters might be accepted, but only after the student on his own had demonstrated to himself their validity. In a sense, they were rebellious, but they did not run counter to the standards out of sheer rebelliousness. Rather, they were spirited in their disagreement and one gets the impression that they learned most from those who were not easy with them. But clearly many of them were not easy to take. One of the most rebellious, but as it turned out, one of the most creative, was advised by the Dean of his School to quit because he had no talent; and another, having been failed in his design dissertation which attacked the stylism of the faculty, took his degree in the art department.

The self-assertive independence which they showed early and manifested so clearly in school and college still characterizes the creative architect. In the total sample two Institute scales, one measuring self-assertiveness, the other independence, correlate $+0.34$ and $+0.43$ with rated creativity.

Psychological Health and Creativity

The most striking aspect of the Minnesota Multiphasic Personality Inventory (Hathaway and McKinley, 1945) profiles for all three groups of architects, as Figure 2 shows, is an extremely high peak on the Mf (femininity) scale. This peak has appeared also for all other highly creative male groups that we have studied. Though architects II score almost as high on femininity as architects I, the difference in mean score between architects I and III is significant at the 0·01 level. For the total sample Mf (femininity) correlates with rated creativity $+0.29$.

The tendency for the more creative architects to score higher on femininity is also demonstrated on the Strong Vocational Interest Blank (Strong, 1959) where scores on the masculinity–femininity scale (high scores indicating more masculinity) correlate -0.48 with rated creativity.

The more creative the architect the more he reveals an openness to his own feelings and emotions, a sensitive intellect and understanding self-awareness, and wide-ranging interests including many which in the American culture are thought of as feminine. In the realm of sexual identifications and interests, our creative subjects appear to give more expression to the feminine side of

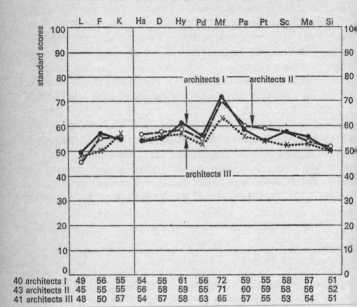

	L	F	K	Hs	D	Hy	Pd	Mf	Pa	Pt	Sc	Ma	Si
40 architects I	49	56	55	54	56	61	56	72	59	55	58	57	51
43 architects II	45	55	55	56	58	59	55	71	60	59	58	56	52
41 architects III	48	50	57	54	57	58	53	65	57	55	53	54	51

Figure 2 M M P I: standard scores with K factor added to five variables

their nature than do less creative persons. If one were to cast this into Jungian terms one would say that these creative persons are not so completely identified with their masculine persona roles as to blind themselves to or deny expression to the more feminine traits of the anima. For some the balance between masculine and feminine traits, interests and identifications is a precarious one, and for several it would appear that their presently achieved reconciliation of these opposites of their nature has been barely achieved and only after considerable psychic stress and turmoil.

In this connexion it may be noted that our architects' mean scores on the eight clinical scales of the **MMPI** (see Figure 2) range from five to ten points above the general population's standard score of fifty (57·1 for architects I, 57·7 for architects II and 55·3 for architects III). While elevations of this magnitude are, in general, less suggestive of psychopathology than of good intellect, richness and complexity of personality, and a general lack of defensiveness, we must also note that there is in the MMPI profiles of many of our creative subjects rather clear evidence of psychopathology, but also evidence of adequate control mechanisms, as the success with which they live their productive lives testifies.

In passing it may be noted that, in addition to Mf, the MMPI scales that correlate significantly in the total sample with rated creativity are the validity scale (F) +0·27, Pd (psychopathic deviate) +0·22, and Sc (schizophrenia) +0·19. But the meanings of these correlations for such an effective, reality-correlating sample as our 124 architects, are not those which would apply in psychopathological groups. In the present context they are indicative of greater unusualness of thought processes and mental content and less inhibition and freer expression of impulse and imagery.

Personality Structure and Creativity

The creative architects' relative rejection of external restraints, freedom from crippling inhibitions, and independence in thought and actions are further evidenced by the group profiles of architects I, II and III on the California Psychological Inventory (Gough, 1957) as shown in Figure 3.

The eighteen scales of this test, designed to measure the inter-personal and positive aspects of personality, provide a comprehensive survey of an individual from the point of view of his social and everyday behavior. They fall into four classes:

1. Measures of poise, ascendency and self-assurance: Do (dominance), Cs (capacity for status), Sy (sociability), Sp (social presence), Sa (self-acceptance), Wb (sense of well-being).

2. Measures of socialization, maturity and responsibility: Re (responsibility), So (socialization), Sc (self-control), To (tolerance), Gi (good impression), Cm (communality).

307

3. Measures of achievement potential and intellectual efficiency: Ac (achievement via conformance), Ai (achievement via independence), Ie (intellectual efficiency).

4. Measures of intellectual and interest modes of functioning: Py (psychological mindedness), Fx (flexibility), Fe (femininity).

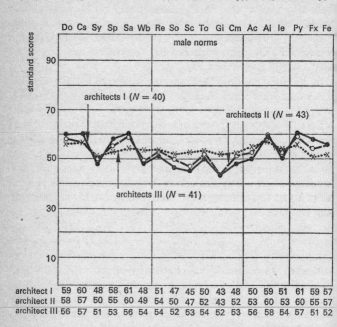

architect	Do	Cs	Sy	Sp	Sa	Wb	Re	So	Sc	To	Gi	Cm	Ac	Ai	Ie	Py	Fx	Fe
architect I	59	60	48	58	61	48	51	47	45	50	43	48	50	59	51	61	59	57
architect II	58	57	50	55	60	49	54	50	47	52	43	52	53	60	53	60	55	57
architect III	56	57	51	53	56	54	54	52	53	54	52	53	56	58	54	57	51	52

Figure 3 Profile sheet for the California Psychological Inventory: male

The profile for architects III (dotted line), the least creative architects, is a remarkably favorable one, and an unusually even one, too, with scores above the mean. The high points are on Ai (the drive to achieve in an independent fashion), Cs (capacity for status), and Py (indicative of interest in and responsiveness to the inner needs, motives and experiences of others). The impression which the group 3 profile conveys is of men who are good citizens, responsible, productive, sensitive and effective.

In contrast, the profile of the highly creative architects (solid line) is a much more uneven one, with striking dips as well as peaks. Eight of the eighteen scores are at or below the mean of fifty, while ten are above the mean.

From left to right those scales on which architects I score differently from architects III (at or beyond the 0·05 level of significance) are as follows: they score higher on Sp (social presence), and Sa (self-acceptance); lower on Wb (sense of well-being), Re (responsibility), So (socialization), Sc (self-control), To (tolerance), Gi (good impression), Cm (communality), and Ac (achievement via conformance); and higher on Py (psychological mindedness), Fx (flexibility), and Fe (femininity).

On the measures of poise, ascendency and self-assurance, creative architects reveal themselves as dominant (Do); possessed of those qualities and attributes which underlie and lead to the achievement of social status (Cs); poised, spontaneous, and self-confident in personal and social interaction (Sp); though not of an especially sociable or participative temperament (low Sy); intelligent, outspoken, sharp-witted, demanding, aggressive, and self-centered; persuasive and verbally fluent, self-confident and self-assured (Sa); and relatively uninhibited in expressing their worries and complaints (low Wb).

But it is on the second cluster of scores, those having to do with responsibility, socialization and self-control that architects I differ most widely from architects III. Their scores reveal the creative architects to be relatively free from conventional restraints and inhibitions (So and Sc), not preoccupied with the impression which they make on others and thus perhaps capable of greater independence and autonomy (Gi), and relatively ready to recognize and admit self-views which are unusual and unconventional (Cm).

As for the next cluster of scales, creative architects, like architects in general, are strongly motivated to achieve in situations in which independence in thought and action are called for (Ai). But, unlike their colleagues, they are less inclined to strive for achievement in settings where conforming behavior is expected or required. In efficiency and steadiness of intellectual effort, however, they do not differ from their fellow workers.

Their scores on the last three scales reveal the creative architects as definitely more psychologically minded (Py), more flexible (Fx), and having more femininity of interests (Fe) than architects III.

On the dimensions of the CPI, scores of architects II fall between those of architects I and architects III, but definitely closer to the former than to the latter. Indeed, there is only one scale, Cm (communality), on which architects II are significantly different from architects I: their responses more closely resemble the modal or common pattern for the inventory.

Much of our data has yet to be analysed. The full and complete image of the creative architect which is still emerging from our research will surely present an infinitely more detailed and differentiated picture than I have drawn for you today. Indeed our image of the creative architect is fast becoming several images of different types of creative architect. But if I were to summarize what is most generally characteristic of the creative architect as we have seen him, it is his high level of effective intelligence, his openness to experience, his freedom from petty restraints and impoverishing inhibitions, his esthetic sensitivity, his cognitive flexibility, his independence in thought and action, his high level of energy, his unquestioning commitment to creative endeavor and his unceasing striving for creative solutions to the ever more difficult architectural problems which he constantly sets for himself.

References

ALLPORT, G. W., VERNON, P. E., and LINDZEY, G. (1951), *Study of Values* (*Rev. edn.*): *Manual of Directions*, Houghton Mifflin.

BARRON, F., and WELSH, G. S. (1952), 'Artistic perception as a possible factor in personality style: its measurement by a figure preference test', *J. Psychol.*, vol. 33, pp. 199–203.

BLOCK, J. (1961), *The Q-sort Method in Personality Assessment and Psychiatric Research*, Thomas.

CRUTCHFIELD, R. S., WOODWORTH, D. G., and ALBRECHT, R. E. (1958), *Perceptual Performance and the Effective Person*, Personnel Laboratory, Wright Air Development, Lackland Air Force Base, Texas.

GOUGH, H. G. (1954), *The General Information Survey, Forms A and B*, University of California, Institute of Personality Assessment and Research.

GOUGH, H. G. (1957), *California Psychological Inventory Manual*, Consulting Psychologists Press.

GOUGH, H. G. (1960), 'The Adjective Check List as a personality assessment research device', *Psychol. Rep. Monogr.*, *Suppl. 2*, vol. 6, pp. 107–22.

HALL, W. B. (1958), 'The development of a technique for assessing aesthetic pre-dispositions and its application to a sample of professional research scientists', *Amer. Psychol.*, vol. 13, p. 510.

HATHAWAY, S. R., and MCKINLEY, J. C. (1945), *Minnesota Multiphasic Personality Inventory*, Psychological Corporation.

MYERS, I. B. (1958), Some findings with regard to type and manual for Myers–Briggs type indicator, Form E., unpublished.

SCHUTZ, W. C. (1958), *FIRO: A Three-Dimensional Theory of Interpersonal Behavior*, Rinehart.

STRONG, E. K., JR (1959), *Manual for Strong Vocational Interests Blanks for Men and Women, Revised Blanks (Forms M and W)*, Consulting Psychologists Press.

TERMAN, L. M. (1956), *Concept Mastery Test, Manual, Form T*, Psychological Corporation.

23 R. B. Cattell and H. J. Butcher

Creativity and Personality

Excerpts from R. B. Cattell and H. J. Butcher, *The Prediction of Achievement and Creativity*, Bobbs-Merrill, 1968, pp. 276–8, 289–96.

The Roots of Creativity in Personality Studied Biographically

Although the modern study of creativity and personality rightly makes use of and largely depends upon experiment, clinical observation, psychological testing, statistical analysis, follow-up studies, and so forth, it would be foolish to neglect entirely the illuminating clues and suggestions provided by historical and biographical studies. Impressive pioneer studies of this kind, attempting to reassess outstanding men and women of the past in terms of modern psychological knowledge and concepts were made by Galton (1870), Cox (1926) and Havelock Ellis (1946), among others.

More recently, Cattell (1959) has surveyed the lives of a large number of eminent research scientists and has summarized his findings in terms of the primary personality factors described in chapter 4 of this book [not included here]. It is important to note that this summary of findings, which will be briefly reproduced in this section, although first made widely accessible in 1963, was arrived at some ten years earlier, before the empirical studies, such as those with Drevdahl, and was presented to the New York Academy of Sciences in 1954. It would have been a pity to study the biographies only after a knowledge of the psychometric results on eminent contemporaries. As it is, however, the extent of concordance between the two approaches can be guaranteed not to be an artifact. The biographical survey, although the result of perhaps a thousand hours' reading, was in the nature of a first attempt to assess retrospectively the personalities of scientists of genius in terms of recently described personality factors. It was not on the scale of, say, Cox and Terman's monumental similar study in terms of intelligence. A arger and more detailed systematic and confirmatory research f this kind would still be well worthwhile, in spite of its formidble difficulties. We hope that a research team with a generous upply of energy and funds will undertake it.

To report the biographical findings factor by factor or man by nan and to illustrate them with the wealth of fascinating and ften amusing anecdotal support available would make this ection disproportionately long. Here are some of the salient oints.

First, in terms of broad, second-order factors, the typical esearch scientist of genius appears introverted and stable. The redominant, although obviously not universal, tendency to ntroversion observed particularly among physical scientists .g. Lord Cavendish, Dalton, Priestley, Lavoisier, Scheele, Avogadro, J. J. Thomson) is logically not surprising in view of he nature of fundamental research. Today, scientific research is ncreasingly a matter of teamwork, and the leader, or innovator, r inventor may appear to be highly dependent on effective ooperation and even on conventional social skills. But even in hese conditions and in the field of technology and applied esearch, it has been frequently pointed out (e.g. Tuska, 1957) hat the individual, fertile originator remains the crucial factor in cientific progress; and this applies even more strongly in heoretical fields, perhaps especially in mathematics (Hadamard, 945). On the whole, therefore, one would expect that the ability, haracteristic of introverts, to withdraw, to exclude the outside vorld in long periods of concentrated thought and speculation, vould outweigh in creative scientists (and even more in creative rtists) the superior ability of the extravert to communicate ocially. This is indeed what was generally found.

On the other hand, to say that creative scientists appear from he biographical evidence to be introverted rather than extraerted is too simple a statement and needs some qualification. he very broad second-order concepts of introversion and extraersion are useful for a first approximation, but can conceal as nuch as they illuminate, and a description in terms of primary actors may be needed to make the picture clearer and more onsistent. Certainly, this seems to be so for eminent scientists. he general tendency to introversion just mentioned does not

apply to all the components, but seems to be largely concentrate
in the A factor, of which a detailed description was given i
chapter 4. Our reference in this section to the apparently intro
verted nature of Lord Cavendish, Dalton and others wa
mainly referable to a typical A-character – skeptical, withdraw
unsociable, critical, precise. Cavendish's biographer, for instance
gives a vivid picture of his dislike of formal, pretentious socia
gatherings and describes one occasion when, required to mee
eminent foreign scientists, he broke away and ran down th
corridor 'squeaking like a bat'! But if it appears to be generall
true from the study of biographies that eminent scientists hav
been low on factor A, the same is not true of another componer
of introversion–extraversion, factor H. Here the strong impres
sion is that they are, in general, well up at the positive end of th
scale, with high 'parasympathetic immunity', and displaying
characteristic resourcefulness, adaptability and adventurousnes
(probably largely constitutional). On factor F, however (Surg
ency–Desurgency), one gets the overwhelming impression tha
eminent scientists of the past have been low (desurgent), com
pared with the general population and with many particula
professions and callings. One has only to think, for instance, c
Pascal, William Hamilton, Newton, Boyle, Dalton and Farada
to form the opinion that introspection, restraint, brooding an
solemnity of manner, all indicators of desurgency, have bee
highly characteristic.

These observations suggest a certain paradoxical structur
within the general introversion second stratum factor, in tha
traits that generally tend to correlate positively in the genera
population may very well correlate negatively among creativ
scientists, and this may be the basis of Kretschmer's notion o
'warring heredity', in that such people appear to have a con
stitutionally low susceptibility to inhibition, as would be show
by a low score on factor H, while yet being highly inhibited, a
would be shown by a low score on factor F. Similarly, it may b
noted that Abeim (*The Psychology of the Philosopher*) found i
high degree of inhibition to be characteristic, though not s
generally combined (as in scientists) with an essentially dominan
personality.

So much for the apparently rather complex question of intro

version. The general impression of stability among scientists requires less discussion. One must agree with Terman that, among scientists at least, the average level of ego strength and emotional stability is noticeably higher among creative geniuses than among the general population, though it is possibly lower than among men of comparable intelligence and education who go into administrative and similar positions. High anxiety and excitability appear common (e.g. Priestley, Darwin, Kepler), but full-blown neurosis quite rare.

To digress for a moment, it is probably in this respect that creative scientists and artists diverge most markedly. Among the latter, particularly perhaps in the nineteenth and twentieth centuries, neurotic, psychotic and addictive tendencies are so frequent as hardly to need illustration. This applies least, perhaps, to composers, though from Beethoven to Ravel, Bartok and Peter Warlock (Philip Heseltine) their lives have often been stormy or unhappy. The tendency among writers, from Flaubert, Ruskin, Nietzsche and Strindberg in the nineteenth century to Proust, Eugene O'Neill and Dylan Thomas in the twentieth is clearer, and possibly clearest of all among painters (Van Gogh, Utrillo, Modigliani). Many different explanations, temperamental, sociological and economic, could be given for this greater susceptibility to nervous disorder among artistic than among scientific geniuses. In this sphere the 'great wits to madness near allied' contention has most plausibility, but has little explanatory value. The topic is a fascinating one, and a gram or two of scientific research would be welcome in contrast to the mountains of romantic speculation that have been piled up.

Returning to the characteristics of creative scientists, one or two further features stood out from a wide reading of their biographies. They appeared to have the socially rather uncongenial and 'undemocratic' attitudes, associated with dominance, E, and perhaps also with the L factor. We have already described somewhat similar findings by Roe and by Barron. This dominance, amounting to a belief that most people are rather stupid, seems to be the root of a rugged independence of mind, and a readiness to face endless difficulties and social discouragement, which are needed in any pursuit of a completely novel project.

Last, these people have a quite exceptional degree of *intellectual* self-sufficiency. They depart freely from all the customary judgements of the world, yet are not appalled by their isolation. They appear, indeed, barely to notice that they are eccentric, and they expect as a natural right the freedom to be 'odd' that they themselves would fairly grant to others, but that the average man is often quite unwilling to grant. In personality research, a dimension of this kind, labeled Q_2 in our series, has long been known. It is interesting to see that what it usually connotes – a rich supply of inner resources and interests – is typically present in the biographical evidence, too.

To cut short what really justifies a wide anecdotal illustration, we summarize the personality profile that appears to have distinguished the creative scientist from both the average man and the professional man successful in a routine occupation. It is a profile of sizothyme hardness, high intelligence, stability, dominance, desurgent taciturnity, and high self-sufficiency. [. . .]

Creativity Prediction by Psychological Tests Aimed at a 'Creative Type'

It is necessary to bear in mind the distinction between *adjustment* and *effectiveness* calculations of fitness for a task. In the former, we ask what characteristics distinguish the person in the job from those in other jobs. In the latter, we obtain regression coefficients of personality, ability and motivation factors upon a criterion of effectiveness or efficiency among those actually in the job. Both these criteria have been used in research on creativity. With a few exceptions, however, both have very often been studied with *ad hoc* scales and supposed measures of creative ability of unknown factor composition and meaning, so that psychological insight and generalization have been impaired. Among the exceptions are the studies of Drevdahl ('adjustment' criterion), Jones, Chambers and Tollefson ('effectiveness' criterion).

The first study using primary personality factors was carried out by Drevdahl (1956) with graduate students. His criterion was the creativity shown by these students in essays, research, and class discussion, as evaluated by professors familiar with them. He found statistically significant differences between students of high and low creativity on the 16 PF test in that the former were more sizothyme (A—), self-sufficient (Q_2), desurgent ($F-$) and radical (Q_1).

The more extensive study that was next made was concerned specifically with creativity in the scientific field. A careful search was made for forty-six leading research physicists, forty-six distinguished research biologists and fifty-two productive researchers in psychology (all selected by committees in their particular fields, and all of whom completed both A and B forms of the 16 PF Questionnaire). A full account of this investigation is given elsewhere (Cattell and Drevdahl, 1955), but chief among the questions that can be asked are:

1. In what way does the personality profile of the creative scientist differ from that of the average man?
2. How does it differ from persons of equal intelligence and similar education whose eminence is in teaching or administration rather than research?
3. How is the profile of those talented in science different from that of innovators in radically different areas, as in art and literature?

The answer to the first question is shown in Figure 1, from which it will be seen at once that the personality profile is very different from that of the average man (indicated by the central dark band), no fewer than five factors deviating at a $p = 0.01$ significance or beyond.

Moreover, the differences in every case support, through measures on contemporary research leaders, the kind and direction of deviation we had inferred from the biographical accounts of historically important researchers. Notably, the researcher is decidedly more sizothyme, more intelligent, more dominant, and more inhibited or desurgent. As we pass toward the bottom of the diagram, into dimensions we have not previously discussed, we notice other divided peaks and troughs indicating that researchers are also significantly more emotionally sensitive ($I+$), more radical (Q_1+), and somewhat more given to controlling their behavior by an exacting self-concept. It is noteworthy that in so far as the conclusions from our different instruments can overlap, Anne Roe's results, already described in the previous chapter, and our own are in essential agreement.

As far as comparison with the general population is concerned, physicists, biologists and psychologists are close together and form one family. However, if space permitted, we could study

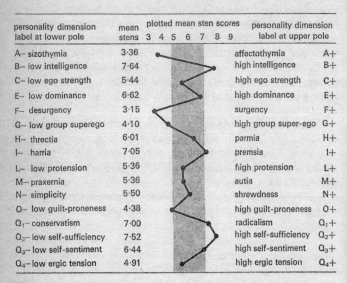

personality dimension label at lower pole	mean stens	plotted mean sten scores 3 4 5 6 7 8 9	personality dimension label at upper pole	
A– sizothymia	3·36		affectothymia	A+
B– low intelligence	7·64		high intelligence	B+
C– low ego strength	5·44		high ego strength	C+
E– low dominance	6·62		high dominance	E+
F– desurgency	3·15		surgency	F+
G– low group superego	4·10		high group super-ego	G+
H– threctia	6·01		parmia	H+
I– harria	7·05		premsia	I+
L– low protension	5·36		high protension	L+
M– praxernia	5·36		autia	M+
N– simplicity	5·50		shrewdness	N+
O– low guilt-proneness	4·38		high guilt-proneness	O+
Q_1– conservatism	7·00		radicalism	Q_1+
Q_2– low self-sufficiency	7·52		high self-sufficiency	Q_2+
Q_3– low self-sentiment	6·44		high self-sentiment	Q_3+
Q_4– low ergic tension	4·91		high ergic tension	Q_4+

Figure 1 Mean 16 PF profile of eminent researchers ($N = 144$) in physics, biology and psychology. (A new 'control' group for the general adult male population has become available since this profile was first published. The slight changes in norms do not affect the stated conclusions)

some interesting minor differences, e.g. the finding that the physicists are even more sizothyme than other researchers, and the psychologists (perhaps we should say with embarrassment!), more dominant and less desurgent.

In answer to our second question, it is clear that, when compared with the general population, eminent researchers have a good deal in common with those who have achieved an outstanding reputation for teaching and administration. For example, both are decidedly above the population average in ego strength, intelligence, dominance and social obligation as shown in the self-sentiment. Nevertheless, it would be foolish to leave out of our calculations, or our selection formulas, whatever makes for high achievement *as such*, regardless of field. In separating the potential creative researcher from the equally able administrator and scholar, we must discern where to drive in the wedge. At the 1 per cent significance level, researchers are more sizothyme, less emotionally stable, more self-sufficient, more bohemian, and more radical than are successful administrators and teachers. Compared next with the general college population from which they come (using the general undergraduate population norms), researchers are again more sizothyme and more intelligent, more self-sufficient, more withdrawn, more paranoid and anxious and more inhibited $(F-)$.

When we consider second-order personality factors, the most striking fact is that the researcher is uniformly lower on all primary personality factors involved in the second-order *extraversion* factor. On the implications of this decided introversion of the researcher, we shall have more to say in a moment. But there is a relevant, detailed discussion by Broadbent (1958) of the application of information theory to brain action, in which one of his main propositions is that as long as you use a lot of the channels for input, you have too few free channels for scanning. That could explain a good deal here. The typical extravert conceivably has too many channels taking in information – or at least, alert to the external trivia of everyday life – and not enough for scanning accepted material. Or, to quote Wordsworth instead of information theory: 'The world is too much with us.' And if we paraphrase his next line: 'Talking and visiting, we lay waste our powers.'

Let us turn to the third question, namely, 'To what extent are creative persons in one field like those in another, e.g. those in science like those in the arts?' (Or, in other words, 'Is the creative personality a recognizable type despite differences in the area of operation?') Here we again receive a definite answer.

In the first place, within science itself, we have evidence from the work of Jones (1964, 1966) on groups very different from the leading academic researchers here considered. With groups of chemists and chemical engineers in New England, forty-five and thirty-five of whom were very carefully rated for their creativity and inventiveness in the work situation, he obtained correlations with personality factors as shown:

	C	E	G	H	O
Chemists	0·27*	0·64*	−0·29	0·48*	−0·64*
Engineers	0·38*	0·28*	−0·07	0·27*	−0·43*

	Q_1	Q_2	Q_3	Q_4
Chemists	0·64*	0·04	0·43*	−0·49*
Engineers	0·38*	0·40*	0·24*	−0·29*

It is interesting to compare this also with the correlations obtained by Meredith for creativity on students ($N = 162$) as measured by the Maddi SPI:

A	B	C	E	F	G	H	I
−0·04	0·17*	0·08	0·27**	0·06	−0·25**	0·11	0·24**

L	M	N	O	Q_1	Q_2	Q_3	Q_4
−0·03	0·35**	0·05	−0·14	0·17*	0·19*	−0·06	−0·12

A commendably large sample for contrasting creative areas was investigated by Chambers (1964, 1966), who checked the relation to personality factors E, H and Q_2 on 400 chemists and 340 psychologists, carefully evaluated for creativity. The general findings for E and Q_2 stood up on both samples, with t-values ranging from 2 to 5. Unfortunately, the full range of source traits on the 16 PF was not included, but the importance of high dominance, E, and high self-sufficiency can be considered now thrice demonstrated.

Finally, we can look at the pooled results of the most substantial research (in numbers, criterion objectivity, and breadth of personality factors involved) yet accomplished in this area, combining the Drevdahl, Jones, Tollefson and Chambers findings and comparing pure and applied researchers (Figure 2).

As more research on creativity is done, increasing the accuracy of determination of personality by using two or more forms of the 16 PF, and by extending measurement to include motivation factors in the MAT, it will become appropriate to concentrate on what test factor weights determine creativity in different fields. At present, we have to deal only with 'indications' of differences, but the common pattern is strongly evident. The latter is not necessarily that of an accommodating and popular personality, and its qualities of independence and forthrightness would commonly evoke the criticism 'tactless'. As Lowell Kelly's results with medical men show, this pattern of personality tends to be subjected to group antipathy and derogation. Central in it

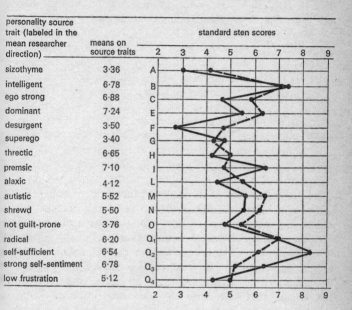

personality source trait (labeled in the mean researcher direction)	means on source traits	standard sten scores
sizothyme	3·36	A
intelligent	6·78	B
ego strong	6·88	C
dominant	7·24	E
desurgent	3·50	F
superego	3·40	G
threctic	6·65	H
premsic	7·10	I
alaxic	4·12	L
autistic	5·52	M
shrewd	5·50	N
not guilt-prone	3·76	O
radical	6·20	Q_1
self-sufficient	6·54	Q_2
strong self-sentiment	6·78	Q_3
low frustration	5·12	Q_4

——————— academic creative researchers

— — — — —industrial, applied creative researchers

Figure 2 Profile of basic and applied (industrial) researchers. This combines with suitable weighting results from Cattell, Chambers, Drevdahl, Jones and Tollefson researches referred to in the text

is a dominant independence, E, some high inhibition (in F, not unlike that in the neurotic), low conformity (on G), high self-sufficiency (Q_2), high adventurousness (H), high radicalism (Q_1), and tough disregard for sentimentality (A—). (The high premsia, I, seems to be characteristic of certain groups, e.g. it is marked in Meredith's students, and in Drevdahl's artists, but absent, as a true *contributor* to the criterion, from Jones's chemists and engineers of mature years. (Possibly it is a necessary youthful 'process variable'.)

An equally clear answer can now be given, through the work of Drevdahl, to the question of whether creativity in the arts depends on similar personalities or very different ones. A study of 153 writers of imaginative literature (Drevdahl and Cattell, 1958) shows a profile on the 16 PF that, by any pattern similarity coefficient (an index designed to express over-all similarity between two profiles), would definitely be placed in the same family as the profiles for the creative scientists; and the same is true of artists, taken from persons listed in *Who's Who in American Art*. This similarity also holds, as Drevdahl (1956) has shown, for those who are graduate students in the field of liberal arts and who are selected as highly creative.

In setting up these experiments, we had actually expected some major differences between those talented in science and those creative in the arts. Doubtless, further search will reveal other dimensions, but even on these primary dimensions a few statistically significant differences can be found. For example, artists and literary men provide some contrast with scientists in being more bohemian (M factor), more emotionally sensitive (I factor), and at a higher ergic tension level (Q4 factor) (Cross, Cattell, and Butcher, 1967). This may well be a more specific statement of that general tendency to greater instability and emotionality that Terman found in historical instances of men eminent in the arts, compared with those eminent in the sciences. However, the emotional 'instability' or 'immaturity' here is that of the high I factor rather than ego weakness (C−). That autism (M factor), the tendency to follow through one's inmost urges regardless of external demands, should distinguish artistic from scientific creativity is exactly what one would expect from an analysis of the essential differences between these types of creativity. The creativity of the scientist is always tempered by a host of brutally unsympathetic and inexorable facts, for his theory must always in some sense work out in practice. The higher ergic tension of the artist may sustain the conclusion that the artist is a more frustrated person, or that high anxiety is less inimical to artistic than to scientific production.

322

Although such differences of personality and motivation between artistic, scientific, and other areas of creativity can be found and will doubtless continue to be found in more refined studies, the really remarkable feature of these research findings, especially for our present concentrated survey, is the high degree of similarity and consistency of the personality picture across *all* areas. It would almost seem as if the differences between science, art and literature are differences of particular skills and interests only, and that the fundamental characteristic of the creative, original person is a type of personality.

It is on this basis that we have argued above that the diversity of criterion factors found by Taylor is likely to converge on one general second order creativity factor, loading particularly his primaries 1 and 7, for in all these diverse fields of performance there is evidently something substantially in common.

Creativity Prediction by Regression on a Criterion of Effectiveness within a Research Group

So far we have asked what distinguishes the *type* of the creative student, in terms of abilities and personality traits, from the average one, or from the equally intelligent but uncreative adult. But let us now turn to the alternative examination by a *weighting of attributes* calculation. The weakness of the adjustment criterion is that it merely defines who stays in the job, and that it indicates not only those who are good at that job but also inevitably to some extent those who have failed alternative jobs. For example, it used to be not uncommon to find among psychology students some who had wanted to follow a science but had failed the mathematics necessary for chemistry or physics. And we have all heard of academic men who became administrators because they failed to find a successful research trail.

It is conceivable, of course, that a person in research is a failed teacher, but there are reasons for believing that the selection that has produced the personality profile typical of research workers is not, in the main, a backfiring selection. It is a selection tending to concentrate in the field the people who are better at it. However, the defects in the 'job adjustment' profile assumptions make it vital also to have data showing the relation of personality

323

factors and actual research effectiveness. We need, in fact, data in terms of regression of personality measures upon a criterion of research productivity. Usually, we seek at first a linear regression equation, but it can progress to nonlinear prediction. What data we have so far are as precious as they are fragmentary. But at least these exploratory studies, e.g. by Jones and Cattell (1966), Tollefson (1961), and Chambers (1964) on predictors and by Taylor (1955, 1957) and his colleagues on the criteria, are highly encouraging.

Among the first studies of research efficiency or productivity measured on the job, one should note that of Van Zelst and Kerr (1954), who found, among other characteristics of productive researchers, a disbelief in egalitarian 'committee-like' practices in research groups and a need for withdrawal and cogitation. This finding again appears reasonably in line with the personality characteristics we have already shown to be typical.

A first study to deal with well-known, replicable personality factors is that of Tollefson (1961), measuring fifty-three Ph.D. chemists in the research department of a nationally known oil company. Here the indicated correlations between primary factors on the 16 PF and rated magnitude of contribution to research were as in the following specification equation:

$$\text{Research performance} = 0.25B + 0.46C + 0.32E - 0.46I + 0.33N + 0.45Q_1 + 0.29Q_2 - 0.35[1]$$

Here B is general intelligence, C is ego strength, E is dominance, I is emotional sensitivity, N is shrewdness, Q_1 is radicalism, Q_2 is self-sufficiency. The criterion in this study was based partly on the number of papers produced and partly on their rated importance. This is reasonably in line with what would be expected from the differences between researchers and other academics listed in the preceding section, except for source trait I, Premsia-versus-Harria, which needs comment. Evidence is accumulating that the I source-trait dimension is related to early home background. It appears that 95 per cent of the variance arises from environmental determination and only

1. This is a constant added so that when the individual's 16 PF scores are entered as stens the performance estimates will come out in stens. When the regressions are zero, the factor is not entered.

5 per cent from hereditary determination. So far as preliminary evidence can show, the increase of Premsia, i.e. of protected emotional sensitivity, has to do with overprotection and indulgence in childhood. Because this factor was found by Cattell and his associates to be negatively related to various kinds of achievement, and by Cattell and Stice (1960) to be related to 'hindering' and 'self-centeredness' in small group behavior, it is hard to interpret the rather high I found in academic researchers (not, be it noted, with industrial researchers) as advantageous. More likely, we are dealing here with an incidental and nonuseful characteristic of academic selection!

References

BROADBENT, D. E. (1958), *Perception and Communication*, Pergamon.

CATTELL, R. B. (1959), 'The personality and motivation of the researcher from measurements of contemporaries and from biography', in C. W. Taylor (ed.), *The 1959 University of Utah Research Conference on the Identification of Creative Scientific Talent*, University of Utah Press, pp. 77–93.

CATTELL, R. B., and DREVDAHL, J. E. (1955), 'A comparison of the personality profile (16 PF) of eminent researchers with that of eminent teachers and administrators, and of the general population', *Brit. J. Psychol.*, vol. 46, pp. 248–61.

CATTELL, R. B., and STICE, G. F. (1960), *The Dimensions of Groups and Their Relations to the Behavior of Members*, Institute of Personality and Ability Testing.

CHAMBERS, J. A. (1964), 'Relating personality and biographical factors to scientific creativity', *Psychol. Monogr.*, vol. 78, no. 584.

CHAMBERS, J. A. (1966), *Selecting the Potentially Creative Scientist*, University of Southern Florida, Psychology Department (unpublished paper).

COX, C. M. (1926), *Genetic Studies of Genius, Vol. II. The Early Mental Traits of Three Hundred Geniuses*, Stanford University Press.

CROSS, P., CATTELL, R. B., and BUTCHER, H. J. (1967), 'The personality pattern of creative artists', *Brit. J. educ. Psychol.*, vol. 37, pp. 292–9.

DREVDAHL, J. E. (1956), 'Factors of importance for creativity', *J. clin. Psychol.*, vol. 12, pp. 21–6.

DREVDAHL, J. E., and CATTELL, R. E. (1958), 'Personality and creativity in artists and writers', *J. clin. Psychol.*, vol. 14, pp. 107–11.

ELLIS, H. (1946), *A Study of British Genius*, Houghton Mifflin.

GALTON, F. (1870), *Hereditary Genius: An Inquiry into its Laws and Consequences*, Appleton.

HADAMARD, J. (1945), *The Psychology of Invention in the Mathematical Field*, Princeton University Press.

JONES, F. E. (1964), 'Predictor variables for creativity in industrial science', *J. appl. Psychol.*, vol. 48, pp. 134–6.

JONES, F. E. (1966), *Prediction of High-Level Creativity in Industrial Scientific Work* (private circular), Renssalaer Polytechnic Institute, Troy, New Jersey.

JONES, F. E., and CATTELL, R. B. (1966), *Weighting of the 16 PF Questionnaire Factors in Predicting Industrial Creativity* (private circular), Renssalaer Polytechnic Institute, Troy, New Jersey.

TAYLOR, C. W. (ed.) (1955), *The 1955 University of Utah Research Conference on the Identification of Creative Scientific Talent*, University of Utah Press.

TAYLOR, C. W. (ed.), (1957), *The 1957 University of Utah Research Conference on the Identification of Creative Scientific Talent*, University of Utah Press.

TOLLEFSON, D. (1961), Response to humor in relation to other measures of personality, *Ph.D. Dissertation*, University of Illinois. Unpublished.

TUSKA, C. D. (1957), *Inventors and Inventions*, McGraw-Hill.

VAN ZELST, R. H., and KERR, W. A. (1954), 'Personality self-assessment of scientific and technical personnel', *J. appl. Psychol.*, vol. 38, pp. 145–7.

24 C. W. Taylor and R. L. Ellison

Prediction of Creativity with the Biographical Inventory

Excerpts from C. W. Taylor and R. L. Ellison, 'Predicting creative performance from multiple measures', in C. W. Taylor (ed.), *Widening Horizons in Creativity*, Wiley, 1964, pp. 230–40, 253.

Biographical Studies of NASA Scientists and of Science Students

In our studies of the relationship of biographical information to success in science, approximately 1600 scientists have filled out one of our 300-item multiple-choice questionnaires. The vast majority of this work has been conducted in conjunction with NASA (National Aeronautical and Space Administration). In a discussion of the biographical items in the Biographical Inventory, the term 'biographical information' is in one sense a misnomer. The Biographical Inventory contains a wide variety of questions about childhood activities, experiences, sources of derived satisfactions and dissatisfactions, descriptions of the subject's parents, academic experiences, attitudes and interests, descriptions of leisure activities, value preferences, self-descriptions and evaluations, etc. The items thus encompass a wide variety of information because they are not limited to a narrow definition of what constitutes biographical experiences. By using such a broad biographical approach, potentially we can attempt to measure not only previous life history experiences, including past environmental effects on a person, but also to assess the outcome or manifestation of the hereditary-environment combination as it is personified in the individuals studied.

Before the NASA project, two studies had been conducted to explore the relationship of biographical information to scientific accomplishment, one by Ellison (1960) and one on Air Force scientists. The validities found between biographical scores from the empirically derived keys (scoring keys built on the data at hand) for each criterion and the scores on the corresponding criterion were extremely high on the initial sample in both studies. No (double checking) cross validation was attempted in either of these two preliminary studies because of the relatively small sample size, but the best items from both studies were identified and retained for future use in the NASA project. However, *a priori* scoring keys (keys built on our best hunches at that time) for the biographical responses also worked well on the sample of Air Force scientists, yielding better validities than any of the other 100 nonbiographical psychological test scores.

We have not been completely orthodox in our Biographical Inventory research. In both these studies, the items that were keyed and retained for use in future research were somewhat arbitrarily selected. In other words, they were not identified strictly in terms of the usual level-of-significance requirements. These requirements were waived with the conviction that a consistent relationship, even in the lower levels of validity across studies and samples, was more important in the long run than a single statistically significant correlation in any one study. Our approach has admittedly been actuarial in nature, being built upon 'experience-table' information for each item, so that the total information accumulated is utilized in order to maximize the results obtained. The items so identified across a series of studies would probably meet the requirements of statistical significance as the sample size increased. The typical alternative-criterion correlations obtained and scored tended to be rather low, ranging from about 0·20 to 0·40, with at least a certain minimal percentage of the sample choosing each alternative to the item. The items so selected to form a longer combined test resulted in the high initial validities even though each item-alternative accounted for only a small percentage of the valid variance. We have sometimes described the Biographical Inventory with its many items and alternatives as an instrument consisting of a great many little oars, with each oar pulling only slightly in the right direction, but with all the oars in concert exerting a powerful pull. We also caution people not to lean too heavily on any single oar.

C. W. Taylor and R. L. Ellison

The First Study of the Biographical Inventory

Based on the two Utah studies [see original text], a new form (Form A) of the Biographical Inventory was constructed and administered to 354 NASA scientists. The form consisted of 300 items which were subjectively classified into four sections: developmental history (up to age twenty-one), parents and family life, academic background and adult life and interests. The criteria used in the study of NASA scientists can be classified into three types: criteria available as official records at each of the NASA research centers, two criteria on the number of publications and the number of patents collected from the scientist and criteria constructed by the investigators for research purposes only. For the first administration an over-all evaluation measure, which we have termed an official rating, was already available at the research center. Three criteria were administered for research purposes only, a productivity check list, a creativity check list and, three months later, a seven-step creativity rating scale. Both the creativity check list and the creativity rating scale were constructed on the basis of Lacklen's formulation as previously described.[1] The correlation between the creativity check list and the creativity rating administered three months later was 0·69. Considering the time interval and the radically different nature of the criterion forms, this reliability estimate was considered satisfactory.

In the data analysis, the sample of 354 scientists was arbitrarily divided (on an approximately random basis) into two subsamples of 178 and 176. A separate item-alternative analysis was performed on each sample against each of three criteria. In the item-alternative analysis, biserial correlations were computed for each alternative in each item against each of the criteria. Large computers have been utilized for all statistical work.

1. It was defined as follows: 'Rate the product of the man's work as to its creativity. Consider the implications of his work, its impact, the originality of the approaches used by the scientist, the comprehensiveness and novelty of the solutions, the degree to which his work has opened the way and stimulated further research and has raised new, unforeseen problems. In short, evaluate the importance of his work in terms of its *breadth of applicability*, *do not* consider other aspects of his performance – *only* the creativity of his work'. [*Ed.*]

Following the item-alternative analysis, we tried a variety of scoring keys and weighting of alternatives and have retained from 125 to 150 items per scoring key, with one or more alternatives entering into the scoring of each item. Empirically derived keys were constructed on each of the two samples and applied to the opposite sample, so that a double cross-validation study was carried out. The average cross-validity coefficient on the two samples was 0·55 on the official over-all rating criterion and 0·52 on the creativity criterion. In one of the two subsamples, complete data were available on the two creativity criteria. The cross-validity coefficient of the best biographical score against a combination of the two creativity criteria was 0·59, a remarkably high cross validity for only a single test and for such an early period in the history of creativity research and measurement.

If the above validity coefficient of 0·59 was corrected for attenuation (unreliability) *in the criterion only* (a justifiable correction), the corrected validity coefficient increased so that it reached approximately 0·70. Thus, with a perfectly reliable criterion measure, approximately half of the variation in creative performance could be accounted for with only one total biographical score – an extremely high degree of prediction. Further leverage on predicting this criterion could be obtained by multiple correlation techniques, that is, by a best-weighted combination of biographical subscores.

The four subscores of the Biographical Inventory, ordered in terms of their validity, were, first, adult life and interests; second, academic background; third, developmental history; and last, parents and family life.

The Second Study of the Biographical Inventory

Before the second study, a new form (Form B) of the Biographical Inventory was constructed; this form was based on the best items of the previous administration. The 'deadwood' items were eliminated to make room for new items to be evaluated in this form, with the hope that in the new set of 300 items the percentage of 'livewood' would be increased. The best items from Form A (i.e. those which worked consistently across both subsamples) were subjectively reclassified into the following four substantive categories: (a) independence, (b) professional self-confidence, (c) general intellectuality and (d) miscellaneous. These four keys were applied to the biographical responses of the scientists at the second research center to obtain four subscores and a total score.

At this center a revised form of the creativity rating scale was administered as the sole criterion score collected for research purposes only. A number of official evaluations were available, and data were collected on the most appropriate ones. These ratings were the following: knowledge of work, initiative, judgement, industry, reliability and cooperation. In addition, the number of publications and the number of patents were obtained for each scientist.

Although these scientists had different work specialties, were at different geographic allocations, and were measured on a slightly different creativity criterion than was used at the first administration, the average cross-validity coefficient for the total creativity biographical score based on the previous study was 0·47 against the creativity criterion on scientists at the new research center. With the use of multiple correlation techniques on the four subscores of the inventory, correlations in the low 50s were obtained, with 'professional self-confidence' being the most valid subscore.

Again the same procedure was followed in analysing the data. Briefly, the total sample of 300 scientists was split into two sub-samples of 148 and 152, and an item-alternative analysis was carried out for each sample in a double cross-validation design. The cross-validation results from the item analysis at the second center were generally not as high as those obtained from the analysis at the first center, although a cross-validity coefficient of 0·60 was obtained in predicting publications. The average cross-validity coefficient for predicting creativity across the two sub-samples at the second research center was 0·48. A comparison of this correlation of 0·48 with the correlation of 0·47 obtained by using the keys from the previous study indicates a high degree of stability in the biographical keys; it also indicates that it probably will not be necessary to build separate keys for each NASA research installation. The extent to which these keys would hold up in an industrial situation remains to be determined. The official rating scores which were available at the research center were without exception not very predictable, evidently because of the manner in which the official ratings were obtained.

The Third Study of the Biographical Inventory

Another form of the inventory was constructed in which the best items from all the previous studies were used. This form (Form C) has recently been administered to over 800 scientists at a third NASA research center, where 97 per cent of the biographical inventories distributed were completed or otherwise accounted for.

At the third NASA research center, in contrast to the other two research centers visited, there is no existing rating procedure for the evaluation of the scientific personnel. Promotions are handled by means of letters of recommendation and by meetings of those concerned. Thus, the criterion measures collected at this center may have been influenced by this comparative lack of rating experience. The only criteria collected were ratings on scales constructed by the investigators, consisting of the following: quantity of work, skill in getting along with people, creativity and an over-all evaluation.

The procedures followed in this third study were again the same as in the previous administrations. After the total sample was divided into various organizational subsamples, cross-validation coefficients were obtained which ranged from 0·41 to 0·48 for the creativity criterion. For the prediction of the number of publications the average cross-validity coefficient on the total sample was 0·62. We have not yet obtained the results from applying the keys from the previous studies of the inventory to this sample.

Examples of Item Content of the Biographical Inventory

In this section a few examples of some of the better biographical items will be presented with a brief discussion of the types of items which have generally failed to contribute to the identification of scientific talent. A factor analysis of the discriminating items in the Biographical Inventory, presently under way, will contribute additional information about both the interpretation of the items and their interrelationships. It should be remembered that the following relationships are characteristic only of the majority; there would be some individuals whose responses to each item would be exceptions to the general finding. All the items cited related to the creativity criterion and on occasions to other criteria as well. Since there may have been some distortion in the responses of the subjects, the extent to which these responses correspond to the actual situation remains to be determined.

A number of items demonstrated that characteristics of self-determination and individualistic orientation (or inner directedness) are positively related to the criteria. A facet of this is concerned with how the individual scientist elects to expend his energies and to what area of his life he devotes himself. For example, a definite task orientation appears to be involved in the following question. If an individual responds that, to a great extent, he is the kind of person who becomes so absorbed in his work and interests that he does not mind a lack of friends, this response was positively related to the criteria, whereas another person's response that this does not describe him at all was negatively related to the criteria. Another example of an item in this areas is as follows:

Assume that you are in a situation in which the following two alternative courses of action arise. Which one of the two would you be more likely to do? (A) Be a good team man so that others like to work with me, or (B) gain a reputation through controversy, if necessary, as one whose scientific word can be trusted.

Response A was correlated negatively with the criteria, and response B was positively related. Wherever this attitude of independence originated, it evidently tended to have been present during the student's academic career. For example, if the scientist reported that he questioned his professors on subject matter considerably more often than average, his response was positively related to the criteria.

The relationship of undergraduate college grade-point average to success as a scientist has been shown by many investigations to be at best low; however, occasionally a few items in the academic section of the Biographical Inventory which are concerned with self-reported academic performance emerge with a low but consistent relationship to supervisor ratings. For example, a B.A. or B.Sc. degree or less has a negative relationship to the criteria, whereas the Ph.D. degree has a positive relationship. If a student describes his college undergraduate work as being well above average and himself as being satisfied with his progress, this response is positively related to the criteria. If the student succeeded exceptionally well in his *engineering* or *biological* science courses, this has a positive relationship to the criteria, while a response of succeeding fairly well has a negative relationship. Other items, such as those concerned with success in *mathematics*, *physics* and *chemistry*, have *not* consistently shown a relationship with the creativity criterion.

One of the more consistently surprising items which has demonstrated a positive relationship to creativity is concerned with attitudes toward making repairs around the house before the age of eighteen. If the subject responds that he had a *strong dislike* of making such repairs, this response is positively related to creative performance. It is suspected that this item is related to the personality factor of femininity. Previous research has shown that this dimension has some relationship to creativity. It may also reflect certain sensitivities and an orientation toward ideas as opposed to more mechanical interests.

This discussion would not be complete without a brief statement of the types of items that have failed to discriminate. Generally speaking, items that measure a small specific segment of previous experience or a specific fact in a life history have not been fruitful. For example, items such as the extent of participation in childhood job enterprises (cutting lawns, washing cars, etc.) or the number of times that the subject had changed residence by the time he entered college, or the age at which he held his first paying job, or the highest level of achievement he obtained in the boy scouts, have not survived the validation process. Another area which has so far proved barren for identifying scientific talent concerns descriptions of various parental characteristics, such as a mother's or father's dominance, affection, encouragement, strictness or permissiveness. Although it is expected that this is an area of definite importance, it has proved to be extremely difficult to cultivate successfully. One of the reasons is probably the complex network of interactions that exists between the subject's parents, so that when any one facet of their behavior has been measured it does not provide enough information about how the other parental characteristics interact; thus, by itself the characteristic being measured appears unimportant.

It would be difficult to estimate the number of items which either have been tried out in one form of our inventory or have been carefully examined for their potential discriminating power. Certainly the number exceeds 1000. Undoubtedly it would be possible to construct additional valid items to add to the Biographical Inventory, but according to our current understanding and measurement skills most of the fertile ground has already been plowed. Consequently, gains in the near future through item construction will probably be small, although not necessarily unimportant. [. . .]

A study on this problem supported by the National Science Foundation (Taylor, Cooley and Nielsen, 1963) highlights some of the complexities involved in early identification of scientific talent, since it implies that our present educational program is not geared to give the most appropriate kind of training as far as creative scientific achievement is concerned. In the N.S.F.-supported summer science program for high school students, some of the students have the unusual opportunity to participate full time in research activities. Others participate in advanced classroom-only work. The main interest of our study was to determine whether the creative and productive characteristics found for scientists on the job, as discovered in recent studies of Air Force, NASA and other scientists, were measurable on high school students in these programs and whether these same characteristics were more closely related to the performance of the students in these research activities than to classroom-only performances.

The data analysis has revealed that two distinct groups can be identified, a research achievement group and an academic achievement group. In general, the predictors with validity for the academic program tended to have low, zero or negative validities in the research programs, and vice versa. In this study the Biographical Inventory was modified to be appropriate for younger age groups. It was found that the vast majority of the items could be used without modification; a few were revised, and a few dropped. Because some items had to be rewritten, because scoring keys were constructed on mature scientists, and because predictive (follow-up) validities rather than concurrent validities were to be determined, we expected the revised Biographical Inventory not to work very well, if at all, in such short-range predictions. However, the results indicated that, of all instruments used in this study, the Biographical Inventory was the best over-all predictor of creative performance. In one of the research participation groups in which we felt we obtained the most valid criteria, the Biographical Inventory scores correlated 0·47 with supervisory ratings on creativity. Needless to say, this is a remarkably satisfactory test of cross validation. Certain biographical keys that worked well in the research programs did not work well for the academic programs and vice versa. The two extreme examples are that the scores from the 'professional self-confidence' key were valid for two-thirds of the criteria in the research programs but had no significant validities whatsoever in the academic sample, whereas scores from the 'miscellaneous' biographical key were as good as any biographical scores in the academic programs but had no significant validities in the research programs. [. . .]

Future Biographical Research Activities

An examination of the different types of items included in the various biographical inventories shows that, in the number of characteristics measured, they are very heterogeneous and complex. One of the activities under way is an intercorrelation and factor analysis of the biographical items, along with appropriate criterion scores. Such an analysis will yield a great deal of information about this type of inventory. Of special interest is the possibility that factor analysis will contribute to the development of more independent and efficient subscores within the inventory than our existing subjective classification of developmental history, parents and family life, etc. has yielded. This in turn should contribute to higher validity coefficients from combined subscores, thus increasing the predictive poten. of the

Biographical Inventory. Another type of useful information from a factor analysis of the items will be the identification of the most promising areas in the inventories. From these leads, it should be possible to construct new items and thereby further improve the instrument.

An additional future research activity concerns the problem of determining the long-range follow-up (predictive) validity of the Biographical Inventory. That is, what will the validity of the inventory be when it is administered to a group of new college graduates or other NASA applicants who are then followed up to determine their degree of success on the job? For this purpose, a short form of the inventory can be developed in order to decrease the time necessary for an applicant to complete it. Another problem which may arise in the administration of the inventory to potential employees is the possibility of distortion or deliberate falsification. Some work has already been completed on this problem. Various types of correction scores (such as an exaggeration score and a false modesty score) have been developed, so that the distortions or falsifications that do occur can hopefully be identified and used to improve the instrument's efficiency.

The Biographical Inventory has usually been found to measure somewhat different criterion variance from other traditional types of selection tests. It therefore seems advisable to consider studies on some of these other kinds of measures found to have promise in research on creative scientific talent to see how well they supplement the Biographical Inventory scores. Such additional validation work could take full advantage of the criterion data as well as the biographical data already available on NASA scientists.

In summary, all our research results obtained to date indicate that biographical information is a very promising, if not the most promising single means of identifying creative and other types of science talent.

The cross-validity coefficients obtained are considerably higher than those typically reported for the prediction and identification of creative or of other types of scientific talent by means of other kinds of predictors, such as high-level aptitude tests, intelligence measures, college grade-point average and personality test measures. It is our conviction that continued research should be carried out to exploit thoroughly the potential in the biographical approach so that the identification of creative scientific talent can be accomplished with as much accuracy as possible. [. . .]

We then raise the question about the price of measuring creative potential. If creative performance is highly desirable and highly valuable, perhaps at our present stage of knowledge and state of measurement we must be willing to pay a price of considerable testing time and expense in order to function at a very high percentage of efficiency in identifying creative potential. These requirements may not really be as great as they seem if we realize that this nation has spent a great deal of time and money for education *per se*, even though we are now discovering that the costly grades which evaluate student performances may have very limited validities in terms of later creative and other important performances. In fact, it could be said that our educational program is the longest and most expensive test ever built, so that we have good reason to hope in the future for greater validities from school grades.

In these lengthy school programs, it may be wise to make time available for creative and other kinds of performances and assessments which might predict future performances with greater validity than grades now do. We should probably also give students creative and other kinds of experience during their educational programs which will enable them to complete self-ratings and other self-report forms after having had more full personal experiences with the nature of these types of performances. These last recommendations we make strongly and with confidence because self-ratings and other self-reports, including the biographical reports, appear to us to be the most single promising approach at present to the identification of creative potential.

References

ELLISON, W. L. (1960), The relationship of certain biographical information to success in science, *Master's Thesis, University of Utah*.

TAYLOR, C. W., COOLEY, G. M., and NIELSEN, E. C. (1963), *Identifying High School Students with Characteristics Needed in Research Work*, National Science Foundation.

Part Six **Stimulating Creativity**

Attempts to stimulate the production of creative ideas actually
started in American industrial firms, though foreshadowed by
Wallas's *The Art of Thought* (see Reading 8). A. F. Osborn's
(1953) 'brain-storming' and W. J. J. Gordon's (1961)
'synectics' are now being taken up by university departments,
as shown in Reading 25 by Parnes. The main object of brain-
storming is to facilitate the expression of the preconscious
imagination in a group situation, by deferring conscious critical
evaluation. E. P. Torrance (see Reading 26) has written
extensively on the repression of creativity among children by the
conformist pressures of American school teachers, parents
and peer groups, and on ways to counteract this. He has also
carried out numerous experimental studies with his Minnesota
Test of Creative Thinking.

It is difficult to find sober psychological assessments of the
effectiveness of work in this area. The advocates of creativity
training are enthusiasts who tend to rely on anecdotal
evidence, or whose experiments are rather poorly controlled.
However Haddon and Lytton's investigation (Reading 27), in
English primary schools, illustrates that it is possible to
demonstrate the effects of different types of school climate on
children's performance at creativity tests. It is interesting to
note, finally, that Crutchfield and Covington, in California, are
developing programmed texts for training children in creative
thinking (Crutchfield, 1967).

References

CRUTCHFIELD, R. S. (1967), 'Instructing the individual in creative thinking', in R. L. Mooney and T. A. Razik (eds.), *Explorations in Creativity*, Harper & Row.

GORDON, W. J. J. (1961), *Synectics: The Development of Creative Capacity*, Harper.

OSBORN, A. F. (1953), *Applied Imagination*, Scribner.

25 S. J. Parnes

Education and Creativity

S. J. Parnes, 'Education and creativity', *Teachers College Record*, vol. 64, 1963, pp. 331–9.

More and more research projects have been pointing up the part that education can play in the development of creative efficacy. At the University of Chicago, the studies of J. W. Getzels and P. W. Jackson (1958) have found that, among bright students, the most highly creative ones excel in achievement to as great a degree as do the highest I.Q. students. This has been corroborated by E. Paul Torrance of the University of Minnesota (1959).

This finding has kindled interest in creative performance as a criterion in the selection of 'gifted' children, a supplement to the traditional criteria of I.Q. and teacher's preference. (Incidentally, research suggests that highly creative children are often disliked by their teachers, a fact with broad implications for educational thought and practice.) With respect to these traditional criteria, John Holland, director of research at the National Merit Scholarship Corporation, has claimed: 'Generally, such measures (as I.Q. and teacher's preference) are moderately accurate for predicting college grades, but they have little relation to post-college achievement.' His organization has now embarked on a study of achievement in a group of boys and girls chosen mainly on the basis of exceptional creative performance.

Elnora Schmadel (1960) of the University of Southern California sounds a widely echoed note: 'The findings of this study indicate that creative thinking abilities do contribute to currently measured achievement and to measures of desirable achievement.' Similarly, Torrance (1961) argues that: 'Perhaps the most promising area, if we are interested in what can be done to encourage creative talent to unfold, is that of experimentation with teaching procedures which will stimulate students to think independently, to test their ideas, and to communicate them to others.'

Research Developments

Research on the development of creative behavior has been conducted on an increasing scale ever since the presidential address of J. P. Guilford (1950) to the American Psychological Association. He emphasized the 'appalling neglect' of the study of creativity, indicating that of some 121,000 titles indexed in *Psychological Abstracts* from its beginning until 1950, only 186 were definitely related to the subject of creativity. In the summer of 1958, the Creative Education Foundation published the first *Compendium of Research on Creative Imagination* (Parnes, 1958), covering thirty research studies concerned with the identification and development of creative ability. This comprised all recent studies in the field at that time. Then, within approximately eighteen months, thirty new research studies were reported and summarized in a second *Compendium* (Parnes, 1960). This also listed twenty-eight additional research projects that had just been started – about double the number apparently under way when the first *Compendium* was compiled.

A new trend was indicated by the nature of the research reported in the later *Compendium*. Until a few years ago, projects dealt mainly with the *identification* of creative talent. About half the studies reported in the second *Compendium* were devoted to the deliberate *development* of creative ability – a far cry from the bare two included in the earlier edition.

At the 1959 University of Utah Research Conference on the Identification of Creative Scientific Talent, a committee was appointed for the first time to report on 'the role of educational experience in the development of creative scientific talent'. The committee reported that at least six research projects had indicated that creative productivity can be developed by deliberate procedures (Taylor, 1959). No research yet reported is inconsistent with this view. Thus, there is a firm basis for the conviction expressed by Guilford (1952): 'Like most behavior, creative activity probably represents to some extent many learned skills. There may be limitations set on these skills by heredity; but I am convinced that through learning one can extend the skills within those limitations.' In the same vein, Irving Maltzman and his associates (Maltzman, Simon and Licht, 1959) at the University of California concluded a group of research studies on originality training by asserting that the results support the hypothesis that 'originality is a learned form of behavior which does not differ in principle from other forms of operant behavior'.

An illustration of the relevant evidence is the thirteen-year experience with a course in creative problem solving at the University of Buffalo. Two research studies have evaluated this creative problem-solving course. The first revealed that on five of seven measures of creative ability, the students who had taken the one-semester course were significantly superior to the group of matched control subjects who had not taken the course. The former group also showed significant gain on a scale devised 'to assess factors of leadership ability, dominance, persistence, and social initiative' (Meadow and Parnes, 1959).

The second study examined the persistence or carry-over effects of the creative problem solving courses. Results indicated that the improvement in creative productivity persisted for more than eight months after completion of the course (Schmadel, 1960). Criteria used in evaluation of the ideas produced included both uniqueness and usefulness.

Research into the effects of creative problem solving programs conducted at other institutions has supported the findings (Parnes, 1958, 1960; Sommers, 1961). The University of Chicago has conducted several research projects on the effects of teaching creative problem solving to governmental and industrial administrators (James, 1960).

Educational Programs

Since research has demonstrated that a considerable part of creative behavior is *learned*, courses in creative problem solving have been multiplying. At the University of Buffalo, the principles and procedures taught in the elective one-semester course have also been used in special programs for groups of students in engineering, law, medicine, education, business, physics, psychology and ROTC. Similar courses and programs, patterned after those of the University of Buffalo (Parnes, 1959), have become widespread in educational institutions, in industrial organizations, in the military and in governmental agencies (Osborn, 1961).

At Buffalo, students are taught the concepts in Alex F. Osborn's (1953) textbook, *Applied Imagination*. The text emphasizes the importance of imagination in all walks of life, the universality of imaginative talent, and the use of creativeness in all stages of problem solving, from orientation to evaluation.

Perceptual, emotional and cultural blocks to creative thinking are demonstrated and discussed in the course. Under perceptual blocks are covered such matters as the difficulty in isolating problems, difficulty from narrowing the problem too much, inability to define or isolate attributes, failure to use all the senses in observing. Under cultural and emotional blocks are emphasized the effects of conformity, overemphasis on competition or cooperation, excessive faith in reason or logic, self-satisfaction, perfectionism, negative outlooks, reliance on authority and fear of mistakes, failure, or looking foolish.

Early in the course, students learn the principle of deferred judgement. In essence, this principle calls for the deliberate separation of idea production from evaluation. In other words, during the effort to generate ideas, the judicial process is deliberately suspended; evaluation is deferred in order to allow full play to imagination.

To estimate the efficacy of the deferred-judgement principle as applied to individual idea production, experimental subjects were given the task of thinking up tentative solutions to assigned problems for periods of five minutes, each student working on an individual (non-group) basis. On one problem, the students operated in the conventional way, concurrently applying evaluation as they tried to think up ideas. On the second problem, they operated in accordance with the deferred-judgement principle, deliberately postponing evaluation. The former method produced an average of 2·5 good ideas. The latter produced an average of 4·3 good ideas, criteria of quality being based on uniqueness and usefulness.

These results indicate that, for this type of creative task, a 72 per cent better productivity can result from the deliberate deferment of evaluation during the idea production process, a difference which is highly significant statistically (Meadow, Parnes and Reese, 1959; Parnes and Meadow, 1959). This deliberate separation of the creative and judicial functions is emphasized throughout the course.

Within the permissive atmosphere that the principle of deferred judgement provides, students are given practice in attribute listing (learning to look at problems from a variety of viewpoints). For example, in considering other uses for such an object as a piece of paper, students are taught to look at each attribute of the paper – its whiteness, its four corners, its straight edges, etc. Each of the attributes then suggests a number of possible uses.

Check Lists

Check-list procedures are also encouraged, such as Osborn's check-list of idea-spurring questions. Students are thus taught to process a problem by means of a number of questions: How can we simplify? What combinations can be utilized? What adaptations can be made?

Forced-relationship techniques are similarly covered. For example, after a list of ideas is produced as tentative solutions to a problem, each of these ideas is then artificially related to each other idea on the list in order to force new combinations. Sometimes a somewhat ridiculous idea is taken as a starting point. By connecting the idea with the actual problem, a series of associations is produced, and this often leads in some novel direction towards a new solution of the problem.

Throughout the course, three points are stressed: the importance of taking notes (keeping a record of ideas that come to one at any and all times, rather than only while one is working on a problem), the value of setting deadlines and quotas for production of ideas and the advantage of setting aside certain times and places for deliberate idea production. Much opportunity is given for deliberate practice in problem solving on a variety of problems, including many of those brought in by the students out of their personal experience.

Students are taught to sense problems in their studies, work and throughout their lives, and to define these problems properly for creative attack. The separation of creative and judicial functions is then practiced in all stages of solution. For example, during analysis, students are taught to list every fact that could be related to the problem. After they have completed this step, they then apply judgement in order to cull out the most important facts. Students next create the longest possible list of questions and sources of additional data that could be useful. Then they go back to the judicial process of selecting the most important questions and sources of data. This procedure continues throughout the final stages of evaluation and presentation of ideas.

When it comes to evaluation, students are taught to develop the longest possible list of criteria by which to evaluate their tentative solutions. They then apply judgement in order to select the most useful ones for the purpose. Thus, the principle of deferred judgement is emphasized, both in individual and in group thinking, in all aspects of the course.

Informal procedures are utilized throughout. Chairs are arranged in a semi-circle in order to encourage the maximum amount of group participation and discussion. The class is often divided into small groups in order to provide practice in team and group collaboration for the production of ideas. Students are given opportunities to serve as leaders of these small groups on various aspects of their own problems as well as on those assigned for practice.

Some Outcomes

In one of a series of studies (see Meadow and Parnes, 1959; Parnes and Meadow, 1959, 1960) at the University of Buffalo, the research staff utilized a battery of ten measures which had previously been demonstrated by other investigators to distinguish creative from non-creative persons. These tests were given to students at the beginning and again at the conclusion of three creative problem-solving courses. These students were considered the experimental subjects (Meadow and Parnes, 1959). Other students, not taking the creative problem-solving course, were given the same tests at the beginning and end of the semester; they were considered the control subjects. Thus, any comparatively greater gains by the creative problem-solving students could reasonably be attributed to the course.

The experimental and control students were carefully matched for intelligence, age, sex and time of class. For example, a bright, twenty-year-old, female, day-school student in the creative problem-solving course was matched for comparison with a bright, twenty-year-old, female, day-school student in another course. All of the students were told that they were participating in an experiment designed to measure changes in their thinking as a result of a semester's work at the University.

Analyses of the results of this phase of the research included these major findings:

1. The creative problem-solving students showed substantial gains in the *quantitative* production of ideas on two tests of idea quantity. Students in the control group showed relatively insignificant gains on these tests.

2. In three tests of the *qualitative* production of ideas, the experimental subjects showed clear superiority over the control group. On a fourth test in this area, the creative problem-solving students showed improvement greater than that shown by the control students, but not sufficiently greater to be regarded as significant. The fifth measure of qualitative production showed no superiority for the creative problem-solving students.

3. Three tests were designed to measure improvement in the personality traits of *dominance*, *self-control* and *need to achieve*. The creative problem-solving students gained substantially in dominance as a result of the course, but showed no significant changes in self-control or need to achieve. The dominance scale used is regarded by psychologists as measuring such characteristics as confidence, self-reliance, persuasiveness, initiative, and leadership potential (Gough, 1957). Other workers have previously found that dominance is a personality trait associated with creative persons (Parnes, 1958, 1960).

It is significant that dominance was the single personality trait in which the creative problem-solving students showed an increase. This is the particular trait which the course methods were designed explicitly to develop.

Most of the tests designed to measure improvement in quantity and quality of ideas were based on a practical type of creative ability. Psychologists describe these tests as measuring the factors of originality, sensitivity to problems, spontaneous flexibility, and ideational fluency. It was on these tests that the students who took the course registered substantial gains.

Two of the tests emphasized a more literary type of creative ability. Students were required to create clever story titles and original plots. On neither of these tests were the gains registered by the students who took the course large enough to indicate superiority over the control students. The test requiring clever story titles, however, showed the greater gain by the course students, and a later experiment showed significant evidence of carry-over effects in this type of creative ability.

Utility for Whom?

In general, the creative problem-solving courses were found to be equally helpful to students of low and high initial creative ability, and equally helpful to those with low and high intelligence levels. This finding is in line with Guilford's conclusion that although heredity may place limitations on the skills involved in creative ability, these skills can be extended within those limitations through education.

In general, the older students (aged twenty-three to fifty-one) in evening classes gained as much from the course as did younger students (aged seventeen to twenty-two) in day classes. Likewise, males and females demonstrated equivalent gains.

There is also evidence that when creative efficacy has been developed by education, the improvement endures (Parnes and Meadow, 1960). Matched experimental and control subjects were compared on six tests of creative ability. The experimental subjects were students who had completed the creative problem-solving course an average of eighteen months prior to the experiment. The control subjects were students *registered* but *uninstructed* in the creative problem-solving course. None of the students had ever before taken the creative-thinking tests.

Course graduates outperformed two separate groups of control subjects on all six measures, including two quantity and four quality tests. All differences were statistically significant in the comparisons with one of the control groups. All but two were significant in comparisons with the second control group.

Incidentally, a popular misconception exists to the effect that the deferment-of-judgement principle is applicable only to group idea production. The fallaciousness of this impression is demonstrated by the fact that all measurements in the studies at the University of Buffalo were made on the basis of individual thinking, not on group collaboration.

These studies have produced countless collateral data which have become available as a result of the electronic processing of the information obtained. These data are being put to valuable use. For example, further analyses have been made to discover the proportion of *good* ideas in the first half of a subject's total output of ideas versus the last half of his sustained effort. Findings of one such study have shown 78 per cent *more* good ideas to be among those produced in the last half than in the first half. Here, again, qualitative scoring was based on the criteria of uniqueness and usefulness. A subsequent experiment indicated a trend towards *increasingly* greater proportions of good ideas as a subject's total quantity increased. The results of both experiments were found to be statistically significant (Parnes, 1961).

The above findings support Osborn's theory that in idea production, quantity leads to quality. The results also seem to concur with William J. J. Gordon's (1956) explanation of 'deferment' in the creative process. He describes deferment as 'the capacity to discard the glittering immediate in favor of a shadowy but possibly richer future'. The *non-creative* problem solver gets an idea, sees it as a possible solution to his problem, and settles for that without further ado. The *creative* problem solver is not satisfied with his first idea. Like the person who invests money to obtain greater rewards later, the creative person foregoes the immediate reward of applying his first idea in expectation of an ultimately better solution (greater reward). A further hypothesis suggested by Osborn's and Gordon's theories is that the *best* idea will come late in the total production period. Experiments are currently being prepared to test this particular hypothesis.

Modification of Courses

In addition to the teaching of creative problem solving *per se*, there have also been successful projects based on the integration of creative principles and procedures with conventional courses. Two outstanding examples of courses which have thus been modified are Jere Clark's economics course at the University of Chattanooga and Harry Hansen's marketing course at Harvard.

The value of such modifications has been indicated by research on the effectiveness of the similar incorporation of creative principles and procedures into courses in language arts (Torrance, 1960). Also, a study by Sommers (1961) reported that mastery of subject matter increased, along with creative ability scores, as a result of weaving creative problem solving into existing courses.

At the University of Buffalo, pilot research has been conducted with physics students who were given a six-session condensation of the creative problem-solving course. Analysis of the data has indicated that these subjects performed better on creative ability tests than a comparable control group of physics students who had no training in creative problem solving. Furthermore, on anonymous questionnaires given to the fifty-five experimental (trained) subjects, 83 per cent expressed the belief that the study of creative problem solving should be required of physics students and others. Nearly all of the others felt that creative problem solving should be offered as an elective. 75 per cent indicated a willingness to continue the creative problem-solving sessions for the entire semester.

Several special institutes and workshops have been held regarding the integration of creative problem-solving methodologies with the teaching of other academic subjects. The first was a one-day workshop at the University of Buffalo for teachers of American history. On the West Coast, San Jose State College has taken the lead with an annual five-day Creative Education Institute which offers graduate credit. At this Institute, several hundred teachers devise ways to integrate creative methodologies within their respective subject-matter fields. Frank Williams is in charge of the program.

Education in the Future

In a recent prediction of forthcoming changes in colleges, Paul H. Davis (1962) states: 'In the last one hundred years, the medical profession has changed from folklore to science, from opinions based on hunches to judgements based on controlled experiments. Now the teaching profession is starting a similar transition.' One of his predictions is that there will be less emphasis on memory and more on creative thinking.

As we all know, change is bewilderingly rapid in our present nuclear and space age – far more rapid than ever before. The discoveries and innovations of the next twenty years will probably make the previous 100 years seem to have progressed at a snail's pace. Therefore, a person cannot foresee exactly what knowledge he will need five or ten years from now to meet his life's problems. He can, however, develop the attitudes and abilities that will help him meet *any* future problem creatively and inventively.

Furthermore, we receive so much spoon-feeding in our present society in terms of how-to-do-it instructions – in school, at home and at work – that most of us lack almost any opportunity for being creative. If this is so, we may be developing a society of 'sick' people. A. H. Maslow (1954) postulates that a person who does not have a basic need fulfilled is sick, just as a man is sick who lacks vitamins and minerals. The five basic needs to which Maslow refers are (a) physiological needs, (b) safety needs, (c) love, affection and belongingness needs, (d) esteem needs and (e) need for self-actualization.

Maslow emphasizes that the need for self-actualization is a healthy man's prime motiyation. Self-actualization means actualizing one's potential, becoming everything one is capable of becoming. Maslow says: 'What a man *can* be, he *must* be.' Education can help provide for this need by building the environmental turnpikes on which the individual may drive once he has removed the mental governors that restrict his creative ability.

In Carl Rogers's terms, education can help provide the 'psychological safety' and 'psychological freedom' necessary to the creative individual. This does not mean license for heedless

351

non-conformity. But it does mean complete freedom for non-conformity of *thought*, even if not for nonconformity in behavior. An old adage says: 'Give me the courage to change those things that can and should be changed, the strength to accept those things that cannot be changed and the wisdom to distinguish between the two.' This then must be the creed of the creative person.

We still know little about what 'creativity' really is. But we do know how to stimulate greater creative behavior in individuals. It is a matter of helping them to release whatever creative potential they possess, like removing the governor from an automobile. The individual's creative ability is frequently so repressed by his education and experience that he cannot even *recognize* his full potential, let alone *realize* it. Once he can be helped to do so, he may attain what Maslow calls 'self-actualization'.

Education can do much to help the individual achieve this fullest self-realization, whatever his level of native capacity. Many people seem to possess the seeds of creativeness, but the environment fails to provide the proper nourishment for growth. Therefore, these persons never fully live.

Education can provide for 'creative calisthenics' to counteract this atrophying of our talents, And just as camping out can be rewarding even though we have homes, creative exercise can be rewarding even though we have access to ready-made solutions. Just as physical education does not take for granted the physical development of our students, likewise creative education must provide deliberately for their creative development. And research does seem to warrant the postulate that the gap between an individual's innate creative talent and his lesser creative output can be narrowed by deliberate education in creative thinking.

In 1948, Carl H. Grabo wrote:

Considering man's hostility to change and innovation . . . it is astonishing that so much of creative and imaginative genius has contrived to leave its impress on the human race. Yet who can doubt that more, habited in weak bodies, blasted early by ignorance and cruelty and superstition, has perished with no record? In our comparatively low civilization, a little is done under favorable circumstances to salvage great talent, to give it opportunity to grow and express itself. Yet how

pitifully meager is our salvage and how great the waste! We know that
this is so. A more civilized time than ours will strive to develop this, the
greatest of all natural resources.

Let's hope that this 'more civilized' day is now dawning.

References
DAVIS, P. H. (1962), 'Changes are coming in the colleges', *J. higher
Educ.*, vol. 23, pp. 141–7.
GETZELS, J. W., and JACKSON, P. W. (1958), 'The meaning of
"giftedness": An examination of an expanding concept', *Phi Delta
Kappan*, vol. 40, pp. 75–7.
GORDON, W. J. J. (1956), 'Operational approach to creativity', *Harv.
bus. Rev.*, vol. 34, pp. 41–51.
GOUGH, H. C. (1957), *Manual for the California Psychological Inventory*,
Consulting Psychologists Press.
GRABO, C. H. (1948), *The Creative Critic*, University of Chicago Press.
GUILFORD, J. P. (1950), 'Creativity', *Amer. Psychol.*, vol. 9, pp. 444–54.
GUILFORD, J. P. (1952), 'Some recent findings on thinking abilities and
their implications', *Inform. Bull.*, vol. 3, pp. 48–61.
JAMES, B. J. (1960), *Education for Innovative Behavior in Executives*,
Research Grant from U.S. Office of Education to University of Chicago.
MALTZMAN, I., SIMON, S., and LICHT, L. (1959), The persistence of
originality-training effects, *University of California, Department of
Psychology, Technical Report*, no. 4.
MASLOW, A. H. (1954), *Motivation and Personality*, Harper.
MEADOW, A., and PARNES, S. J. (1959), 'Evaluation of training in
creative problem-solving', *J. appl. Psychol.*, vol. 43, pp. 189–94.
MEADOW, A., PARNES, S. J., and REESE, M. (1959), 'Influence of
brainstorming instructions and problem sequence on a creative
problem-solving test', *J. appl. Psychol.*, vol. 43, pp. 413–16.
OSBORN, A. F. (1953), *Applied Imagination*, Scribner.
OSBORN, A. F. (1961), Is education becoming more creative?, *An
Address Given at the Seventh Annual Creative Problem-Solving
Institute, University of Buffalo*.
PARNES, S. J. (ed.) (1958), *Compendium of Research on Creative
Imagination*, Creative Education Foundation, Buffalo, New York.
PARNES, S. J. (1959), *Instructor's Manual for Semester Courses in
Creative Problem-solving*, Creative Education Foundation, Buffalo,
New York.
PARNES, S. J. (ed.) (1960), *Second Compendium of Research on Creative
Imagination*, Creative Education Foundation, Buffalo, New York.
PARNES, S. J. (1961), 'Effects of extended effort in creative problem-
solving', *J. educ. Psychol.*, vol. 52, pp. 117–22.
PARNES, S. J., and MEADOW, A. (1959), 'Effects of "brain-storming"
instructions on creative problem-solving by trained and untrained
subjects', *J. educ. Psychol.*, vol. 50, pp. 171–6.

PARNES, S. J., and MEADOW, A. (1960), 'Evaluation of persistence of effects produced by a creative problem-solving course', *Psychol. Rep.*, vol. 7, pp. 357–61.

SCHMADEL, ELNORA (1960), The relationship of creative thinking abilities to school achievement, *Unpublished Doctoral Dissertation, University of Southern California*.

SOMMERS, W. S. (1961), The influence of selected teaching methods on the development of creative thinking, *Unpublished Doctoral Dissertation, University of Minnesota*.

TAYLOR, C. W. (ed.) (1959), *Research Conference on the Identification of Creative Scientific Talent*, University of Utah Press.

TORRANCE, E. P. (1959), *Explorations in Creative Thinking in the Early School Years*, Bureau of Educational Research, University of Minnesota.

TORRANCE, E. P. (1960), *Conditions for Creative Growth*, Bureau of Educational Research, University of Minnesota.

TORRANCE, E. P. (1961), 'Status of knowledge concerning education and creative scientific talent', Working paper for a project on the Status of Knowledge about Creative Scientific Talent, directed by Calvin W. Taylor, University of Utah, with support by the National Science Foundation.

26 E. P. Torrance

Causes for Concern

Chapter 1 of E. P. Torrance, *Guiding Creative Talent*, Prentice-Hall, 1962, pp. 1–15.

Why should counselors, teachers and administrators be concerned with the problems of creative individuals? What business is it of theirs whether or not one is highly creative? Doesn't everybody know that the highly creative person is 'a little crazy' and that you can't help him anyway? If he's *really creative*, why does he need guidance anyway? He should be able to solve his own problems. He's creative, isn't he?

Unfortunately, these are attitudes which have long been held by some of our most eminent scholars and which still prevail rather widely. Most of the educators I know perk up when they discover a child with a high I.Q. or a high score on some other traditional measure of intellectual talent. They are impressed! Most of them are rather impressed if they discover in a child some outstanding talent for music, or art, or the like. Some counselors and psychologists even go to the trouble of testing such things as finger dexterity and speed in checking numbers and names. Not a counselor or psychologist among my acquaintance, however, bothers about obtaining measures of their client's creative thinking abilities. I was trained in counseling myself and did work as a high school and college counselor for several years, and for two years I served as the director of a university counseling bureau. In all this time, I never did hear anyone mention a test of creative thinking. I certainly never used one!

What puzzles me, however, is why I remained so ignorant of such instruments. I find now that many such tests have been developed only during the past seventy years. Descriptions of these tests are now fairly detailed and scoring procedures can be satisfactorily reproduced. The reason for this state of affairs is simply that we have not really considered this kind of talent important. This kind of talent has not been valued and rewarded in our educational system, so guidance workers have seen little reason to identify it and to try to contribute to its growth.

Some Legitimate Concerns of Educators

There are very legitimate reasons why educators should be concerned about assessing and guiding the growth of the creative thinking abilities. I would like to discuss a few of these.

Mental health

Schools are legitimately concerned about the mental health of children, adolescents, college students and adults. They would like to be able to help their students avoid mental breakdowns and achieve healthy personality growth. These are legitimate concerns of education. But what does all this have to do with creativity?

Actually, it has a great deal to do with creativity. There is little question but that the stifling of creativity cuts at the very roots of satisfaction in living and ultimately creates overwhelming tension and breakdown (Patrick, 1955). There is also little doubt that one's creativity is his most valuable resource in coping with life's daily stresses.

In one study (Hebeisen, 1960), a battery of tests of creative thinking was administered to a group of schizophrenics who appeared to be on the road to recovery. Many of them were being considered for vocational rehabilitation by the State Department of Welfare. These individuals manifested an astonishingly impoverished imagination, inflexibility, lack of originality and inability to summon any kind of response to new problems. Their answers gave no evidence of the rich fantasy and wild imagination popularly attributed to schizophrenics. There was only an impoverished, stifled, frozen creativity. They appeared to be paralysed in their thinking, and most of their responses were the most banal imaginable.

Although it will be difficult to prove, I suspect that schizophrenics and others who 'break down' under stress constitute one of the most unimaginative, noncreative groups to be found. I also suspect that it was their lack of creativity rather than its presence which brought about their breakdowns. Certainly the schizo-phrenics tested lacked this important resource for coping with life's stresses. Creativity is a necessary resource for their struggle back to mental health.

Fully functioning persons

Schools are anxious that the children they educate grow into fully functioning persons. This has long been an avowed and widely approved purpose of education. We say that education in a democracy should help individuals fully develop their talents. Recently there have been pressures to limit this to intellectual talents. There has been much talk about limiting the school's concern to the full development of the intellect only.

Even with this limited definition of the goals of education, the abilities involved in creative thinking cannot be ignored. There has been increasing recognition of the fact that traditional measures of intelligence attempt to assess only a few of man's thinking abilities. In his early work, Binet (1909) recognized clearly this deficiency. It has taken the sustained work of Guil-ford (1959) and his associates to communicate effectively the complexity of man's mental operations.

Certainly we cannot say that one is fully functioning mentally, if the abilities involved in creative thinking remain undeveloped or are paralysed. These are the abilities involved in becoming aware of problems, thinking up possible solutions and testing them. If their functioning is impaired, one's capacity for coping with life's problems is indeed marginal.

Educational achievement

Almost no one disputes the legitimacy of the school's concern about educational achievement. Teachers and guidance workers are asked to help under-achievers to make better use of their intellectual resources and to help over-achievers become better 'rounded' personalities. But, how do you tell who is an under- or over-achiever? In my opinion, recent findings concerning the role of the creative thinking abilities in educational achievement call for a revision of these long-used concepts.

We are finding (Getzels and Jackson, 1958; Torrance, 1960) that the creative thinking abilities contribute importantly to the acquisition of information and various educational skills. Of course, we have long known that it is natural for man to learn creatively, but we have always thought that it was more economical to teach by authority. Recent experiments (Moore, 1961; Ornstein, 1961) have shown that apparently many things can be learned creatively more economically than they can by authority, and that some people strongly prefer to learn creatively.

Traditional tests of intelligence are heavily loaded with tasks requiring cognition, memory, and convergent thinking. Such tests have worked rather well in predicting school achievement. When children are taught by authority these are the abilities required. Recent and ongoing studies, however, show that even traditional subject matter and educational skills can be taught in such a way that the creative thinking abilities are important for their acquisition.

Most of these findings are illustrated dramatically in a study conducted during three years in the University of Minnesota Laboratory Elementary School. We differentiated the highly creative children (as identified by our tests of creative thinking) from the highly intelligent (as identified by the Stanford–Binet, an individually administered test). The highly creative group ranked in the upper 20 per cent on creative thinking but not on intelligence. The highly intelligent group ranked in the upper 20 per cent on intelligence but not on creativity. Those who were in the upper 20 per cent on both measures were eliminated, but the overlap was small. In fact, if we were to identify children as gifted on the basis of intelligence tests, we would eliminate from consideration approximately 70 per cent of the most creative. This percentage seems to hold fairly well, no matter what measure of intelligence we use and no matter what educational level we study, from kindergarten through graduate school.

Although there is an average difference of over twenty-five I.Q. points between these two groups, there are no statistically significant differences in any of the achievement measures used either year (Gates Reading and Iowa Tests of Basic Skills). These results have been duplicated in a Minneapolis public high school, the University of Minnesota High School and two graduate school situations. Getzels and Jackson (1959) had earlier obtained the same results in a private secondary school. These results were not confirmed in a parochial elementary school and a small-town elementary school known for their emphasis on 'traditional virtues in education'. Even in these two schools, however, achievement is significantly related to measures of creative thinking and the highly creative group is 'guilty' of some degree of over-achievement, as assessed by usual standards.

It is of special interest that the children with high I.Q.s were rated by their teachers as more desirable, better known or understood, more ambitious and more hardworking or studious. In other words, the highly creative child appears to learn as much as the highly intelligent one, at least in some schools, without appearing to work as hard. My guess is that these highly creative children are learning and thinking when they appear to be 'playing around'. Their tendency is to learn creatively more effectively than by authority. They may engage in manipulative and/or exploratory activities, many of which are discouraged or even forbidden. They enjoy learning and thinking, and this looks like play rather than work.

Vocational success

Guidance workers[1] have traditionally been interested in the vocational success of their clients. Indeed, the guidance movement got much of its impetus from this concern. Of course, it has long been recognized that creativity is a distinguishing characteristic of outstanding individuals in almost every field. It has been generally conceded that the possession of high intelligence, special talent and technical skills is not enough for outstanding success. It has also been recognized that creativity is important in scientific discovery, invention, and the arts.

We are discovering now that creative thinking is important in success even in some of the most common occupations, such as selling in a department store (Wallace, 1960). In one study it was found that saleswomen ranking in the upper third in sales in their departments scored significantly higher on tests of creative thinking than those who ranked in the lower third in sales. An interesting point in this study, however, is that the tests did a

1. The term 'guidance workers' will be used to refer to all school personnel who perform guidance functions and includes teachers, administrators, counselors, psychologists, social workers, deans of boys and/or girls.

better job of discriminating the high and low selling groups in what the personnel managers considered routine sales jobs requiring no imagination than in the departments rated as requiring creative thinking. Thus, creative thinking appears to be important, even in jobs which appear to be quite routine.

Social importance

Finally, educators are legitimately concerned that their students make useful contributions to our society. Such a concern runs deep in the code of ethics of the profession. It takes little imagination to recognize that the future of our civilization – our very survival – depends upon the quality of the creative imagination of our next generation.

Democracies collapse only when they fail to use intelligent, imaginative methods for solving their problems. Greece failed to heed such a warning by Socrates and gradually collapsed. What is called for is a far cry from the model of the quiz-program champion of a few years ago. Instead of trying to cram a lot of facts into the minds of children and make them scientific encyclopedias, we must ask what kind of children they are becoming. What kind of thinking do they do? How resourceful are they? Are they becoming more responsible? Are they learning to give thoughtful explanations of the things they do and see? Do they believe their own ideas to be of value? Can they share ideas and opinions with others? Do they relate similar experiences together in order to draw conclusions? Do they do some thinking for themselves?

We also need more than well-rounded individuals. We ordinarily respect these well-rounded individuals, broad scholars and men of many talents. Dael Wolfle (1960) has made a case for those who develop some of their talents so highly that they cannot be well-rounded. He argues that it is advantageous to a society to see the greatest achievable diversity of talent among those who constitute the society.

A warning by Henry Murray (1960, p. 10), a well-known Harvard psychologist, sounds very much like the one Socrates gave in his day. It reads as follows in part:

An emotional deficiency disease, a paralysis of the creative imagination, an addiction to superficials – this is the diagnosis I would offer to account for the greater part of the widespread desperation of our time. Paralysis of the imagination, I suspect, would also account, in part, for the fact that the great majority of us, wedded to comfort so long as we both shall live, are turning our eyes away from the one thing we should be looking at: the possibility or probability of co-extermination.

Guidance roles

Many will say, 'Surely, schools have a right to be concerned about mental health, full mental functioning, educational achievement and vocational success. They ought to be concerned that coming generations contribute productively to our society. *But* how can school guidance workers contribute to the creative growth necessary for these things?'

This is a legitimate question. Parents and peers play such important roles in the encouragement or discouragement of creative expression and growth, what can school guidance workers do? There are at least six special roles which school guidance workers can play in helping highly creative children maintain their creativity and continue to grow. Each of these is a role which others can rarely fulfil. Our social expectations frequently prevent even teachers and administrators from effectively fulfilling these roles. Thus, in some cases, only counselors, school psychologists and similar workers will be able to fulfil these roles. In many cases, however, teachers and administrators can supply these needs, if they differentiate their guidance roles from other socially expected roles.

The six roles which I have in mind are: (a) providing the highly creative individual a 'refuge', (b) being his 'sponsor' or 'patron', (c) helping him understand his divergence, (d) letting him communicate his ideas, (e) seeing that his creative talent is recognized, and (f) helping parents and others understand him. I shall now discuss each of these roles briefly.

Provide a 'refuge'

Society in general is downright savage towards creative thinkers, especially when they are young. To some extent, the educational system must be coercive and emphasize the establishment of behavior norms. Teachers and administrators can rarely escape this coercive role. Counselors and other guidance workers are in a much better position to free themselves of it. Nevertheless, there are ways teachers and administrators can free themselves of this role long enough to provide refuge, if they are sensitive to the need.

From the studies of Getzels and Jackson (1958), we know that highly creative adolescents are estranged from their teachers and peers. Our Minnesota studies indicate that the same holds true for children in the elementary school. The reasons are easy to understand. Who can blame teachers for being irritated when a pupil presents an original answer which differs from what is expected? It does not fit in with the rest of the grading scheme. They don't know how the unusual answer should be treated. They have to stop and think themselves. Peers have the same difficulty and label the creative child's unusual questions and answers as 'crazy' or 'silly'.

Thus, the highly creative child, adolescent, or adult needs encouragement. He needs help in becoming reconciled and, as Hughes Mearns (1941) once wrote, in being 'made cheerful over the world's stubborn satisfaction in its own follies'. The guidance worker must recognize, however, that the estrangement exists and that he will have to create a relationship in which the creative individual feels safe.

Be a sponsor or patron

Someone has observed that almost always wherever independence and creativity occur and persist, there is some other individual or agent who plays the role of 'sponsor' or 'patron'. This role is played by someone who is not a member of the peer group, but who possesses prestige and power in the same social system. He does several things. Regardless of his own views, the sponsor encourages and supports the other in expressing and testing his ideas and in thinking through things for himself. He protects the individual from the reactions of his peers long enough for him to try out some of his ideas and modify them. He can keep the structure of the situation open enough so that originality *can* occur.

It is my contention that the school counselor or guidance worker is in a better position than anyone else in the social system to play this role, especially if such a role for him is sanctioned by the teachers and principal. Since few elementary schools have counselors or guidance workers, this role is usually assumed by principals. It is a difficult role for a principal, however. Think of the role conflicts which must be involved in the following case of a principal whose school participated in our research.

In an experiment conducted on a Monday, I had observed the exceptional creative talent of Tom, a fourth grader. Before leaving the school, I asked the teacher about Tom. She volunteered the information that he had had a struggle with most of his teachers, but that he had had a very successful experience in the third grade.

On Friday, we returned to the school to conduct the experiment in some other classes. In the meantime, the principal had observed this boy's class for an hour. During the mathematics class, Tom questioned one of the rules in the textbook. Instead of having Tom try to prove his rule and perhaps modify it or explain the textbook rule, the teacher became irate, even in the presence of the principal. She fumed, 'So! You think you know more than this book!' (holding the book and tapping it with her hand).

Tom replied meekly, 'No, I don't think I know more than the book, but I'm not satisfied about this rule.'

To get on safer ground, the teacher then had the class solve problems in their workbook. Tom solved the problems easily and about as rapidly as he could read them. This too was upsetting to the teacher. She couldn't understand how he was getting the correct answer and demanded that he write down all of the steps he had gone through in solving each problem.

Afterwards, the teacher asked the principal to talk to Tom. The principal explained to Tom that many things came easy to him, such as solving problems and perhaps he really didn't need to write out all of the steps. The principal also explained that there are some other things like handwriting which came easier to others than to him and that he might have to work harder than some of the others on these things.

Apparently, this principal had been able to provide enough of the 'patron' role to permit him to keep alive his creativity up to this time. Soon afterwards, Tom's family moved to a nearby suburb and he was duly enrolled in a new school. On Tom's very first day in the new school, the principal of the new school called the principal of the school from which Tom had transferred. He wanted to know immediately if Tom is the kind of boy who has to be squelched rather roughly. His former 'patron' explained that Tom was really a very wholesome, promising lad who needed understanding and encouragement. The new principal exclaimed rather brusquely, 'Well, he's already said too much right here in my office!'

We can certainly sympathize with the new principal. He must support his teachers and maintain good discipline in the school. It is frequently difficult for a principal to play the 'sponsor' or 'patron' role. It is far more harmonious with the position of the school counselor. Nevertheless, it is a role which administrators and teachers may have to play. Otherwise, promising creative talent may be sacrificed.

Help him understand his divergence

A high degree of sensitivity, a capacity to be disturbed and divergent thinking are essentials of the creative personality. Frequently, creative children are puzzled by their own behavior. They desperately need help in understanding themselves, particularly their divergence. The following story written by a fourth grader about a lion that won't roar illustrates the divergent child's search for someone who will understand him:

Charlie had just one great wish. It was to be able to roar. You see when Charlie was born he quickly turned hoarse. As soon as he was nine years old, he went to ask Polly the parrot. But she said, 'Go ask Blacky the crow.'

So off went poor Charlie to see Blacky. When he got there, he asked, 'Blacky, why, oh why can't I roar?'

But Blacky only replied, 'Don't you see, Charlie, I'm busy. Go see Jumper the kangaroo. She can help you.'

Jumper didn't understand Charlie's problem. But she did give him some advice. Jumper said, 'Go ask the wise old owl.'

The wise old owl understood everything. He told Charlie, 'I hate to say this, but if you really want to know, you're scared of everything.'

Charlie thanked him and hurried home. To this day Charlie can't roar but how happy he is to know why he can't.

There are crucial times in the lives of creative children when being understood is all that is needed to help them cope with the crisis and maintain their creativity.

Let him communicate his ideas

The highly creative child has an unusually strong urge to explore and to create. When he thinks up ideas, or tests them and modifies them, he has an unusually strong urge to communicate his ideas and the result of his tests. Yet both peers and teachers named some of the most creative children in our studies as ones who 'do not speak out their ideas'. When we see what happens when they do 'speak out their ideas', there is little wonder that they are reluctant to communicate their ideas. Frequently, their ideas are so far ahead of those of their classmates and even their teachers that they have given up hope of communicating.

All school guidance workers need to learn to perform this function more effectively. They must genuinely respect the questions and ideas of children to sustain the highly creative child so that he will continue to think.

See that his creative talent is recognized

Information from many sources indicates that much creative talent goes unrecognized. In our own studies at all educational levels (Torrance, 1960), you will recall that over 70 per cent of those in the upper 20 per cent on tests of creative thinking would be eliminated if only an intelligence or scholastic aptitude test had been used.

Of all of Elizabeth Drews' (Drews, 1961) three gifted groups (social leaders, creative intellectuals and studious achievers), the lowest teacher grades were achieved by the creative intellectuals. When the others were studying for examinations, they would be reading a book on philosophy or a college textbook, activities with almost no payoff in the teacher's grade book. Thus, on standardized achievement tests, the creative intellectuals surpassed the other groups as a result of their wide reading and uncredited, self-initiating learning.

Holland and Kent (1960), of the National Merit Scholarship Corporation, have questioned the effectiveness of present scholarship programs. They think that much of the $100,000,000 now available annually for college scholarships may be going to the wrong individuals, the good grade-getters who often have little creative talent. In the corporation's studies of scholarship winners, Holland (1961) found that 'for samples of students of superior scholastic aptitude, creative performance is generally unrelated to scholastic achievement and scholastic aptitude'. He suggests the use of nonintellectual criteria in the selection of students for scholarships and fellowships. A bold step was taken by the National Merit Scholarship Corporation in 1961 when it awarded twenty-five of its scholarships to individuals who had high creative promise but would not otherwise have won awards.

Getzels and Jackson (1960) have also pointed out that the tests, recommendations and rank in class now relied upon so heavily in college admission are biased in favor of the student with 'convergent' intellectual ability and social interests. They made a plea at the 1960 meeting of the American Educational Research Association that colleges recognize and find a place for superior divergent students as well as the superior convergent ones. Mednick (1961) made a similar plea at the 1961 meeting of the Association for Higher Education. He pointed out that although modern technology might soon enable colleges to admit only a relatively pure strain of 'grade-getters', they may in so doing breed some extremely desirable characteristics *out* of college populations.

In the second chapter [not included here], attention will be given to methods for identifying creative talent and ways by which guidance workers can fulfil their role of seeing that creative talent is recognized.

Help parents understand their creative child

One of the most tragic plights I have witnessed among highly creative individuals stems from the failure of their parents to understand them. Frequently destructive or incapacitating hostility is the result of this failure. When teachers fail to understand highly creative children, refusal to learn, delinquency or withdrawal may be a consequence. In some cases, the quiet and unobtrusive intervention of the counselor offers about the only possibility whereby parents and teachers may come to understand them and thus salvage much outstanding talent.

Guidance workers need to help parents and teachers recognize that everyone possesses to some degree the ability involved in being creative, that these abilities can be increased or decreased by the way children are treated and that it is a legitimate function of the home and the school to provide the experiences and guidance which will free them to develop and function fully. Of course, these abilities are inherited, in the broad sense, that one inherits sense organs, a peripheral nervous system and a brain. The type of pursuit of these abilities and the general tendency to persist in their search is largely a matter of the way parents and teachers treat children's creative needs.

Guidance workers can, as I see it, help parents to guide highly creative children in two major ways. The first concerns the parent's handling of the child's unusual ideas and questions, and the other involves helping such a child become less obnoxious without sacrificing his creativity.

The school should help parents recognize that criticism – making fun of the child's ideas or laughing at his conclusions – can prevent his expression of ideas. The parent's experienced eyes and ears can help the child learn to look for and to listen to important sights and sounds. The parent should stimulate the child to explore, ask questions and try to find answers.

Many parents attempt too early to eliminate fantasy from the thinking of the child. Fantasy is regarded as something unhealthy and to be eliminated. Fantasies such as imaginative role playing, fantastic stories, unusual drawings and the like are normal aspects of a child's thinking. Many parents are greatly relieved to learn this and out of this understanding grows a better parent–child relationship. Certainly we are interested in developing a sound type of creativity, but this type of fantasy, it seems to me, must be kept alive until the child's intellectual development is such that he can engage in sound creative thinking. I have seen many indications in our testing of first and second graders that many children with impoverished imaginations have been subjected to rather vigorous and stern efforts to eliminate fantasy too early. They are afraid to think.

Counselors and administrators can be sympathetic with teachers and parents who are irritated by the unending curiosity and manipulativeness of highly creative children. Endless questioning and experimenting can be inconvenient. Parents may not appreciate the child's passion for first-hand observation. Persistent questioning can be very annoying. A mother of a three-year-old complained: 'He wears me out just asking questions. He won't give up either, until he gets an answer; it's just awful when he gets started on something!'

Counselors, teachers and administrators can help parents recognize the fact that there is value in such curiosity and manipulativeness and that there can be no substitute for it. Parents should be encouraged to help the child learn to ask good questions, how to make good guesses at the answers and how to test the answers against reality.

Most parents find it extremely difficult to permit their children to learn on their own – even to do their school work on their own. Parents want to protect their children from the hurt of failing. Individual administration of problems involving possible solutions to frustrating situations has shown that the imagination of many children is inhibited by the tremendous emphasis which has been placed on prevention. For example, many of our third graders were so obsessed with the thought that Mother Hubbard should have prevented her predicament that they were reluctant to consider possible solutions to her problem. This may possibly be related to the criticism of some observers that American education prepares only for victory or success and not for possible frustration or even failure.

Certainly teaching of all kinds of failure is important, but overemphasis may deter children from coping imaginatively and realistically with frustration and failure, which cannot be prevented. It may rob the child of his initiative and resourcefulness. All children learn by trial and error. They must try, fail, try another method and, if necessary, try even again. Of course, they need guidance, but they also need to find success by their own efforts. Each child strives for independence from the time he learns to crawl, and independence is a necessary characteristic of the creative personality.

Summary

Schools have cause for concern about the creative talent and creative growth of children which stems from their legitimate and traditional concerns about mental hygiene, fully functioning personalities, educational achievement, vocational success and social welfare. Guidance workers are in a unique position to encourage creative talent by providing highly creative children with a refuge from vicious attacks by the world, being a sponsor or patron, helping him understand and accept his divergence, letting him communicate his ideas, seeing that his creative talent is recognized and helping parents and teachers understand him.

References

BINET, A. (1909), *Les Idées Modernes sur les Enfants*, Flammarion, Paris.

DREWS, E. M. (1961), 'A critical evaluation of approaches to the identification of gifted students', in A. Traxler (ed.), *Measurement and Evaluation in Today's Schools*, American Council on Education, pp. 47–51.

GETZELS, J. W., and JACKSON, P. W. (1958), 'The meaning of "giftedness" – an examination of an explanatory concept', *Phi Delta Kappan*, vol. 40, pp. 75–7.

GETZELS, J. W., and JACKSON, P. W. (1959), 'The highly intelligent and the highly creative adolescent', in C. W. Taylor (ed.), *The 1959 University of Utah Research Conference on the Identification of Creative Scientific Talent*, University of Utah Press.

GETZELS, J. W., and JACKSON, P. W. (1960), 'Occupational choice and cognitive functioning: career aspirations of highly intelligent and highly creative adolescents', *J. abnorm. soc. Psychol.*, vol. 61, pp. 119–23.

GUILFORD, J. P. (1959), *Personality*, McGraw-Hill.

HEBEISEN, A. A. (1960), 'The performance of a group of schizophrenic patients on a test of creative thinking', in E. P. Torrance (ed.), *Second Minnesota Conference on Gifted Children*, University of Minnesota, pp. 125–9.

HOLLAND, J. L. (1961), 'Creative and academic performance among talented adolescents', *J. educ. Psychol.*, vol. 52, pp. 136–47.

HOLLAND, J. L., and KENT, L. (1960), 'The concentration of scholarship funds and its implications for education', *College and University*, vol. 35, pp. 471–83.

MEARNS, H. (1941), *The Creative Adult*, Doubleday.

MEDNICK, S. A. (1961), 'Development of admission criteria for colleges and universities', in *Current Issues in Higher Education*, National Education Association, pp. 87–8.

MOORE, O. K. (1961), 'Orthographic symbols and the pre-school child – a new approach', in E. P. Torrance (ed.), *Third Minnesota Conference on Gifted Children*, University of Minnesota, pp. 51–101.

MURRAY, H. A. (1960), 'A mythology for grownups', *Saturday Rev.*, vol. 43, no. 4, pp. 10–12.

ORNSTEIN, J. (1961), 'New recruits for science', *Parents Mag.*, vol. 36, no. 2, p. 42.

PATRICK, C. (1955), *What is Creative Thinking?*, Philosophical Library.

TORRANCE, E. P. (1960), *Eight Partial Replications of the Getzels–Jackson Study*, Bureau of Educational Research, University of Minnesota.

WALLACE, H. (1960), 'Tests of creative thinking and sales performance in a large departmental store', in E. P. Torrance (ed.), *Second Minnesota Conference on Gifted Children*, University of Minnesota.

WOLFLE, D. (1960), 'Diversity of talent', *Amer. Psychol.*, vol. 15, pp. 535–45.

27 F. A. Haddon and H. Lytton

Teaching Approach and Divergent Thinking Abilities

F. A. Haddon and H. Lytton, 'Teaching approach and the development of divergent thinking abilities in primary schools', *British Journal of Educational Psychology*, vol. 38, 1968, pp. 171–80.

Introduction

Despite the attention which 'Creativity' has received as a fashionable topic for research there is, as yet, as Vernon (1964) and Hudson (1966) point out, no clear evidence for the assumption that high scorers on tests of 'divergent thinking' in Guilford's terminology, will be particularly fertile in creative original production in their own life situation. Nor is there evidence for the converse, that high scorers on tests of 'convergent thinking' alone, will lack such creativity. The best way of looking at this question probably is to regard high scores on divergent thinking tests as an indication of lack of anxiety about nonconformist responses, a necessary, but not a sufficient condition for creative work. To avoid undue claims, we have used the term 'divergent thinking', rather than 'creativity' throughout.

As Guilford has shown in his many studies (summarized in Guilford, 1956) divergent abilities can be distinguished factorially from convergent abilities which have hitherto formed the main component of general ability tests. It is important to explore divergent abilities since they hold some promise of providing new insights into cognitive functioning. Tests of those abilities may provide a welcome supplement to 'intelligence tests' as we have so far known them, and indicate the type rather than the level of future performance (Hudson, 1966). This model of cognitive abilities implies that divergent and convergent thinking are complementary aspects or different styles of intellectual functioning.

Whilst a great deal has been written on the guidance of creative ability, very little work appears to have been published investigating the effects of particular school situations. Torrance does hint briefly at the effects of school orientation towards learning

(Torrance, 1962), and Hasan and Butcher (1966) report his view to the effect that the success of predominantly divergent thinkers is directly related to the degree of freedom and permissiveness and the lack of authoritarian discipline within a school. Vernon (1964), in a review of creativity and intelligence, also comments: 'I strongly suspect some schools do much more to stimulate and foster, or else to inhibit, creative talent than others.' Sears and Hilgard (1964) quote Spalding (1963) as finding strong negative relations between the expression of creativity in elementary-aged children and teacher behaviour characterized as formal group instruction, using shame as a punishment technique, whilst Sears (1963) found positive correlations between creativity and teachers' use of the technique of rewarding children by personal interest in their ideas rather than by evaluation.

The research reported here was concerned with evaluating the effects of contrasted formal and informal schools upon performance on tests of divergent thinking abilities. It was felt that teaching approach might be a variable affecting the degree of divergency exhibited in children's thinking. Two other aspects have also been examined. First, the relationship between I.Q. and performance on divergent tests has been looked at in some detail. Secondly, the relationship between performance on divergent tests and peer popularity has been compared with the relationship between V.R.Q. (verbal reasoning quotient) and peer popularity in each of the schools used.

Basic Hypothesis and Research Design

It is generally accepted that abilities and personality characteristics are, to a large extent, moulded by environmental influences such as family and school. Since the school, however, is only one factor in the development of a child's personality, the basic structure of which has very largely been laid down by the time the child arrives there, measurable differences between school and school are likely to be small. The basic hypothesis is that some differences in divergent thinking abilities can, nevertheless, be detected between comparable children who have spent formative years in contrasted environments such as different primary schools provide. Schools may differ in many ways, one of which is the degree of formality or informality which permeates the approach to learning. The two types of schools which have been contrasted here are the formal, or traditional, school which places emphasis upon convergent thinking and authoritative learning, and the informal or progressive school, where the emphasis is upon self-initiated learning and creative activities. It was predicted that children from the formal school will have lower mean scores on 'divergent' tests than children from the informal school, which, it was thought, encourages the growth of personality traits associated with divergency.

A further area of interest was the relation between I.Q. or V.R.Q. and measures of divergent thinking. It was thought that given a high general cognitive potential, development along either convergent or divergent lines may receive considerable emphasis at the expense of the other, but that the informal school, more than the formal school, would develop both convergent and divergent thinking in line one with the other. Conversely, when intelligence is limited, V.R.Q. and divergent thinking ability are likely to display greater correlation. In other words, the differentiation of divergent from convergent abilities is likely to show itself more clearly at higher than at lower levels of general intellectual ability (whether measured via convergent or divergent abilities). This prediction is in accordance with Yamamoto's (1965) findings. To summarize the predictions: (a) Mean scores on divergent tests would be significantly higher in the informal schools than in the formal schools. (b) Correlation between V.R.Q. and divergent thinking abilities would decrease as the mean V.R.Q. and mean divergent tests scores of subgroups rose, but the values obtained would throughout be higher in the informal school.

The tests

Full details of the tests and the system of scoring, adapted from that used by Torrance for the Minnesota Tests of Creative Thinking, are given in the Appendix. Briefly, the tests were:

The non-verbal or 'iconographic' tests. (a) Circles (Torrance, 1962); (b) vague shape of dots (developed from Torrance, 1962, Picture Construction Task); (c) block printing (new test).

373

The verbal tests. (d) Uses for a shoe-box (modified from uses for a can, Torrance, 1962); (e) problems which might arise in taking a bath (Torrance, 1962, common problems); (f) imaginative stories (Torrance, 1962); (g) the camping expedition, a disguised socio-metric test (new test).

From each test two scores were obtained, one of which was originality (except for test b – see Appendix). The total for each test was the total of the two component scores.

The subjects and schools

The schools used were selected after consultation with lecturers from a college of education who were familiar with the area, and after advice from a local inspector of schools. Two pairs of contrasted primary schools matched for socio-economic background were chosen. A and C are the formal, B and D the informal schools. Schools A and B are in a predominantly middle-class urban area, the mean V.R.Q. being 106·5 and 103·5, respectively. Schools C and D draw their children from a more mixed social background in a different urban area, the mean V.R.Q. being 96·1 and 98·3, respectively. The mean V.R.Q. of the formal schools combined (A and C) is 101·75, and that of the informal schools (B and D) 101·14.

The tests were administered to all the children eligible for transfer to secondary schools the following term. In all, 211 children, eleven to twelve years old, were tested and the whole ability range in the schools was covered.

There were several advantages in choosing to administer the tests to children within a few days of completing their primary education:

1. Such children had been subjected to the effect of their particular school for the maximum amount of time.

2. Selection for secondary education had already taken place, so that the children were not concerned about possible effects upon their future schooling.

3. I.Q.s (or V.R.Q.s) for all the children were made available by the Chief Education Officer. These were based on Moray House Verbal Reasoning Test no. 72, which was used throughout

the county as part of the selection procedure for allocation to secondary education.

Results and Discussion

Comparisons between two types of school

The results of the tests are set out in Table 1. Each component was marked separately and the component scores combined to obtain a test score for each child. Mean scores for the group were calculated from these.

Table 1

Comparison of Mean Test Scores (Raw Scores)

	Formal schools			Informal schools			t-value of difference combined means	P
	A mean	C mean	combined mean A+C	B mean	D mean	combined mean B+D		
V.R.Q.	106·50	96·1	101·75	103·50	98·30	101·14	0·31	N.S.
Test 1	12·00	9·1	10·55	15·55	10·10	12·80	3·07	<0·01
2	5·72	5·92	5·82	7·48	7·52	7·50	5·48	<0·01
3	7·50	4·88	6·19	9·05	11·64	10·35	6·50	<0·01
4	4·98	6·58	5·78	6·86	7·62	7·25	2·11	<0·05
5	10·56	10·08	10·32	15·20	8·41	11·81	1·61	N.S.
6	12·46	12·50	12·48	14·75	13·54	14·15	2·51	<0·05
N	54	50	104	59	48	107		

N for test 3 (numbers reduced on account of practical testing difficulties).

| | 29 | 25 | 54 | 35 | 25 | 60 | | |

The results in Table 1 in general confirm the main prediction of significantly higher scores being obtained from the informal schools. Even in test 5, where the difference does not reach statistical significance at the 0·05 level, the direction of the difference is in line with the other results. There is, of course, no appreciable difference in mean V.R.Q. between the two groups of schools.

The iconographic tests – numbers 1, 2 and 3 – all show highly significant differences between the two groups. This is not unexpected. It is reasonable to suppose that the effect of the different approaches will show to its maximum here, in that no child will be handicapped by having to respond in writing. This not only allows the less able child to make a response but applies particularly to the boys who often seem either unable or reluctant to express themselves in writing with the same fluency as girls of similar age. Conversely, one would expect lesser differences between the two groups on the verbal tests. This is generally true again, tests 4 and 6 showing a difference of means significant at the 0·05 level, whilst test 5 just fails to reach this level.

Table 2

Comparison of Mean Scores of Test Components (Standard Scores)

Component	Tests from which obtained	Formal schools means	Informal schools means	t-value of difference	P
Fluency	6	7·26	7·67	1·78	N.S.
Flexibility	1, 4, 5	57·31	61·39	2·62	<0·01
Originality	1, 4, 5, 6	61·61	70·10	2·71	<0·01
Fit of concept	2	3·26	3·81	3·12	<0·01
Elaboration	2	2·58	3·69	5·30	<0·01

Having confirmed the main prediction, further analyses were made. The component raw scores which were used for the previous table were changed to standard scores with a mean of 20 and a standard deviation of 5 to make them comparable. It was then possible to extract the component scores from each test to obtain a total component score for originality, etc., for the whole battery. The results are shown in Table 2. Scores for test 3 were not included here because only 50 per cent of the children were tested.

An alternative way of looking at the results is shown in Table 3, in which the scores were added to give mean scores for iconographic tests, verbal tests and all divergent tests. Comparisons are made over different ranges of V.R.Q. Results from test 2 were not included in these calculations since the test was scored in a somewhat experimental manner.

The results again gave a clear indication of the superiority of the informal schools in performance on the tests. It seemed important next to examine the differences between the two types of school over high and low ranges of V.R.Q. Whilst it is recognized that the V.R.Q. is in some ways an unsatisfactory indication of general intelligence because it samples too narrow a range of intellectual abilities, nevertheless, considerable importance is attached to this index and to the abilities it measures, and it usually carries considerable weight in selection procedures. If, as

Table 3

Comparison of Mean Scores Over Various Ranges of V.R.Q. (Standard Scores)

	Formal schools means	Informal schools means	t-value of difference	P
Over full range of V.R.Q.:				
V.R.Q.	101·75	101·14	0·31	N.S.
Iconographic	18·96	21·29	4·16	<0·01
Verbal	19·50	20·72	2·71	<0·01
All tests	38·34	41·87	4·15	<0·01
V.R.Q. 100 and above:				
V.R.Q.	113·47	110·57	1·88	N.S.
Iconographic	20·18	22·37	2·88	<0·01
Verbal	20·29	21·97	3·18	<0·01
All tests	40·36	44·18	3·62	<0·01
V.R.Q. below 100:				
V.R.Q.	88·59	89·11	0·32	N.S.
Iconographic	17·59	19·92	3·11	<0·01
Verbal	18·61	19·13	0·76	N.S.
All tests	36·06	38·92	2·41	<0·05

has been claimed, the informal schools are fostering the development of divergent thinking abilities, then one would expect a greater difference between the two types of school over the higher ranges of V.R.Q. where there is greater intellectual potential. Conversely, over the lower ranges of V.R.Q., the expected differences would be less. Table 3 compares the two types of school over the range V.R.Q. 100 and above, and V.R.Q. below 100, respectively.

The results shown in the lower part of Table 3 support the

main hypothesis, but the prediction of greater differences with higher V.R.Q.s is borne out only as regards the verbal, not the iconographic tests. It is worth noting that for V.R.Q.s above 100 the differences are in the reverse direction to the differences on the divergent tests, yet in spite of this, the informal schools achieve results which are significantly superior.

Table 4

Correlation of V.R.Q. and Divergent Thinking Tests

All schools. Subgroups based on V.R.Q. ranges

	N	r
Full range of V.R.Q. 70–135	211	0·480
V.R.Q. 115 and above	35	0·076
V.R.Q. 100 and above[1]	115	0·164
V.R.Q. below 100	96	0·512

All schools. Subgroups based on divergent thinking scores

Mean divergent thinking score = 40	N	r
Full range	211	0·480
Divergent score 40 and above	103	0·230
Divergent score below 40	108	0·440

1. This includes the category V.R.Q. 115 and above.

The evidence from correlations

The main prediction with regard to correlation, it will be recalled, was that the correlation between V.R.Q. and divergent thinking abilities would decrease as V.R.Q. rose. This is demonstrated by Table 4 which used the combined data from the four schools. The results here are in agreement with Yamamoto (1965) who reports 'a consistent decrease in the size of correlation as the I.Q. level of subgroups became higher' (although the values quoted by him are considerably smaller in both the school systems used for his investigations than the values obtained here). In the lower half of Table 4 the data have been re-grouped on the basis of total scores on the tests of divergent thinking.

These findings strongly confirm the view that convergent thinking and divergent thinking are two complementary aspects of intellectual ability in general (styles of functioning). They separate from each other, each attaining a more clearly independent status of its own, at higher levels of ability, and they overlap more closely at lower levels, whether ability is measured by convergent or by divergent tests.

Table 5

Correlations between V.R.Q. and Divergent Thinking Tests

V.R.Q.	N	Formal schools			N	Informal schools		
		Icono-graphic r	Verbal r	All tests r		Icono-graphic r	Verbal r	All test r
Full range	104	0·335	0·418	0·454	107	0·379	0·618	0·560
115 and above	22	−0·041	−0·011	−0·050	13	0·018	0·026	0·036
100 and above [1]	55	−0·051	0·159	0·059	60	0·204	0·483	0·366
Below 100	49	0·245	0·576	0·487	47	0·367	0·578	0·548

1. This includes the category 115 and above.

Within this general concept of a diminishing relationship at higher levels of ability, a subsidiary hypothesis was that the correlation would be somewhat higher in the informal schools. It was argued that in these schools, because of their particular approach to learning, the link between the two aspects would be maintained to a greater extent. The idea is more forcibly expressed by saying that formal education will tend to destroy this connexion by putting a premium on convergent thinking and conformist behaviour. Table 5 explores this connexion over various V.R.Q. groupings.

The evidence in this table is quite convincing in its support of the hypothesis. In every instance the value of r is higher in the informal schools. This is especially noticeable in the range V.R.Q. 100 and above, which suggests that formal education fails to develop latent ability to think along divergent lines among the most able children.

It is interesting to compare these results with the outcome of a pilot study in Birmingham (Kellmer Pringle and McKenzie, 1965) which involved two contrasted primary schools selected on criteria similar to those used in this study. The object of the research was to examine teaching methods as a factor influencing the degree of rigidity in problem solving. The definition of rigidity as 'the inability to restructure a field in which there are alternative solutions to a problem in order to solve that problem more efficiently', is almost a negative definition of divergency and it might have been expected that the Informal school would have shown a significantly less rigidity among its pupils. In fact, no over-all difference was found, but since the comparison was made on the degree of set found in performance on one arithmetic test, this is hardly sufficient evidence for any definite conclusions to be drawn.

Sociometric analysis

Considerable attention has been given in America to the social relationships of creative individuals – in our terminology, those who do well on tests of divergent thinking abilities. The general view seems to be that such children are subjected to pressure to conform and to conceal their divergent characteristics. It is suggested that the creative child will be lacking in popularity and that social pressures may well be a factor inhibiting the development of divergent abilities (Torrance, 1962).

However, it was felt that the qualities associated with the divergent personality – fluency, flexibility and sensitivity – might well be qualities which make for good social relationships in a society in which originality was valued, and that there could, therefore, be a positive relationship between popularity and divergent personality. Test 7 was included in the battery to explore this connexion. It was expected that any correlation found would be low, but that the values would be higher in the informal schools. The argument here was that in so far as a school is able to transmit its cultural values, those values should be reflected in the general appreciation of the individuals who exhibit them in action. As a corollary to this, the correlation between V.R.Q. and popularity should show a higher value in the formal schools.

Table 6 sets out these correlations. These have been calculated on a school by school basis because the value of sociometric status as expressed here varies according to the number of children in the class, and so it was not possible to combine the schools for comparisons. Spearman's rank order correlation has been used.

There is partial support for the prediction, but two values require some discussion. In school A the top class contained only children of V.R.Q. 100 and above. The probable result of this is to give a much lower value for both correlations. However,

Table 6

Rank Order Correlation Coefficients between V.R.Q. and Sociometric Status, and between Divergent Thinking Scores and Sociometric Status

School	N	V.R.Q. range	V.R.Q. and sociometric status	Divergent thinking and sociometric status
A. Formal	33	135–100	0·137	−0·128
C. Formal	50	126–70	0·337	0·279
B. Informal	47	135–85	0·058	0·363
D. Informal	37	131–71	0·462	0·382

the important point here is not so much the value of the co-efficients as the relationships between them. V.R.Q. has a positive correlation with sociometric status, whereas divergent test scores have a negative one – as they did in Getzels' and Jackson's study.

The second point to discuss is the values obtained from school D. The three other schools all show the predicted direction in the differences between the two values. This is not only reversed in school D but the values themselves are the highest obtained. This school is a particularly delightful one to visit and gives one the impression of friendly informality combined with high standards of work and behaviour. It may be that the ethos of this school ensures esteem for both types of ability and thus makes for popularity of both high convergent and high divergent thinkers, who indeed are often the same children.

The over-all results suggest that the school ethos as formulated by the head and the staff plays an important role in determining the children's values during the primary stage. This would seem to explain the inter-school differences in our investigations.

Conclusions

The analysis of the test results provided considerable evidence in support of the chief hypothesis. This was, to repeat it briefly, that the informal schools provide an environment which develops qualities of personality that result in a high level of divergent thinking ability. This has been supported by comparisons of mean test scores classified in a variety of ways. The means from the informal schools have in most cases been significantly higher than those from the formal schools. In those cases where the difference in means has not reached the level of statistical significance the direction of the difference has confirmed the general trend. In *no* case has there been a difference in the unpredicted direction.

The evidence from correlations was again in support of the contention that the informal school succeeded in developing more of the divergent potential, since the correlation coefficients between V.R.Q. and divergent test scores were consistently higher in the informal schools. The general hypothesis of a decrease in the correlation value as both the V.R.Q. and the divergent ability level of subgroups rose was also confirmed.

The results from the sociometric analysis are inconclusive, but there is some indication that there is a positive connexion between divergent ability and peer popularity in the informal schools. This differentiation appears to increase if the lower V.R.Q.s are excluded (schools A and B).

This study has not been comparing good versus bad schools, but good schools which operate with a somewhat different emphasis. It is certainly not permissiveness which is the distinguishing criterion of informality as opposed to formality. The most striking difference lies in the degree of emphasis laid upon self-initiated learning. Behind this emphasis in the informal schools and fundamental to its success, lies the pattern of interpersonal relationships within the school. One's impression in the informal school is of a relaxed, friendly atmosphere in which children move freely, both within the classroom and in the school generally. Particularly noticeable is the freedom of access to the libraries and the extent to which children work in them unsupervised. The formal schools are not unfriendly but one senses a tighter rein and a firmer directive. Class work is more in evidence.

The investigation has shown that the optimum development of divergent thinking abilities is related to a certain teaching approach. As to what lies at the roots of this relationship we can only speculate. But it would seem that it is based on the teacher's confidence in the child's ability to think adventurously and in new directions, which in turn, will determine the child's estimation of himself and of his abilities. If the teacher can enter into the child's thinking, if she is prepared to let work develop in unexpected directions according to the child's needs and interests, if she can find and express genuine pleasure in the child's efforts, then self-initiated learning can be developed. It is in this climate that divergent thinking abilities are seen to flourish.

Appendix

The tests of divergent thinking abilities and scoring procedures
Unless otherwise indicated, the tests are all taken from the Minnesota Tests of Creative Thinking (Torrance, 1962). The scoring procedures are adapted from the same source. The titles of the Minnesota tests are given in brackets.

Test 1 – the circles test (Circles and Squares Task). Scoring – flexibility: one point for each category of response; originality: one point for each response outside listed common responses.

Test 2 – the vague shape of dots test (derived from Picture Construction Task). Scoring – elaboration: one point for each new idea added to the initial response; fit to concept: this was the new category of score which attempted to score for sensitivity to the qualities of the stimulus on a scale of 1–5 points.

Test 3 – the block-printing test (New Test). In this test the children were given an ink pad and a small block of wood, 2-in $\times$ $1\frac{3}{4}$-in

× ½-in and a booklet of absorbent paper. They were required to discover how many different kinds of mark they could make and to use these as they liked. (There were twenty-six possible types of mark.) Scoring – flexibility: one point for each category of mark discovered, e.g. long edge print, short-side print, etc.; originality: one point for each image, each pattern, each textural experiment or for making letters or figures.

Test 4 – uses for a shoebox (Unusual Uses). Scoring – flexibility: one point for each category of response; originality: on the following basis, twelve or more children giving responses, score 0, six to eleven children giving responses, score 1, three to five children, score 2, two children, score 3, one child, score 4.

Test 5 – problems that might arise in taking a bath (Common Problems). Scoring – flexibility: one point for each response. (In this test each response constituted a new category); originality: As for test 4.

Test 6 – imaginative stories (Imaginative Stories). Scoring – fluency: points awarded for length on a scale of 1–3; originality: one point for each of the following characteristics if they appeared at all: description, vividness, indication of feelings, personal involvement, original solution or ending, original plot or setting, humour, inventive language, other original twists not covered by previous categories.

The scripts were scored by three judges, two of whom were unaware which schools were classed as formal and informal. The scores were then averaged for fluency and originality.

Test 7 – the camping party test (New Test). This was a simple sociometric test disguised as another test of divergent thinking ability. A simple sociometric status was obtained by counting the number of nominations to join the expedition which each child received. This information was not obtained for all the children who were tested since in three of the schools used, the children of lower ability were spread through other classes from which they were extracted for testing purposes. This meant that they were unable to receive a proper number of nominations.

References

ANDERSON, J. E. (1960), 'The nature of abilities', in E. P. Torrance (ed.), *Education and Talent*, University of Minnesota Press, pp. 9–31.

GUILFORD, J. P. (1956), 'The structure of intellect', *Psychol. Bull.*, vol. 53, pp. 267–93.

HASAN, P., and BUTCHER, H. J. (1966), 'Creativity and intelligence: a partial replication with Scottish children of Getzels' and Jackson's study', *Brit. J. Psychol.*, vol. 57, pp. 129–35.

HUDSON, L. (1966), *Contrary Imaginations*, Methuen. (Penquin Books edn., 1967.)

KELLMER PRINGLE, M. L., and MCKENZIE, I. R. (1965), 'Teaching method and rigidity in problem solving', *Brit. J. educ. Psychol.*, vol. 35, pp. 50–59.

SEARS, P. S. (1963), *The Effects of Classroom Committee Conditions on the Strength of Achievement Motivation and Work Output in Children*, Stanford University Press.

SEARS, P. S., and HILGARD, E. R. (1964), 'The teacher's role in the motivation of the learner', in *Theories of Learning and Instruction* (63rd N.S.S.E. Yearbook), University of Chicago Press.

SPALDING, R. (1963), *Achievement, Creativity and Self-concept Correlates in Elementary Schools*, University of Illinois (mimeo.).

TORRANCE, E. P. (1962), *Guiding Creative Talent*, Prentice-Hall.

VERNON, P. E. (1964), 'Creativity and intelligence', *Educ. Res.*, vol. 6, pp. 163–9.

YAMAMOTO, K. (1965), 'Effects of restriction of range and test unreliability on correlation between measures of intelligence and creative thinking', *Brit. J. educ. Psychol.*, vol. 35, pp. 300–305.

Further Reading

General

H. H. Anderson (ed.), *Creativity and its Cultivation*, Harper & Row, 1959.

F. Barron, 'The psychology of creativity', in T. M. Newcomb (ed.), *New Directions in Psychology*, *II*, Holt, Rinehart & Winston, 1965, pp. 1–134.

S. E. Golann, 'Psychological study of creativity', *Psychol. Bull.*, vol. 60 (1963), pp. 548–65.

H. E. Gruber, G. Terrell and M. Wertheimer (eds.), *Contemporary Approaches to Creative Thinking*, Atherton Press, 1962.

R. L. Mooney and T. A. Razik (eds.), *Explorations in Creativity*, Harper & Row, 1967.

M. I. Stein and S. J. Heinze, *Creativity and the Individual*, Free Press, 1960.

C. W. Taylor (ed.), *Creativity: Progress and Potentiality*, McGraw-Hill, 1964.

C. W. Taylor (ed.), *Widening Horizons in Creativity*, Wiley, 1964.

C. W. Taylor and F. Barron (eds.), *Scientific Creativity: Its Recognition and Development*, Wiley, 1963.

M. Tyson, 'Creativity', in B. M. Foss (ed.), *New Horizons in Psychology*, Penguin Books, 1966, pp. 167–82.

P. E. Vernon, 'Creativity and intelligence', *Educ. Res.*, vol. 6 (1964), pp. 163–9.

P. E. Vernon, 'Psychological studies of creativity', *J. child Psychol. Psychiat.*, vol. 8 (1967), pp. 153–64.

Introspective materials and cognitive theories

K. Duncker, 'On problem solving', *Psychol. Monogr.*, vol. 58 (1945), no. 270.

B. Ghiselin, *The Creative Process: A Symposium*, University of California Press, 1952. (Mentor Books edn, 1955.)

B. Ghiselin, 'The creative process and its relation to the identification of creative talent', in C. W. Taylor and F. Barron (eds.), *Scientific Creativity: Its Recognition and Development*, Wiley (1963), pp. 355–64.

J. Hadamard, *The Psychology of Invention in the Mathematical Field*, Dover, 1945.

R. Harding, *An Anatomy of Inspiration*, Cass, 1940.

A. Huxley, *The Doors of Perception*, Harper & Row, 1954.

A. Koestler, *The Act of Creation*, Hutchinson, 1964.

P. McKellar, *Imagination and Thinking*, Cohen & West, 1957.

N. R. F. Maier, 'Reasoning in humans', *J. comp. Psychol.*, vol. 10 (1930), pp. 115–43; vol. 12 (1931), pp. 181–94.

S. A. Mednick, 'The associative basis of the creative process', *Psychol. Rev.*, vol. 69 (1962), pp. 220–32.

Further Reading

A. Newell, J. C. Shaw and H. A. Simon, 'The process of creative thinking', in H. E. Gruber *et al.* (eds.), *Contemporary Approaches to Creative Thinking*, Atherton Press, 1962, pp. 63–119.

C. Patrick, 'Creative thought in poets', *Arch. Psychol.*, vol. 26 (1935), pp. 1–74.

C. Patrick, 'Creative thought in artists', *J. Psychol.*, vol. 4 (1937), pp. 35–73.

I. A. Taylor, 'The nature of the creative process', in P. Smith (ed.), *Creativity: An Examination of the Creative Process*, Hastings House, 1959, pp. 51–82.

W. E. Vinacke, *The Psychology of Thinking*, McGraw-Hill, 1952.

N. Wertheimer, *Productive Thinking*, Tavistock, 1959.

Psychometric approaches

H. E. Brogden and T. B. Sprecher, 'Criteria of creativity', in C. W. Taylor (ed.), *Creativity: Progress and Potential*, McGraw-Hill, 1964, pp. 155–76.

C. L. Burt *et al.*, 'A study in vocational guidance', *Industr. Hlth Res. Board Rep.*, no. 33, 1926.

R. J. Goldman, 'The Minnesota tests of creative thinking', *Educ. Res.*, vol. 7 (1964), pp. 3–14.

J. P. Guilford, 'Creativity', *Amer. Psychol.*, vol. 5 (1950), pp. 444–54.

J. P. Guilford, *The Nature of Human Intelligence*, McGraw-Hill, 1967.

H. L. Hargreaves, 'The "faculty" of imagination', *Brit. J. Psychol. Monogr. Suppl.*, no. 10, 1927.

P. Hasan and H. J. Butcher, 'Creativity and intelligence: a partial replication with Scottish children of Getzels' and Jackon's study', *Brit. J. Psychol.*, vol. 57 (1966), pp. 129–35.

C. W. Taylor, 'Measurement of creativity', *Proceedings of the Sixteenth International Congress on Applied Psychology*, Swets & Zeitlinger (in press)

R. L. Thorndike, 'Some methodological issues in the study of creativity', *Proceedings of the 1962 Invitational Conference on Testing Problems*, Educational Testing Service, 1962, pp. 40–54.

L. L. Thurstone, 'Creative talent', in L. L. Thurstone (ed.), *Applications of Psychology*, Harper & Row, 1952, pp. 18–37.

R. C. Wilson, J. P. Guilford and P. R. Christensen, 'The measurement of individual differences in originality', *Psychol. Bull.*, vol. 50 (1953), pp. 362–70.

R. C. Wilson, J. P. Guilford, *et al.*, 'A factor-analytical study of creative thinking abilities', *Psychometrika*, vol. 19 (1954), pp. 297–311.

Personality studies and dynamic theories

F. Barron, *Creativity and Psychological Health*, Van Nostrand, 1963.

C. M. Cox, *Genetic Studies of Genius. Vol. II. The Early Mental Traits of Three Hundred Geniuses*, Stanford University Press, 1926.

R. S. Crutchfield, 'Conformity and creative thinking', in H. E. Gruber *et al.* (ed.), *Contemporary Approaches to Creative Thinking*, Atherton Press, 1962, pp. 120–40.

J. E. Drevdahl, 'Factors of importance for creativity', *J. clin. Psychol.*, vol. 12 (1956), pp. 21–6.

B. T. Eiduson, 'Artist and non-artist: a comparative study', *J. Person.*, vol. 26 (1958), pp. 13–28.

H. Ellis, *A Study of British Genius*, Hurst & Blackett, London, 1904.

S. Freud, 'Leonardo da Vinci and a memory of his childhood', in J. Strachey (ed.), *The Standard Edition of the Complete Psychological Works of Sigmund Freud*, Hogarth Press, 1958, pp. 63–137. (First published 1910.)

L. S. Hollingworth, *Gifted Children, their Nature and Nurture*, Macmillan, 1926.

L. Hudson, *Frames of Mind*, Methuen, 1968.

E. Kretschmer, *The Psychology of Men of Genius*, Kegan Paul and Harcourt, Brace, 1931.

E. Kris, *Psychoanalytic Explorations in Art*, International Universities Press, 1952.

L. S. Kubie, *Neurotic Distortion of the Creative Process*, University of Kansas Press, 1958.

H. C. Lehman, *Age and Achievement*, Princeton University Press, 1953.

D. C. McClelland, 'On the psychodynamics of creative physical scientists', in H. E. Gruber *et al.* (eds.), *Contemporary Approaches to Creative Thinking*, Atherton Press, 1962, pp. 141–74.

D. W. MacKinnon, 'The highly effective individual', *Teachers Coll. Rec.*, vol. 61 (1960), pp. 367–78.

A. H. Maslow, 'Creativity in self-actualizing people', in H. H. Anderson (ed.), *Creativity and Its Cultivation*, Harper & Row, 1959, pp. 83–95.

A. Roe, *The Making of a Scientist*, Dodd Mead, 1952.

L. M. Terman *et al.*, *Genetic Studies of Genius*, Stanford University Press, vol. I, *Mental and Physical Traits of a Thousand Gifted Children* (1926); vol. III, *The Promise of Youth* (1930); vol. IV, *The Gifted Child Grows Up* (1947); vol. V, *The Gifted Group at Mid-Life* (1959).

Environmental factors and training creativity

C. H. Ammons and R. B. Ammons, 'How to prevent geniuses: McCurdy revisited', *Proc. Montana Acad. Sci.*, vol. 21 (1962), pp. 145–52.

J. McK. Cattell, 'A statistical study of American men of science. III. The distribution of American men of science', *Science*, vol. 24 (1906), pp. 732–42.

R. S. Crutchfield, 'Instructing the individual in creative thinking', in R. L. Mooney and T. A. Razik (eds.), *Explorations in Creativity*, Harper & Row, 1967.

W. J. J. Gordon, *Synectics: The Development of Creative Capacity*, Harper & Row, 1961.

R. H. Knapp, 'Demographic cultural and personality attributes of scientists', in C. W. Taylor and F. Barron (eds.), *Scientific Creativity: its Recognition and Development*, Wiley, 1963, pp. 205–16.

Further Reading

A. F. Osborn, *Applied Imagination*, Scribner, 1953.

S. J. Parnes and H. F. Harding, *A Source Book for Creative Thinking*, Scribner, 1962.

E. P. Torrance, *Rewarding Creative Behavior*, Prentice-Hall, 1965.

W. D. Wall, 'Highly intelligent children', *Educ. Res.*, vol. 2 (1960), pp. 101–11, 207–17.

P. Witty (ed.), *The Gifted Child*, D. C. Heath, 1951.

Acknowledgements

Permission to reproduce the Readings in this volume is acknowledged from the following sources:

Reading 1   The Macmillan Company
Reading 2   The Eugenics Society
Reading 3   Scientific American, Inc.
Reading 6   University of California Press
Reading 7   Dover Publications, Inc.
Reading 8   Harcourt, Brace & World, Inc., and Jonathan Cape Ltd
Reading 9   George Allen & Unwin Ltd and Basic Books, Inc.
Reading 10   Harper & Row, Publishers, Inc.
Reading 11   Longmans, Green & Co. Ltd
Reading 12   The Hogarth Press Ltd, Sigmund Freud Copyrights Ltd, The Institute of Psycho-Analysis, Basic Books, Inc., George Allen & Unwin Ltd and Liveright Publishing Corporation
Reading 13   The International Society for General Semantics
Reading 14   Harper & Row, Publishers, Inc.
Reading 15   Harper & Row, Publishers, Inc.
Reading 16   John Wiley & Sons, Inc., J. W. Getzels and Calvin Taylor
Reading 17   British Journal of Educational Psychology
Reading 18   Methuen & Co. Ltd and Shocken Books, Inc.
Reading 19   Holt, Rinehart & Winston, Inc.
Reading 20   Psychologia Africana
Reading 21   American Psychological Association and Frank Barron
Reading 22   Munksgaard Ltd and Donald W. MacKinnon
Reading 23   The Bobbs-Merrill Co. Inc.
Reading 24   John Wiley & Sons, Inc.
Reading 25   Teachers College Record and Sidney J. Parnes
Reading 26   Prentice-Hall, Inc.
Reading 27   British Journal of Educational Psychology

Author Index

Subject Index